FORWARD TO THE PAST?

FORWARD TO THE PAST?

Continuity and Change in Political Development in Hungary, Austria, and the Czech and Slovak Republics

*Edited by Lene Bøgh Sørensen and
Leslie C. Eliason*

AARHUS UNIVERSITY PRESS

Copyright: Aarhus University Press, 1997
Printed on acid-free paper by SCE Printing, Mauritius
ISBN 87 7288 652 8

AARHUS UNIVERSITY PRESS
Building 170, Aarhus University
DK-8000 Aarhus C, Denmark
Fax + 45 86 19 84 33

73 Lime Walk,
Headington, Oxford OX3 7AD
Fax (+ 44) 1865 750 079

Box 511,
Oakville, Conn. 06779
Fax (+ 1) 860 945 9468

Preface

This book is a collection of essays stemming from a conference held in October 1994 at the University of Aarhus' course estate, Sandbjerg Manor, in southern Jutland. The promoter of the conference was a group of Danish social science researchers sharing a common interest and research background in Central and East European history, as well as recent social and political developments. The transition to democratic regimes in 1989-90 opened up new opportunities for cooperating with Central and East European scholars and the conference "Forward to the Past?" reflected a need that we all felt to establish a cross-national forum for open discussions and research. We were particularly interested in enhancing our appreciation of the role of the past in shaping current behaviour and institutional development in Central and Eastern Europe. It is our hope that the contributions in this volume will inspire new studies of the general problematic of how historical experiences influence the prospects for future democratic development, peace and stability in Central and Eastern Europe.

The editors wish to thank all the contributors for their patience and cooperation in the process of finishing this book. New research networks have been established and we would particularly like to thank our colleagues from Central and Eastern Europe for the hospitality they have shown us in the years that have followed our original meeting. We also wish to thank Helle Jørgensen of the Department of Political Science at the University of Aarhus for her kind and tactful assistance in typing and preparing this volume. The English language versions of many of the conference papers were considerably improved with help from Leslie C. Eliason. Without a generous grant from the Danish Social Science Research Council, the conference and this book would not have come to fruition. Our Danish research group and the editors would like to thank the Council for their support.

Aarhus, November 1997   *Lene Bøgh Sørensen & Leslie C. Eliason*

Contents

Contents

Introduction

The events of 1989 in Central and Eastern Europe were straight away internationally recognized as a significant break with the past: the end of communist control of the eastern territories of the European continent, the end of a particular type of regime, and the end of an historical era in the development of the societies in the region. Many pundits of the recent transition period speak of the contemporary Central and Eastern European situation as a blank slate, a *tabula rasa*, onto which new institutions and new social, economic and political relations can be projected. Among western politicians and observers, it remains a widespread belief that the collapse of the communist-ruled regimes confirmed the supremacy of western liberal democracy and capitalist market economies (see, for example, Gellner 1996). Sustained by this logic, many observers believed that once freed from communist rule, the Central and Eastern European societies would quickly embark on the appropriate path towards democratic and capitalist development, resuming a process from which they had been cut off in the late 1940s when the Soviet Union asserted its control over the region.

This interpretation of the current situation has been challenged by those who discern a resurgence of history in the Central and Eastern European region following the collapse of the communist-led regimes. Rather than 'breaking with the past', the societies of Central and Eastern Europe are experiencing a reassertion of historical forces and patterns that in some cases fell dormant during the communist era and in other instances were actively repressed by the regime. Those who see a return to history view the 'end of history' approach as immoderate, ideological, shortsighted, and ignorant of the diversity of people and historical experiences in the region. By sweeping away the past, the 'clean slate' approach helps to sustain key aspects of the Cold War mentality that simplified the dynamics of international politics into a bipolar world view. The Cold War framework not only produced a monolithic view of Central and Eastern European communism but also lent credence to the belief that if Soviet hegemony could be broken, the existing political and social order would be swept away — and take history with it. Thus the simultaneous collapse of communist rule throughout the region seemed to confirm the 'end of history' hypothesis asserted by commentators such as Fukuyama (1992).

On the other hand, the 'return of history' approach to the study of the contemporary Central and Eastern European reality over-emphasizes the resurgence of ethnic and nationalist sentiments, including the re-emergence of bloody rivalries as an inevitable and destablizing element in the contemporary politics of the region. This has led some commentators to ponder whether perhaps one of communism's successes was its ability to repress or suppress these age-old rivalries.

Milan Kundera's essay, 'The Tragedy of Central Europe' (1994), gives voice to another version of the 'return to history' perspective. Russian dominance of Central Europe during the communist era represented an imposition of a foreign culture on the people of the region. Deprived of their own history, Central Europeans were kidnapped and forced to live under a system of rule that was not of their own making. Thus the end of Soviet domination in Central Europe represents a return to their own history and the possibility of reclaiming their own culture. While his is a somewhat more optimistic view of Central Europe's present possibilities, Kundera's argument can nevertheless be used by others to reinforce a world view that rejects the last half century as part of an ongoing process of historical development and instead sees it as an aberration rather than an integral part of the legacy Central European states and peoples must now come to terms with. Other scholars have insistently criticized the tendency of presenting all things Russian as barbaric and non-European (Garton Ash, 1989). They remind us that Hitler's Germany — a central European power — was responsible for the destruction of the young democracies in Central Europe (Šimečka, 1989). Thus all barbarism that has befallen the region cannot be equated solely to extra-territorial (Russian) influence.

In contemporary discussions we face two countervailing and almost diametrically opposed constructions of Central and Eastern Europe. Those who have yet to escape the Cold War world-view see a place where the past is irrelevant and western institutions can be transplanted if only reactionary tendencies (i.e., a reassertion of communist authoritarian rule) can be harnessed so that competitive elections can form the basis for a policy consensus on rapid market-oriented reforms. Less optimistic observers regard Central Europe as a place where ethnic and national conflict define social relations, destining the region to internal strife and rendering its people incapable of democratic self-governance. In either case, the outcome of the transition period seems to be a foregone conclusion.

While these two approaches seem to offer two strikingly different alternatives, neither the utopian end of history view nor the cataclysmic primordial conflict view provides a viable analytical framework for making sense of the contemporary situation in Central and Eastern Europe. Instead we need to assess the interplay of both old and new elements in order to identify a range of possibilities. A realistic analysis of Central European development today requires an appreciation of the role of the past, including the role of popular mythologies as well as historical facts in shaping current behavior and institutional development. But we must also acknowledge the particular challenges faced by societies with few, if any, relevant precedents for popular participation and democratic representation in government.

The backdrop for any serious consideration of the prospects for democratization in the Central European region is the legacy of the Austro-Hungarian Empire. Austria, Hungary, the Czech Republic, and Slovakia share this common historical background. However, each country occupied a distinct position within the dual monarchy of the Habsburgs and this produced quite different experiences with the processes of nation and state-building. The 'Ausgleich' of 1867 put Austria and Hungary on equal footing within the monarchy. Within the Austrian part of the dual monarchy, Czech nationalists sought a status equal to that of Hungary within the empire although they did not seek full political independence. In Hungary, the Magyar political elite could justify their aggressive assimilationist policies towards the various nationalities within their domain on their privileged status within the dual monarchy. Thus Slovaks, Croats, Serbs, Romanians, and Germans residing within the Hungarian state's territory retain a hostility towards the legacy of Hungarian rule. The Treaty of Versailles did little to put these conflicts to rest. Instead, the territorial settlement rearranged the political map, thereby introducing yet another historical layer to the complex pattern of nation and state-building in the region. Contemporary tensions among the peoples and states that make up the mosaic of Central Europe are in part the product of these earlier experiences. The history of the region does not destine the people and places to irresolvable conflict. However, these historical experiences do influence the paths towards the development of peace, stability, and democratic development in Central Europe.

The contributions in this volume aim to bridge the gap between the two extreme images of Central European society at the present time by focusing on the consequences of past regime types, social structures and cultural contexts for democratic development today in the Central and Eastern European countries. The studies presented here examine critically the processes of state and nation-building in relation to regime change. We explore the historical legacy of earlier efforts at building political entities (states) with particular institutional characteristics (regime type). These macropolitical processes have intertwined with efforts to define and mobilize collective identities associated with a particular geographic space (nation). These processes have a long and complex history within the region circumscribed by the limits of the old Austro-Hungarian Empire of the Habsburgs. Various successful and unsuccessful attempts at all three of these processes — nation-building, state-building, and regime change — have left important birthmarks on the map of the region and on identity formation and social movements. There are particular connotations attached to ideas of nation, state and their connection to the land and geography that can only be understood through a deeper appreciation of earlier experiences. Furthermore, the historical experience of any individual political entity (nation or state) cannot be fully understood without reference to the other entities (nation, state, empire) within the region. Thus, many of the difficult issues involved in regime change today have their roots in earlier incomplete or unsuccessful regime changes — or successful regime changes that might have led to democratic regimes but instead ended in authoritarian, fascist or communist regimes.

The contributors to this volume span several disciplines and approaches to studying the region. These include history, political science, sociology, geography, and anthropology. What they share is an appreciation of the role of the past in shaping both the continuities and changes that are part of contemporary Central European politics. Reactions to contemporary developments both among elites and the general population in the region are partly determined by the legacy of past attempts at democratic governance as well as the role of empires and conquering states. Thus social actors today define their roles and strategies at least in part in relation to earlier social and political orders. Some seek a definitive break with the past; others try to revive old mythologies and identities to mobilize support. The patterns of seeking or rejecting the past vary from country to country and from social group to social group and can best be understood by a closer examination of each locale within a broader comparative framework. That is the central goal of this book.

Chapter Overview

The first three contributions in this volume take an explicitly comparative perspective. In the first study, *Curt Sørensen* discusses the lost dimension of social movements and classes in recent research on political development. According to Sørensen, the current lack of attention to the role of social movements and social classes seriously limits our basis for theorizing more generally about the nature of democratic development. Referring to and comparing the Central European and Northern European historical experiences, he shows how the complicated relationship between capitalist and democratic development has actually evolved. His central point is that nowhere did democracy emerge as an automatic product of capitalist expansion. Sørensen convincingly demonstrates how the fate of attempts to establish democracy in the interwar period in Western and Eastern Europe was highly contingent on protracted social, political and cultural struggles in which social classes and class alliances played a vital role. Sørensen then suggests that research into the present complex processes of economic and political change in Central and Eastern Europe must to a greater extent feature differences in historical preconditions and the legacy of the past. The past, therefore, plays an important role in contemporary decision-making. Our attention to the past must be complemented by studies examining how social relations are crystalliz-ing today at both the elite and mass levels of society.

In the second contribution, *Heinz Gärtner* explores the relationship between the concepts of 'nation' and 'state' within the historical context of European international relations. These two concepts are critical elements in under-standing the interplay of people and places over time, a dynamic that heavily influences the context within which democratic regimes are consolidating today. His central thesis is that the concept of nation should be divorced from the definition of who belongs to a particular state, that is, from the question of societal identity. Gärtner argues that as long as states are constituted as entities with a specific *national* identity, ethnic groups may lay claim to the state at the expense of the basic rights and influence of other ethnic groups located within the territorial boundaries of that state. Unless and until nation and state are separated — both in theory and in practice — the assertion of the right of self-determination by ethnic (national) minority groups poses a significant threat to peace and stability in Europe. In this sense, both the internal development of democratic states as well as the peaceful relations among states in the region depend on how the relationship between state and nation is defined by each and every country in the region.

When this question is then posed in the broader context of (West) European integration, Gärtner points out how the development of the European Union at the same historical moment further complicates the successful resolution of conflicts arising from the interaction of nation and state-building in Central Europe. By undermining state sovereignty, European integration increases the probability of ethnic conflict in Central Europe. Only democracy can protect minority rights and only states are democratic. Supranational entities such as the European Union are not constituted with the same conception of citizenship and rights that are part and parcel of democratic theory and practice. States are based on the principle of territorial sovereignty and as integration proceeds, the territorial sovereignty of democratic states is undermined. But given the economic power and wealth of the European Union, the prospect of member-ship constitutes a virtually irresistible temptation for almost every Central and East European state. European integration, however, threatens the institutional framework that provides constitutional guarantees of minority civil rights, a crucial but precarious element necessary for the successful consolidation of democracy in Central Europe.

Gärtner does not seek to analyze the specific rights of ethnic minorities in the nature of cultural identity. Rather he offers a framework for thinking about the interaction between the physical or geographical dimensions of states and the distribution of collective identities within that space. Seen from a state-system perspective, working out the questions related to who 'belongs' is one of the most pressing and important tasks confronting the fledgling democracies of Central and Eastern Europe, and Hungary is no exception in this regard.

While Austria did not belong to the group of states undergoing the transition from communism in 1989, our approach emphasizes the importance of understanding the complex interrelationships among emergent states in the region over the past century. Thus Austria's central role, particularly during the reign of the Habsburgs, is an important aspect of any examination of the historical legacy confronting the newly democratizing states of the region. In his examination of the Austrian transition to democracy, *Gerhard Botz* takes up several theses advanced by Stein Rokkan concerning the relationship between the development of states and their geographical location with respect to the centre of the European continent. Rokkan, a Norwegian political scientist, was especially interested in understanding the developments in the periphery and semi-periphery of Europe and why more centralized states tended to develop as one drew farther away from the city-state belt running from the northwest to the southeast of the continent.

Rokkan's model helps explain the variations in political development and consolidation of centralized authority in the Austrian area. Regions closer to the central urban belt in Europe were slower in developing into centralized provinces, while those on the outskirts centralized earlier. This may help to explain the development of separatism and federalism in Austria. These geopolitical relationships that are the product of long historical processes are often downplayed or ignored by sociologists and political scientists even though they may provide us with important insights into the historical roots of contemporary political developments. Botz suggests in his conclusion that Rokkan's geopolitical model might also be useful in examining developments in the post-communist states of Central Europe which in any event will provide additional cases for confirming, falsifying, or modifying this particular explanatory model of state development.

In the emergence and consolidation of democratic regimes, the development of political parties and party systems play a central role in linking the population to political institutions. Representation, the cornerstone of democratic governance, is mediated by the competition of political parties in free and fair elections. Until recently, most of the theoretical literature on political parties and party system development was based on empirical analyses of the West European and Anglo-American cases. *Attila Ágh* calls for a rethinking of the dynamics of party system development in light of the Central European cases. He examines both the internal developments in the formation and institutionalization of individual parties and the overall evolution of Central European party systems.

Ágh argues that the relationship between parties and the electorate inverts the relationship between the parties and voters that would be predicted based on West European developmental patterns. Party elites make up the bulk of party support. Thus the Central European parties are not (yet) mass parties because they have little or no connection to an identifiable social base. He finds little party organization beyond a few politicians and party activists. Therefore, the parties cannot perform their otherwise expected role as aggregators of public opinion or interest mediators. The Central European parties thus pursue a 'catch-all' party (Kirchheimer 1920) strategy, with competing claims to represent 'the people' rather than a particular social class or set of political interests. Since the parties have yet to distinguish themselves according to particular policies or programmes, their only recourse is to campaign against the validity of the claims of other parties. Each party asserts that it is the only true representative of the people's interests.

Attila Ágh suggests four different aspects or dimensions of parties in his analysis: membership, organization, programmatic commitment, and power. These dimensions interact to produce somewhat different profiles reflecting the dominant preoccupation of party leadership within the context of each parties particular stage of development. Where one of these dimensions is under-developed, the party (and thus the party system as a conduit of political participation) hinders the development of effective and legitimate democratic parliamentary politics. By introducing the concepts of 'overparliamentarization' and 'overparticipation', Ágh suggests that politics in Central Europe today rest too heavily on what happens in parliament — often at the expense of recognizing the role of broader social movements and a societal debate on political choices. Furthermore, the drive by party elites to attain power has produced a situation in which the parties become the only relevant actors in the political arena. Other social groups including labour unions, interest groups, and social classes are frozen out of the political sphere, producing a situation where the parties 'hover' above the electorate in a highly politicized parliament that is largely out of touch with the people it is supposed to represent. The result is widespread popular alienation not just from parties and the parliament, but from politics in general.

The Czechoslovak case raises important and complex issues regarding the influence of nation and state-building processes on regime type. Czechoslovakia, as one of the newly created nation-states after World War I, succeeded in sustaining a democratic regime during the interwar period. *Peter Bugge* argues that this fact has led to many myths about an especially strong Czech and Slovak humanistic, liberal and democratic tradition. However, a closer examination of the role and status of the Czech (oslovak) parliament, past and present, leads him to modify this image of an almost innate disposition towards democratic culture and government. Drawing on examples from the past as well as the present, Bugge discerns a tendency in Czech and Slovak politics to give high priority to political efficiency at the expense of democratic principles.

The existing Czech and Slovak Republics both contend with claims made by neighbouring states arising from national minorities' rights. These controversies over minority rights policies that have reemerged after the withdrawal of Soviet power are deeply rooted in the history of the region. The treaty systems following World War I dictated a new arrangement of nation-states in Central and Eastern Europe and created a tapestry of national minorities throughout the region as many groups found themselves residing outside the national territory of their homeland.

At the end of World War II, a substantial number of people were collectively deprived of their existing citizenship rights and forced to resettle elsewhere. In the Czech case, the Sudeten-German problem, discussed here by *Eva Hahn*, is one important manifestation of the difficulties involved in mediating resurgent claims arising from the incomplete process of building integrated nation-states prior to the communist era. The expulsion in the aftermath of World War II of around three million former Czechoslovak citizens of German nationality from the Bohemian and Moravian Lands have important consequences for present day Czech politics. Czech political leaders are faced with demands from the *Sudetendeutsche Landsmannschaft*, which include the right of return for the expelled Sudeten Germans and the restitution of their property. Hahn convincingly argues that this is a very real problem and that the way the problem is perceived by the various actors involved (the Czech government, the Sudeten Germans, the German government, and the Czech people) influences the solutions each is willing to pursue. Hahn's recommendation is that without forgetting the past, the injustice of the forced resettlement off the Sudeten Germans over half a century ago must be acknowledged. However, public recognition of a past injustice is not sufficient grounds for attempting to reconfigure property rights. This will require an softening of the decades-old, die hard perceptions of the Sudeten Germans, in order to reflect contemporary reality rather than old stereotypes. Furthermore, the resolution of this issue has important implications not only for Czech domestic politics, but also for external relations, especially with Germany.

In a similar vein, *Christiane Brenner* explains how the new debate about Czech history has stirred old conflicts in Czech society. Brenner argues that each successive change of the Czech political situation has launched a major debate among historians and a new interpretation of the past. The change of regime initiated in 1989 has been no exception in this regard and thus captures both continuity and change. While the perception of the past may be changing among historians, it is a fact that the debate about how to interpret historical events and their meanings is a recurrent feature of Czech political culture. The major contours of the Czech debate include the question of whether to take a critical stance or accept the past in its entirety. This part of the debate has important implications for the question of the rights and claims of the Sudeten Germans. Second, the question of German occupation and the Czech situation at the end of World War II has become an explosive one. Some historians would prefer to put this part of Czech history aside entirely without further discussion. Perhaps most importantly, the discomfort Czech historians and Czech society in general encounter in dealing with these difficult issues of their history reveals precisely what Bugge argues in his chapter, namely that Czech society is not nearly so humanistic and liberal as the popular mythology might lead one to believe.

Tibor Pichler provides an important contribution to our study of the region by examining political developments in the Slovak republic. The Slovak case reminds us that the processes of state and nation-building, which began in the previous century, remain incomplete and therefore offer only remnants of a participatory tradition in politics to draw upon in the current situation. Pichler provides us with some important insights into the roles of *elites* in putting the identity issue on the political agenda. In the previous century, attempts to define an independent Slovak political identity remained largely a matter of elite discourse without popular mobilization. In this way the process of nation-building was overwhelmed by external actors and events that defined the situation for the following century. Without enlisting the support and involvement of society in general, the process of building a general sense of political identity as a country cannot be fully realized.

A common theme in the Hungarian case is what *Lázló Kürti* refers to as the 'reproduction of the inegalitarian nature of power politics'. Kürti provides an anthropological analysis of the processes and consequences of regime change in Hungary. The interaction of social classes and political elites during the past hundred years has left a legacy of nepotistic and clientelistic relations that continues to restrict the willingness and capacity of other social groups to participate in the new democratic regime. He emphasizes the potentially disastrous consequences of the growing gap between the rich and poor along with the economic decline of the middle class. Inequality and social atomization, although present to some extent in every society, is particularly destructive in the Hungarian case given the current external political situation, especially the ongoing struggle in the territories of the former Yugoslav Federation. The failure of the Hungarian government to address economic and social needs in the population only serves to strengthen tendencies towards alienation and the development of a potentially aggressive form of nationalism. For this reason the legitimacy problems of the new Hungarian democracy are exacerbated by both the internal economic context and instability beyond the borders of the state.

Bill Lomax concentrates on the emergence and development of the Hungarian party system between 1989 and 1994. These formative years resulted in the formation of a tripolar system around which the parties and their various internal factions cluster. The three poles — National-Conservative, Liberal, and Socialist — diverge from traditional (West) European left-right dimensionality in part because of differences in political traditions as well as differences in the property relations that undergird these political traditions in the west. These poles provide the basis for understanding the emergent six-party system that appears to be stabilizing in Hungarian political life. The central challenge of party system development in Hungary is for the parties to acquire or develop a more organic connection to the wider society. The parties do not represent particular social groups or strata, nor is it easy to identify politically organized groups sufficiently developed to articulate demands to which the political parties might respond. What the Hungarian experience confirms is that the theoretical and empirical literature on party system development has largely been based on the historical experiences in Western Europe and North America. But its major constructs, including left-right dimensionality, are ill-suited to the analysis of party system development in Central and Eastern Europe where socio-political relations, both now and in the past, have followed a very different trajectory. For this reason, the development of party systems in the current East European context requires an expansion or reformulation of extant theories of party system development.

Lene Bøgh Sørensen, in examining the relationship between the emergence of democratic politics and the role of organized interests, further emphasizes the consequences of a party system and parliament that lack an organic connection to the broader society. As she points out, this has been a recurrent, if not consistent, aspect of state-society relations in Hungary. The 'entry into politics crisis' must therefore be seen not only as a consequence of the immediate strategies of political elites during the transition to, and consolidation of, democracy in today's Hungary. It also results from the absence of a meaningful participatory tradition in Hungarian society. The absence of a strong independent labour movement, for example, has meant that unions have expended considerable energy coping with internal conflicts and power struggles. This has hampered their ability to present a unified bargaining position in emergent corporatist structures. However, these difficulties are beginning to be resolved and therefore, she concludes, Hungary has made an important first step towards the inclusion of non-state social actors in the democratic process.

Taken together, these chapters represent a significant step towards establishing a foundation for appreciating the political history of Central Europe that continues to play an important role in shaping the contours of democratic development in the region. The political landscape in each country, including the emergence of political parties, the dynamics of the nascent party systems, the relationship between political actors and social groups and movements, and the general public's attitude towards both domestic politics and international relations cannot be divorced from past experiences and continuing interpretations of the so-called lessons of history. While these historical precedents are important constraints on the development of democratic institutions and political processes in the region, they do not constitute irretrievable deformations or impossible obstacles to democracy. What the contributions to this volume suggest is that the pattern of relations between the past and present varies from country to country and that the particular trajectory of each state remains open although contingent on the past history (or lack thereof) of attempts to establish participatory democratic politics.

Bibliography

Fukuyama, Francis 1992. *The End of History and the Last Man*, New York: Free Press.

Garton Ash, Timothy 1989. 'Does Central Europe Exist?', in George Schöpflin and Nancy Wood, *In Search of Central Europe*, Cambridge: Polity Press: 191-215.

Gellner, Ernest, 1996. 'Return of a Native', *Political Quarterly* 67 (1): 4-14.

Kirchheimer, Otto, 1966. 'The Transformation of the Western European Party Systems' in *Political Parties and Political Development*, eds. J. La Palombara and M. Weiner, Princeton: Princeton University Press: 177-200.

Kundera, Milan, 1994. 'The Tragedy of Central Europe', *New York Review of Books*, 26 April.

Simečka, Milan, 1989. 'Another Civilization? An Other Civilization?', in George Schöpflin and Nancy Wood, *In Search of Central Europe*, Cambridge: Polity Press: 155-62.

Social Classes and Democracy — Different Trajectories

Curt Sørensen

The development of democracy and the question of the role of social classes

During the last two decades a remarkable number of regime changes have taken place around the world: in Southern Europe, in Latin America and most recently in Eastern Europe and in the former Soviet Union. Some observers have seen these political transformations as part of a global trend that is both irresistible and irreversible and the process of democratization that has swept across many countries and regions has been portrayed as part of a 'democratic wave'.[1]

However, attempts to establish democratic regimes are neither new nor unique. At the end of World War I there was also something like a 'democratic wave'. But within a relatively short time these newly established democratic regimes broke down and were replaced by right-wing authoritarian or fascist dictatorships.[2] While Juan Linz refers to this as the 'breakdown of democratic regimes',[3] perhaps it would be more accurate to analyze the interwar period in terms of failed attempts to establish democracies.[4] If we shift the emphasis in this way, we begin to focus on the problems associated with the precariousness of establishing and institutionalizing democracies. Furthermore, the abysmal failure of the last large-scale attempt in European history to establish democratic systems should serve as a reminder to temper our enthusiasm for recent developments with a more prudent and reflective approach. This requires cogent analyses of conditions and strategies favouring or impeding the development of democratic systems today.

Recent developments also raise a number of theoretical concerns for social researchers. The many changes of regime and the apparent general trend towards democracy has revitalized general theoretical interest within political science and political sociology in questions concerning the relationship between capitalist economic development and political development, regime formation and the development of democracy.

Political development and regime changes during the last decades have been described and explained in the growing literature on processes of 'transition' and 'consolidation' with an emphasis on the choices and actions of key actors and the processes of establishing, institutionalizing, and legitimizing democratic systems.[5] While these are important processes and problems, this overall approach has some serious limitations as a basis for theorizing about the nature of democratic development.

The transition and consolidation approach tends to downplay or even neglect the importance of historical conditions that predate the shorter timespan of the immediate 'crisis and re-equilibration'. The absence of a longer time horizon in this approach means that we may fail to adequately theorize the implications of different historical preconditions and the legacy of the past in contemporary decision-making. Furthermore, this approach tends to emphasise the role of key actors in the transition and consolidation processes, abstracting from the historical-structural conditions within which they operate. A further consequence of this emphasis on elites is the underestimation of the importance of popular social movements and social classes.[6] The abstraction from historical preconditions, the structural limitations and the underlying dynamics of social forces and classes also help to explain why some early contributors to the transition literature were overly optimistic about the possibility of establishing and consolidating democratic regimes. Some scholars argued that a 'window of opportunity' has opened, allowing us to create or 'craft' democracy anywhere, regardless of circumstances. In a similar vein, some authors argued that democracy produces its own 'preconditions'.[7]

Another approach to the study of political development, regime formation and development of democracy — the historical-structuralist approach — does not suffer from the same short-sightedness.[8] Within this research tradition, scholars have attempted to identify the historical-structural conditions conducive to development of democracy.[9] These researchers have tended to be much more pessimistic in their assessments of the future of democracy in the modern world.[10] From their point of view, democracy is something which developed under very specific circumstances at a particular moment in the history of Western Europe and North America:

The development of democracy in the nineteenth century was a function of an unusual configuration of historical circumstances which cannot be repeated. The European-American route to democracy is closed.[11]

Here, as in Barrington Moore's seminal work on roads to modernization, the conditions that fostered the development of democracy in certain parts of Europe and America are thought to be unique, historically contingent, and unlikely to be repeated.[12]

Much earlier, Max Weber pointed to the historically contingent nature of the simultaneous development of capitalism and democracy. Unlike Marx, who in retrospect appears to have been surprisingly optimistic about the compatibility of capitalism and liberal democracy, Weber articulated a much more pessimistic view. In his 1906 analysis of Russian development,[13] for example, he stated that democratic development in this country was very unlikely.[14] According to Weber, freedom and democracy emerged together only under the conditions present in the early period of capitalist development. This constellation of conditions was unique and unrepeatable.[15]

Despite this early pessimistic view, contemporary scholars have continued to look for conclusive evidence to support a causal connection between capitalist economic development and the development of democracy.[16] Many scholars of the optimistic tradition seem to see a straightforward connection between capitalist development and democracy. Capitalist economic development automatically produces both material affluence and democracy. This conception is also inherent in the shock therapy philosophy and strategy.[17] If only one can unleash unrestricted capitalist economic development, affluence and democracy will automatically follow in due time. Austerity programmes and suffering[18] at the present time will be rewarded by a happy life in the future.[19]

We must remember, however, that capitalist economic development has not always led to democracy. In countries such as Germany and Japan and in many Latin American countries, for example, capitalist economic development was associated with authoritarian political structures and politics. Capitalist economies have supported authoritarian regimes for long periods and had it not been for the outcome of World War II, we might today find examples of fascist dictatorships with well-functioning capitalist economies.

In a more sophisticated form, scholars within the optimistic tradition postulate capitalist development as a necessary, but not sufficient, condition of democracy.[20] The opposite, however, could be argued: that the immense concentration of economic wealth and the very unequal distribution of resources produced by capitalism constitutes a serious impediment for the full unfolding of democratic life.[21] Usually in liberal political science theory, the contradiction between the ideal of equal democratic participation and influence on the one hand, and unequal distribution of resources and asymmetrical patterns of participation and influence on the other, has been 'solved' by defining democracy not as popular participation and influence, but as elite competition.[22] I shall, in the context here, leave open this whole question about capitalism as a necessary condition for democracy or on the contrary, as a great obstacle to any real democracy and concentrate on the question: which kind of capitalist development is conducive to democratic development?

Capitalist economic development did not always produce democracy. But even where it did, the process was much more complicated than often assumed. As emphasized by Rueschemeyer et al., 1992, democracy was always a product of long periods of social and political struggle. They further assert that social classes played a special role in the processes of the development of democracy. Democracy never came as an automatic consequence of capitalist development as such, but developed as a product of class struggles unleashed by capitalist economic development:

capitalist development is associated with democracy because it transforms the class struggle, strengthening the working and middle classes and weakening the landed upper class. It was not the capitalist market nor capitalists as the new dominant forces but rather the contradictions of capitalism that advanced democracy.[23]

In what follows, I shall discuss this thesis concerning the role of social classes in the development of democracy. Following Rueschemeyer et al., I shall define democracy as a political system characterized by:

regular, free and fair elections of representatives with universal and equal suffrage, ... responsibility of the state apparatus to the elected parliament ... (and) the freedoms of expression and association as well as the protection of individual rights ...[24]

The process of the development of democracy then, is the process which led to the establishment of political systems characterized in this way.

We can distinguish between five processes: (1) capitalist economic development, (2) the development of democracy, (3) nation- building, (4) state-building, and (5) the development of inter-state relations, including war.[25] These processes are interrelated and often even intertwined, but the analytical emphasis in this chapter is on the second process, the development of democratic institutions and here again with a special focus on the role of social classes .in this process. I further emphasize the 'mixed' character of all these processes, including the process of the development of democracy. Economic, political and ideological factors and relations intermingle all the time. It is not necessary in the context here, however, to enter into a comprehensive theoretical discussion about the relative importance of different 'levels' and 'relations' and the expediency of such conceptions of 'levels' of social reality.[26]

An especially close connection seems to have existed between the development of democracy and nation building.[27] Both are related to the coming of the age of mass politics, the entry of the masses into politics and the general rise of mass participation.[28] The process of class formation, class alliances and confrontations on the one hand and the processes of nation building and development of democracy on the other, can be seen as parallel and inter-connected processes, producing under certain circumstances democracy and moderate nationalism or, alternatively, under other circumstances, authoritarian or totalitarian regimes and excessive nationalism. These processes were never automatic. No nation building occurred without builders,[29] and no democracy was established without people who actively fought for democracy against those who resisted it. Due to different circumstances and different choices and actions, developmental patterns differed across Europe, resulting in variations in national consciousness and regime types.

While acknowledging the close relationship between nation building, state-building and the development of democracy, this study concentrates on the role of social classes in the process of the development of democracy.[30] While other agents and processes are important, in the context of current debates about transitions and consolidations of democratic regimes, we are in need of analyses which highlight the lost dimension of social movements and classes in particular. Furthermore, to understand fully the context within which contemporary struggles to establish democracies in Central and Eastern Europe are taking place, we need to analyse the process of the development of democracy in connection with the rise and development of mass politics especially in the interwar period. In the final section of this chapter, I then turn to a discussion of the question of the utility of historical-sociological and class analyses for understanding developments after World War II and recent transitions as well.

The participation crisis and the fragility of social orders

Amidst the turmoil of the late 1920s and the 1930s, the many and often grim and violent social and political struggles had quite a different outcome in Central Europe than in the Scandinavian countries. Why did the trajectories and the outcomes differ so greatly?

Several sets of interconnected circumstances and processes are important in answering this question: the different general character of these societies, their different political systems, the character of the 'crisis of participation',[31] the character and strategy of their labour movements, the reactions of ruling elites and vested interests, the reactions of other social classes and entrenched political subcultures to increased mass participation and the specific configuration of cleavages[32] and alliances. I shall concentrate here on the reactions of different social classes to the crisis of participation.

A 'developmental crisis' can be understood as a 'serious threat' to an existing political system, as an important institutional change and as a basic problem which must be solved.[33] The 'participation crisis' is such a developmental crisis. The coming of the era of mass politics in Europe[34] produced everywhere an 'entry of the masses into politics' — or 'participation' crisis.[35] In some countries the crisis of participation was solved in a quick and efficient way. The mobilization of the masses and their subsequent entry into politics was canalized through democratic mass parties and a democratic popular culture developed. In other countries the crisis of participation became protracted and deep.[36]

Social mobilization can be seen as a development from an original, amorphous, not yet articulated position to a high degree of organization and ideology.[37] A mobilizing social group will increasingly articulate interests and make demands on other groups in society or on the state apparatus. This whole development takes place as a consequence of increasing social and political participation. Participation has an educative function.[38] But participation does on the other hand not necessarily lead to the development of a democratic political culture.

We must make a distinction between two basic kinds of participation, democratic, genuine on the one hand and non-democratic, pseudo-participation on the other. Crucial in this context is the goal which the social movement in question seek to achieve, the character of the political culture it develops and the amount of influence it attains. Does a social movement promote and protect democracy or does it on the contrary try to prevent or destroy democracy? Does it develop within its organizational network a democratic popular culture based on humanistic and rationalist values or does it on the contrary encourage and cultivate an anti-humanistic and anti-rationalist authoritarian culture? Finally, does it secure and promote the development of participation which secures some degree of influence for the popular participants, or is the participation it encourages a participation completely directed from above and without any influence for the mass of participants?

The different possible trajectories of mass mobilization and participation crystallized in Central Europe already around the turn of the century. In his celebrated work on politics and culture in fin-de-Siecle Vienna,[39] Carl E. Schorske identifies four main 'solutions' to the problem of mass participation in politics. Generalizing Schorske's observations we can distinguish between four main responses to the crisis of participation, three of these constituting three different types of social mobilization and participation. (See Illustration 1).

The traditional continental European liberalist response to the crisis of participation was non-mobilization, i.e., the attempt to exclude the masses from political life and reserve politics for an educated elite. This traditional solution proved inadequate, however, in the new era of mass politics. It was confronted with and defeated by three variants of the new mass politics.

The kind of mobilization and participation promoted by Karl Lueger's populist, authoritarian, and anti-semitic Christian-Social movement in Vienna at the turn of the century was undemocratic. It was a pseudo-participation. So was Georg von Schönerer's ultra-nationalist movement and subsequent fascist mobilization and participation. The social democratic mass mobilization and participation, on the other hand, was democratic and genuine.

Illustration 1 :	Rationalist, Humanist	Anti-Rationalist, Anti-Humanist
Elitist, No Mass Base	Traditional Continental-European Liberalism	Traditional German Right
Mass Base	Social Democratic Labour Movement	Georg v. Schönerer's German-Nationalist Karl Lueger's populist and anti-Semitic Christian-Social Movement Extremist Nationalism Fascism Nazism

The Communist type of mobilization and participation constitutes a further category of mass mobilization not captured by the four-fold table above. Communist movements try to establish a mass base and their ideology is within the rationalist tradition, but they differ from social democratic movements by their different goal and type of organization. The adoption from an early time of the goal, strategy and party model of the Russian Bolsheviks strongly determined the development of the policy and structure of the communist parties in the West.[40]

Political participation and mobilization in Hitler's Germany or Stalin's Russia are examples of undemocratic, pseudo-participation and mobilization.[41] In general political participation and mobilization in democracies are genuine, but have usually been very restricted. Mobilization and political participation of workers in the Scandinavian and Central European labour movements were genuine and democratic, whereas fascist or Stalinist mobilizations were not. Labour mobilization was also broad, covering whole areas of life, whereas mobilization and participation in modern 'polyarchies' are restricted, mainly to electoral participation.

The provocative question now is the question of democratic mass participation. Is mass mobilization and participation on a rational and humanistic basis possible? The most serious and comprehensive attempt to accomplish this kind of mass mobilization in European history was the social democratic labour movement. But it lost to fascism, which represented quite another type of mass mobilization: mass mobilization on an anti-rationalist, anti-humanistic basis.

Mass mobilization and participation obviously can take different directions. Instead of democratic participation and democratic popular culture, ultra-nationalist and fascist forms of participation and political culture can develop. And, as indicated by the communist type, un-democratic mobilization can even develop on a rational ideological base.[42] Mass mobilization is risky seen from a democratic point of view. But at the same time, mass mobilization and participation are also indispensable in any genuine process of democratization. 'Democratization' without both mass participation and the development of popular democratic culture does not result in democracy, but a system of 'competitive elitism'.[43]

Under what circumstances does one or the other kind of participation develop? A preliminary answer could be that the type of mass participation unfolding in a European society in the period studied here, depended on the general character of the existing social order and political system, the character and the strategy of the labour movement, the reaction of vested interests, and other threatened classes and political subcultures, and the underlying pattern of cleavages and alliances. The existing social order and political system can be seen as a given system of structural conditions which restrict and enable social action. Previous and present cleavages and alliances form an important part of this always existing universe of structural conditions. The European labour movement as it unfolded in the age of mass politics can then be seen as an active and new force impinging on the traditional European social and political order, provoking different reactions from different elites and social classes.

The main beneficiary of the European extension of 'citizen rights'[44] and the main force in promoting universal suffrage was the working class. Working class action was also important for the character and development of the participation crisis and the subsequent development of different kinds of participation. But what determined the character and the strategy of the labour movement?

Economic and social factors have often been identified as especially important influences on the character of the labour movement. A classic explanation of working class radicalization has pointed to the impact of the timing, character and pace of industrialization. In 1922 the Norwegian historian Edward Bull, for example, published a famous paper on the question of differences in the degree of radicalization of the three Scandinavian labour movements.[45] In his explanation, he emphasized the differences in the timing and the speed of industrialization and in the size of industrial units in the three countries. The Bull thesis was later adopted by the labour relations researcher Walter Galenson[46] and the political sociologist S.M. Lipset.[47] For many years the Bull-Galenson-Lipset thesis about a causal relationship between late and rapid industrialization, the creation of uprooted social groups and the formation of big industrial units on the one hand, and political radicalization on the other, was almost commonplace within the sociology of labour movements and industrial relations.

The Bull-Galenson-Lipset thesis has, however, been contested by later research. According to Lafferty, for example, political structures were more important in explaining differences in ideology and politics between the Scandinavian labour movements.[48] This thesis on the importance of the surrounding political system for the character of the labour movement has also been advanced as a general thesis by scholars like Dick Geary and S.M. Lipset.[49] In the present context, I find this thesis especially interesting because it directs attention to the question of relations between the labour movement and the surrounding political system, and the political reactions of other social classes to the rise of organized labour.

The working class and the labour movement acted and reacted in different ways depending on the character of the political system and the different actions and reactions of the other classes in the total social actor system. But the working class and the labour movement also influenced the surrounding political system and the other social classes, provoking different responses.

How did vested interests react when confronted with the challenge of mobilization and increasing participation of the subaltern classes? The way ruling classes and elites handled the problem of mass participation deeply influenced political development in each society.

The reaction to the advancement of the labour movement is illustrative here. In the Scandinavian countries the traditional ruling elites and economically dominant classes eventually accepted the ascending political elite of the labour movement, and a sort of truce and mutual understanding between capital and labour was established giving rise to a corporatist system.[50]

In countries like Austria, Italy and Spain, on the other hand, organized labour was 'kept out' of politics and the labour political elite were denied access to governmental power. Eventually the ruling classes and elites were even prepared to dismantle democratic institutions and accept a fascist dictatorship in order to protect their vested interests and crush the labour movement.[51]

The German case lies between these two extremes. Back in the old Wilhelmine Germany, the social democratic labour movement had been discriminated in several ways and social democratic workers had been looked upon as outcasts (*Vaterlandslose Gesellen*).[52] This changed apparently with the arrival of Weimar democracy. During the first years of the Weimar Republic and again from 1928-30, the SPD participated in government coalitions at the level of the Reich. For a longer period the SPD also governed at the state level, and notably its Prussian position was important here.[53] But in the final phase of the Weimar Republic the SPD was sidetracked and a series of intrigues prepared the way for the Nazi takeover on 30 January, 1933.[54] And down at the bottom of Weimar society, the social democratic workers remained almost as outcasts, as they had been in pre-1914 Germany.[55]

This emphasises the quite different reaction of the traditional ruling elites and classes to the fascist mass movement and the rising fascist elite. The main question here is that of moral and political support and a willingness to allow Nazi access to governmental power. It was the lack of democratic convictions and values and the general preference of the traditional elites and ruling classes for an authoritarian solution more than financial support which paved the way for the Nazi takeover.[56] As Eberhard Kolb puts it:

The business world did not create Hitler's government ... But by their opposition to parliamentary democracy and preference for an authoritarian system, the bosses had accelerated the break up of the Weimar Republic and played into the hands of a dictatorship.[57]

Important in the process of Nazi ascendency to power was also the role played by the agrarian upper class and by the Reichswehr-elite.[58]

Much energy has been spent discussing the question: 'Who paid Hitler?'[59] Heavy industry certainly contributed financially to the Nazi movement[60] but as convincingly argued by Turner they also contributed to the conservative DNVP and to the DVP.[61] The Norwegian political scientist Bernt Hagtvet is probably correct in characterizing the whole issue of financing as a 'side issue'.[62]

One can, as suggested by Reinhard Kühnl, view the relationship between the traditional ruling classes and elites on the one hand, and the rising Nazi elite on the other, as a sort of alliance.[63] The Nazi movement was not just an instrument of big capital, it was an independent force that increasingly gained access to the centres of power in Weimar society. Its road to power was mediated by bargains struck with the traditional elites and ruling classes as previously had been the case in Italian fascism's rise to power.[64]

As pointed out by Luebbert, however, there was in this respect an important difference between West European and East European development.[65] East European societies were traditional societies and social mobilization was weak. In these societies a traditional dictatorship was sufficient to subdue the subaltern classes and protect the vested interests of the traditional ruling classes and elites. There was no need here for an alliance with fascism and the establishment of a fascist dictatorship. On the contrary, in Eastern Europe a relationship of rivalry and contest developed between the forces of the old order on the one hand, and the new fascist elites and movements on the other. Especially in Hungary and Romania, the struggle between 'the old' and 'the new' Right became a conspicuous feature of political life in the interwar period. In Romania this contest exploded into armed struggle.[66]

Otherwise in countries such as Germany, Austria, Italy and Spain. Here the labour movements were strong and the social order was characterized by a high level of social mobilization and social unrest. In these countries the ruling classes and elites felt sufficiently threatened to actively and forcibly repress the subaltern classes. Eventually an alliance between the forces of the old order and fascism crystallized and a fascist dictatorship was established.[67]

The different reactions of the ruling classes and elites to increasing mass participation of the subaltern classes thus produced divergent alliances and strategies in different regions of Europe. But it would be a mistake only to consider the reactions of the ruling classes and elites. The reactions of the urban middle class and the peasantry were also important.

The reaction of these classes to the increasing participation of the subaltern classes in politics has often been described and explained in terms of the 'middle class panic' thesis: Due to their exposed position between capital and labour, their economic marginality and the threat of 'proletarianization' the lower sections of these classes panicked and moved to extremist positions, to extremist nationalism at the end of the nineteenth century and to fascism in the twentieth century.[68]

Lipset's theory on 'middle class extremism' rests on this broader panic thesis. According to Lipset middle class extremism developed in countries characterized by both large scale capitalism and a strong labour movement. The middle class, squeezed between big capital and labour, then often turned to Fascism. Lipset spoke here of an 'extremism of the middle' clearly distinguishable from the traditional right-wing authoritarianism.[69]

Both the broader thesis on the panic of the lower layers of the middle-class and Lipset's more specific thesis on position and movement of the German middle class can be criticized.[70] As demonstrated by Hamilton, not only the lower middle class but also, and to an even higher degree, the upper middle class and the upper classes increasingly voted for the NSDAP.[71] The scope of the thesis must be extended: It was not only a great part of the lower-middle class, but of the whole middle class as well as the bourgeoisie who panicked and turned to fascism.[72]

Secondly, what was at stake was not primarily material interests, but a clash of values. The middle class citizens as well as the peasantry and the bourgeoisie were scared and aggressive because they perceived the labour movement in the Central European social order as a threat to their basic cultural values and whole way of life.[73] This point, made by Bernt Hagtvet, is supported by local community studies such as those of William Sheridan Allen and Jeremy Noakes.[74] Like Hagtvet, they stress the strong class polarization at the bottom of Weimar society, the ideological-cultural dimension of this basic conflict and the strategic exploitation of this situation by the Nazi movement:

... the most important factor in the victory of Nazism was the active division of the town along class lines...The victory of Nazism can be explained to a large extent by the desire on the part of Thalburg's middle class to suppress the lower class and especially its political representative, the Social Democratic party.[75]

In the countryside as well, the German and Austrian peasantry reacted violently against what they viewed as the threat from the labour movement. Especially in Austria, a country without a large bourgeoisie comparable to the Rhine-bourgeoisie or a Junker class as in Prussia, the main dimension of conflict emerged between the socialist labour movement of the towns and industrial areas and the Catholic, authoritarian peasants of the countryside. This class conflict was also mainly an ideological-cultural conflict.[76]

In the towns of Central Europe and almost everywhere in the countryside an overwhelming alliance rose up against working class parties. Almost everywhere a bloc of parties from the right to the centre formed a so-called 'citizen alliance' (*Bürgerblock*) or 'camp' (*Lager*) to fight the labour movement and to keep it from political influence.[77] Eventually in Germany, the Nazi movement took the lead in these alliances, in many places swallowing the whole electoral basis[78] of the citizen alliances, thus integrating the bourgeois and petty bourgeois masses into the Nazi movement:

With its vicious attacks on the 'Marxists', the NSDAP actively took the lead in the class conflict at the local level, a conflict which was being intensified by the depression. With this tactic the NSDAP won over a large number of the middle class who no longer felt capable of mastering the situation and feared the coming of Bolshevism.[79]

The situation in Austria was in one respect more complicated due to the existence here of different variants of fascism.[80] In another respect the Austrian case was more polarized because the complicating element of two rival labour parties was absent here.

We can now draw some provisional conclusions on the role of different social classes in the historical process of development of democracy in Europe. Usually scholars have pointed to the bourgeoisie as the main social agent for democracy. 'No bourgeoisie, no democracy', as Barrington Moore put it.[81] A similar view has been articulated by Seymour Martin Lipset and Robert A. Dahl.[82] This thesis has had a strong comeback in the prevailing political and ideological climate after the breakdown of the former Soviet Union and the communist regimes in Eastern Europe and in the current public debate market, bourgeoisie and liberalism have almost been synonymous with democracy.[83]

Rueschemeyer et al., on the other hand, emphasize the role played by the European working class in the actual historical process of democratization:

democratization was both resisted and pushed forward by class interest. It was the subordinate classes that fought for democracy. By contrast, the classes that benefitted from the status quo nearly without exception resisted democracy. The bourgeoisie wrested its share of political participation from royal autocracy and aristocratic oligarchy, but it rarely fought for further extensions once its own place was secured ... the working class was the most consistently pro-democratic force.[84]

This thesis, that the working class is 'the most consistently pro-democratic force' seems to be confirmed by historical facts. In countries such as Germany and especially Austria, the working class was almost the only force pushing for democratization. In the Scandinavian countries, labour movements have been a major force in the development of democracy, albeit not the only one.

The agrarian upper class, especially in countries like Germany, Hungary, Italy, Spain and Sweden and to a certain extent Denmark, was the main social force opposing democratization. But other forces were at work too. In Norway, Sweden and Germany, the bureaucratic elite, for example, also resisted democracy and the fatal role played by the Reichswehr elite in German development is well known.

In Germany and Austria, the peasants and the petty bourgeoisie in the towns long resisted democracy and in the late 1920s and the 1930s, they supported fascism. But in Denmark and Sweden, and to a certain extent Norway, part of the middle class and the peasantry turned to democracy instead, and the Scandinavian countries took the social democratic road. The bourgeoisie wavered, fighting against the old monarchy for constitutional government and legal rights, but generally resisting an extension of suffrage to the lower classes. In the inter-war period the European bourgeoisie was generally sceptical about democracy and especially in Central Europe, sentiments for an authoritarian 'solution' grew strong in the late twenties.

In the Weimar Republic and the First Austrian Republic, a substantial part of these classes turned to fascism and it was left to the workers to sustain political democracy. This was reflected in the strength of political parties too. In Germany, the Liberal Party (Deutsche Demokratische Partei) almost vanished at the end of the Weimar period,[85] and in the Austrian Republic a liberal party was totally absent from the political scene. The social democratic labour movement was the only strong and visible force sustaining democracy and fighting fascism.

The assertion advanced by Barrington Moore, S.M. Lipset and Robert A. Dahl that a strong bourgeoisie and a strong middle class are essential for political democracy thus seems to be a dubious assertion. The Barrington Moore-Lipset-Dahl thesis must be rejected, or at least modified, and the Rueschemeyer et al. thesis seems confirmed. But it needs some further clarification and modification. Firstly, the working class movement must not be defeated, as were the German and Austrian labour movements in 1933/34, in order for democracy to succeed. Secondly, Rueschemeyer, et al. do not pay sufficient attention to the importance of developing a strong democratic political culture based on popular movements. The development of such movements was essential for the development of democracy in the Scandinavian countries. The development of similar popular cultures within the organizational networks of the Central European labour movements did not, however, secure democratic political systems in this region of Europe. Here the 'surroundings', including oppositional traditional elites and ruling classes, plus the rising fascist movements, forced political development in quite another direction. Thirdly, although Rueschemeyer, et al. mention the importance of alliances, this element should be stressed much more. The alliance established between peasants and workers in the Scandinavian countries during the thirties constitutes one of the decisive differences between Scandinavian and Central European developments. Finally, workers everywhere did not always fight for democracy. In Germany, communist workers certainly fought against fascism, but they did not fight for democracy. Working class support for the 'Arrow Cross' movement in Hungary in the 1930s and the Peronist movement in Argentina in the fifties are further examples of deviations from the general rule.

This again underlines the importance of the development of democratic traditions and of popular democratic culture. As noted by S.M. Lipset, organization and political culture are crucial. According to Lipset, the 'raw' working class is not especially democratic; on the contrary, unmobilized and unorganized workers often display what he called 'working class authoritarianism'.[86] But on the other hand, he recognized that in Europe the organized labour movement, not liberalism, has been the main force pushing for democracy.[87] This emphasis on organization and ideology has, of course, been a consistent part of the socialist tradition.[88]

But the very fact that some social classes promoted democracy and other classes resisted it, is not in itself sufficient to explain the stability or instability of social orders, the different trajectories of European societies and the very different outcomes. We must explore the deeper configurations of socio-economic, political and ideological cleavages and the resulting patterns of alliances and confrontations.

This has been recognized by several scholars within this field. In his classic explanation of the German *Sonderweg*, Lipset points to the importance of the character of earlier cleavages and the way they were handled as deeply affecting subsequent development.[89] Especially important here are the sequence of crises and the phenomenon of crises accumulation:

Were these issues dealt with one by one, with each more or less solved before the next arose; or did the problems accumulate, so that traditional sources of cleavage mixed with newer ones? Resolving tensions one at a time contributes to a stable political system; carrying over issues from one historical period to another makes for a political atmosphere characterized by bitterness and frustration rather than tolerance and compromise. Men and parties come to differ with each other, not simply on ways of settling current problems, but on fundamental and opposed outlooks.[90]

In his recent work on social classes and the origins of different political regimes in interwar Europe, Gregory M. Luebbert further develops the Lipset-Rokkan thesis on the importance of earlier cleavages and the phenomenon of crisis accumulation.[91] Luebbert points to the existence before 1914 of two different types of regimes in Europe: countries with liberal hegemony (for example, Britain, France and Switzerland) and countries without liberal hegemony (for example, Germany, Italy, Spain, Sweden, Norway and Denmark). In the liberal hegemony systems, where liberalism was strong, it could afford to make concessions to the working-class movements, which in turn became moderate. This resulted in the development of a kind of 'alliance' or 'compromise', 'Lib-Labism', as Luebbert calls it.[92]

In countries were liberalism was weak, it took a hard and unsympathetic attitude towards workers' movements and demands. Consequently the labour movements in these countries developed in sharp opposition to liberalism and to the existing social order in general. In a manner reminiscent of William Lafferty's explanation of the different character and development of the three Scandinavian labour movements and Dick Geary's general account of the different trajectories of European labour,[93] Luebbert thus explains the different character and development of the European labour movements by reference to the different character of the surrounding political systems emphasizing especially the importance of the strength and character of liberalism in the respective countries.[94]

But why was liberalism strong in some countries and weak in others? Adhering to the Lipset-Rokkan thesis, Luebbert explains the weakness of liberalism in countries such as Germany, Italy, Spain, Sweden and Norway by pointing to divisions within the middle class and liberalism, divisions rooted in cleavages of the pre-industrial period. Conversely, where the old cleavages and problems of the pre-industrial period were overcome before the emergence of new cleavages caused by industrialization and the rise of new social classes, liberalism remained united and therefore strong. This was the case in Britain, for example.[95]

After World War I, the Lib-Lab systems collapsed as class struggles intensified. But due to the successful integration of the working class in the pre-1914 Lib-Lab systems, these countries remained stable, despite the aggravated social and economic circumstances and the increasing conflicts of the interwar period.[96]

In countries where liberalism was weak before 1914 and where working class opposition was strong, attempts after the war to form coalitions based on the Lib-Lab model were short-lived and unsuccessful. Two different 'solutions' occurred: either the peasants aligned themselves with the urban middle class against the workers or they aligned themselves with the urban workers against the urban middle class and the bourgeoisie. The first type of coalition led to fascism and authoritarian corporatism, as in Germany and Italy. The second type of coalition led to social democratic hegemony and a democratic variant of corporatism. This was the Scandinavian solution.[97]

Luebbert convincingly demonstrates the effects of cleavages and alliances, but there are several debatable points in his analysis. Firstly, he is not sufficiently clear about the particular social class base of liberalism. Did the entire middle class support liberalism? What was the role of the bourgeoisie? Luebbert does not seem to distinguish between bourgeoisie and middle class.[98] Secondly, his classification of countries according to the strength of liberalism is debatable. Is it for example true that liberalism in pre-1914 Germany was as weak as he assumes?[99] Thirdly, was strong liberalism always conciliatory towards the labour movement, whereas weak liberalism always intransigent and hostile towards working class demands? Luebbert's thesis concerning the relationship between liberalism and labour movement must be carefully examined in light of the historical record in each of the countries under study.

Luebbert's emphasis on liberalism as a political force, and the middle class as its social basis, leads him to ignore or minimize the role of conservative forces and the agrarian aristocracy in the different countries. He totally denies, for example, the role of the agrarian upper class as an anti-democratic force in Germany's political development. He argues that the economic power of the Weimar Junker class did not translate into political power.[100] However, Barrington Moore, Hans-Ulrich Wheeler, Ralph Dahrendorf, Gerschenkron, and others, take a more sophisticated approach.[101] They do not claim that the members of the agrarian upper class were politically active all the time, constantly seeking to transform their economic power into political power. Rather the predominant position of the agrarian upper class from an early time in German history produced the specific social and political order of Wilhelmine Germany, an order which, despite the interruption of war and revolution, determined the basic character of the subsequent Weimar Republic.[102] Furthermore, actors with a background in the Junker class actually did play an important role in the decisive, final process of intrigues and struggles which led to the collapse of the Weimar Republic.[103]

Finally, Luebbert's analysis suffers in general from super-structuralism.[104] He almost seems to deny completely the importance of political action:

One of the cardinal lessons of the story I have told is that leadership and meaningful choice played no role in the outcome.[105]

This being so, he consequently pays little attention to the importance of political action and cultural struggle. But even if historical and structural circumstances conditioned different trajectories in Northern and Central Europe, the outcome was never pre-ordained. Political struggle in which some lost and some won determined the outcome. Different historical prerequisites and structural circumstances explain a great deal. But the actions of the actors involved were crucial too. Neither social democratic rule in Northern Europe nor fascist dictatorship in Central Europe was predestined.

Structures and social agents

Luebbert's super-structuralism raises important theoretical questions, too. A structural, historically oriented approach must be combined with an actor and presence-oriented approach. (See Illustration 2).

The social science literature often engages in a pronounced 'either-or' way of thinking. For example, either one applies a structuralist approach,[106] or conversely, an actor-oriented approach.[107] I shall assert the expediency of a less orthodox attitude. It is both necessary and possible to combine the two approaches in an effort to embrace structural as well as behaviourial elements of social reality.[108] One can abstract momentarily from structural and historical conditions and concentrate on analyzing the interaction between actors or one can concentrate on structural conditions, ignoring for the moment social action. But one cannot pretend that social reality is either actors floating in an empty space[109] or structures totally dominating and determining the behaviour of social actors reducing them in this way to mere 'agents'.[110]

Illustration 2:

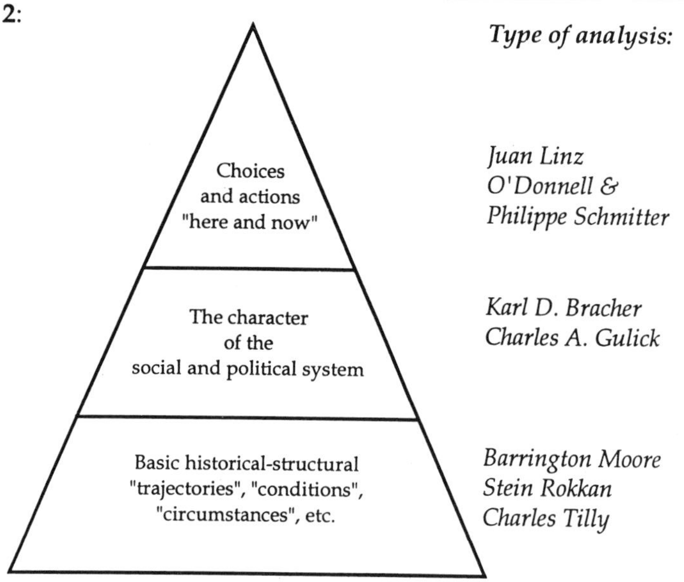
Type of analysis:
Choices
and actions
"here and now"
Juan Linz
O'Donnell &
Philippe Schmitter
The character
of the
social and political system
Karl D. Bracher
Charles A. Gulick
Basic historical-structural
"trajectories", "conditions",
"circumstances", etc.
Barrington Moore
Stein Rokkan
Charles Tilly

Now, it is easy to say, of course, that one should just combine actor and structure-oriented approaches. It is, as noted by Charles Tilly, surprisingly difficult to accomplish.[111] Perhaps this cannot be done once and for all at a high level of abstraction.[112] The answer then is to demonstrate in each concrete historical case the interdependence of structural conditions and social actions. But this raises new problems: where has comparative analysis gone? Has it not been transformed into a purely historical study of quite unique situations?

Leaving this problem aside, I shall provisionally, and on a high level of abstraction, define social structures as the acknowledged and unacknowledged conditions for, and the intended as well as unintended consequences of, social action. I find Giddens' conception of social structures, as only the unacknowledged and unintended conditions and consequences, too narrow.[113] Conditions will often be acknowledged and at least some conditions are the outcome of previous purposive social action. Consequences, too, will often be acknowledged and intended.

Structures restrict as well as enable.[114] Structures restrict and condition the choices and actions of social agents, but they also allow certain types of behavior and shape opportunities for social action. Not only the limits, but also the possibilities of choices and actions of social agents will depend on the pattern of structural positions and the distribution of resources.[115]

Social structures are not given by nature but products of human action. The choices and actions of various social agents constantly produce social structures which again, at any given moment, condition subsequent choices and actions of social agents, and so on, in a never-ending process.[116]

Social agents can be individuals, social groups, elites, and social classes. I have chosen to concentrate on a discussion of the role of social classes in the processes of the development of democracy. This does not entail a denial of the importance of other social agents although I conceive class relations, alliances and actions as especially important here.[117]

Unfortunately many scholars seem to have given up completely any attempt at a more precise definition of the concept of social class. Barrington Moore, Lipset and Luebbert, for example, are all surprisingly vague here.[118] A more precise delimitation and determination of social classes is certainly also extremely complicated and highly contested.[119] The main criteria used here are actual social control, by economic as well as ideological and political means, over the means of production, disposition over the surplus social product, and the pattern of authority relations in the work process. The determination of classes is complicated in three respects: their formation and persistence, their interests and their influence.

As to formation and persistence, social classes can be discerned on three levels of reality: as objective positions in the economic and social structures, as spontaneously developed attitudes and conceptions, and as organized and conscious action.[120] A social class can exist on all three levels or on only the first or the first and the second level. The effects of social classes are by no means restricted to the influence resulting from conscious, organized action. Stated in another way, it can be said that classes are complicated because they embrace the level of structures as well as the level of social action.

It is also necessary to stress the contingency of class formation. Developments from objective positions to conscious social agents are by no means automatic and pre-destined. As emphasized by Rueschemeyer, et al.:

In contrast to the traditional view, we see the subjective and organizational expressions of class interests contingent on complex and variable historical conditions and not as an invariant and near-automatic outgrowth of the objective class structure.[121]

Class interest is complicated too. It can by no means be defined narrowly as comprising only economic interests. European peasants and the town middle classes reacted violently to what they conceived as a threat to their subculture and traditional way of life. The reactions of traditional elites and ruling classes, too, were conditioned by their fear of a dissolution of traditional values and symbols. And the European labour movements were, finally, not only movements for the promotion of narrow economic interests, but to a very high degree cultural movements.

As to influence, social classes and class relations have ultimately been important in the processes of development of democracy, not only due to the direct clashes of interests, but also through the complicated systems of alliances and confrontations. These systems were determined not only by the actual positions of the different classes in the social and economic system, but also by the pattern of past and present cleavages and the sequence in the development of these. This again determined different trajectories in European development.

Different trajectories

The thesis on the importance of social classes argued by a number of scholars[122] and the thesis on the importance of the sequence of the development and solution of cleavages, forwarded by Rokkan, Lipset and Luebbert, lead to the further question of the type of social order produced by class relations and actions and the unfolding of cleavages and alliances. What was the result of the ongoing interplay of social action and social structures? What kind of social order prevailed in Europe during the fateful period from the 1860's to the end of World War II?

This was a period which saw the formation of a number of important nation states, the entry of the masses into politics, the development of the European labour movement and of socialist and internationalist ideas, but also the rise of extreme nationalism and later fascism. It was the period of two world wars and repeated economic and political crises, a period of the birth — as well as — the breakdown of democracies.

In his provocative work on 'The Persistence of the Old Regime', Arno Mayer has questioned a number of dominant views on the character of this period and its social order.[123] Mayer challenges the prevailing view, that the main feature of this period was capitalist development and modernization. On the contrary, he claims, the period was first and foremost characterized by the persistence of the old order. This predominance of the old order is, according to Mayer, the main cause of the turbulent, explosive character of the whole period. In the end, the persistence of the old order produced what he calls 'the European 30 years' war' from 1914 to 1945. It was the savage struggle of traditional elites and ruling classes to preserve, by any means necessary, the old order and their privileged positions within this same order which propelled European societies into first World War I, then fascism and subsequently World War II:

> the Great war of 1914, or the first and protogenic phase of this general crisis, was an outgrowth of the latter-day remobilization of the European anciens régimes. Though losing ground to the forces of industrial capitalism, the forces of the old order were still sufficiently wilful and powerful to resist and slow down the course of history, if necessary by recourse to violence. The Great War was an expression of the decline and fall of the old order fighting to prolong its life rather than of the explosive rise of industrial capitalism bent on its primacy ... after 1918-19 the forces of perseverance recovered sufficiently to aggravate Europe's general crisis, sponsor fascism, and contribute to the resumption of total war in 1939.[124]

Arno Mayer has been accused of failing to appreciate the force of capitalist development in this period and the endemic contradictions and conflicts in capitalism. Thus he acquits capitalism of any responsibility 'for the horrors of the first half of the century'.[125] This criticism forwarded by Callinicos resembles the criticism advanced by Blackburn and Eley against Hans-Ulrich Wehler, Dahrendorf and others on the character of Imperial Germany.[126] But what is at stake here is not the moral question of guilt or innocence. The question raised by Arno Mayer is the question of the main character of the European social order in the whole period from about 1860 to 1945. It is a question of recognizing the very complexity of European societies in this period and of different trajectories in different regions of Europe.

    The main point is to recognize the penetration of industrial capitalism into the old order, the struggle between old and new and the ensuing complicated patterns of cleavages and conflicts. Even Callinicos recognizes the complex and 'mixed' character of societies in this period of European history due to the survival of elements and relations from the old agrarian order. He also emphasizes a decisive difference here between Britain and East and Central Europe:

> Explaining the eruption of military and social conflict after 1900 in terms of contradictions internal to the capitalist mode of production does not imply that the survivals of the old order on which Mayer concentrates can be ignored...Britain by the late nineteenth century did not offer the sharp contrast between old and new

provided by the comparatively sudden onset of industrial capitalism in genuinely ancien régime orders such as Prussia, Russia and Austria-Hungary.[127]

The Central European societies,[128] especially Germany and Austria, were to an exceptional degree 'mixed' societies characterized by the clash between and the violent penetration of two competing social orders. The sudden intrusion of industrial capitalism into the old order, intermingling old and new, produced an accumulation of many different cleavages. Reinforcing each other, they created explosive developments.

It is possible then to discern several trajectories in European political development:

Central European societies, due to their explosive mixture of new and old, had an unusually troublesome and conflict ridden political development in the period from 1860 to 1945. Central European societies saw the development of a strong and radicalized labour movement. Not only the traditional ruling elites and classes and big capital, but also the middle classes resented the labour movement. Eventually, under the impact of successive economic and political crisis, large sections of the middle classes turned to fascism. The peasants too reacted violently against what they perceived to be a deadly threat to their entrenched subculture and traditional way of life. Furthermore, an alliance between the traditional ruling elites and classes on the one hand and the rising fascist elite on the other, crystallized, paving the way for a fascist take-over.

The trajectory of Scandinavian development came closer to the British path. The Scandinavian countries were in the fortunate situation that most of the old cleavages had been overcome before the development of new cleavages rooted in industrial capitalism. Thus, the Scandinavian social order was less explosive than the Central European social order. In the Scandinavian countries, both liberalism and the labour movement became moderate and conciliatory and, moreover, the important alliance between workers and peasants succeeded. This again laid the foundation for the peaceful ascent of the labour movement to political power, the rescue of democracy in the turmoil of the thirties and the construction of the Scandinavian welfare state model.

In Eastern and Central-Eastern Europe, the general development of society lagged behind Central European development (except in Bohemia). East European societies were more traditional and less mixed than the Central European societies. The subaltern classes were completely subjugated and displayed a very low degree of mobilization and participation. In times of crisis, therefore, a traditional dictatorship sufficed to keep them down and secure the privileged position of the ruling classes and elites. In these countries, there was no need for any alliance between fascism and the forces of the old order. Consequently a situation of contest and struggle developed between 'the old' and 'the new Right'.

The Russian trajectory, finally, was in certain respects similar to the East European, but due to the country's status as an 'underdeveloped Great Power'[129] and the attempt from the 1890's onwards to carry out a rapid industrialization initiated from above,[130] the Russian trajectory in certain respects also resembled the German. The combination of accumulated internal cleavages and pressures along with defeat in war produced the revolutions of 1905, and February and October 1917. After the Bolsheviks took over, the new elite resumed Sergei Witte's old policy of rapid modernization directed from above, but on an enlarged scale. After Stalin's victory at the end of the twenties, industrialization progressed at a rapid speed, displaying what Alec Nove has called 'excessive excesses'.[131] In this process of rapid and forced modernization, the ideology, created by Stalin and Bukharin in the twenties, of 'socialism in one country' came to function as the Russian equivalent of 'the Protestant ethic' in the West.[132]

Conclusions and hypotheses

In this chapter, I have explored the relationship between the development of democracy and the role of social classes. The argument presented here stresses that we cannot hope to understand today's transitions to democracy without studying the class dynamics unfolding during these transitions and without a clear understanding of how the current situation is predicated upon a history of class formation, class conflicts, and class alliances. The patterns of conflicts and alliances, as well as the ideologies and values that supported and penetrated these social relations, have been historically and culturally specific. In other words, while we can discern certain common tendencies and trends, we must also explore the specific conditions and history of different social classes within their particular societies in order to grasp fully the course of development of democracy — the successes and failures — across Europe. These assertions and my whole argument can be summarized as follows:

1) Economic development alone has never produced democracy. Even if a certain degree of economic development is a necessary condition for democracy, it is not a sufficient condition. Democracy was everywhere a product of action, of protracted social and political struggles where different social classes played different roles. As pointed out by Rueschemeyer et al., capitalist economic development has favoured the development of democracy because it changed the class structure, weakening the classes which most resisted the

development of democracy, and strengthening the classes that promoted democracy.

2) There has never been an automatic relationship between liberalism and democracy. In Central Europe in particular, political liberalism resisted democracy for a long period and in the interwar period during the decisive struggle for democracy, liberalism was either absent from the political scene or too weak to make a difference. The social democratic labour movement was left to fight for, and sustain, democracy. The different reactions to the entry of the masses into politics and development of democracy must be explained by the different class interests underlying political liberalism and social democracy. In this period of European history, these interests were in political life articulated in relation to the question of democracy. But we must be careful here: the relations between classes and politics are complicated.

3) Liberalism has usually been associated with the rising bourgeoisie and/or with the town middle classes.[133] But in Denmark after 1848, for example, liberalism was associated with the peasant movement.[134] In Hungary, liberalism was a movement of the gentry.[135] Liberalism has had different social bases. In many countries, the bourgeoisie and the middle classes found other political ideologies to embrace.[136] Liberalism's ideological content also differed from place to place and time to time.[137] Nevertheless, in a broad and approximate sense, liberalism can be seen as a political expression of the interests of the rising bourgeoisie and of sections of the town middle classes.[138]

4) Conservatism was born as a reaction to the Enlightenment and to the political ideas and forces of liberalism, socialism and democracy.[139] Conservatism long resisted democracy and, as late as the interwar period, the greater part of continental European conservatism was either hostile or skeptical towards democracy. The social base of conservatism has varied a great deal. In its origins, and for a long time thereafter, conservatism was sustained by the agrarian upper class and the peasantry. Later on however, in other places, it gained support from part of the bourgeoisie, the middle classes and even some workers.[140] As long as its main social support resisted democracy, political conservatism was anti-democratic.

5) As Rueschemeyer et al. argue, the working class has been the most consistently pro-democratic force. But it must be emphasized that it was the organized social democratic labour movement which fought for, and sustained, democracy. The development of democratic popular participation and a democratic popular culture — the behavioural and normative dimensions of

democracy — was rooted in the activism within the organizational network of European labour.[141]

6) In its birth and development in the West, socialism was a vision nurtured within the labour movement and among groups of intellectuals. The vision embraced a continued extension of political democracy, universal suffrage, the involvement of the masses in politics, the breakdown of barriers between rulers and the ruled, the extension of democracy into the realm of economic life, the end of exploitation and oppression, democratic control and planning, and the free and versatile realization of human potential.[142]

7) In the East, socialism was reduced to state ownership and Stalinist planning. Communism can, in the Russian context, be seen as a system and strategy of rapid, forced modernization initiated and directed 'from above'.[143] In this process, the *nomenklatura* came to function as a ruling class, which as a group exercised real social control over the means of production and disposed of the surplus social product.[144] In this context, the theory of 'socialism in one country' came to function as a modernizing ideology and as a legitimizing device for the new ruling class, the nomenklatura.[145] After 1945, this system and strategy was forced upon the East European societies. Communism in the West, on the other hand, was in its mass base an expression of working class radicalism. Its leadership and organizational structure, however, were subjected to a process of Stalinization that completely changed the original parties.[146]

8) Fascism can be seen as an independent social and political movement which took different courses in Eastern and Western Europe.[147] In the East, fascism never came to terms with the traditional elites and ruling classes. On the contrary, competition, and even conflict, developed.[148] In the West, on the other hand, an alliance between the rising fascist elite and the traditional elites and ruling classes eventually developed.[149] These different patterns can only be explained by a theory of class interests, conflicts and alliances. However, the social basis of fascism can only partly, and not completely, be explained by class theory.[150]

9) In European political development, the reaction of different social classes was a crucial factor during the emergence and unfolding of mass politics. As ruling classes and governing elites came to see the mobilization and increasing participation of subaltern classes as a threat to their positions and vested interests, they reacted strongly. In such situations there was a risk of a counter-democratic backlash. Depending on the general character of the social order, a breakdown of democracy and the establishment of a dictatorship could take

place. The reaction of the urban middle classes and the peasants also influenced events. In cases where they reacted violently against threats to their culture and traditional way of life, the road to a fascist dictatorship was cleared.

10) A satisfactory solution to the crisis provoked by the entry of the masses into politics depended on the development of democratic mass participation and a popular democratic culture, both of which were essential and indispensable for the development of democracy . At the same time, however, it is evident from the European experience that mass mobilization and participation can also be dangerous. As demonstrated by fascism and extreme nationalism, mobilization and participation can take quite different directions and assume different forms and goals. The particular form and ideology of the mass mobilization and mass participation of the European labour movement was not the only possible one.

11) In general, the relationship between the old European order and rising industrial capitalism which gradually penetrated this order played a crucial role in European political development. The most 'dangerous' (seen in the context of the development of democracy) types of societies and periods were those which were extraordinarily 'mixed' due to the relatively sudden, rapid and massive penetration of rising industrial capitalism into the existing old order. This produced a very complex interplay of relations between traditional elites and ruling classes, peasants and the old petty bourgeoisie on the one hand, and industrial capitalists, workers and the new middle class on the other, and between the political ideologies and movements of conservatism, fascism, liberalism, socialism and democracy. In these cases, the accumulation of mutually reinforcing cleavages and conflicts produced a highly turbulent path of political development.

12) The class-analytic approach seems to be a valuable, even indispensable, tool in long-term analyses of political development and regime formation, including the development of democracy. It is also possible, as indicated in sub-section IV, to discern some main trajectories in European political development, trajectories which to a high degree have been determined by different patterns of class conflicts and alliances and the underlying patterns of cleavages and the sequences in the development of these.

13) Class analysis must be applied cautiously and carefully, however. The relationships among social classes, political ideas and organizations are highly complex. S.M. Lipset's famous three part division of social classes, political ideas, and forces, is rudimentary and it only catches some main tendencies and

trends.[151] The relations are complex because class interests are not directly and automatically translated into political ideas and organizations, and because political ideas and organizations have been determined not only by class interests but by other factors as well. On the other hand, it would be impossible to explain long-term political development in Europe, the formation of different types of regimes, the crystallization of the main trajectories, the strengths and weaknesses of major political movements and ideas etc., without relying heavily on a theory of social classes. Class theory does not explain everything, but it explains a great deal.

14) Social classes do not emerge instantly and automatically from an objective base. Class formation is a long and complicated process.[152] Furthermore, social classes must not be conceptualized as pure economic categories. Not only economic, but also political and ideological factors play a part in the processes of class formation. Class interests are determined not only by economic position, but by politics and ideology as well. Class interests include values and norms as well as material demands. Class domination also involves political and ideological relations as well as purely economic relations. The rule of the nomenklatura in the former Soviet Union, for example, was exercised primarily by political and ideological means. In this respect, the rule of the nomenklatura was more like the rule of the feudal ruling class of the past, than the domination of the capitalist class in modern societies.

15) The previous argument also stresses the importance of class conflicts as well as class alliances. Patterns of class conflicts and class alliances are influenced by previous cleavages and sequences in the development of such cleavages. These cleavages have often been of a non-economic nature. Finally, class analysis cannot stand alone: it must be completed by an analysis of elites,[153] that is elaborated theoretically and investigated empirically.[154]

16) The fact that class analysis has proved indispensable for understanding the development of democracy and failed attempts to develop democracy in Europe up to the present time is, of course, no proof of its universal indispensability for analyses of present and future developments.[155] But it seems to be a theoretical approach worth considering. The prevailing one-sided focus on declared ideology and leaders in the study of political development in Eastern Europe and the former Soviet Union is not very fertile or promising.[156] The real class character of the Soviet Union and of the Stalinist societies in Eastern Europe after 1945 must be analyzed.[157] We must study not only leaders and elites but also the social processes going on at the bottom of these societies,[158] and necessary conceptual adjustments and theory building must be carried

out.[159] Social research within this field has too long been seriously hampered by Cold War rhetoric and official ideology. Instead of penetrating to the level of real social power relations and conflicting interests, many scholars have stuck to the adhesive surface of ruling ideology, accepting at its face value the ideological claim of the former Soviet regime and Eastern European communist regimes that they had accomplished 'real existing socialism'.[160]

17) Research on recent processes of transition, too, has been one-sided in its focus on leaders, factions and proclaimed ideology.[161] Attention must be directed towards questions like: Do recent processes of transformation in Eastern and Central Eastern Europe constitute a 'conversion of power' carried out by the old ruling class of the nomenklatura? Can the present period of consolidation best be understood as characterized by the formation of a new ruling class consisting of the transformed nomenklatura and the new rich?[162] And, what is happening at the bottom of these societies?

18) One must recognize the very complex character of recent developments in Eastern and East-Central Europe. Everything seems to have been turned upside down: members of the former nomenklatura emerge in the post-Stalinist societies as capitalists, political leaders who yesterday spoke of 'proletarian internationalism', today indulge in the wildest nationalist excesses and ethnic cleansings.[163] Former Communist politicians and 'Marxist' intellectuals have been converted into super-liberalist adherents of unrestricted market economies and monetarist policy.[164] Past ideologies, idiosyncrasies and xenophobia are aroused and transferred to the present, intermingling with, or confronting, modern ideologies, values and attitudes.[165] Ideologies seem to be 'movable' and 'convertible'. Old ideologies which originated under definite historical circumstances with specific functions have been moved, converted, and attached to new elites and classes, assuming quite other functions than the original ones.[166] The whole East European region seems to be a great melting pot where old elites, classes and ideologies are forged into new elites, classes and ideologies.

19) If it is true that the period from about 1860 to 1945 can be seen as a sort of transition period during which industrial capitalism on the European continent penetrated the previous existing social order, then capitalism is still young and not at all *spät* or 'post'. Capitalism in Central Europe was then only fully established as late as 1945, and what we are witnessing now is capitalism triumphantly spreading to the last of the areas of the world which were still outside its orbit. Whether this new world will be peaceful and democratic

without serious problems and deep cleavages — the proclaimed end of history[167] — remains to be seen.

20) It remains also to be seen whether current developments in Eastern and East-Central Europe are analogues to developments in the interwar period, a period in Central European history when the clash between — and the mutual penetration of — two different social orders produced an extraordinary accumulation of conflicts and a turbulent political development.

Thus the transitions underway today in East-Central and Eastern Europe are neither pre-determined nor random. The success or failure of the dramatic social, economic, and political, transformations in so many different countries, depends in each case on the specific historical preconditions, previous patterns of cleavages, and on the historical legacy of previous attempts or failures of mass mobilization and democratization. In our research on the contemporary period in the development of democracy, we need to pay greater attention to the long historical trajectories of each case in order to develop a theoretical framework for understanding the range and variations of outcomes and possible explanations for emergent patterns. Democratic development will also be influenced by the relationships between both new and existing social groups and whether, and how, they organize as elites and classes to pursue their economic, political and cultural interests. The future of democracy in Eastern and Central Europe depends to a large degree on how social relations crystallize, not only among elites and parties, but also throughout society.

Notes

1. Samuel P. Huntington, 1991. *The Third Wave. Democratization in the Late Twentieth Century.* Norman and London: University of Oklahoma Press.
2. Juan Linz & Alfred Stepan (eds.), 1978. *The Breakdown of Democratic Regimes. Europe.* Baltimore.
3. Juan Linz, 1978. *The Breakdown of Democratic Regimes: Crisis, Breakdown and Reequilibration.* Baltimore.
4. The collapse of the Weimar Republic, for example, should be seen as an unsuccessful attempt to consolidate a democratic regime rather than the 'breakdown' of a well-established democracy.
5. Cf. Guillermo O'Donnell & Philipe C. Schmitter, 1991. *Tentative Conclusions about Uncertain Democracies*, Baltimore & London; Guillermo O'Donnell, Philippe C. Schmitter & Laurence Whitehead, 1986. *Transitions from Authoritarian Rule. Southern Europe.* Baltimore & London; Philippe C. Schmitter, 1991. 'The Consolidation of Democracy and the Choice of Institutions', paper, Stanford; Philippe C. Schmitter, 1991. 'The Consolidation of Political Democracies:

Processes, Rhytms, Sequences and Types', paper, Stanford; and John Herz (ed.), 1989. *From Dictatorship to Democracy: Coping with the Legacies of Authoritharianism and Totalitarianism*. London.

6. See also the penetrating analysis and criticism of this approach in Lene Bøgh Sørensen, 'Political Development and Regime Transformations. The Hungarian Case', dissertation, Institute of Political Science, University of Aarhus, Denmark.

7. See for example Terry Karl, 1990. 'Dilemmas of Democratization in Latin America', *Comparative Politics*, October; Guiseppe di Palma, 1990. *To Craft Democracies, An Essay on Democratic Transitions*. Berkeley; and for a criticism Lene Bøgh Sørensen, *op.cit:* 142ff.

8. Lene Bøgh Sørensen, *op.cit.*, makes a basic distinction between 'actor-oriented approaches' and 'historical-structural approaches'. Rueschemeyer et al. distinguish between 'cross-national quantitative research' and 'comparative historical research', recognizing, however, within the latter category the existence of a sub-tradition which focuses on agents and operates with a very narrow time horizon — Dietrich Rueschemeyer, Evelyne H. Stephens & John D. Stephens, 1992. *Capitalist Development and Democracy*. Chicago. In what follows I shall use the basic distinction made by Lene Bøgh Sørensen.

9. Cf. Barrington Moore, 1966. *Social Origins of Dictatorship and Democracy*. Boston; and Karl de Schweinitz, 1964. *Industrialization and Democracy: Economic Necessities and Political Possibilities*. New York.

10. Barrington Moore, *op.cit.*; and Karl de Schweinitz, *op.cit.*

11. Karl de Schweinitz, *op.cit:* 10-11.

12. Barrington Moore, *op.cit.*

13. This observation has also been made by Rueschemeyer et al., *op.cit:* 20-21.

14. Max Weber, 1980. 'Zur Lage der bürgerlichen Demokratie in Russland, 1906', in Johannes Winckelmann (ed.), *Max Weber. Gesammelte Politische Schriften*, Tübingen: 33-68; and Max Weber, *Russland. Übergang zum Scheinkonstitutionalismus, op.cit:* 69-111.

15. Max Weber, *Zur Lage der bürgerlichen Demokratie in Russland:* 64.

16. See for a survey of debates and findings, Rueschemeyer et al., *op.cit:* 13ff.

17. See Jeffrey Sachs, 1990. 'What is to be Done?', *Economist*, 13 January; and Jeffrey Sachs, 1993. *Poland's Jump to the Market Economy*, Cambridge Mass. And for a critique Alice Amsden, Jacek Kochanowicz & Lance Taylor, 1994. *The Market Meets its Match*, Princeton; and Peter Gowan, 1995. 'Neo-Liberal Theory and Practice for Eastern Europe', *New Left Review*, (213): 3-60.

18. See for a revealing survey of poverty, malnutrition and health crisis produced by shock therapy economic policy in Eastern Europe and the former Soviet Union: *UNICEF, Economies in Transition Studies, Regional and Monitoring Report, 1994. Crisis in Mortality, Health and Nutrition*, Florence, 1994. According to UNICEF the 'excess mortality' in Russia, Ukraine, Bulgaria, Hungary and Poland between 1989 and 1993 was 800,000.

19. This projection of asserted positive effects of present policy into an indeterminate distant future very much resembles the Stalinist logic of sacrificing the present to 'History'. Often the very same people who yesterday lauded the blessings of

'socialist development of productive forces' today applaud the unrestricted 'development of market forces' as the universal road to affluence and democracy.

20. Cf., for example, S.M. Lipset, 1959. 'Some social requisites of democracy: economic development and political legitimacy', *American Political Science Review*, 53; Philips Cutwright & James Wiley, 1969. 'Modernization and political representation: 1927-66', Studies in Comparative International Development; and Janos Kornai, 1990. *The Road to a Free Economy*. New York & London.

21. This has, of course, been a main argument within the socialist tradition. See for example Michael Harrington, 1990. *Socialism. Past and Future*. New York: Plume; Ellen Meiksins Wood, 1995. *Democracy Against Capitalism*. Cambridge: Cambridge U.P.; Ralph Miliband, 1989. *Divided Societies*. Oxford: Clarendon Press; and Michael Parenti, 1988. *Democracy for the Few*. New York: St. Martin. It is notable, however, that also scholars of a liberalist persuasion have been concerned about the impact of unequal distribution of resources on the democratic political process, see for example Robert A. Dahl, 1985. *A Preface To Economic Theory*. Cambridge: Polity Press; C.B. Macpherson, 1973. *Democratic Theory. Essays in Retrieval*. Oxford: Clarendon; C.B. Macpherson, 1977. *The Life and Times of Liberal Democracy*. Oxford U.P.; and Charles E. Lindblom, 1977. *Politics and Markets*. New York. See further note 154.

22. See the now classical definition by Joseph Schumpeter. *Capitalism, Socialism and Democracy*. New York: Harper, 1975 (1942): 269; and for a survey of conceptions and arguments David Held. *Models of Democracy*. Cambridge: Polity Press, 1987.

23. Dietrich Rueschemeyer, Evelyne H. Stephens & John D. Stephens, 1992. *Capitalist Development and Democracy*. Chicago: 7.

24. Rueschemeyer et al., *op.cit*: 43.

25. See also Michael Mann who speaks of four 'higher level crystallizations', Michael Mann, 1993. *The Sources of Social Power*, vol. 2, *The rise of classes and nation-states, 1760-1914*. Cambridge: Cambridge U.P.: 81ff.

26. Cf. for example the discussions in Alex Callinicos, 1987. *Making History*, Cambridge: Polity Press; Anthony Giddens, 1981. *A Contemporary Critique of Historical Materialism*, vol. 1. London: Macmillan; Anthony Giddens, 1986. *The Constitution of Society*. Berkeley; Michael Mann, *op.cit.*; and Ellen Meiksins Wood, 1995. *Democracy Against Capitalism. Renewing Historical Materialism*. Cambridge: Cambridge U.P.

27. By Nation-building I shall understand the development and consolidation of modern national communities. By state-building I shall understand the development and consolidation of modern states, including modern bureaucracies. See for analyses of state- and nation-building Reinhard Bendix, 1977, *Nation-Building and Citizenship*. Berkeley; Ernest Gellner, 1983. *Nations and Nationalism*. Oxford; Anthony Giddens, 1987. *The Nation-State and Violence*. Cambridge: Polity Press; Raymond Grew, 1978. *Crises of Political Development in Europe and the United States*. Princeton; E.J. Hobsbawm, 1992. *Nations and Nationalism Since 1780*. Cambridge: Cambridge U.P.; Samuel P. Huntington, 1968. *Political Order in Changing Societies*. Yale; Michael Mann, 1986 & 1993. *The Sources*

of Social Power, vols. 1-2. Cambridge: Cambridge U.P.; Charles Tilly (ed.), 1975. *The Formation of National States in Western Europe*. Princeton; and Charles Tilly, 1992. *Coercion, Capital and European States AD 990-1992*. Cambridge Mass. & Oxford: Blackwell.

28. See note 35 and note 36.

29. See the point made by Peter Bugge, 1994, in his criticism of Ernest Gellner's super-functionalism — 'Czech Nation-Building, National Self-Perception and Politics 1780-1914'. Dissertation, Institute of Slavonic Studies, University of Aarhus: 9.

30. Cf. my general discussion in section 3 and section 5 of the concept of 'social class' and the fertility of class analyses.

31. See for this concept of 'participation crisis' (Grew) or 'entry into politics crisis (Lipset), Raymond Grew (ed.), 1978. *Crises of Political Development in Europe and the United States*. Princeton: 7ff. and 21ff.; and S.M. Lipset, 1963. *Political Man*, London: 79ff.

32. See for the concept of 'cleavage' S.M. Lipset & Stein Rokkan, 1967. 'Cleavage Structures, Party Systems and Voter Alignments: An Introduction', in S.M. Lipset & Stein Rokkan (eds.), *Party Systems and Voter Alignments: Cross-National Perspectives*. New York: 1-64.

33. Cf. the discussion in Grew, *op.cit:* 10ff. and 21ff.

34. See note 36.

35. Grew, *op.cit.*; Lipset, *op.cit.*; and Hobsbawm, *op.cit.* See also E.J. Hobsbawm, 1992. *Nations and Nationalisms Since 1780*. Cambridge: Cambridge U.P., ch. 4.

36. Cf. in addition to Grew, *op.cit.*; Hobsbawm *op.cit.*; Dick Geary, 1981. *European Labour Protest 1848-1939*. London; Robert Gildea, 1987. *Barricades and Borders. Europe 1800-1914*. Oxford; Theodore Hamerow, 1983. *The Birth of a New Europe: State and Society in the Nineteenth Century*. Chapel Hill and London: University of North Carolina Press; Harvey Mitchell & Peter N. Stearns, 1971. *Workers and Protest: The European Labour Movement, the Working Classes and the Origins of Social Democracy, 1890-1914*. Itaca Ill.; Peter N. Stearns, 1967. *European Society in Upheaval. Social History Since 1800*. New York & London; Norman Stone, 1983. *Europe Transformed 1878-1919*. London; and Charles Tilly, Louise Tilly & Richard Tilly, 1975. *The Rebellious Century 1830-1930*. London.

37. See Charles Tilly, 1978, *From Mobilization to Revolution*. New York.

38. Cf. Graeme Duncan, 1973. *Marx and Mill*. Cambridge: Cambridge U.P.; and Norman Geras, 1976. *The Legacy of Rosa Luxemburg*. London.

39. Carl E. Schorske, 1980. *Fin-de-Siecle Vienna: Politics and Culture*. New York.

40. It also means that it is necessary to distinguish between endogenous developed features and 'imported' features and between the stalinist leadership and the mass base of the Western communist parties. See for example the German KPD, Ossip K. Flechtheim, 1969, *Die KPD in der Weimarer Republik*. Frankfurt a.M.; and Herman Weber, 1969, *Die Wandlung des deutschen Kommunismus. Die Stalinisierung der KPD in der Weimarer Republik*, Bnd. 1-2. Frankfurt a.M. See further note 41.

41. An important difference between communism and fascism was the different content of the two ideologies. Communism, after all, was within the rationalist tradition with roots in the Enlightenment whereas fascism was anti-rationalist.In communism there was a discrepancy between theory and practice; in fascism, on the contrary, practice was in full accordance with ideology.

42. See for differences between communism and fascism note 40 and note 41.

43. For this concept and the theory on competitive elitism, see David Held, 1987. *Models of Democracy*. Cambridge: Polity Press, ch. 5.

44. See Reinhard Bendix, 1977. *Nation Building and Citizenship*. Berkeley: University of California Press; and T.H. Marshall, 1950. *Citizenship and Social Class*. Cambridge: Cambridge U.P.

45. Edvard Bull, 'Arbeiderbevegelsens stilling i de tre nordiske lande 1914-1920', (1922), reprinted in *Tidsskrift for arbeiderbevegelsens historie*, 1, 1976, 3-28.

46. Walter Galenson (ed.), 1952. *Comparative Labour Movements*, New York. Cf. also Niels Elvander, 1980. *Skandinavisk arbetarrörelse*. Stockholm: Liber-Förlag, 47-48.

47. S.M. Lipset, 1963. *Political Man*. London.

48. W.M. Lafferty, 1971. *Economic Development and the Response of Labour in Scandinavia: a Multi-Level Analysis*. Oslo.

49. Dick Geary, 1984. *European Labour Protest 1848-1939*. London; and S.M. Lipset, 1985. 'Radicalism or Reformism: The Sources of Working-Class Politics', in S.M. Lipset (ed.), *Consensus and Conflict. Essays in Political Sociology*. New Brunswick & Oxford, 219-51. Lipset adds to the thesis on the importance of the general political system a further thesis on the importance of the presence or absence of a feudal system in the pre-industrial capitalist period.

50. Walter Korpi, 1978. *The Working Class in Welfare Capitalism*. London: Routledge & Kegan Paul; Walter Korpi, 1983. *The Democratic Class Struggle*. London: Routledge & Kegan Paul; John D. Stephens, 1986. *The Transition from Capitalism to Socialism*. Chicago: University of Illinois Press; Nils Elvander, 1980. *Skandinavisk arbetarrörelse*. Stockholm; and Gregory M. Luebbert, 1991. *Liberalism, Fascism or Social Democracy. Social Classes and the Political Origins of Regimes in Interwar Europe*. Oxford, 121ff and 267ff.

51. Charles A. Gulick, 1948. *Austria. From Habsburg to Hitler*, vols. 1-2. Berkeley; Gerald Brenan, 1960. *The Spanish Labyrinth*. Cambridge: Cambridge U.P.; and Hugh Seton-Watson, 1963. *Italy from Liberalism to Fascism*. Cambridge, Mass. And for comparative analyses, Dick Geary, 1981. *European Labour Protest 1848-1939*. London; and Gregory M. Luebbert, *op.cit.*

52. See Dieter Groh, 1973. *Negative Integration und revolutionärer Attentismus. Die deutsche Sozialdemokratie am Vorabend des Ersten Weltkriges*. Frankfurt a.M.: Ullstein; Vernon L. Lidtke, 1966. *The outlawed Party. Social Democracy in Germany 1878-90*. Princeton, N.J.; Günther Roth, 1963. *The Social Democracy in Imperial Germany*. Totowa, N.J.: Bedminster; and Carl E. Schorske, 1965. *German Social Democracy 1905-17*. New York: Wiley & Sons.

53. Hagen Schulze, 1977. *Otto Braun oder Preussens demokratische Sendung*. Berlin; in general W.L. Guttsmann, 1981. *The German Social Democratic Party 1875-1933*. London; and Georg Fülberth & Jürgen Harrer, 1977. *Die deutsche Sozialdemokratie*

1890-1933. Darmstadt & Neuwied.

54. See Karl Dietrich Bracher, 1955. *Die Auflösung der Weimarer Republik*. Villingen; and Hans Mommsen, 1989. *Die verspielte Freiheit. Der Weg der Republik von Weimar in den Untergang 1918 bis 1933*. Berlin.

55. Guttsmann, *op.cit.* See also William Sheridan Allen, 1966. *The Nazi Seizure of Power. The Experience of a Single German Town*. London.

56. I agree with Bernt Hagtvet, *op.cit.*: 114; and Eberhard Kolb, *op.cit.*: 193. H.A. Turner is focusing much too narrowly on the question of economic financing.

57. Eberhard Kolb, *op.cit.*: 193.

58. Bracher, *op.cit.*; Mommsen, *op.cit.*; Kolb *op.cit.*, ch. 6; Kühnl, *op.cit.*; and F.L. Carsten, 1966. *The Reichswehr and Politics 1918-33*. Oxford.

59. Cf. for a survey of the discussion, Eberhard Kolb, 1988. *The Weimar Republic*. London: 191ff.

60. Cf. Eberhard Czichon, 1967. *Wer verhalf Hitler zur Macht?*. Köln; Dick Geary, 1983. 'The Industrial Elite and the Nazis in the Weimar Republic' in Peter Stachura (ed.), *The Nazi Machtergreifung*. London; George W.F. Hallgarten & Joachim Radkau, 1974. *Deutsche Industrie und Politik von Bismarck bis heute*. Frankfurt a.M.: 195ff.; and D. Stegmann, 1973. 'Zum Verhältnis von Grossindustrie und Nationalsozialismus 1930-33', in *Archiv für Sozialgeschichte*, vol. 13: 399-482. For another view, see H.A. Turner, 1985. *German Big Business and the Rise of Hitler*. New York & Oxford.

61. H.A. Turner, *op.cit.* It is worth noting, however, that heavy industry never dreamt of supporting the SPD, let alone the KPD. In this respect class interests certainly set some limits!

62. Bernt Hagtvet, 'The Theory of Mass Society and the Collapse of the Weimar Republic: A Re-Examination', in Stein Ugelvik Larsen et al., *op.cit.*: 114.

63. Kühnl, *op.cit.*

64. Lyttelton, *op.cit.*; Seton-Watson, *op.cit.*; and Tasca, *op.cit.*

65. Gregory M. Luebbert, *op.cit.*: 258-66.

66. See F.L. Carsten, 1980. *The Rise of Fascism*. Berkeley, ch. 5; Andrew Janos, 1982. *The Politics of Backwardness in Hungary 1825-1945*. Princeton, ch. 5 and 6; and Joseph Rotschild, 1974. *East Central Europe between the Two World Wars*. Seattle: University of Washington Press.

67. Cf. in general F.L. Carsten, *op.cit.*; and Gregory M. Luebbert, *op.cit.* For Germany, Bracher, *op.cit.*; Mommsen *op.cit.*; Kolb *op.cit.*; and Reinhard Kühnl, 1980. 'Pre-Conditions for the Rise and Victory of Fascism in Germany', in Stein Ugelvik Larsen et al., *Who Were the Fascists?* Bergen-Oslo-Tromsø: Universitetsforlaget, 118-30. For Austria, Charles A. Gulick, *op.cit.*, Gerhard Botz, 'Introduction' and 'The Changing Patterns of Social Support for Austrian National Socialism (1918-45)', in Ugelvik Larsen et al., *op.cit.*: 192-201 and 202-25; and Bruce F. Pauley, 'Nazis and Heimwehr Fascists: The Struggle for Supremacy in Austria, 1918-38', in U. Larsen et al., *op.cit.*: 226-38. For Italy, Adrian Lyttelton, 1973. *The Seizure of Power. Fascism in Italy 1919-29*. London; Seton-Watson, *op.cit.*; and Angelo Tasca, 1969. *Glauben, Gehorchen, Kämpfen. Aufstieg des Faschismus*, (1938). Wien; and for Spain, Poul Preston, 1983. *The Coming of the Spanish Civil War*. London.

68. For the middle class panic thesis, see for example Theodor Geiger, 1932. *Die soziale Schichtung des deutschen Volkes: Soziographischer Versuch auf statistischer Grundlage.* Stuttgart: Enker Verlag: 109-22; William Kornhauser, 1959. *The Politics of Mass Society.* Glencoe: The Free Press; Harold Laswell, 1933. 'The Psychology of Hitlerism', *Political Quarterly*, 4, 373-84; S.M. Lipset, 1963. 'Fascism — Left, Right and Centre', in S.M. Lipset: *Political Man*. London: Mercury, 131-76; Sigmund Neumann, 1956. 'Germany: Changing Patterns and Lasting Problems', in Sigmund Neumann (ed.), *Modern Political Parties: Approaches to Comparative Politics*. Chicago: University of Chicago Press, 354-92. See for a critique of the thesis Richard F. Hamilton, 1982. *Who Voted for Hitler?* Princeton: Princeton U.P., ch. 2.

69. S.M. Lipset, 1963. 'Fascism — Left, Right and Center', in S.M. Lipset, *Political Man*. London: Mercury: 131-76.

70. See Richard Hamilton, *op.cit.*; and the criticism advanced by Hagtvet and Kühnl - Bernt Hagtvet & Reinhard Kühnl, 'Contemporary Approaches to Fascism: A Survey of Paradigms', in Ugelvik Larsen et al., *op.cit.*: 26-51, criticism 29-31.

71. Hamilton, *op.cit.*

72. Hagtvet's comment on Hamilton's results is worth citing here: 'in essence what he has done is to replace the traditional argument that the social specificity of Nazi support may be identified with the lower middle classes with the view that this specificity must be extended to include higher echelons of society.' Hagtvet, *op.cit.*: 110.

73. Bernt Hagtvet, 'The Theory of Mass Society...', *op.cit.*

74. William Sheridan Allen, 1966. *The Nazi Seizure of Power. The Experience of a Single German Town.* London; and Jeremy Noakes, 1971. *The Nazi Party in Lower Saxony, 1921-33.* Oxford.

75. W.S. Allen, *op.cit.*: 274.

76. See Gerhard Botz, 1987. *Krisenzonen einer Demokratie. Gewalt, Streik und Konfliktunterdrückung in Österreich seit 1918.* Frankfurt & New York: Campus; Charles A. Gulick, 1948. *Austria from Habsburg to Hitler*, vols. 1-2. Berkeley; Anson Rabinbach, 1983. *The Crisis of Austrian Socialism. From Red Vienna to Civil War 1927-34.* Chicago: University of Chicago Press; Curt Sørensen, 1992. *Mellem Demokrati og Diktatur*, vols. 1-2, dissertation, Institute of Political Science, University of Aarhus; and Adam Wandruszka, 1954. 'Österreichs politische Struktur. Die Entwicklung der Parteien und politischen Bewegungen', in Heinrich Benedikt (ed.), *Geschichte der Republik Österreich*. München: 289-485.

77. Cf. William Sheridan Allen, 1966. *The Nazi Seizure of Power. The Experience of a Single German Town.* London; and Jeremy Noakes, 1971. *The Nazi Party in Lower Saxony 1921-33.* Oxford.

78. A long and comprehensive discussion about the electoral support for nazism continues today. Neither the Bendix thesis focusing on the previous non- voters as the basis for the Nazi upsurge at the general elections in 1930, nor the Lipset thesis, pointing to the radicalization of the middle class as the main explanation for the Nazi victory in 1930 fully explains their support. The pre-1930 Nazi movement can perhaps be characterized as predominantly a petty bourgeois

movement. After 1930, the movement increasingly gained support from other sectors of the population, including, as Hamilton demonstrates, the upper and upper-middle classes. In general social democratic and communist voters and voters for the Zentrum were resistant to the Nazi appeal. Electoral research thus confirms evidence produced by community studies such as the studies of W.S. Allen and Jeremy Noakes. See Thomas Childers, *The Nazi Voter. The Social Foundation of Fascism in Germany, 1919-33*. Chapel Hill and London: University of North Carolina Press; Jürgen W. Falter, 1991. *Hitlers Wähler*. München; and Richard F. Hamilton, 1982. *Who Voted for Hitler?* Princeton.

79. Jeremy Noakes, *op.cit.*: 136.
80. See Gerhard Botz, 'Introduction', in Ugelvik Larsen et al., *op.cit.*: 192-201.
81. Barrington Moore, 1969. *Social Origins of Dictatorship and Democracy, Lord and Peasant in the Making of the Modern World*. London: 418.
82. S.M. Lipset, 1963. 'The Conditions of the Democratic Order', Part I in S.M. Lipset, *Political Man*. London; and Robert A. Dahl, 1971. *Polyarchy*. Yale, ch. 3.
83. For a theoretical critique of this now so prevailing conception, see John Hoffman, 1988. *State, Power and Democracy*, Sussex: Wheatsheaf; C.B. Macpherson, 1977. *The Life and Times of Liberal Democracy*, Oxford: Oxford U.P.; C.B. Macpherson, 1973. *Democratic Theory. Essays in Retrieval*, Oxford: Clarendon; and Ellen Meiksins Wood, 1995. *Democracy Against Capitalism*. Cambridge: Cambridge U.P. Referring to the concrete political level, it can be argued that liberalism existed for centuries before it became democratic and that liberalism in real history often resisted the process of democratization, opposing, for example, extensions of suffrage — see Luebbert, *op.cit.*; and Ruschemeyer et al., *op.cit.*
84. Rueschemeyer et al., *op.cit.*: 46 and 8.
85. Thomas T. Mackie & Richard Rose, 1982. *The International Almanac of Electoral History*. London: 154-55.
86. S.M. Lipset, 1963. *Political Man*. London, ch. 4.
87. S.M. Lipset, *op.cit.*: 128.
88. A main point made by theoreticians, otherwise as different as Karl Kautsky, Rosa Luxemburg and Otto Bauer.
89. S.M. Lipset, 'Social Conflict, Legitimacy, and Democracy', ch. 3, in *Political Man, op.cit.*, cf. especially 83ff.
90. Lipset, *op.cit.*: 83.
91. Gregory M. Luebbert, 1991. *Liberalism, Fascism or Social Democracy. Social Classes and the Political Origins of Regimes in Interwar Europe*. Oxford; also Luebbert's explicit reference to S.M. Lipset & Stein Rokkan, 1967. 'Cleavage Structures, Party Systems and Voter Alignments: An Introduction', in S.M. Lipset & Stein Rokkan (eds.), *Party Systems and Voter Alignments: Cross-National Perspectives*. New York: 1-64; in Luebbert, *op.cit.*: 327, note 24.
92. Luebbert, *op.cit.*, ch. 2.
93. W.M. Lafferty, 1971. *Economic Development and the Response of Labour in Scandinavia: a Multi-Level Analysis*. Oslo; and Dick Geary, 1981. *European Labour Protest 1848-1939*. London.
94. Luebbert, *op.cit.*, ch. 2, 3, 4 and 5.

95. Luebbert, *op.cit.*
96. Luebbert, *op.cit.*, ch. 6.
97. Luebbert, *op.cit.*, ch. 7 and 8.
98. The bourgeoisie is the class of big and medium capitalists, the middle class consists of two categories: the 'old middle class' of small artisans, shopkeepers and retailers and the 'new middle class' of white collar workers and civil servants.
99. See the discussion in David Blackburn & Geoff Eley, 1984. *The Peculiarities of German History*. Oxford.
100. Luebbert, *op.cit.*: 309.
101. Barrington Moore, 1966. *Social Origins of Dictatorship and Democracy*. Boston; Hans-Ulrich Wehler, 1985. *The German Empire*. Hamburg-New York; Ralf Dahrendorf, 1968. *Gesellschaft und Demokratie in Deutschland*. München; Alexander Gerschenkron, 1943. *Bread and Democracy in Germany*. Berkeley; and for another interpretation, David Blackbourn & Geoff Eley, 1984. *The Peculiarities of German History*. Oxford.
102. Cf. for a similar criticism of Luebbert, Lene Bøgh Sørensen, 1995. *Political Development and Regime Transformations. The Hungarian Case*. Institute of Political Science, University of Aarhus: 101-2.
103. See Bracher, *op.cit.*; Mommsen, *op.cit.*; and Carsten, *op.cit.*
104. Cf. again for a similar criticism, Lene Bøgh Sørensen, *op.cit.*: 101-2.
105. Luebbert, *op.cit.*: 306.
106. This position is shared by Theda Skocpol, *States and Social Revolutions*. Cambridge: Cambridge U.P., 1979. All other theories of social revolutions are accused of 'voluntarism'. Within the marxist tradition, Nicos Poulantzas and G.D. Cohen have maintained similar positions. Nicos Poulantzas, *Political Power and Social Classes*. London, 1973; and G.D. Cohen, *Karl Marx's Theory of History*. Oxford, 1978.
107. Jon Elster, 1985. *Making Sense of Marx*. Cambridge: Cambridge U.P.; and Jon Elster, 1982. 'Marxism, Functionalism and Game Theory. The Case for Methodological Individualism', *Theory and Society*, 11: 453-82.
108. Cf. for this position, Michael Taylor, 1988. 'Rationality and Revolutionary Collective Action', in Michael Taylor (ed.), *Rationality and Revolution*. Cambridge: Cambridge U.P.: 63-97; Anthony Giddens, 1984. *The Constitution of Society*. Cambridge; and Alex Callinicos, 1989. *Making History*. Oxford: Polity Press. The effort to embrace structural as well as behavioral elements of social reality was also the ambition of Karl Marx. For years he has wrongly been interpreted as a mere structuralist (the Althusser school and the German Capital-Logical school). Now it is claimed that he shall be seen as a mere rational choice analyst (see, for example, Jon Elster, *Making Sense of Marx*). But this is a one-sided interpretation, too. The interplay between 'Verhalten' and 'Verhältnisse' is exactly the core of Karl Marx's sociology. See especially Karl Marx & Friedrich Engels, *Die deutsche Ideologie*, 1846, *MEW*, (3), Berlin, 1969: 9-530.
109. Cf. for this position, for example, Ernesto Laclau & Chantal Mouffe, 1985. *Hegemony and Socialist Strategy*. London.

110. Cf. for this position Louis Althusser, 1973. *Pour Marx*, Paris; and Nicos Poulantzas, 1973. *Political Power and Social Classes*. London.
111. Charles Tilly, 1978. *From Mobilization to Revolution*. New York: Random House, 6.
112. Cf. for a not too convincing attempt, Anthony Giddens, 1984. *The Constitution of Society*. Cambridge.
113. Anthony Giddens, 1979. *Central Problems in Social Theory*. London: 69-70; and Anthony Giddens, 1986. *The Constitution of Society*. Berkeley: University of California Press: 25ff.
114. Giddens, *op.cit.* See also Alex Callinicos, 1987. *Making History*. Cambridge: Polity Press: 84-86.
115. Giddens, *op.cit.*; and Callinicos, *op.cit.*
116. Giddens *op.cit.*; Callinicos *op.cit.*; and of course, Marx.
117. Cf. the arguments in Rueschemeyer et al., *op.cit.*; Luebbert, *op.cit.*; Callinicos *op.cit.*; Erik Olin Wright, 1978. *Class, Crisis and the State*. London: NLB; Erik Olin Wright, 1985. *Classes*. London: Verso; and Ellen Meiksins Wood, 1986. *The Retreat from Class*. London: Verso.
118. Rueschemeyer et al., on the other hand, discuss the concept of class and try to give it a more precise content — see Rueschemeyer et al., *op.cit.*: 51ff.
119. Cf. See for a survey of concepts and debates, Anthony Giddens & David Held (eds.), 1982. *Classes, Power and Conflict. Classical and Contemporary Debates*. London: Macmillan; and Stephen Edgell, 1993. *Class*. London & New York: Routledge. My own conception has been much influenced by Erik Olin Wright, 1978. *Class, Crisis and the State*. London: NLB; Erik Olin Wright, 1985. *Classes*, London: Verso; Ellen Meiksins Wood, 1986. *The Retreat from Class*. London: Verso; Ira Katznelson & Aristide R. Zolberg (eds.), 1986. *Working-Class Formation*. Princeton; E.P. Thompson, 1968. *The Making of the English Working Class*. London: Penguin; and Rueschemeyer et al., *op.cit.*
120. Rueschemeyer et al., *op.cit.*: 53. See also Ira Katznelson & Aristide Zolberg (eds.), 1986. *Working Class Formation*. Princeton.
121. Rueschemeyer et al., *op.cit*: 315, no. 13. Cf. also Katznelson & Zollberg, *op.cit.*
122. Perry Anderson, *op.cit.*; Callinicos, *op.cit.*; S.M. Lipset, *op.cit.*; Gregory M. Luebbert, *op.cit.*; Barrington Moore, *op.cit.*; Rueschemeyer et al., *op.cit.*; Meiksins Wood, *op.cit.*; and Olin Wright, *op.cit.*
123. Arno J. Mayer, 1981. *The Persistence of the Old Regime*. London: Croom Helm.
124. Arno Mayer, *op.cit.*: 4.
125. Alex Callinicos, 1990. *Against Postmodernism*, New York: 43.
126. See note 99 and 101.
127. Callinicos, *op.cit.*: 43-4.
128. I use the term 'Central Europe' in three senses. In the narrowest sense it covers Germany and Austria, in a second sense it covers the core area of the former dual monarchy, namely, Austria, Hungary and Czechoslovakia. In the broadest sense it designates this core area plus Germany. This simultaneous use of three concepts reflects the general confusion and disagreement on the delimitation of the Central European region.

129. For such a characterization, see Skocpol, *States and Social Revolutions*: 81ff.
130. Skocpol, *op.cit.*; Theodore H. Von Laue, 1963. *Sergei Witte and the Industrialization of Russia*. New York & London: Columbia University Press; and Theodore H. Von Laue, 1966. *Why Lenin? Why Stalin?*, London: Weidenfeld & Nicholson.
131. Alec Nove (ed.), 1993. *The Stalin Phenomenon*. London: 28.
132. This interpretation of Russian development and of Stalinism as modernization strategy and policy has been inspired by among others John H. Kautsky, 1968. *Communism and the Politics of Development: Persistent Myths and Changing Behavior*. New York: Wiley & Sons; John H. Kautsky, 1972. *The Political Consequences of Modernization*. New York: Wiley & Sons; John H. Kautsky, 1975. *Patterns of Modernizing Revolutions: Mexico and the Soviet Union*. Los Angeles & London: Sage; Theodore von Laue, Sergei Witte, 1965. *Sergei Witte and the Industrialization of Russia*. New York & London: Columbia U.P.; Theodore von Laue 1966. *Why Lenin?, Why Stalin?* London; Barrington Moore, 1966. *Social Origins of Dictatorship and Democracy*. Boston: Beacon Press; Alec Nove, 1993. *The Stalin Phenomenon*. London; Alec Nove, 1964. *Was Stalin Really Necessary?* London: Allen & Unwin; A.F.K. Organski, 1965. *The Stages of Political Development*. New York: Alfred Knopf; and Theda Skocpol, *op.cit.*
133. Scholars have unfortunately not always been very precise here. Often the expressions 'middle class' and 'bourgeoisie' seem to be used almost indiscriminately — see for example S.M. Lipset, *op.cit.*; Barrington Moore, *op.cit.*; and Gregory M. Luebbert, *op.cit.*
134. See Luebbert, *op.cit.*: 73ff., and 133ff. Cf. also Per Salomonsson (ed.), 1968. *Den politiske magtkamp 1866-1901*. København.
135. Andrew Janos, 1982. *The Politics of Backwardness in Hungary, 1825-1945*. Princeton, ch. 3.
136. In Germany part of these classes supported the conservative DNVP or the Catholic Zentrum. In Austria the Christian Social Movement captured a great part of the middle class. It is notable, also, that Liberalism lost much support and influence in both countries. In Germany it was seriously weakened, in Austria it disappeared completely from the political scene. See Thomas Childers, *op.cit.*; and Adam Wandruszka, *op.cit.*
137. See for a survey of different variants, conceptions and interpretations Andrew Vincent, 1992. *Modern Political Ideologies*. Oxford: Blackwell, ch. 2; see for the special German liberalist tradition — Leonard Krieger, 1972. *The German Idea of Freedom*. Chicago: University of Chicago Press; and James J. Sheehan, 1978. *German Liberalism in the Nineteenth Century*. Chicago: University of Chicago Press.
138. S.M. Lipset, *op.cit.*; Gregory M. Luebbert, *op.cit.*; Barrington Moore, *op.cit.*; and Rueschemeyer et al., *op.cit.*. See further A. Arblaster, 1984. *The Rise and Decline of Western Liberalism*. Oxford: Blackwell; C.B. Macpherson, 1964. *The Political Theory of Possessive Individualism*. Oxford: Oxford U.P.; C.B. Macpherson, 1977. *The Life and Times of Liberal Democracy*. Oxford: Oxford U.P.; and Karl Polanyi, 1957. *The Great Transformation*. Boston: Beacon.

139. See Ted Honderich, 1991. *Conservatism*, London: Penguin; Noël O'Sullivan, 1976. *Conservatism*, London: Dent & Sons; and Andrew Vincent, *op.cit.*, ch. 3. For different conceptions of democracy and the reaction of conservatism and liberalism to democracy, see also Jens Christophersen, 1956. 'An historical outlook on the different usages of the term "democracy"', in Arne Naess et al., *Democracy, Ideology and Objectivity*. Oslo: Oslo U.P.: 77-138.

140. See for the so called 'Tory-workers' in England, Robert T. McKenzie & Allan Silver, 1968. *Angels in Marble*, Chicago: University of Chicago Press; and Eric Nordlinger, 1968. *Working Class Tories*. Berkeley: University of California Press; and for the similar German phenomenon, Richard Hamilton, *op.cit.*: 386ff.

141. Cf. for the cultural activities of for example the Austrian labour movement: Julius Deutsch, 1931. *Unter Roten Fahnen. Vom Rekord zum Massensport*. Wien; Brigitte Emig, 1980. *Die Veredelung des Arbeiters. Sozialdemokratie als Kulturbewegung*. Frankfurt a.M.; Alfred Georg Frei, 1984. *Rotes Wien. Austromarxismus und Arbeiterkultur. Sozialdemokratische Wohnungs- und Kommunalpolitik 1919-34*. Berlin; Helmut Gruber, 1991. *Red Vienna. Experiment in Working Class Culture 1919-34*. Oxford; Hans Hautmann & Rudolf Hautmann, 1980. *Die Gemeindebauten des Roten Wien 1919 bis 1934*. Wien; Reinhard Kanonier, 1981. *Zwischen Bethoven und Eisler. Zur Arbeitermusikbewegung in Österreich*. Wien; Helene Maimann, 1981 (ed.), *Mit uns zieht die neue Zeit. Arbeiterkultur in Österreich 1918-34*. Wien; Wolfgang Neugebauer, 1975. *Bauvolk der kommenden Welt. Geschichte der sozialistischen Jugendbewegung in Österreich 1919 bis 1934*. Wien; and Joseph Weidenholzer, 1981. *Auf dem Weg zum 'Neuen Menschen'. Bildungs- und Kulturarbeit der österreichischen Sozialdemokratie in der ersten Republik*. Wien.

142. See also notes 50, 52 ,76 and 141. Cf. further Wolfgang Abenroth, 1965, *Sozialgeschichte der europäischen Arbeiterbewegung*. Frankfurt a.M: Suhrkamp; Julius Braunthal, 1966. *History of the International*, vol. 1, *1864-1914*. London: Nelson & Sons; Julius Braunthal, 1967. *History of the International*, vol. 2, *1914-43*. London: Nelson & Sons; Julius Braunthal, 1971. *Geschichte der Internationale*, (3). Hannover: Dietz; David Caute, 1966. *The Left in Europe since 1789*. London: Weidenfeld and Nicolson; G.D.H. Cole, 1959-60. *A History of Socialist Thought*, vols. 1-5. London: Macmillan; Dick Geary, 1984. *European Labour Protest 1848-1939*. London: Methuen; Dick Geary (ed.), 1989. *Labour and Socialist Movements in Europe Before 1914*. Oxford, New York & Munich: Berg; Michael Harrington, 1972. *Socialism*, New York: Saturday Review Press; George Lichtheim, 1970. *A Short History of Socialism*. London: Weidenfeld & Nicolson; and Adolf Sturmthal, 1944. *The Tragedy of European Labour 1918-39*. London: Victor Gollancz. See for especially Marx's conception Shlomo Avineri, 1968. *The Social and Political Thought of Karl Marx*. Cambridge: Cambridge U.P.; Alan Gilbert, 1981. *Marx's Politics*. Oxford: Martin Robertson; Hal Draper, 1977-90. *Karl Marx's Theory of Revolution*, vols. 1-4. New York & London: Monthly Review; and David McLellan, 1971. *The Thought of Karl Marx*. London: Macmillan.

143. See note 132.

144. The question of the class character of the Soviet Union has always been a main concern within the critical marxist tradition. See for example Antonio Carlo 1972. *Politische und ökonomische Struktur der UdSSR (1917-75)*. Berlin: Wagenbach; Tony Cliff, 1988. *State Capitalism in Russia*. London: Bookmarks; Milovan Djilas, 1957. *The New Class*, New York: Praeger; Leon Trotsky, 1970. *The Revolution Betrayed*. New York: Pathfinder; and outside this tradition, but clearly inspired by it, the remarkable George Konrád & Ivan Szelenyi, 1979. *The Intellectuals on the Road to Class Power*. New York: Harcourt Brace. The problem with Trotsky is that he does not recognize the nomenclatura as a ruling class. Konrad and Szelenyi prefer for mysterious reasons to speak of 'state socialism' whereas Djilas speaks of 'communism'. Antonio Carlo insists on the completely new and unique character of stalinist societies. Cliff, on the other hand, speaks of 'state capitalism'. I shall prefer to conceive Russian society under stalinism as a society undergoing a process of forced and state organized primitive accumulation. This accumulation was perhaps, perhaps not, 'capitalist' or 'pre-capitalist', but certainly not 'socialist' as claimed by Preobrazenskij (see E. Preobrazenskij, *Die Neue Oekonomik*. Berlin: Neuer Kurs, 1971 (1926). See also notes 132 and 157.

145. See note 132.

146. See note 40 and note 41.

147. Luebbert, *op.cit.*: 265-66. See further F.L. Carsten, 1982. *The Rise of Fascism*. Berkeley: University of California Press; Hans Rogger & Eugen Weber (eds.), 1965. *The European Right*. London: Weidenfeld & Nicholson; and Peter F. Sugar (ed.), 1971. *Native Fascism in the Successor States 1918-45*. Santa Barbara: Clio.

148. See note 65 and note 147.

149. See note 67.

150. See Thomas Childers, *The Nazi Voter. The Social Foundation of Fascism in Germany, 1919-33*. Chapel Hill and London: University of North Carolina Press; Jürgen W. Falter, 1991. *Hitlers Wähler*, München; and Richard F. Hamilton, 1982. *Who Voted for Hitler?* Princeton. Cf. also Bernt Hagtvet's comment on Hamilton's results cited in note 72.

151. Namely that right wing and conservative parties are associated with the upper classes, the left and socialist parties with the lower classes and the liberalist centre parties with the middle classes — See S.M. Lipset, 1963. *Political Man*. London: Mercury, ch. 7 and 8.

152. See note 119.

153. Elites are small groups of especially powerful persons such as members of the government, the top bureaucracy, military leaders, the cultural and mass media elite etc. — see further T.B. Bottomore, 1993. *Elites and Society*. London & New York: Routledge. Whereas social classes are constituted by their relationship- which can embrace economic as well as political and ideological resources and relations- to the means of production and investment policy, elites are constituted by their control over resources not directly involving control over the means of production and investment policy. Elites are powerful due to other ressources and relations than ruling classes. Both elites and ruling classes are very important in any process of political development and regime formation.

154. For such attempts, see the analyses and discussions in T.B. Bottomore, *op.cit.*; T.B. Bottomore & Robert J. Brym (eds.), 1989. *The Capitalist Class: An International Study.* London: Harvester Wheatsheaf; Steward Clegg et al., 1986. *Class, politics and the economy.* London: Routledge & Kegan Paul; G. William Domhoff, 1990. *The Power Elite and the State. How Policy is Made in America.* New York: de Gruyter; John Scott, 1991. *Who Rules Britain?* Cambridge: Polity Press; John Scott, 1979. *Corporations, Classes and Capitalism.* London: Hutchinson; and Maurice Zeitlin, 1989. *The Large Corporations and Contemporary Classes.* Cambridge: Polity Press.

155. For the general discussion on the value of and problems in class analyses of modern societies, see note 119 and note 154. See also Alex Callinicos & Chris Harman, 1987. *The Changing Working Class.* London: Bookmarks; Fiona Devine, 1992. *Affluent Workers Revisited.* Edinburgh: Edinburgh U.P.; Stephen Edgell, 1993. *Class,* London & New York: Routledge; Anthony Giddens & David Held (eds.), 1982. *Class, Power, and Conflict. Classical and Contemporary Debates.* London: Macmillan; and Gordon Marshall et al., 1988. *Social Class in Modern Britain.* London: Hutchinson.

156. See the general discussion and criticism in Stephen Cohen, 1985. *Rethinking the Soviet Experience. Politics and History Since 1917.* New York & Oxford: Oxford U.P.; and Edward Acton, 1990. *Rethinking the Russian Revolution.* London: Edward Arnold. See also the contributions by J. Arch Getty and Sheila Fitzpatrick in Alec Nove (ed.), 1993. *The Stalin Phenomenon.* London: Weidenfeld & Nicolson.

157. This, of course, has traditionally been a main focus within the critical marxist tradition. A major problem here has been that the different schools within this tradition have used much time and energy quarrelling about the general characterisfic of the Soviet Union, whether it should be seen as a 'deformed workers state', as a 'bureaucratic collectivist' system or as 'state capitalism'. See for example Leon Trotsky, 1970. *The Revolution Betrayed,* (1937). New York: Pathfinder; Antonio Carlo, 1972. *Politische und ökonomische Struktur der USSR (1917-75).* Berlin: Wagenbach; and Tony Cliff, 1988. *State Capitalism in Russia,* (1955). London: Bookmarks. See also the shrewd contribution by Alex Callinicos, 1991. *The Revenge of History. Marxism and the East European Revolutions.* The Pennsylvanian State U.P. See also note 144.

158. See for examples of such studies, Moshe Lewin, 1968. *Russian Peasants and Soviet Power.* London: Allen & Unwin; Moshe Lewin, 1985. *The Making of the Soviet System.* London: Methuen; Sheila Fitzpatrick, *Education and Social Mobility in the Soviet Union, 1921-34;* Lynne Viola, 1987. *The Best Sons of the Fatherland: Workers in the Vanguard of Soviet Collectivization.* Oxford; and Hirokai Kuromiya, 1990. *Stalin's Industrial Revolution. Politics and Workers, 1928-32.* Cambridge. The remarkable studies by Bill Lomax and Miklos Molnar of the 1956 Hungarian revolution can also be seen as examples of such studies 'from below' — see Bill Lomax, 1976. *Hungary 1956.* London; Bill Lomax (ed.), 1990. *Hungarian Worker's Councils in 1956.* New York: Columbia U.P.; and Miklos Molnar, 1971. *The History of the Hungarian Revolution.* London. See also Chris Harman, 1988. *Class Struggles*

in *Eastern Europe 1945-83*. London: Bookmarks.

159. Fortunately there have been a number of deviations from the main trend criticized here. See notes 132, 144, 157 and 158. As to Eastern Europe especially, there exists a whole sub-tradition of penetrating analyses from Milovan Djilas, 1957. *The New Class*. New York: Praeger; and Francois Fejtö, 1974. *A History of the People's Democracies*. London, over the remarkable contribution by George Konrad & Ivan Szelenyi, 1979. *The Intellectuals on the Road to Class Power*. New York: Harcourt Brace; to Elemér Hankiss, 1990. *East European Alternatives*. Oxford; and Jadwiga Staniszkis, 1991. *The Dynamics of the Breakthrough in Eastern Europe*. Berkeley: University of California Press. Despite considerable differences as to concepts, analyses and conclusions, they all share a will to go beneath the surface of official ideology, judicial structures and political leaders and penetrate to the level of social forces, conflicts and interests.

160. The almost endless stream of studies on 'collapse of socialism', 'end of socialism', 'post-socialist societies', post-communism' etc, etc. testifies the persistent strength of this regrettable fixation on declared ideology and submission to cold war rhetoric. Even Konrad and Szeleny for mysterious reasons stubbornly insist on clinging to the ideologically biased cold war concept of 'state socialism', Konrad & Szeleny, *op.cit.*

161. See note 5.

162. For analyses of such questions, see, for example, Elemér Hankiss, 1990. *East European Alternatives*. Oxford; James Petras, 1991. 'Eastern Europe: Restoration and Crisis', *Journal of Contemporary Asia*, Vol. 21, (3); Jadwiga Staniszkis, 1991. *The Dynamics of the Breakthrough in Eastern Europe*. Berkeley: University of California Press; and Lene Bøgh Sørensen, *op.cit.*, ch. 9, section 4.

163. Most evident in the former Yugoslavia, of course. But see in general Paul Hockenos, 1994, *Free to Hate. The Rise of the Right in Post-Communist Eastern Europe*. New York & London: Routledge.

164. See for a penetrating analysis and criticism James Petras, 1991, 'Eastern Europe: Restoration and Crisis', in *Journal of Contemporary Asia*, Vol. 21, (3): 301-26.

165. See Paul Hockenos, *op.cit.*

166. The most conspicuous example here is perhaps the ideology of socialism which was 'lifted' from its original environment in Western European labour movement and 'moved' to the Russian context undergoing at the same time profound changes as to content and functions. Other examples are 'nationalism', 'democracy', 'liberalism' etc.

167. Francis Fukuyama, 1992. *The End of History and the Last Man*. New York. For quite another perspective on capitalist development and history, see Karl Polanyi, 1957. *The Great Transformation*, (1944). Boston: Beacon; Eric Hobsbawm, 1962. *The Age of Revolution 1789-1848*. New York: Mentor; Eric Hobsbawm, 1995. *The Age of Capital 1848-75*. London: Weidenfeld & Nicholson; Eric Hobsbawm, 1994. *The Age of Empire 1875-1914*. London: Abacus; and Eric Hobsbawm, 1994. *Age of Extremes. The Short Twentieth Century History 1914-91*. London: Penguin.

Bibliography

Abendroth, Wolfgang 1965. *Sozialgeschichte der europäischen Arbeiterbewegung*. Frankfurt a.M.: Suhrkamp.

Acton, Edward 1990. Rethinking the Russian Revolution., London: Edward Arnold.

Allen, Sheridan William 1966. *The Nazi Seizure of Power. The Experience of a Single German Town*. London: Eyre & Spottswoode.

Althusser, Louis 1973. *Pour Marx*, Paris.

Amsden, Alice, Jacek Kochanowicz & Lance Taylor 1994. *The Market Meets its Match*. Cambridge MA.: Harvard U.P.

Arblaster, 1984. *The Rise and Decline of Western Liberalism*. Oxford: Blackwell.

Avineri, Shlomo 1968. *The Social and Political Thought of Karl Marx*. Cambridge: Cambridge U.P.

Bendix, Reinhard 1977. *Nation Building and Citizenship*. Berkeley: University of California Press.

Blackburn, David & Geoff Eley 1984. *The Peculiarities of German History*. Oxford: Oxford U.P.

Bottomore, T.B. & Robert J. Brym (eds.), 1989. *The Capitalist Class: An International Study*. London: Harvester Wheatsheaf.

Bottomore, T.B. 1993. *Elites and Society*. London & New York: Routledge.

Botz, Gerhard 'Introduction', in Ugelvik Larsen et al. (eds). *Who were the Fascists, Social roots of European Fascism*. Bergen: Universitetsforlaget: 192-201.

Botz, Gerhard 1987. *Krisenzonen einer Demokratie. Gewalt, Streik und Konfliktunterdrückung in Österreich seit 1918*. Frankfurt & New York: Campus.

Bracher, Karl Dietrich 1955. *Die Auflösung der Weimarer Republik*. Villingen: Ringverlag

Braunthal, Julius 1967. *History of the International*, vol. 2, *1914-43*. London: Nelson & Sons.

Braunthal, Julius 1966. *History of the International*, vol. 1, *1864-1914*. London: Nelson & Sons.

Braunthal, Julius 1971. *Geschichte der Internationale*, (3). Hannover: Dietz.

Brenan, Gerald 1960. *The Spanish Labyrinth*. Cambridge: Cambridge U.P.

Bugge, Peter 1994. 'Czech Nation-Building, National Self-Perception and Politics 1780-1914'. PhD Dissertation, Institute of Slavonic Studies, University of Aarhus.

Bull, Edvard 1922. 'Arbeiderbevegelsens stilling i de tre nordiske lande 1914-1920', reprinted in *Tidsskrift for arbeiderbevegelsens historie*, 1, 1976: 3-28.

Callinicos, Alex 1990. *Against Postmodernism*. New York: St. Martin's Press.

Callinicos, Alex 1991. *The Revenge of History. Marxism and the East European Revolutions*. Pittsburgh: Pennsylvania State U.P.

Callinicos, Alex 1987. *Making History*. Cambridge: Polity Press.

Callinicos, Alex & Chris Harman 1987. *The Changing Working Class*. London: Bookmarks.

Carlo, Antonio 1972. *Politische und ökonomische Struktur der UdSSR (1917-75)*. Berlin: Wagenbach.

Carsten, F.L. 1966. *The Reichswehr and Politics 1918-33.* Oxford.

Carsten, F.L. 1982. *The Rise of Fascism.* Berkeley: University of California Press.

Caute, David 1966. *The Left in Europe since 1789.* London: Weidenfeld and Nicolson.

Childers, Thomas. *The Nazi Voter. The Social Foundation of Fascism in Germany, 1919-33.* Chapel Hill and London: University of North Carolina Press.

Christophersen, Jens 1956. 'An historical outlook on the different usages of the term "democracy"', in Arne Naess et al., *Democracy, Ideology and Objectivity.* Oslo: Universitetsforlaget: 77-138.

Clegg, Steward, et al. 1986. *Class, politics and the economy.* London: Routledge & Kegan Paul.

Cliff, Tony 1988. *State Capitalism in Russia.* London: Bookmarks.

Cohen, G.D. 1978. *Karl Marx's Theory of History.* Oxford.

Cohen, Stephen 1985. *Rethinking the Soviet Experience. Politics and History Since 1917.* New York & Oxford: Oxford U.P.

Cole, G.D.H. 1959-60. *A History of Socialist Thought,* vols. 1-5. London: Macmillan.

Cutwright Philips & James Wiley 1969. 'Modernization and political representation: 1927-66', Studies in Comparative International Development.

Czichon, Eberhard 1967. *Wer verhalf Hitler zur Macht?* Köln: Paul Rugenstein Verlag.

Dahl, Robert A. 1985. *A Preface To Economic Theory.* Cambridge: Polity Press.

Dahl, Robert A. 1971. *Polyarchy.* Yale: Yale U.P.

Dahrendorf, Ralf 1968. *Gesellschaft und Demokratie in Deutschland.* München: Anchor Books.

Deutsch, Julius 1931. *Unter Roten Fahnen. Vom Rekord zum Massensport.* Wien.

Devine, Fiona 1992. *Affluent Workers Revisited.* Edinburgh: Edinburgh U.P.

Djilas, Milovan 1957. *The New Class.* New York: Praeger.

Domhoff, G. William 1990. *The Power Elite and the State. How Policy is Made in America.* New York: de Gruyter.

Draper, Hal 1977-90. *Karl Marx's Theory of Revolution,* vols. 1-4. New York & London: Monthly Review.

Duncan, Graeme 1973. *Marx and Mill.* Cambridge: Cambridge U.P.

Geras, Norman 1976. *The Legacy of Rosa Luxemburg.* London: NLB.

Edgell, Stephen 1993. *Class.* London & New York: Routledge.

Elster, Jon 1985. *Making Sense of Marx.* Cambridge: Cambridge U.P.

Elster, Jon 1982. 'Marxism, Functionalism and Game Theory. The Case for Methodological Individualism', *Theory and Society.* 11: 453-82.

Elvander, Niels 1980. *Skandinavisk arbetarrörelse.* Stockholm: Liber-Förlag.

Emig, Brigitte 1980. *Die Veredelung des Arbeiters. Sozialdemokratie als Kulturbewegung.* Frankfurt & New York: Campus.

Falter, Jürgen W. 1991. *Hitlers Wähler.* München: Verlag C.H. Beck.

Fejtö, Francois 1974. *A History of the People's Democracies.* London: Pelican Books.

Fitzpatrick, Sheila 1979. *Education and Social Mobility in the Soviet Union, 1921-34.* Cambridge: Cambridge U.P.

Flechtheim, Ossip K. 1969. *Die KPD in der Weimarer Republik.* Frankfurt a.M: Euro-päische verlagsanstalt.

Frei, Alfred Georg 1984. *Rotes Wien. Austromarxismus und Arbeiterkultur. Sozialdemo-kratische Wohnungs- und Kommunalpolitik 1919-34.* Berlin: DVK-Verlag.

Fukuyama, Francis 1992. *The End of History and the Last Man.* New York: Free Press.

Fülberth Georg & Jürgen Harrer 1977. *Die deutsche Sozialdemokratie 1890-1933.* Darmstadt & Neuwied: Luchterhand.

Galenson, Walter (ed.) 1952. *Comparative Labour Movements.* New York.

Geary, Dick 1981. *European Labour Protest 1848-1939.* London: Methuen.

Geary, Dick 1983. 'The Industrial Elite and the Nazis in the Weimar Republic' in Peter Stachura (ed.), *The Nazi Machtergreifung.* London: Allen and Unwin.

Geary, Dick (ed.), 1989. *Labour and Socialist Movements in Europe Before 1914.* Oxford, New York & Munich: Berg.

Geiger, Theodor 1932. *Die soziale Schichtung des deutschen Volkes: Soziographischer Versuch auf statistischer Grundlage.* Stuttgart: Enker Verlag.

Gellner, Ernest 1983. *Nations and Nationalism.* Oxford: Blackwell.

Gerschenkron, Alexander 1943. *Bread and Democracy in Germany.* Berkeley: University of California Press.

Getty, J. Arch and Sheila Fitzpatrick in Alec Nove (ed.), 1993. *The Stalin Phenomenon.* London: Weidenfeld & Nicolson.

Giddens, Anthony 1981. *A Contemporary Critique of Historical Materialism,* vol. 1. London: Macmillan.

Giddens, Anthony 1987. *The Nation-State and Violence.* Cambridge: Polity Press.

Giddens, Anthony 1986. *The Constitution of Society.* Berkeley and Los Angeles: University of California Press.

Giddens, Anthony & David Held (eds.), 1982. *Classes, Power and Conflict. Classical and Contemporary Debates.* London: Macmillan.

Giddens, Anthony 1979. *Central Problems in Social Theory.* London: Macmillan.

Gilbert, Alan 1981. *Marx's Politics.* Oxford: Martin Robertson.

Gildea, Robert 1987. *Barricades and Borders. Europe 1800-1914.* Oxford: Oxford U.P.

Gowan, Peter 1995. 'Neo-Liberal Theory and Practice for Eastern Europe', *New Left Review.* (213): 3-60.

Grew, Raymond 1978. *Crises of Political Development in Europe and the United States.* Princeton: Princeton U.P.

Groh, Dieter 1973. *Negative Integration und revolutionärer Attentismus. Die deutsche Sozialdemokratie am Vorabend des Ersten Weltkrieges.* Frankfurt a.M.: Ullstein.

Gruber, Helmut 1991. *Red Vienna. Experiment in Working Class Culture 1919-34.* Oxford: Oxford U.P.

Gulick, Charles A. 1948. *Austria from Habsburg to Hitler,* vols. 1-2. Berkeley: University of California Press.

Guttsmann, W.L. 1981. *The German Social Democratic Party 1875-1933.* London: Allen and Unwin.

Hagtvet, Bernt & Reinhard Kühnl, 'Contemporary Approaches to Fascism: A Survey of Paradigms', in Ugelvik Larsen et al. (eds.) *Who Were the Fascists, Social roots of European Fascism.* Bergen: Universitetsforlaget: 26-51.

Hagtvet, Bernt. 'The Theory of Mass Society and the Collapse of the Weimar Republic: A Re-Examination', in Stein Ugelvik Larsen et al.(eds.). *Who Were the Fascists, Social Roots of European Fascism.* Bergen: Universitetsforlaget: 114.

Hallgarten, George W.F. & Joachim Radkau, 1974. *Deutsche Industrie und Politik von Bismarck bis heute.* Frankfurt a.M.: Europäische Verlagsanstalt.

Hamerow, Theodore 1983. *The Birth of a New Europe: State and Society in the Nineteenth Century.* Chapel Hill and London: University of North Carolina Press.

Hamilton, Richard F. 1982. *Who Voted for Hitler?* Princeton: Princeton U.P.

Hankiss, Elemér 1990. *East European Alternatives.* Oxford. Clarendon Press.

Harman, Chris 1988. *Class Struggles in Eastern Europe 1945-83.* London: Bookmarks.

Harrington, Michael 1990. *Socialism. Past and Future.* New York: Plume.

Harrington, Michael 1972. *Socialism.* New York: Saturday Review Press.

Hautmann, Hans & Rudolf Hautmann. 1980. *Die Gemeindebauten des Roten Wien 1919 bis 1934.* Wien.

Held, David 1987. *Models of Democracy.* Cambridge: Polity Press.

Herz, John (ed.), 1989. *From Dictatorship to Democracy: Coping with the Legacies of Authoritharianism and Totalitarianism.* London.

Hobsbawm, Eric 1994. *The Age of Empire 1875-1914.* London: Abacus.

Hobsbawm, E.J. 1992. *Nations and Nationalisms since 1780.* Cambridge: Cambridge U.P.

Hobsbawm, Eric 1995. *The Age of Capital 1848-75.* London: Weidenfeld & Nicholson.

Hobsbawm, Eric 1994. *Age of Extremes. The Short Twentieth Century History 1914-91.* London: Penguin.

Hobsbawm, Eric 1962. *The Age of Revolution 1789-1848.* New York: Mentor.

Hockenos, Paul 1994. *Free to Hate. The Rise of the Right in Post-Communist Eastern Europe.* New York & London: Routledge.

Hoffman, John 1988. *State, Power and Democracy.* Sussex: Wheatsheaf.

Honderich, Ted 1991. *Conservatism.* London: Penguin.

Huntington, Samuel P. 1991. *The Third Wave. Democratization in the Late Twentieth Century.* Norman and London: University of Oklahoma Press.

Huntington, Samuel P. 1968. *Political Order in Changing Societies.* Yale: Yale U.P.

Janos, Andrew 1982. *The Politics of Backwardness in Hungary 1825-1945.* Princeton: Princeton U.P.

Kanonier, Reinhard 1981. *Zwischen Bethoven und Eisler. Zur Arbeitermusikbewegung in Österreich.* Wien: Europaverlag.

Karl, Terry 1990. 'Dilemmas of Democratization in Latin America', *Comparative Politics.* October.

Katznelson, Ira & Aristide R. Zolberg (eds.), 1986. *Working-Class Formation.* Princeton: Princeton U.P.

Kautsky, John H. 1968. *Communism and the Politics of Development: Persistent Myths and Changing Behavior.* New York: Wiley & Sons.

Kautsky, John H. 1975. *Patterns of Modernizing Revolutions: Mexico and the Soviet Union.* Los Angeles & London: Sage.

Kautsky, John H. 1972. *The Political Consequences of Modernization.* New York: Wiley & Sons.

Kolb, Eberhard 1988. *The Weimar Republic.* London: Unwin Hyman.

Konrad, George & Ivan Szelenyi 1979. *The Intellectuals on the Road to Class Power.* New York: Harcourt Brace.

Kornai, Janos 1990. *The Road to a Free Economy.* New York & London: Norton.

Kornhauser, William 1959. *The Politics of Mass Society.* Glencoe: The Free Press.

Korpi, Walter 1978. *The Working Class in Welfare Capitalism.* London: Routledge & Kegan Paul.

Korpi, Walter 1983. *The Democratic Class Struggle.* London: Routledge & Kegan Paul.

Krieger, Leonard 1972. *The German Idea of Freedom.* Chicago: University of Chicago Press.

Kuromiya, Hirokai 1990. *Stalin's Industrial Revolution. Politics and Workers, 1928-32.* Cambridge: Cambridge U.P.

Kühnl, Reinhard 1980. 'Pre-Conditions for the Rise and Victory of Fascism in Germany', in Stein Ugelvik Larsen et al.(eds). *Who Were the Fascists?* Bergen: Universitetsforlaget: 118-30.

Laclau, Ernesto & Chantal Mouffe 1985. *Hegemony and Socialist Strategy.* London: Verso.

Lafferty, W.M. 1971. *Economic Development and the Response of Labour in Scandinavia: a Multi-Level Analysis.* Oslo: Universitetsforlaget.

Laswell, Harold 1933. 'The Psychology of Hitlerism', *Political Quarterly*, 4: 373-84.

Laue, Theodore von 1963. *Sergei Witte and the Industrialization of Russia.* New York & London: Columbia U.P.

Laue, Theodore H. Von 1966. *Why Lenin? Why Stalin?* London: Weidenfeld & Nicholson.

Lewin, Moshe 1968. *Russian Peasants and Soviet Power.* London: Allen & Unwin.

Lewin, Moshe 1985. *The Making of the Soviet System.* London: Methuen.

Lichtheim, George 1970. *A Short History of Socialism.* London: Weidenfeld & Nicolson.

Lidtke, Vernon L. 1966. *The Outlawed Party. Social Democracy in Germany 1878-90.* Princeton N.J.: Princeton U.P.

Lindblom Charles E. 1977. *Politics and Markets.* New York: Basic Books.

Linz, Juan & Alfred Stepan (eds.), 1978. *The Breakdown of Democratic Regimes in Europe.* Baltimore and London: Johns Hopkins U.P.

Linz, Juan 1978. *The Breakdown of Democratic Regimes: Crisis, Breakdown and Reequilibration.* Baltimore and London: Johns Hopkins U.P.

Lipset, S.M. 1963. *Political Man.* London: Mercury.

Lipset S.M. 1959. 'Some social requisites of democracy: economic development and political legitimacy', *American Political Science Review*: 53.

Lipset, S.M. 1985. 'Radicalism or Reformism: The Sources of Working-Class Politics', in S.M. Lipset (ed.), *Consensus and Conflict. Essays in Political Sociology.* New Brunswick & Oxford: Transaction Books.

Lipset, S.M. & Stein Rokkan 1967. 'Cleavage Structures, Party Systems and Voter Alignments: An Introduction', in S.M. Lipset & Stein Rokkan (eds.), *Party Systems and Voter Alignments: Cross-National Perspectives*. New York: 1-64.

Lipset, S.M. 1963. 'Fascism — Left, Right and Centre', in S.M. Lipset, *Political Man*. London: Mercury: 131-76.

Lomax, Bill 1976. *Hungary 1956*. London: Allison and Busby.

Lomax, Bill (ed.), 1990. *Hungarian Worker's Councils in 1956*. New York: Columbia U.P.

Luebbert, Gregory M. 1991. *Liberalism, Fascism or Social Democracy. Social Classes and the Political Origins of Regimes in Interwar Europe*. Oxford: Oxford U.P.

Lynne, Viola 1987. *The Best Sons of the Fatherland: Workers in the Vanguard of Soviet Collectivization*. Oxford: Oxford U.P.

Lyttelton, Adrian 1973. *The Seizure of Power. Fascism in Italy 1919-29*. London: Princeton U.P.

Machpherson, C.B. 1977. *The Life and Times of Liberal Democracy*. Oxford: Oxford U.P.

Mackie, Thomas T. & Richard Rose 1982. *The International Almanac of Electoral History*. London: Macmillan.

Macpherson, C.B. 1964. *The Political Theory of Possessive Individualism*. Oxford: Oxford U.P.

Macpherson, C.B. 1977. *The Life and Times of Liberal Democracy*. Oxford: Oxford U.P.

Macpherson, C.B. 1973. *Democratic Theory. Essays in Retrival*. Oxford: Clarendon.

Maimann, Helene, 1981 (ed.), *Mit uns zieht die neue Zeit. Arbeiterkultur in Österreich 1918-34*. Wien: Habarta & Habarta.

Mann, Michael 1986 & 1993. *The Sources of Social Power*, vols. 1-2. Cambridge: Cambridge U.P.

Marshall, T.H. 1950. *Citizenship and Social Class*. Cambridge: Cambridge U.P.

Marshall, Gordon et al., 1988. *Social Class in Modern Britain*. London: Hutchinson.

Marx Karl & Friedrich Engels 1969. *Die deutsche Ideologie*, 1846, MEW, (3). Berlin: Dietz Verlag.

McKenzie, Robert T. & Allan Silver 1968. *Angels in Marble*. Chicago: University of Chicago Press.

McLellan, David 1971. *The Thought of Karl Marx*. London: Macmillan.

Miliband, Ralph 1989. *Divided Societies*. Oxford: Clarendon Press.

Mitchell, Harvey & Peter N. Stearns 1971. *Workers and Protest: The European Labour Movement, the Working Classes and the Origins of Social Democracy, 1890-1914*. Itaca, Ill.

Molnar, Miklos 1971. *The History of the Hungarian Revolution*. London: Allen and Unwin.

Mommsen, Hans 1989. *Die verspielte Freiheit. Der Weg der Republik von Weimar in den Untergang 1918 bis 1933*. Berlin: Propyläen Verlag.

Moore, Barrington 1969. *Social Origins of Dictatorship and Democracy, Lord and Peasant in the Making of the Modern World*. London: Penguin Press.

Neugebauer, Wolfgang 1975. *Bauvolk der kommenden Welt. Geschichte der sozialistischen Jugendbewegung in Österreich 1919 bis 1934*. Wien: Europaverlag.

Neumann, Sigmund 1956. 'Germany: Changing Patterns and Lasting Problems', in Sigmund Neumann (ed.), *Modern Political Parties: Approaches to Comparative Politics.* Chicago: University of Chicago Press: 354-92.

Noakes, Jeremy 1971. *The Nazi Party in Lower Saxony 1921-33.* Oxford: Oxford U.P.

Nordlinger, Eric 1968. *Working Class Tories.* Berkeley: University of California Press.

Nove, Alec 1964. *Was Stalin Really Necessary?* London: Allen & Unwin.

Nove, Alec (ed.), 1993. *The Stalin Phenomenon.* London: Weidenfeld & Nicolson.

Organski, A.F.K. 1965. *The Stages of Political Development.* New York: Alfred Knopf.

O'Donnell Guillermo & Philipe C. Schmitter 1991. *Tentative Conclusions about Uncertain Democracies.* Baltimore & London: Johns Hopkins U.P.

O'Donnell, Guillermo, Philippe C. Schmitter & Laurence Whitehead 1986. *Transitions from Authoritarian Rule: Southern Europe.* Baltimore & London: Johns Hopkins U.P.

O'Sullivan, Noël 1976. *Conservatism.* London: Dent & Sons.

Palma, Guiseppe di 1990. *To Craft Democracies, An Essay on Democratic Transitions.* Berkeley and Los Angeles: University of California Press.

Parenti, Michael 1988. *Democracy for the Few.* New York: St. Martin.

Pauley, Bruce F. 1980. 'Nazis and Heimwehr Fascists: The Struggle for Supremacy in Austria, 1918-38', in Ugelvik Larsen et al. (eds).*Who Were the Fascists, Social Roots of European Fascism.* Bergen: Universitetsforlaget: 226-38.

Petras, James 1991. 'Eastern Europe: Restoration and Crisis', *Journal of Contemporary Asisa*, 21, (3).

Polanyi, Karl 1957. *The Great Transformation*, (1944). Boston: Beacon.

Poulantzas, Nicos 1973. *Political Power and Social Classes.* London: Verso.

Preobrazenskij, E. 1971 (1926). *Die Neue Oekonomik.* Berlin: Neuer Kurs.

Preston, Poul 1983. *The Coming of the Spanish Civil War.* London: Methuen.

Rabinbach, Anson 1983. *The Crisis of Austrian Socialism. From Red Vienna to Civil War 1927-34.* Chicago: University of Chicago Press.

Rogger, Hans & Eugen Weber (eds.), 1965. *The European Right.* London: Weidenfeld & Nicholson.

Roth, Günther 1963. *The Social Democracy in Imperial Germany.* Totowa, N.J.: Bedminster.

Rotschild, Joseph 1974. *East Central Europe between the Two World Wars.* Seattle: University of Washington Press.

Rueschemeyer, Dietrich, Evelyne H. Stephens & John D. Stephens 1992. *Capitalist Development and Democracy.* Chicago: University of Chicago Press.

Sachs, Jeffrey 1990. 'What is to be Done?', *Economist*, 13 January.

Sachs, Jeffrey 1993. *Poland's Jump to the Market Economy.* Cambridge MA.

Salomonsson, Per (ed.) 1968. *Den politiske magtkamp 1866-1901.* Copenhagen.

Schmitter Philippe C. 1991. 'The Consolidation of Democracy and the Choice of Institutions', unpublished paper. Stanford.

Schmitter Philippe C. 1991. 'The Consolidation of Political Democracies: Processes, Rhytms, Sequences and Types'. Unpublished paper. Stanford.

Schorske, Carl E. 1965. *German Social Democracy 1905-17.* New York: Wiley.

Schorske Carl E. 1980. *Fin-de-Siecle Vienna: Politics and Culture.* New York: Vintage, Random House.

Schulze, Hagen 1977. *Otto Braun oder Preussens demokratische Sendung.* Berlin.

Schumpeter, Joseph 1975 (1942). *Capitalism, Socialism and Democracy.* New York: Harper.

Schweinitz, Karl de 1964. *Industrialization and Democracy: Economic Necessities and Political Possibilities.* New York: Free Press.

Scott, John 1991. *Who Rules Britain?* Cambridge: Polity Press.

Scott, John 1979. *Corporations, Classes and Capitalism.* London: Hutchinson.

Seton-Watson, Hugh 1963. *Italy from Liberalism to Fascism.* Cambridge, Mass: Methuen.

Sheehan, James J. 1978. *German Liberalism in the Nineteenth Century.* Chicago: University of Chicago Press.

Skocpol, Theda 1979. *States and Social Revolutions.* Cambridge U.P.

Staniszkis, Jadwiga 1991. *The Dynamics of the Breakthrough in Eastern Europe.* Berkeley: University of California Press.

Stearns, Peter N. 1967. *European Society in Upheaval. Social History Since 1800.* New York & London.

Stegmann, D. 1973. 'Zum Verhältnis von Grossindustrie und Nationalsozialismus 1930-33', in *Archiv für Sozialgeschichte.* 13: 399-482.

Stephens, John D. 1986. *The Transition from Capitalism to Socialism.* Chicago: University of Illinois Press.

Stone, Norman 1983. *Europe Transformed 1878-1919.* London: Fontana.

Sturmthal, Adolf 1944. *The Tragedy of European Labour 1918-39.* London: Victor Gollancz.

Sugar Peter F. (ed.), 1971. *Native Fascism in the Successor States 1918-45.* Santa Barbara: Clio.

Sørensen, Curt 1992. *Mellem Demokrati og Diktatur,* vols. 1-2. Doctoral dissertation. Institute of Political Science, University of Aarhus.

Sørensen, Lene Bøgh, 1995. 'Political Development and Regime Transformations. The Hungarian Case', PhD dissertation, Institute of Political Science, University of Aarhus.

Tasca, Angelo 1969. *Glauben, Gehorchen, Kämpfen. Aufstieg des Faschismus* (1938). Wien: Europaverlag.

Taylor, Michael 1988. 'Rationality and Revolutionary Collective Action', in Michael Taylor (ed.), *Rationality and Revolution.* Cambridge: Cambridge U.P.: 63-97.

Thompson, E.P. 1968. *The Making of the English Working Class.* London: Penguin.

Tilly, Charles 1992. *Coercion, Capital and European States AD 990-1992.* Cambridge, Mass. & Oxford: Blackwell.

Tilly, Charles 1978. *From Mobilization to Revolution.* New York: Random House.

Tilly, Charles (ed.) 1975. *The Formation of National States in Western Europe.* Princeton: Princeton U.P.

Tilly, Charles, Louise Tilly & Richard Tilly 1975. *The Rebellious Century 1830-1930.* London: Dent and Sons.

Trotsky, Leon 1970. *The Revolution Betrayed*, (1937). New York: Pathfinder.

Turner, H.A. 1985. *German Big Business and the Rise of Hitler*. New York & Oxford: Oxford U.P.

UNICEF, 1994, *Economies in Transition Studies, Regional and Monitoring Report, Crisis in Mortality, Health and Nutrition*. Florence.

Vincent, Andrew 1992. *Modern Political Ideologies*. Oxford: Blackwell.

Wandruszka, Adam 1954. 'Österreichs politische Struktur. Die Entwicklung der Parteien und politischen Bewegungen', in Heinrich Benedikt (ed.), *Geschichte der Republik Österreich*. München: Verlag Oldenburg: 289-485.

Weber, Max *1980. Zur Lage der bürgerlichen Demokratie in Russland*, 1906, in Johannes Winckelmann (ed.), *Max Weber. Gesammelte Politische Schriften*, Tübingen: J.C.B. Mohr, 33-68.

Weber, Herman 1969. *Die Wandlung des deutschen Kommunismus. Die Stalinisierung der KPD in der Weimarer Republik*, Vol. 1-2. Frankfurt a.M.: Europäische Verlagsanstalt.

Wehler, Hans-Ulrich 1985. *The German Empire*. Hamburg & New York: Berg Publishers.

Weidenholzer, Joseph 1981. *Auf dem Weg zum 'Neuen Menschen'. Bildungs- und Kulturarbeit der österreichischen Sozialdemokratie in der ersten Republik*. Wien: Europaverlag.

Wood, Ellen Meiksins 1995. *Democracy Against Capitalism. Renewing Historical Materialism*. Cambridge: Cambridge U.P.

Wood, Ellen Meiksins 1986. *The Retreat from Class*. London: Verso.

Wright, Erik Olin 1985. *Classes*. London: Verso.

Wright, Erik Olin 1978. *Class, Crisis and the State*. London: NLB.

Zeitlin, Maurice 1989. *The Large Corporations and Contemporary Classes*. Cambridge: Polity Press.

State, Nation, and Security in Central Europe: Democratic States without Nations

Heinz Gärtner

Introduction

Two debates on different levels have influenced our understanding of the role of the state in international politics: the debate about the relationship between state and nation, on the one hand, and the contribution of International Relations Theory to the debate about the state, on the other. This paper argues that these debates fail to fully capture the developments in Central and Western Europe. The solution to nationality problems does not lie in the relations between nation and state, but rather in the separation of the state from the nation. Furthermore, it is not the anarchical character of the state system that threatens Western and Central Europe, but nationalism as a force within the state.

The new discovery of *national identity* in the East Central European States[1] is occurring simultaneously with the process of *European integration* in Western Europe.[2] While the search for national identity has revived the principle of nationality and ethnicity, the European integration process has forced Western European states to redefine their national identities. The meaning of 'identity' is by no means clear. There can be a variety of national identities including cultural, linguistic, ethnic, and national elements. But all of these identities become exclusionist if they intensify. Their inherent danger lies in their potential to lead to cultural discrimination, ethnic conflict or separation, and nationalism. There is, for example, no definite clear-cut distinction between linguistic and racial nationalism. Ethnicity can be defined as a group of persons with 'common ancestry' or sharing a 'common cultural heritage' or as an alternative term for 'race'.[3] In nationalist doctrine, as in Nazi Germany, language, race and culture constitute different aspects of the same entity, the nation.[4] Max Weber defines nations as ethnic communities 'unified by a myth of common descent'.[5]

This essay does not discuss the rights of ethnic minorities or the nature of cultural identity; rather, it is about the positioning of nationalism within the international state system. Nationalism is related to the state: it tries to get its own statehood and it opposes state interference.[6] The paper argues that it is possible, and necessary, to separate the concept of the state from that of the nation. Without this separation unrest, conflict, instability and, in certain cases, even war will result. The literature very often confuses state and nation. Most scholars maintain that in Western Europe, nations have become synonymous with the state, whereas in Eastern Europe the transition from the nation to statehood is incomplete.[7] I will argue that the compatibility of state and nation does not explain why nationalism is less of a problem in Western Europe. Rather it is because Western Europe is built upon strong, developed, and democratic statehood based on the rule of law. However, it would be wrong, even disastrous, for Central and Eastern Europe, to assume that the relatively homogeneous states of Western Europe could serve as models. The consequence would be a rearrangement of borders and the complete dissolution of the Versailles settlement, and cause dangerous instability.

The study further argues that the dissolution of statehood in Western Europe through integration, regionalization or globalization processes may give rise to ethnic nationalism and not to overlapping identities with individuals or social movements as the main actors. Theories which consider the anarchical character of the state system as the main source of war (neo-realism, institutionalism) miss the point, because the causes of instability lie within the characteristics of states themselves.

Historical aspects of 'state' and 'nation' in Western and Central Europe

Until the beginning of the nineteenth century, the meaning of 'nation' was not defined by language, culture or ethnicity. For Montesquieu the 'nation' was synonymous with the nobility and aristocracy. In France and England, the 'nation' was clearly distinguished from the 'people' or population. In the sixteenth and seventeenth centuries in France, the 'state' was associated with the King and his royal government. The idea of the nation was then used in opposition to the Crown by resentful aristocracies and/or in encounters with external powers (anti-English in France, anti-French in England). Once dissociated from the person of the King after the French revolution, the French 'state' became synonymous with the French 'nation'.[8]

In the seventeenth century, 'nations' in Central Europe consisted of the nobles or gentry who together with the King or Emperor lived off the peasants and other suppliers of labour and goods.[9] The original nations had no unitary ethnic base.[10] During the eighteenth century, no distinction was drawn between an homogenous people and the nation. In Germany, the 'state' remained a separate concept until the nineteenth century. The meaning of the word nation was then shaped by German Romanticism (Fichte, Herder, Schlegel). 'Nation' became synonymous with 'Volk', but was also frequently used interchangeably with 'state'.[11] The rise of romantic nationalism in the nineteenth century fueled the desire of every nationality to have its own nation-state. The late nineteenth and the early twentieth century saw the birth of an aggressive and expansionist nationalism.

As a political and ethnic concept, the 'nation' was established much later than the state. The nation therefore is not a primordial and natural entity.[12] It is a modern phenomenon with an archaic face.[13] While there may be 'primordial sentiments',[14] the ethnic nation is a modern invention[15] and a political artefact. Since the nineteenth century, however, the nation has gradually been identified with the state.[16] Nationalism has been both a cause as well as a consequence of the demise of multinational state systems.[17] Nevertheless, the rulers of these multinational systems regarded their territories as states. The collapse of the Habsburg, Ottoman and Russian empires in 1918 led to the creation of Poland, the Baltic states, Czechoslovakia, Hungary, Yugoslavia, Austria, and very nearly, a Ukrainian state. But like the former empires which spawned them, these entities did not emerge as homogeneous nation-states. Filled with national minorities, these states were linguistically and culturally mixed.[18] The Wilsonian principle of self-determination could not be applied at the same time to ethnic nationalities and the territorial integrity of states. The self-determination of peoples and the territorial integrity of states are not identical. Thus, the principle of self-determination may cause and legitimize nationalism and fragmentation.[19] There is no way to distinguish between the 'good self-determination' and 'bad nationalism'.[20] For example, the Romanians who support a unification of Moldova with Romania on an ethnic basis would not accept a separation of Romanian territories with substantial Hungarian minorities.

The aspiration that nation and state borders should coincide has been a decisive cause of European wars since the middle of the nineteenth century — including the wars in former Yugoslavia since 1991. In Central Europe in the nineteenth century, the German (Herderian) idea of the nation, defined by ethnicity, culture, language, and an emphasis on 'common' history has always been predominant. The nation should be defended by a powerful state. The Hungarian and Slovakian nationalism was mainly based on language. Lúdovít Stúr (1815-56), the theorist of Slovak nationalism, developed a real 'language philosophy' based on Herder's ideas of community building.[21] A somewhat similar version of this linguistic and cultural nationalism had been developed by the Czech historian Frantisek Palacky, the Ukrainian Michael Hrushevsky, and the Romanian Nicolae Iorga.[22] Nationhood in Central Europe can be defined in terms of lineage. The attributes of the ethnic nation include culture, language, and a common ancestry. Most of the time these characteristics are blurred and cannot be separated.[23]

The transition from this concept to a more political definition of the nation as a community of citizens inspired by the French Revolution has never really succeeded although there were some attempts before and after 1918.[24] Tomás Masaryk, for example, tried to find a solution to the nationality problem within a reformed Austrian state before he founded Czechoslovakia.

In 1915, Friedrich Naumann developed a theory of 'Mitteleuropa' in which Prussia-Germany would unite with Austria-Hungary to form a Central European 'world power'. All other states of the region would be satellites. In the 1930s, Hitler argued that protecting German minorities required expanding the German 'Lebensraum' in the East. He found allies in Hungary because of their opposition to the Versailles system — among the Romanians because of the Soviets' annexation of Bessarabia — among the Slovaks because of their anti-Czech nationalism — and among the anti-Serbian Croats.[25] Conversely, Stalin used the German enemy as a pretence to dominate the Slavic nations. After 1945, ethnic-based nationalism became invisible to the West. Neither the genocide of World War II nor the post-war withdrawal and expulsion of the Germans created homogeneous nation-states in Central Europe.[26] The 'Yalta system' resulted from the failure to resolve, or at least keep under control the national and ethnic problems and conflicts prior to World War II. After the lid of the Cold War was lifted, however, the national aspirations unleashed and the dilemmas afflicted by the break-up of the Austro-Hungarian Empire after World War I and Stalin's realignment of borders after World War II have re-emerged.

'Nation-state' or 'state'?

The term 'nation-state' implies that national and state identity are congruent.[27] In order to emphasise the ethnic dimension of the state in Central Europe, scholars frequently use the term 'national state'. Scholars of nationalism concentrate mainly on the question of whether states create nations, or nations bring about states, and to what degree state and national boundaries are identical.[28] As a consequence of this debate, states without nations are considered incomplete.

Benedict Anderson[29] describes how states transform themselves into nations, which he calls 'imagined communities'. For Eric Hobsbawm, the state induces nationalism primarily as an instrument to create loyalty.[30] Ernest Gellner's[31] main interest is the close relationship between culture and state. He defines nationalism as a 'principle which holds that the political and national unit should be congruent'. He describes the way in which the 'marriage of state and culture' works in different parts (time zones) of Europe during the last 200 years. In the most western time zone (the Atlantic shore of Europe), the states correlate with cultural zones. In the next time zone, corresponding to the erstwhile Holy Roman Empire, a homogeneous, standardized culture (bride) was there in the late eighteenth century without a suitable state (bridegroom). In the Eastern part of Europe, the third time zone, there were neither national states nor clear 'staatsfähige' national cultures; both had to be created. The ethnographic map of Eastern Europe from Trieste to St. Petersburg looks like a painting by Kokoschka;[32] it is a mass of multicoloured points. So neither bride nor bridegroom was ready. In the fourth zone, the Red Army imposed a culturally homogeneous ('gleichgeschaltetes') political system on a non-ethnic political system linked to an industrial society. He comes to the same conclusion as did Karl W. Deutsch twenty years ago. Deutsch observed a patchwork consisting of large spots with the same language, the same nationalities, and in large part also the same religion as in Western Europe (France, Great Britain, Germany, and Italy). In contrast, the Eastern European map of languages, religions, and nationalities looked like an irregular pattern of little dots.[33]

Many scholars and politicians in East Central Europe draw the conclusion that nation and state should coincide, or the scholars at least complain about the incompatibility:

In Western Europe essentially homogenous nation states were created while Eastern Europe's traditional Great Empires were always multinational and attempts to homogenise them were doomed to failure, they never developed into nation states.[34]

In many cases, these complaints led to the call for political change. Historians, for example, very soon after the breakup of the Yalta system in 1989/90 began to question the Versailles system. The scholarly debate about the injustices of the Trianon Treaty (1920),[35] in which Hungary lost roughly two-thirds of its territory and one-third of its population,[36] led Hungarian Prime Minister Antall to declare that he was the 'Prime Minister of all Hungarians'.[37]

However, in the eyes of the Hungarian minorities the post-Communist governments in Romania, Slovakia, and Serbia did not guarantee their rights. In December 1991, the Hungarian Democratic Federation of Romania (HDFR) voted against the adoption of the new constitution because it stresses the unity of the Romanian nation and the exclusive official status of the Romanian language. In 1992, the Hungarian parliamentary coalition abstained in the votes on the new constitution because its original draft affirmed the principle of the 'Slovak nation' and failed to provide for official use of minority languages. In 1991, a new law declared Serbian to be the sole official language in the republic, in effect eliminating the administrative use of Hungarian. Only the

Ukrainian and the Croatian governments guaranteed minority rights to the Hungarians' satisfaction.[38]

With Slovenia,[39] the Ukraine[40] and Slovakia[41], and eventually with Romania, Hungary agreed to treaties on minority rights. These treaties should help guarantee the borders between Hungary and its neighbouring countries and protect ethnic minorities.[42]

On the one hand, Hungarian politicians have given public assurances that they will not seek to change the borders. On the other hand, the government has affirmed the Final Act of the Conference on Security and Co-operation in Europe (CSCE). In this document, the participating states 'consider that their frontiers can be changed, in accordance with international law, by peaceful means and by agreement'.[43] Among the Hungarian population the feeling remains that it is not fair that the Hungarian nation is much larger than the territory of the state.

While this debate aims to define the relationship between nation and state, and while politicians try to solve the problem of ethnic minorities inside and outside the state's boundaries, others see the territorial state fading away and social and national identities emerging. Waever et al. recognise the separation of the nation from 'stateness', while pointing to the simultaneous weakening of the territorial state. They do not see the demise of the nation-state, but rather of the state alone, with the nation remaining: 'Left behind we find, nations with less state, culture, with less shell ... Culture has in this sense become security policy'.[44] Therefore they suggest that European integration does not necessarily demand close integration of peoples, shared culture or homogeneity.[45] On the contrary, the process of breaking down state sovereignty leads to a stronger assertion of cultural (national) identity. The authors try to cover the variety of emerging overlapping and competing identities with the concept of 'societal security'.[46] Societal identity should, according to the authors, develop both an ethnonational and a political identity. They argue, however, that threats to ethnonational identity replace military concerns as the central focus of European insecurity. 'The security of a society can be threatened by whatever puts its 'we' identity into jeopardy'.[47]

Yosef Lapid also notes the return of ethnic and national identities. He claims that 'identity is an irreducible category'.[48] Daniel N. Nelson[49] offers the idea of a 'de-statized' security for the next century, because security does not lie in the capacities of states, or groups of states, alone, but is also derived from the strength and resources found in consensual societies, growing economies, and legitimate polities.

The above-quoted authors deal with the phenomena of nation, state, and society as dependent and independent variables. The question should be asked, however, whether states can develop without a nation. Max Weber defined the state as 'an administrative and legal order' with 'binding authority' over 'the area of its jurisdiction'. One might also add the state's monopoly of the legitimate use of force,[50] or Weber's notion of the state as a corporate group. For Weber the state is not necessarily connected to the idea of nation (though it is connected to the Hegelian conception of civil society of which the nation is part). Also the legal definition of the state — population, territory and effective government — makes no mention of culture, religion or ethnicity as defining characteristics of statehood. Neither culture, ethnicity, language, nor religion is necessary to define independent statehood. To obtain statehood the population must occupy an exclusive territory under a national government of its own which is constitutionally independent of all other sovereign states.[51]

For Anthony Giddens, a sovereign state is a political organisation that has the capacity, within a delimited territory or territories, to make laws and effectively sanction their maintenance; exert a monopoly over the disposal of the means of violence; control basic policies relating to the internal political or administrative form of government; and depose the fruits of a national economy that are the basis of its revenue. For Giddens, linguistic or cultural identity is one of the distinctive characteristics of the classical nation-state. 'They are clearly bounded administrative units, in which policies adopted by governments are binding upon whole populations'.[52]

If the state were separated from the nation, then the legitimacy of creating ethnically and culturally homogeneous nation-states would decrease. One could argue that some sort of national identity is essential to keep the state together. This is not necessarily true if the state can define its own identity based on democratic, institutional and legal concepts. In other words, it is possible to have a political identity with cultural variety. Before the question of state identity is addressed, the debate between neo-realists and institutionalists should also be included in the analysis of European developments. In contrast to the debate on the relationship between state and nation, the debate between neo-realists and institutionalists tends to overlook the phenomenon of nationalism within states.

An 'anarchy of states'?

Neo-realists and their traditional realist forefathers consider states the primary unit of analysis and the sole actors in international relations. In addition according to Kenneth Waltz, states form the structure of international political systems through their mutual interaction.[53]

Waltz has been heavily criticized, not only for making states the most important units in the international system, but also for assuming that these units are not affected by the functions they perform or the variations and processes that occur within them.[54]

Everything else is omitted. Concern for tradition and culture, analysis of the character and personality of political actors, consideration of the conflictive and accommodative processes of politics, description of the making and execution of policy ... they are omitted because we want to figure out the expected effects of structure on process and of processes on structure. That can be done only if structure and process are distinctly defined.[55]

For Waltz, domestic systems are centralized and hierarchical; international systems are decentralized and anarchic. Domestic political structures have governmental institutions, while international politics are characterized by the absence of government. In contrast to the international system, domestic systems are characterized by specialization and integration.

For Buzan et al.[56] although the international system has been defined by the ordering principle of anarchy, functional differentiation can change the structure of the international system itself. The consequence is that an international structure that is reproduced intentionally will take a form that is very different from the neo-realist one that is reproduced unintentionally. Units (states) differ according to the extent to which they can claim — not as Waltz argues — full sovereignty, but sovereignty over only a limited range of functions. Because the internal structure of states diverges, diffusion of domestic and international structures occurs. This diffusion makes it possible for states not only to pursue competitive strategies, but also to cooperate even under the condition of anarchy. They can generate a 'cooperative anarchic society'. In such a society the states are reproduced by 'the process of mutual recognition and common practice'.

Institutionalists assert that states are not the sole significant actors in world politics and stress patterns of complex interdependence and institutionalized cooperation.[57] 'Transnational actors sometimes prevail over governments'.[58] They do not question the realist assumption of anarchy. They argue, however, that international institutions mitigate the dangers of the anarchic world of states.

International institutions can facilitate ... a process of cooperation by providing opportunities for negotiations, reducing uncertainty about others' policies, and by affecting leaders' expectations about the future. Thus, international institutions can affect the strategies states choose and the decisions they make.[59]

Both neo-realists and institutionalists recognize the anarchic nature of international relations and view states as the principal actors in world politics, and both 'seek to explain behavioural regularities'. Neo-realists conclude that — because the system is anarchic — each state must provide for its own security (self-help); while for institutionalists, international institutions mitigate the consequences of anarchy. For neo-realists, states are constrained in a structure of anarchy, for institutionalists international institutions affect the states' behaviour,[60] others stress the rules of conduct and discipline.[61]

Some neo-realists[62] predicted the emergence of conflicts among states after the end of the Cold War because this meant a return to a more anarchic system of state relations. Even the 'Western European states will begin viewing each other with greater fear and suspicion'.[63] Renewed interstate conflicts are more likely to break out in Eastern Europe, as Mearsheimer points out, in part because of resurgent 'hyper-nationalism',[64] which was an important cause of the two world wars.

For institutionalists, organizations and regimes are essential in order to constrain state strategies and provide opportunities for collective action, and find support for their perspective in Eastern Europe after the end of the Cold War.[65] Institutions signal the future intentions of governments and legitimize their behavior; institutions can provide governments with information and third party arbitration, and governments can employ security institutions as fora to strike favourable bargains.[66]

Neither neo-realists nor institutionalists adequately take into account changes in the nature of threats, however. Anarchy at the state system level is not much of a problem in Western Europe; it is not even a serious risk among the East Central European states. In Western and Central Europe the risk of inter-state wars is not very high. No immediate military threats exist at the state system level.

Conflicts have shifted from inter-state to intra-state levels. On the one hand, the main threat is ethnic nationalism which is directed against existing democratic statehood. On the other hand, democratic states are best able to respect minority rights on a non-territorial basis.

Nationalism against states

Although East Central European states remain concerned about potential new Russian imperialism, their main security threat is not external, rather it comes from anarchy within these states.[67] Ethno-nationalism does not reside at the level of the state system as it did in the nineteenth century (for example, the unification of Germany and Italy) and before the two world wars. It is directed against the state itself or it is used by an ethnically defined state elite against its own minorities. Nationalism can emerge when state boundaries do not coincide with national boundaries. Hence, the main enemy of the principle of ethnicity and nationalism appears to be the state, which is seen as the major obstacle to achieving a homogeneous nation. As a consequence, conflicts of desire emerge over borders, territories (most of the time both sides claim historical rights), and minorities (within or outside the respective state). Throughout East Central Europe, war is no longer considered a practicable means for resolving disputes between states, but conflicts emerge rather between ethnic communities and states.

Many in East-Central, Eastern and South-Eastern Europe[68] see the end of communism as an opportunity to re-animate the national and ethnic claims of the past to restore an order essential to their identity.[69] The wars between Serbia and Slovenia, and Serbia and Croatia started off as domestic wars about the establishment of ethno-national states before they became international wars following the international recognition of Slovenia and Croatia. The war in Bosnia was a civil war over ethnically defined territories. The most endangered region which has not yet drifted into a war is the Muslim Albanian enclave of Kosovo within Serbia. Problems with nationalities exist with Hungarians in Slovakia, Romania, and Serbia. There are Romanians and Russians (Dnjestr) in Moldova; Romanians, Slovaks and Poles in Ukraine; Russians in the Baltic states; Poles in Lithuania, Ukraine and Belarus; and ethnic tensions in Georgia, Armenia and Azerbaijan. There are strong German communities in Poland, the Czech Republic, Hungary and Romania.[70] Greek minorities live in Albania, Serbia and Bulgaria, and a Bulgarian minority exists in Serbia. The conflict between Greece and Macedonia (Fyrom) is ethnically based. The future of the Albanian minority in Macedonia is uncertain. There are also Turks in Bulgaria. Altogether, if the nation-states declared ethnic homogeneity, about a quarter of the population between the Baltic and Black Sea[71] would be living in the wrong place. Thus establishing ethnically homogeneous nation-states in Central Europe would require not only redrawing internationally recognized borders, but also relocating various population groups currently located in relatively isolated enclaves throughout the region in order to achieve territorially contiguous nation-states.

These ethnic tensions are accompanied by secondary effects such as refugee problems, migration, and demographic strains.[72] Furthermore, imagined homogeneous nations will perceive immigrants with different ethnic backgrounds as a threat to their desired homogeneity.

On the surface, these types of conflicts seem to correspond to the traditional types.[73] But the 'classic' types of conflicts are between states, while new nationalism is directed against the non-ethnic state itself. Realists and neorealists have difficulty capturing the dynamics of this type of nationalism because it does not occur at the state level.[74] Institutionalists also focus on the impact of institutions on the behavior of states and governments in conflict. Cooperation among states in international institutions is primarily designed to prevent conflicts among and between states, not within states. Furthermore, the internal diversity of states need not necessarily lead to the cooperative society which Buzan et al. envisage, especially if the domestic structure is shaped by anti-state nationalisms. International society would not be dominated by co-operative states but the societies within the states could be dominated by nationalism.

Conflict prevention and resolution between or within states?

The Yugoslav case has proved that an international institutional network itself is not sufficient for internal peace building. International cooperation has not been able to prevent or resolve the conflict. Before the Yugoslav crisis, many believed that the enunciation of norms was sufficient to prevent violence and to promote peace-building. This view stemmed from the enthusiasm of politicians and diplomats after the CSCE Charter of Paris was adopted in November 1990. The Charter is based on the assumption that states are willing to comply with the rules, procedures, and norms laid down by the CSCE institutions and 'mechanisms'.[75] These norms would limit the use of force and protect human rights and the rights of national minorities. Indeed, Yugoslavia was one of the most active countries in the CSCE[76] process[77] as a member of the so-called NNA[78] group. Within a very short period, this optimistic view was shattered by armed conflict that has defied all attempts of intervention.

Most of the traditional security concepts are state-based in the sense that they are designed to keep peace and security in the case of conflicts between states.

1) Alliances are seen as a device available to sovereign states[79] to aggregate and augment their individual capacities to bring about greater security.[80]
2) A system of collective security[81] implies that all member states would be willing to come to the assistance of individual member states when attacked or threatened by another member. The member states in the system might not consider an ethnic conflict a threat worthy of collective action. If they do, however, the mechanism would escalate ethnic wars into interstate wars.
3) A concert system based on co-operation among the great powers might reduce the risk of war among themselves, but there is the danger of a breakdown from within as in the nineteenth century Concert of Europe.

Recent events indicate that institutions and their member states seem to learn more quickly than scholars. After the international institutions were caught completely unprepared, lacking experience or appropriate instruments[82] to deal with the challenge of the abrupt re-emergence of uncontrolled inter-ethnic conflicts, they have been active in developing new approaches.

The CSCE (at the Budapest CSCE Summit in December 1995, the CSCE became the OSCE[83]), for example, has made conflict prevention and crisis management an integral part of the process of its functional redefinition and institutional development.[84] The OSCE High Commissioner on National Minorities, established at the Helsinki summit in 1992, has a specific and explicit 'early warning' function. According to his mandate, he provides warning at the earliest possible stage regarding tensions involving national minority issues. These tensions, although not having developed beyond the 'early warning' stage, should have in the judgement of the High Commissioner, the potential to develop into conflict within the OSCE area, thus affecting peace, stability or relations between participating states.[85] Appointed in December 1992, he has had to deal with minority problems in Estonia, Latvia, the former Yugoslav Republic of Macedonia, Albania, Slovakia and Hungary.

The OSCE also makes use of its official representation (missions) to counter, for example, the danger of a spill-over of the conflict in former Yugoslavia (to Macedonia, Kosovo, Sanjak and Vojvodina). The missions in Estonia and Latvia have performed a preventive function. Other missions are charged with mediation and conflict settlement (e.g. Moldova, Georgia, Chechnya). The first OSCE peacekeeping mission in Nagorno-Karabakh has been planned but not carried out yet.[86]

The Budapest summit in 1995 adopted the Code of Conduct on politico-military aspects of security which emphasizes that the participating states will not use armed forces to deprive persons, as individuals or as representatives of groups, of their national, religious, cultural, linguistic or ethnic identity.[87]

The establishment of these mechanisms as such does not, however, tell how effective they will be. At its meeting in Rome in December 1993, the CSCE Council of Ministers[88] also agreed that for the establishment of cooperative arrangements the respect of sovereignty and territorial integrity is one criterion that must be observed.

Despite warnings since November 1990 about the break-up of Yugoslavia, neither NATO nor the WEU became involved until much later. In the three years since NATO emergency meetings on former Yugoslavia began, however, NATO officials have learned something. They acknowledge frankly that alliance structures were, even after the changes initiated in 1990 and 1991, still largely based on the requirements for regional defense vis-à-vis an external threat, and thus not ideally suited to circumstances which called for a broader range and mix of responses with greater flexibility in both structure and means of deployment and support. The idea of Combined Joint Task Forces (CJTF) originated at the Supreme Headquarters of the Allied Powers in Europe (SHAPE) with the aim of providing NATO with a deployable multinational headquarters capability for peacekeeping and any other out-of-area operation.[89]

Skeptics argue, however, that ethnic conflicts — except, perhaps, those that spill-over existing borders or involve clear genocide — are probably beyond settlement through external institutions, particularly once fighting has begun. This would be true for weak institutions like the OSCE which has limited possibilities for sanction, and for peacekeeping operations on the ground, as the Bosnian case illustrates. It is true also for more powerful institutions such as NATO.[90] NATO also lacks the tools that are required to help prevent ethnic tensions from escalating into outright conflict.[91] Furthermore, a military alliance can threaten, or use negative sanctions, but has few positive incentives at its disposal to encourage peaceful settlement.

Membership in NATO and security guarantees cannot adequately respond to this type of pressure. NATO is suitable to counterweigh a potential Russian military threat. Enlarging NATO could mean that its member states will be confronted with threats posed by internal unrest in the new member states, not Russian resurgence. The question remains whether NATO is willing and capable of addressing new types of threats. Why should NATO want to get involved in ethnic conflicts and internal turmoil? It must not give security guarantees that are not credible.

Regional organizations

The East Central European leaders see regional co-operation as a means of becoming members of the EU. The Central European Initiative (CEI, formerly 'Pentagonal' group[92]) is a system of regional co-operation among mainly smaller states. The Central European Initiative was initially considered by some as a counterweight to Germany. But each member considers the initiative a step closer towards Western Europe. Founded in 1989, the CEI had ten full members in 1994 (Austria, Hungary, Italy, Poland, Slovenia, Croatia, Czech and Slovak Republics, Bosnia-Hercegovina, Macedonia[93]). The CEI is not an international organization and has neither the basis, nor the intention, to initiate a Central European integration process. Its purpose is to implement joint regional projects[94] within Central Europe in very concrete and pragmatic fields. It has never dealt with security and defense issues. The 'Policy Document on the Pentagonal Initiative' in November 1989 stated:

The Pentagonal Initiative is a contribution towards creating security and stability ... particularly through establishing and strengthening mutually beneficial partnership

structures based on the shared values of parliamentary democracy and human rights
... cooperating on specific matters ...

The 'Visegrád Initiative' (regional cooperation among Poland, the Czech
Republic, Slovakia and Hungary) failed to establish a regional security and
defense cooperation. The result of the Visegrád initiative was, however, that the
participating states concluded among themselves, and with Western European
states, bilateral treaties with security clauses. Each state pursued its individual
strategy to establish closer ties with NATO.[95] Furthermore, the Visegrád states
have been reluctant to pursue more ambitious regional initiatives because they
were concerned that such initiatives will come at the expense of their
integration into NATO.[96]

Although the European Community requested the establishment of a free
trade zone among the Central European countries (CEFTA) to promote
association agreements with the EU,[97] foreign trade among them remained
under 7 per cent of total trade.

Their products are not complementary; they all sell semi-manufactured
goods and raw materials. All of them compete for markets in the East and the
West. There is almost no mutual investment. Economic recovery and growth
in the Visegrád countries in the medium and long term will not be strong
enough to enable a rapid catching-up with Western Europe. The real per capita
GDPs in the most advanced Visegrád countries (the Czech Republic and
Hungary) are now about 35–44 per cent of the average EU level.[98] In order to
accelerate the integration process, the Visegrád countries do not need regional
cooperation but first and foremost growth in their domestic economies.[99]

Security and integration into the Western system can be secured only
through changes within these countries, and not through formal membership
in international organizations such as NATO or the EU. The establishment of
democratic statehood on the basis of the rule of law, economic development,
and pluralism is the basis for successful integration. The West European states
meet these criteria, hence they have been successful with integration. There is
no comparable economic and political integration outside Western Europe. All
other attempts failed or did not go beyond a certain point (e.g. WTO, OAU,
OAS, ODECA, ASEAN[100]), because they usually comprised non-democratic,
politically and ethnically fragmented, and in many cases economically weak[101]
states. Of course, the formation of democratic states in the West was gradual
and took centuries; in the East it was sudden and fairly recent.[102]

Democracy is a precondition

Non-democratic and less democratic states frequently violate minority rights and suppress their minorities. This suggests a relationship between regime-type and violence within states. State repression is often used to explain and justify nationalist anti-state mobilization.[103] Ethno-political conflicts in autocratic regimes are, however, far more intense than those in democracies.[104] Less than 1 per cent of the world's population killed by violence within the state have resided in democracies.[105]

Since 1989, all countries of the Visegrád group have gradually introduced democracy. European institutions have already developed the instruments to support the strengthening of democracy. According to OSCE documents, three major principles define a democratic political system: the rule of law (which includes the division of power, a representative government, and guarantees against the abuse of state power), political pluralism (with a parliamentary process) and respect for individual rights and freedoms. Outside the normative framework, there are also social, economic, political, and cultural conditions, such as the existence of a 'civil society', which have to be met to ensure democratic processes.[106] The Document of the Copenhagen Meeting of the Conference on the Human Dimension of the CSCE[107] contains a list of human rights and fundamental freedoms in detail, among them: the right to freedom of expression, the right of peaceful assembly and demonstration, the right of association, the right to freedom of thought, conscience and religion. The CSCE Charter of Paris affirms the strong commitment of its member states to democracy. They:

undertake to build, consolidate and strengthen democracy as the only system of government of our nations. ... Democratic government is based on the will of the people, expressed regularly through free and fair elections. Democracy has as its foundation respect for the human person and rule of law. Democracy is the best safeguard of freedom of expression, tolerance of all groups of society, and equality of opportunity for each person. Democracy, with its representative and pluralist character, entails accountability to the electorate, the obligation of public authorities to comply with the law and justice administrated impartially. No one will be above the law.[108]

Modern democracy cannot simply mean majority rule which can threaten minority interests. Minority rights are included explicitly in the 'Declaration on the Guidelines on Recognition of New States in Eastern Europe and the Soviet Union' issued by the EC Foreign Ministers in December 1991. It stated that the recognition of these new states requires:

— respect for the provisions of the Charter of the UN and the commitments
  subscribed to in the Final Act of Helsinki and in the Charter of Páris,
  especially with regard to the rule of law, democracy and human rights;
— guarantees for the rights of the ethnic and national groups and minorities
  in accordance with the commitments subscribed to in the framework of the
  CSCE ...[109]

The Council of Europe has a major function in the process of developing
democratic institutions and the rule of law as well as protection of minority
rights. The 'Framework Convention for the Protection of National Minorities',
signed in February 1995, transformed existing political commitments into legal
obligations. It also contains a special monitoring mechanism. Increasing the
membership of the Council of Europe without lowering its standards is an
important challenge.

So far, there are no other structures which can implement and guarantee
minority rights better than the democratic states. A homogenous nation-state
is not a precondition for democracy;[110] however, Ralf Dahrendorf demonstrated
convincingly that ethnically heterogeneous states are better able to guarantee
basic civil rights than are homogeneous nation-states[111] because democracy is
the basis for the recognition of cultural diversity. Although both nationalism
and democracy may have emerged out of the same process of industrialization,[112] they are not inseparable.[113] It would be like arguing that two trains
leaving the same station at roughly the same time would have to go in the
same direction. Moreover, if democracy and ethnicity are not kept separate,
people would increasingly vote along ethnic lines. The elected leaders would
then pursue narrow ethnic interests.[114]

States without nations and nations without territories

If the state disintegrates but the nation continues, if security becomes 'de-
statized' and ethno-national identity replaces state security, it might well
happen that domestic anarchy prevails over the democratic state. Gottfried
Herder's idea that a variety of nations organized along cultural lines and
supported by strong states could co-exist peacefully, failed. The outcome was
that 'small nations filled with national pride and hatreds and jealousies, egged
on by demagogues, (were) marching against each other'.[115] A study of
European minorities came to the conclusion that:

the concept of self-determination is too destabilizing to be applied broadly as a
solution to ethnic grievances; and that the splintering of state entities into smaller and

smaller ethnic enclaves is destroying both the political and economic cohesiveness of the European continent.[116]

Among others, Barry Buzan distinguishes between weak and strong states. States in which society and government are at odds are weak states. States which are coherent in socio-political terms are strong. 'Reducing contradictions between the state and societal security is thus a precondition for successful 'national' security policy'.[117]

If a society is dominated by ethnicity and nationality, however, the gap between society and state will widen and the state will be weakened,[118] unless the state itself is ethnically homogeneous. Only with a society based on strong political identity (citizenship)[119] rather than on ethnic origin,[120] can society and state be reconciled. Ethno-national identity should not be part of statehood (as the concept of 'societal security' suggests). Hence, to defend democratic statehood it is necessary for Central European states to 'de-nationalize' and 'de-ethnicize' the concept of the state. The state must be defined without reference to the nation. Nor should it matter whether the states are larger than the nations or the nations are larger than the states.[121] There is no convincing reason why people who speak the same language or belong to the same race should form one state.[122] If nations are 'imagined communities' (Anderson) or an instrument to create loyalty and not an enduring characteristic of human nature, then it should be possible to remove them from the concept of the state. Nationality and ethnicity, like religion, should remain a private matter, as a granted right, however. For centuries religion was tied to the state. Eventually the secular state prevailed, at least in Western societies.

Historically, state and nation developed separately. If democratic states (political and administrative units on a legal basis) are dissolved, however, ethnic nations may emerge with local or regional autocratic powers and with their own militias. Leaders of nation-states who consider themselves explicitly as representatives of a particular ethnic group tend to oppress or ignore the rights of other ethnic groups. The Serbian attempt to create a Serbian state is a case in point. But also the Croatian constitution of December 1990 defined the state as a 'nation-state of the Croat people'. The same is true for the Romanian (1991) and Slovak (1992) constitutions.[123]

This essay does not discuss the question whether secession is morally justified or whether there should be a constitutional right to secede.[124] It argues, however, that strong democracies offer the best opportunity for resolving ethnic conflict, but only if ethnic conflicts are addressed carefully.[125] Without the self-limitation that stems from a democratic state, there will be no distinction between citizenship and nationhood.[126]

Non-territorial minority rights

States respect and protect minority rights better than supranational bodies. Hannah Arendt takes a pragmatic view with respect to the League of Nations:

Or when, as in the case of minorities, an international body arrogated to itself a nongovernmental authority, its failure was apparent even before its measures were fully realised; not only were the governments more or less openly opposed to this encroachment on their sovereignty, but the concerned nationalities themselves did not recognize a non-national guarantee, mistrusted everything which was not a clear-cut support of their 'national' ... rights ....[127]

One approach to protecting minority rights[128] on a non-territoral basis is to guarantee personal and functional autonomy in the areas of culture, language, and religion; this was first developed by the Austrian Social Democrats, Otto Bauer and Karl Renner.[129] Renner advocated non-territorial national councils for minority issues (such as culture and education). The councils would be elected independently of the territory in which the minority lived.[130] The Slovenian Social Democracy leader Etbin Kristan proposed an even more radical solution at the Party Congress in 1899: nations can only exist without borders but they consist of the totality of individuals, not of territories. Therefore, Kristan compared 'nation' with the Roman Church. Because the Slovenes lived dispersed throughout the crown lands of the monarchy,[131] Kristan sought a policy that decoupled 'nation' from 'territory'.

Non-territorial solutions[132] can be achieved only if the state remains territorial and is separated from a kind of nationality which remains individual and personal. This includes, of course, the guarantees by the state of cultural identity across borders but with no regional political authority or governance.[133] Non-territoral approaches would also reduce the danger that settlements of the majority population on the territory where the minority lives would undermine minority rights. This approach can, however, also lead to a permanent discussion about ethnic 'over-' and 'under-' representation in every possible institution.

Karl Renner, the Austrian politician and lawyer, wrote in 1902:

Nature knows neither an equality of individuals nor an equality of nations; equality is a creation of law and its greatest benefit for those subject to it.[134]

For Renner, equality is a matter of institutions, law, constitution and administration. These dimensions have developed within the context of statehood and have been provided only by the state.[135]

Can integration be an adequate response to nationalism?

One idea of the founders of the European Community was to ban nationalism. All European states support further progress of European integration. Nationalism on a state level has in fact been left behind. The Union was built on French-German partnership to reduce the fear of German military resurgence. It is unclear, however, how far the integration process will go and what the 'finalité politique' will be. The concept 'of an ever closer union' (Treaty of Rome and Treaty of Maastricht) does not specify the end of the process. Will economic integration processes eventually lead to a European federation?

Nor is the integration theory[136] very specific about the finality of this process. Integration theory is based on the assumption that in some fields and at a certain point, economic integration processes would unavoidably spill over — automatically or politically — to other areas (political and security). It is by no means certain, however, if and when integration processes become irreversible and prevail over state sovereignty. Functionalist theory does not predict the limits of integration.

The European integration process has raised growing concern about national identities, however.[137] Supporters of a deeper Europeanisation are quick to assure skeptics that national identities based on language and culture are not threatened.[138] But promoters of European integration have avoided addressing the complicated relations between integration, nation, and state. If national identities remain, what becomes of the state? Will it become less significant? And if states disappear, what would the new structure look like? What would be the structure of the EU? How democratic would it be?

If states remain the main actors, however, the EU can be seen as a structure[139] of a new type that affects and constrains the behaviour of member states. The units will be constrained to take the same form, pursue a similar range of governmental tasks, and they would adopt a similar internal structure as well. This seems to confirm the view that despite different geostrategic positions, different threat perceptions, and varying economic performance there is a similar debate on security issues in all West European states. The members of the EU have developed a new structure by creating new institutions, norms and rules, even a new code of communication. This is different from the realist picture of the war-prone anarchic structure.

What happens, however, if the integration process results in the dissolution of states?

If states disappear, Hedley Bull[140] foresees a 'neo-medieval' model with 'overlapping authority and multiple loyalty' emerging. In such a system, states must share their authority with 'other associations'.[141] Bull regards the 'neo-medieval' system as incompatible with the state-based international society. Barry Buzan,[142] however, supports the idea that international society is not contradictory, but symbiotic and complementary to a world society, which is based on individuals, non-state organizations, and the population as a whole as functionally differentiated actors with shared identities.

Andrew Moravcsik[143] sees individuals and privately constituted groups as fundamental actors in world politics; governments constitute a subset of domestic social actors. For Mark Zacher,[144] the decaying Westphalian system of sovereignty and state autonomy is directly related to the increasing cooperation among states: 'states are becoming increasingly enmeshed in a network of collaborative arrangements or regimes'. Charles Kegley argues that this process requires the active moral commitment of states to cooperative arrangements:

The voluntary sacrifice of sovereignty for collaborative problem-solving ... requires states to conceive morally of transnational co-operation as compatible with their national interests ...[145]

James Rosenau goes one step further and sees a 'multi-centric world' emerging which 'is in sharp contrast to that which prevails in the state-centric world'.[146] The number of essential actors would increase to 'hundreds of thousands'.[147] The state system would gradually be replaced by the two-fold process of 'globalization' and 'localization', which Rosenau calls 'fragmegration' (fragmentation + integration):[148]

While different sources underlie the operation of fragmegrative dynamics in the political, social, and economic realms, they all contribute to the same major outcome: in each realm the close links between territoriality and the state are breaking down and thereby posing the question of what constitutes the boundaries of communities.

Holm and Sørensen[149] point to the process of 'uneven globalization' resulting from intensification of economic, political, social, and cultural relations across borders. The state plays an active role in this process, however. Michael Zürn looks at the other side of the coin and speaks of 'uneven denationalization'. For Zürn 'denationalization' results from the weakening of the state through globalization and the presence or emergence of 'strong societies'.[150]

Robert W. Cox sees opportunities for social movements:

Moreover, the changes taking place in states (diminished importance) give new opportunities for self-expression by nationalities that have no state of their own, in movements for separation or autonomy; and the same tendencies encourage ethnicities and religiously defined groups that straddle state boundaries to express their identities in global politics. ... Social movements like environmentalism, feminism, and the peace movement transcend territorial boundaries. Transnational co-operation among indigenous peoples enhances their force within particular states.[151]

It is far from being clear whether, or when, Europe will become a super-state or a 'neo-medieval' system. If statehood is dissolved, however, it is very unlikely that a society of overlapping, more or less equal authorities and actors with shared identities will emerge. It is more likely that the most powerful authority will dominate: the nation. If the boundaries of the territorial state are dissolved through 'fragmegration' processes, they will most likely be replaced by borders defined by nationalities, ethnicity, culture, and language. When state structures are weakened, nationalism based on ethnic distinctions is likely to be the consequence, rather than equal rights for individuals or groups.[152]

Stephen Van Evera[153] predicts that nationalisms will pose little risk to peace in Western Europe because they are satisfied, having already gained states. In the East the number of stateless nationalisms is larger, increasing the risk that future conflicts will lead to wars of liberation. He basically follows Ernest Gellner's argument that in the West, in contrast to the East, states correlate with cultural zones.

The potential for the concept of the nation to degenerate into ethno-nationalism is not limited to Eastern Europe. In Western Europe, the Flemings and Walloons in Belgium, the German-speaking minority in Northern Italy (South Tyrol), the Basques and Catalans in Spain, and Corsica are the best known examples. In 1994 the Italian right-wing 'National Alliance' partner in the governing coalition advocated revising the Treaty of Osimo (1975) that recognized the post-war borders between Italy and Yugoslavia (now Croatia and Slovenia).[154] In response, the leader of the major party representing the German-speaking minority in South Tyrol (Northern Italy) said that if borders were under revision, then the border between Italy and Austria should be reconsidered as well.

A 'Europe of the regions' challenges states through decentralization and fragmentation. Where are the borders of the regions?[155] Will there be a Basque region transcending the border between France and Spain? Will there be a Tyrolian region[156] or a Bavarian-Tyrolian region, or will there be a Northern Italian region as the 'Lega Nord' (the second largest party in the Italian government in 1994/95) proposes?[157] What would happen to Switzerland with its linguistic groups? The result of these changes might not be war, but most likely uncertainties, tensions, conflicts, unrest, and perhaps terrorism would increase.

Consider the situation of Austria if state borders were to disappear. Historically, Austria has suffered from an identity crisis, and many leaders of the First Republic (1918-1938) thought that the country was not a viable entity. All political parties had the designation 'deutsch-österreichisch' (German-Austrian) in their programmes or names. Most Austrians considered themselves ethnic Germans. This general sentiment prepared the ground for the 'Anschluss' in 1938. After 1945, Austria developed a strong identity as an independent though small state. Austrian politicians downplayed the idea of the 'nation'[158] or called the state 'nation'. Part of Austria's identity was shaped by its neutrality between the military blocs. Today more than two-thirds of the Austrians believe that they are an independent nation.[159] To a large extent this is due to Austria's successful de-ethnicising of the Austrian state which the Austrians consider their 'nation'. If state borders in Europe were to disappear due to integration, the Austrians could once again consider themselves to belong to the German nation. Europe would once again be confronted with a unified ethnic German majority.[160]

Ethno-nationality as a basis for authority relations challenges the premises of European integration: a society of democratic states with equal citizens. If statehood were dissolved, democracies developed over the last centuries might fade as well. So far there is no developed democracy outside the state, either on a supranational or on a regional or local level. The domestic structures of the member states have shaped the structure of the EU. All member states are democracies with developed economies. In other words, the internal characteristics of the states have reinforced the process of European integration. More European federalism without a developed state would, however, favour nations over the states. Democracy is an attribute of states[161] and should be guaranteed to the democratic member states unless it is replaced in certain areas by a more democratic EU structure, which is not yet on the horizon. States should not give up democracy before it is clear what they get in return. As to the institutional arrangements, the European Commission should not operate independently of the democratic governments of its member states.

Conclusion: states without nationalism

Many observers foresee no withering away of the state systems. They suggest that sovereign states and the state systems formed by them will be around, at least for the time being, and probably for much longer than that.[162] One could argue that European states are no longer sovereign because they have transferred much of their sovereignty to international bodies (e.g., the EU) in any case. The argument that states have lost sovereignty is far from new, however. Hedley Bull maintains that the European state systems have always been part of a wider system of interaction in which groups other than the state (e.g., Catholics and Protestants) are related to each other, to foreign states and to international or supranational bodies, as well as to the state in which they are located.[163] States have always struggled to maintain sovereignty. However, if sovereignty means autonomy, a supreme coercive power, authority not hampered by others,[164] exclusive control over a given territory,[165] and equality and independence in their mutual relations, then states have never been sovereign. Since the Westphalian system of 'sovereign states' there have always been limitations to sovereignty, including national and international law, constraints imposed by the configuration of power and economic inter-dependence.[166] However, the understanding among the members of the international community as to what constitutes sovereign authority during a particular historic period (dynastic state, national state) changes.[167] The state responds to international challenges such as economic and technological internationalization processes. Accommodation to new developments is hardly a new feature of state sovereignty and has been going on ever since the modern sovereign state emerged.

The Westphalian system did not eliminate old entities.[168] The new territorial states emerged as the main actors, however.[169] The new order created a system of states which are at least formally equal, in contrast to the earlier dominance of emperors and popes. In this manner, the non-democratic states of 1648 contained elements on which later pluralist democracies were built, including churches, universities, cities, guilds, merchant leagues, monasteries, and the aristocracy with its sovereigns.

Democratization and economic development in the West were achieved within the framework of the European state. Hedley Bull has observed that the European state system is also the basis of international society:

What is chiefly responsible for the degree of interaction among political systems in all continents of the world, sufficient to make it possible for us to speak of a world political system, has been the expansion of the European states system all over the globe, and its transformation into a states system of global dimension.[170]

The European state is the basis of globalization, integration, and of democracy. There is no developed democracy outside the state. Integration should not go beyond the limit where democratic statehood is dissolved. It might well be that it is replaced by the most powerful new and old actor: the nation defined in ethnic terms. The principle of nationality and ethnicity is far from a unifying force. More likely, nationalism will split existing states. Ethno-nationalism may become the major cause of domestic anarchy in European states. A Europe based on nations without states would most likely reverse the integration process. Only integration, plus statehood, can reduce this danger. Traditionally, international institutions and organizations, such as the League of Nations and the United Nations, sought to protect existing states from external threats (as the liberation of Kuwait demonstrated). Protecting states from internal dissolution and helping them to rebuild their economic, social, and administrative structures is a new function of international organizations. In Europe, international institutions (OSCE, Council of Europe) also seek to protect minority rights; this was not only in order to improve the status of ethnic nationalities, but also to protect states from secession.[171]

Of course, states make war. The history of the rise of the state is linked to violent conflict and military power.[172] Democratic states are usually able to keep peace among themselves, however.[173] Will this be true if they are replaced by something else?[174] International institutions provide important support for democratization. The major threat in Central and Western Europe comes from within the states[175] and not from an anarchic state system. The 'security dilemma' does not simply appear on the ethnic level.[176] Ethnic groups do not act like states as a modified neo-realist approach would see it.[177] Conflict arises not so much between ethnicities, but among different groups concerning the character of the state and whether it is defined ethnically or politically.

Van Evera observes that nationalist movements without states and densely intermingled nationality populations increase the risk of war. The danger of war can be reduced if nationalisms attain statehood and if national populations are compact and homogeneous.[178] But this goal is unrealistic for several reasons.

— One response to intra-national heterogeneity is some sort of 'ethnic cleansing'. The history of Central Europe and the Balkans is full of examples: the Turkish killing of Armenians during the First World War; the exchange of Greek and Turkish populations in 1922; Stalin's evacuation of Poles from the Eastern territories in 1939-1941;[179] the Croat massacres of Serbs during the 1940s; the so-called 'option' when the population of South Tyrol had to decide in 1939 whether to become Italians or leave the country; the expulsion of the German-speaking population from the Sudetenland after the Second World War, and of course the Holocaust; the most recent example is the 'ethnic cleansing' in Bosnia and Croatia.
— Suggestions for peaceful separation[180] rarely work.[181] Success depends on the history of the territory and populations involved and on the degree of ethnic heterogeneity, and most important of all, the political leadership of both sides must want, or at least accept, the separation. One relatively peaceful example is the Czech-Slovak 'civilized divorce' in 1992.[182] The secession of homogeneous Slovenia involved some violence in 1991. Peaceful homogenization (separation or unification) cannot be a general solution.[183] This would create new national problems and new minorities.

If South Tyrol joined Austria again, there would be a significant Italian minority there (one-third of the population). More than two thirds of the population of Transylvania are now Romanians, and Slovakia's Magyars represent about 50 per cent of the inhabitants in towns and villages near the Hungarian border.[184] All these parts of the population belonging to the majority would become new minorities if borders were to be changed. Homogenization as a general principle for peaceful separation would confirm and legitimize efforts to make political and ethnic borders correspond.

— The remaining option is to create states without nations, or to 'de-nationalize' and 'de-ethnicize' the idea of the state gradually. States defined as administrative units do not necessarily have any national or ethnic affiliations. Conversely, ethnically defined states are likely to oppress minorities. Only de-nationalized and de-ethnicized democratic states are fully equipped to protect minorities. This could be done best on a non-territorial basis. Ethnicity and nationality, like religion, should become a private matter recognized by states as a civil right. The 'nation-state' should keep the 'state' and drop the 'nation'.

Notes

1. Thanks to John Bunzl for sharing his knowledge on nationalism and minorities and for his comments on this paper. Helpful suggestions have been given by Jonathan Bach, Robert Jackson, Stephan Kux, Stephen Larrabee, Hanspeter Neuhold, Daniel Nelson, Bruno Schoch, Lene Bøgh Sørensen, and Mark Zacher. In this article the term 'Central Europe' is used for the old lands of the Habsburg Empire. The term 'East Central Europe' mainly refers to the former smaller members of the Warsaw Pact Organization.
2. Regarding the Nordic states (Norway, Finland, Sweden) see Raimo Väyrynen, 1993. 'Territory, Nation State and Nationalism', in Jyrki Iivonen (ed.), The Finnish Institute of International Affairs, *The Future of the Nation State in Europe*, Aldershot: Edward Elgar: 159-78.
3. Definitions by Bernard Phillips, Ashley Montagu, and Encyclopaedia Britannica quoted in Mojmir Krizan, March 1995, 'Postkommunistische Wiedergeburt ethnischer Nationalismen und der Dritte Balkan-Krieg', *Osteuropa* 45, (3): 202.
4. Elie Kedourie, 1960. *Nationalism*, London: Hutchinson: 71.
5. Max Weber, 1948. 'The Nation', in H.H. Gerth and C. Wright Mills (eds.), *From Max Weber: Essays in Sociology*, London: Routledge & Kegan Paul: 171-79.
6. Compare Daniele Conversi, Spring 1995. 'Reassessing Current Theories of Nationalism: Nationalism as Boundary Maintenance and Creation', *Nationalism & Ethnic Politics* 1, (1): 73-85.

7. Stephen Van Evera, Spring, 1994. 'Hypotheses on Nationalism and War', *International Security* 18, (4): 10-12, 33-39; Iván Gyurcsík, 1993. 'New Legal Ramifications of the Question of National Minorities', in Ian M. Cuthbertson and Jane Leibowitz (eds.), *Minorities: The New Europe's Old Issue*, New York: Institute for East-West Studies: 20.

8. Liah Greenfeld, 1992. *Nationalism: Five Roads to Modernity*, Cambridge, Mass: Harvard U.P.: 27-184; Norbert Elias, 1988. *Über den Prozeß der Zivilisation, Soziogenetische Untersuchungen*, Vol. 2, *Wandlungen der Gesellschaft: Entwurf zu einer Theorie der Zivilisation*, Frankfurt: Suhrkamp: 123-311; and Charles Tilly (ed.), 1975. *The Formation of National States in Western Europe*, Princeton.

9. Tony Judt, 1994. 'The New Old Nationalism', *The New York Review of Books*, 26 May: 46.

10. William Pfaff, 1993. *The Wrath of Nations*, New York: Simon & Schuster: 19.

11. Greenfeld, *Nationalism*: 286, 364.

12. Joszef Bayer, 1994. 'Nationalismen in Osteuropa: Sackgasse oder notwendiges Durchgangsstadium zur Demokratie?', in *Friedensbericht 1994: Krieg und gewaltfreie Konfliktlösungen*, Zürich: Verlag Rüegger: 29-42. See also Pfaff, *The Wrath of Nations*: 14; Peter Rutland, 1994. 'State Failure and State Building in Post-Socialist Europe: Implications for Theories of Nationalism' (Paper prepared for the annual convention of the American Political Science Association, New York, 1-3 September, 1994): 5-9.

13. Bruno Schoch, 1992. 'Der neu aufbrechende Nationalismus in Europa als Bedrohung für Stabilität und Frieden', in Achim Güssgen and Rüdiger Schlaga (eds.), *Chancen und Probleme einer zukünftigen europäischen Friedensordnung*, Frankfurt: Hessische Stiftung Friedens und Konfliktforschung: 66-69. See also Bruno Schoch, 1992, *Nach Strassburg oder nach Sarajevo? Zum Nationalismus in postkommunisatischen Übergangsgesellschaften*, HSFK-Report (6), Frankfurt: HSFK.

14. Rupen Cetinyan, 1994. 'The Institution of Ethnicity: The Political Economy of Ethnic Organization and Conflict', (Paper presented at the 1994 Annual Meeting of the American Political Science Association, New York, 1-4 September).

15. Pfaff, *The Wrath of Nations*: 16.

16. Otto Dann, 1991. 'Begriffe und Typen des Nationalen in der frühen Neuzeit', in Bernhard Giesen (ed.), *Nationale und kulturelle Identität: Studien zur Entwicklung des kollektiven Bewußtseins in der Neuzeit*, Frankfurt: Suhrkamp: 56-76.

17. Concerning the disintegration of the Habsburg monarchy see Manfried Rauchensteiner, 1994. *Der Tod des Doppeladlers: Österreich-Ungarn und der Erste Weltkrieg*, Graz: Styria; See also Rutland, 'State Failure and State Building': 19-20.

18. Judt, 'The New Old Nationalism': 46-47.

19. Daniel Patrick Moynihan, 1993. *Pandaemonium: Ethnicity in International Politics*, New York: Oxford U.P.: 63-106.

20. Bach, Jonathan P.G. 1993. 'The Crisis of Democratic Discourse: Nationalism and Eastern Europe', (Paper presented at the 34th Annual International Studies Association Conference, Acapulco, Mexico, 23-27 March): 6 ff.

21. Tibor Pichler, 1994. 'Die Eigenständigkeit als Idee des Slowakischen sprachbegründeten Nationalismus', in Eva Schmidt-Hartmann, *Formen des nationalen Bewußtseins im Lichte zeitgenössischer Nationalismus-theorien*, München: R. Oldenbourg Verlag: 321-30.
22. See also John Breuilly, 1982. *Nationalism and the State*, Manchester: Manchester U.P.: 335-44; John Hutchinson, 1987. *The Dynamics of Cultural Nationalism*, London: Allen and Unwin: 12-19.
23. For the definition of 'ethnic nationalism' see Charles A. Kupchan (ed.), 1995, *Nationalism and Nationalities in the New Europe*, Ithaca and London: Cornell U.P.: 4.
24. See Jacques Rupnik, 1990. 'Central Europe or Middle Europe?', *Daedalus*, 119, (1) Winter: 249-78.
25. *Ibid.*
26. Schoch, 'Der neu aufbrechende Nationalismus': 65; Joseph Rothschild, 1994, 'Nationalism and Democratization in East Central Europe: Lessons from the Past', *Nationalities Papers* 22, (1), Spring: 32.
27. For definitions see Rothshild, 'Nationalism and Democratization': 27-30.
28. Zarko Puhovski, 1994. 'Nationalismus und Demokratie im postkommunistischen Schlüssel', in Margit Pieber (ed.), (Österreichisches Studienzentrum für Frieden und Konfliktlösung), *Europa — Zukunft eines Kontinents: Friedenspolitik oder Rückfall in die Barbarei*, Münster: Agenda Verlag: 132-38.
29. Benedict Anderson, 1983. *Imagined Communities: Reflections on the Origin and Spread of Nationalism*, London: Verso.
30. Eric Hobsbawm, 1990. *Nations and Nationalism since 1780: Programme, Myth, Reality*, Cambridge: Cambridge U.P.
31. Ernest Gellner, 1991. 'Nationalism and politics in Eastern Europe', *New Left Review*, (189), September/October: 127-34.
32. Gellner prefers paintings by Modigliani with clear distinguishable colours.
33. Karl W. Deutsch, 1972. *Der Nationalismus und seine Alternativen*, München: Serie Piper: 41-68. (The American edition *Nationalism and Its Alternatives* was published in New York: Alfred A. Knopf, 1969.)
34. András Balogh, 1993. 'Conventional Wisdoms on National Minorities and International Security', *Defence Studies: Army and Security Policy in Hungary*, (2), Budapest: Institute for Strategic Studies: 35.
35. For example the Hungarian Historian Katalin Soós in a speech in Vienna at the Austrian Institute for Eastern and South Eastern Europe on 6 March, 1990.
36. Hungary lost almost 1.7 million ethnic Hungarians to Romania, about one million to Czechoslovakia, and around half a million to Yugoslavia. Bennett Kovrig, 'Hungarian Minorities in East-Central Europe' (The Atlantic Council of the United State: Occasional Paper, March 1995). Transylvania did not, however, belong to Hungary until 1848. In the seventeenth century it was autonomous, in the eighteenth century it belonged to Austria. From 1848 to 1918 it was Hungarian, it came to Romania after 1918, to Hungary again in 1940, and back to Romania after 1945. Pfaff, *The Wrath of Nations*: 201.

37. Reported by the Hungarian news agency, MTI, 13 August 1990. Other political leaders repeated similar statements afterwards.

38. Kovrig, 'Hungarian Minorities in East-Central Europe': 17-27.

39. Convention on providing special rights for the Slovenian minority living in the Republic of Hungary and for the Hungarian minority living in the Republic of Slovenia, (Ljubljana, 6 November, 1992).

40. Declaration on the Principles of Cooperation between the Republic of Hungary and Ukrainian Soviet Socialist Republic in the guaranteeing of Rights for National Minorities, (Budapest, 31 May, 1991).

41. Hungary and Slovakia signed the treaty short before the 'Pact on Stability in Europe' was adopted in Paris in March 1995.

42. The Hungarian Parliament accepted unilateraly a law on the rights of national and ethnic minorities (Romanians, Slovaks, Rumanians, Croats, Serbs, Slovenes, Germans) in July 1993. Obviously, this law is also considered to be a model for the neighbouring states with Hungarian minorities: 'In its positive interpretation, the principle of reciprocity means that two countries, along the common border of which national minorities are living, try to create proper living conditions for those minorities on the basis of similar principles'. Office for National and Ethnic Minorities, *The principle of reciprocity in the policy towards national minorities*, Budapest, January 1992.

43. 'Final Act of the Conference on Security and Cooperation in Europe', Helsinki, 1 August 1975. Document in Lawrence Freedman (ed.), 1990, *Europe Transformed: Documents on the End of the Cold War, Key Treaties, Agreements, Statements and Speeches*, New York: St. Martin's Press: 87. The Hungarian Government insisted on enshrining this principle into the bilateral treaties with the Ukraine and the Slovak Republic.

44. Ole Waever; Barry Buzan; Morten Kelstrup and Pierre Lemaitre, 1993. *Identity, Migration and the New Security Agenda in Europe*, London: Pinter Publishers Ltd: 68-71.

45. *Ibid.*, 76-78.

46. *Ibid.*

47. *Ibid:* 42.

48. Yosef Lapid, 1993. 'Nationalism, Identity and Security: Global Threats and Theoretical Challenges', (Paper presented at the 34th International Studies Association Convention, Acapulco, 23–27 March): 4ff.

49. Daniel N. Nelson, 1993. 'Great Powers and World Peace', *Österreichische Zeitschrift für Politikwissenschaft* 22, (2): 169-78.

50. Max Weber, 1978. *Economy and Society*, Günther Roth and Claus Wittich (eds.), Berkeley: University of California Press: 54-6.

51. Robert H. Jackson and Alan James, 1993. 'The Character of Independent Statehood', in Robert H. Jackson and Alan James (eds.), *States in a Changing World: A contemporary Analysis*, Oxford: Clarendon Press: 18-19.

52. Anthony Giddens, 1987. *The Nation-State and Violence*, 2 vols. of A Contemporary Critique of Historical Materialism, vol. 2, Berkeley and Los Angeles: University of California Press: 270, 282, 289.

53. Kenneth N. Waltz, 1979. *Theory of International Politics*, New York: McGraw-Hill Publishing Company.
54. William C. Olson and A.J.R. Groom, 1991. *International Relations then and now: Origins and Trends in Interpretation*, London: Harper Collins Academic: 264.
55. Waltz, *Theory of International Politics*: 82.
56. Barry Buzan, Charles Jones and Richard Little, 1993. *The Logic of Anarchy: Neorealism to Structural Realism*, New York: Columbia U.P.
57. Robert O. Keohane, 1989. *International Institutions and State Power: Essays in International Relations Theory*, Boulder: Westview Press.
58. Robert O. Keohane and Joseph S. Nye, 1971. *Transnational Relations and World Politics*, London: Harvard U.P.: 386.
59. Robert O. Keohane, Joseph S. Nye and Stanley Hoffmann, 1993. *After the Cold War: International Institutions and State Strategies in Europe: 1989-91*, Cambridge, Mass./London: Harvard U.P.: 5.
60. Rittberger pointed out that German research centred on international regimes in the East-West context in the issue area of security at a time when the crisis of 'détente' was causing great anxiety in large parts of the populace in Germany and in Europe in general. In contrast, the American regime's analysis concentrated mostly on economic issue areas in East-West relations. See Volker Rittberger, 1993. 'Research on International Regimes in Germany: The Adaptive Internalization of an American Social Science Concept', in *Regime Theory and International Relations*, Oxford: Clarendon Press: 6-8.
61. Charles W. Kegley, Jr., 1993. 'Cold War Myths and the New International Realities: Reconsidering Theoretical Premises', *Österreichische Zeitschrift für Politikwissenschaft* 22, (2): 150.
62. John J. Mearsheimer, 1990. 'Back to the Future: Instability in Europe after the Cold War', *International Security*, 15, (No. 1), Summer: 5-56.
63. *Ibid*: 47.
64. *Ibid*: 7, 20-21, 35.
65. Keohane, Nye and Hoffmann (eds.), *After the Cold War*: 383.
66. Richard Weitz, 'Pursuing Military Security in Eastern Europe', in Keohane, Nye and Hoffmann (eds.), *After the Cold War*: 342-80.
67. See also Peter Coulmas, 1993. 'Das Problem des Selbstbestimmungsrechtes: Mikronationalismen, Anarchie und innere Schwäche der Staaten', *Europa-Archiv* 48, (4), 25 February: 85-92.
68. Not to mention the Russian Federation.
69. William Pfaff, 1994. 'East Europeans Have a Basic Adjustment to make', *International Herald Tribune*, 21-22 May: 4.
70. With all these states Germany concluded treaties on friendship and co-operation, which address minority issues.
71. Giles Merritt, 1993. 'A Charter For Peace In Europe', *International Herald Tribune*, 5 May.
72. One example is Germany. German law defines citizenship by ancestry. Despite Germany's financial, housing and unemployment problems due to the unification costs, it has accepted 340,000 ethnic German immigrants to resettle

in Germany since 1990. In 1993 Germany changed its constitution eviscerating the respective Art. 16, but not abolishing it.

73. For example, Ole Waever and Morten Kelstrup, 'Europe and its nations: political and cultural identities', in Waever, Buzan, Kelstrup and Lemaitre, *Identity, Migration and the New Security Agenda in Europe*: 72.

74. This criticism of neo-realism is different to the argument that neo-realists would not see the different characters of states (democratic or autocratic, capitalist or communist, peace-loving or aggressive). Among others see John Lewis Gaddis, Winter 1992/93. 'International Relations Theory and the End of the Cold War', *International Security* 17, (3): 5-58.

75. Charter of Paris for a New Europe, 21 November 1990.

76. Conference on Security and Cooperation in Europe.

77. Ljubivoje Acimovic, 1987. 'The CSCE Process from a Yugoslav Viewpoint', in Hanspeter Neuhold (ed.), *CSCE: N+N Perspectives: The Process of the Conference on Security and Cooperation in Europe from the Viewpoint of the Neutral and Non-Aligned Participating States*, Vienna: Wilhelm Braumüller: 79-100.

78. Neutral and non-aligned states.

79. For the tendencies of European defence organizations towards 'Renationalization', see Jan Willem Honig, 1992. 'The Renationalization of Western European Defence', *Security Studies* 2, (1), Autumn: 122-38.

80. Various definitions of alliances are given by Stephen Walt, 1987. *The Origins of Alliances*, Ithaca: Cornell U.P.; Brian L. Job and Don Munton, 'Disentangling the Alliance: The Role of Small and Middle States in NATO' (Paper presented at the 33rd International Studies Association Convention, Atlanta, 30 March-4 April, 1991); Katja Weber, 'A New Era in Global Relations: A reassessment of Security Arrangements', (Paper presented at the 35th International Studies Association Convention, Washington, D.C., 28 March-1 April, 1993): 2.

81. For examples of this debate see Richard K. Betts, 1992. 'Systems for Peace or Causes of War? Collective Security, Arms Control, and the New Europe', *International Security*, 17, (1), Summer, pp. 4-43; Inis R. Claude, 1966. *Power and International Relations*, New York: Random House; Heinz Gärtner, 1992. *Wird Europa sicherer? Zwischen kollektiver und nationaler Sicherheit*, Vienna: Braumüller; Joseph Joffe, Spring 1992. 'Collective Security and the Future of Europe: Failed Dreams and Dead Ends', *Survival*: 36-50.

82. Among others compare Andreas Unterberger, 1994. 'Minderheitenschutz und Selbstbestimmung: Die große historische Aufgabe zur Jahrtausendwende', *Europäische Rundschau* 22, (3): 37-50.

83. Organization for Security and Cooperation in Europe.

84. Among others see Hanspeter Neuhold, 1994. 'Conflicts and Conflict Management in a *new* Europe', *Austrian Journal of Public and International Law*, (46): 109-29.

85. *Helsinki Document 1992*, Decisions, II (3).

86. Office of the Secretary General, *CSCS Facts*, Vienna: 15 November 1993. See also Wilhelm Hoynck, 1994. Secretary General of the CSCE, *CSCE Works to Develop its Conflict Prevention Potential*, Brussels: NATO Review 42, (2).

87. CSCE Budapest Document 1994. *Towards a Genuine Partnership in a New Era*.

88. Fourth Meeting of the CSCE Council, Rome, 1993. *CSCE and the New Europe —Our Security is Indivisible,* Decisions II (3).
89. Bruce George (General Rapporteur), 1994. *After the NATO summit: Draft General Report,* Brussels: International Secretariat of NATO, May, II./10-17.
90. Catherine McArdle Kelleher, 1994. 'Cooperative Security in Europe', in Janne E. Nolan (ed.), *Global Engagement: Cooperation and Security in the 21st Century,* Washington, D.C.: The Brookings Institution: 321-22.
91. See also Petr Lunak, 1994. 'Security for Eastern Europe: The European Option', *World Policy Journal* XI, (3), Autumn: 129.
92. Hanspeter Neuhold (ed.), 1991. *The Pentagonal/Hexagonal Experiment: New Forms of Cooperation in a Changing Europe,* The Laxenburg Papers LP 10, Wien: Wilhelm Braumüller.
93. So far there is no consensus on admitting Belarus, Bulgaria, Romania and the Ukraine, which have indicated their interest in membership.
94. The joint projects are formulated and supervised by 16 working groups and a large number of sub-groups. The fields covered are among others: protection of environment; transport and traffic; cooperation between small and medium-sized businesses; culture; education and youth exchanges; technological and scientific co-operation; information; telecommunications; energy; tourism; disaster protection and relief; migratory movements; statistics, and agriculture.
95. In January 1994, a short time before the NATO summit the Czech Republic declared that it did not want collective arrangements.
96. Charles A. Kupchan, 1994. 'Strategic Visions', World Policy Journal XL, (No. 3), Autumn: 117.
97. Although the EU is already Eastern European largest trading partner, the EU states export more to the Visegrád states than they import from these states.
98. Peter Havlik et al., 1994. *More solid recovery in Central and Eastern Europe, continuing decline elsewhere,* Research Report (207), Vienna: The Vienna Institute for Comparative Economic Studies — WIIW, July: 26ff.
99. András Inotai, 1994. 'Die Visegrád-Länder: Eine Zwischenbilanz', *Europäische Rundschau* 22, (1): 51-4.
100. Warsaw Treaty Organization, Organization of African Unity, Organization of American States, Organization of Central American States, Association of South East Asian Nations, etc.
101. Some members of ASEAN meet the criteria of economic development.
102. Compare also Jonathan Eyal, 1994. 'Liberating Europe From Nationalism Will Not Be Easy', *International Herald Tribune,* 24 May.
103. Conversi, 1995. 'Reassessing Current Theories of Nationalism': 76.
104. Ted Robert Gurr, 1994. 'Peoples Against States: Ethnopolitical Conflict and the Changing World System' (1994 International Studies Association Presidential Address), *International Studies Quarterly* 38, (3), September: 362-63.
105. Rudolph J. Rummel, 1994. 'Power, Genocide and Mass Murder', *Journal of Peace Research* 31, (1), February: 1-10.

106. Javier Ruperez (General Rapporteur), 1994. *Democratization in Eastern Europe: an Interim Assessment*, Draft General Report, I and II, May, Brussels: International Secretariat of NATO.

107. 29 June 1990.

108. Charter of Paris for a New Europe, 21 November 1990.

109. Compare also Colin Warbrick, 1992. 'Recognition of States: Recent European Practice', (Paper presented at the 33rd Annual Convention of the International Studies Association, Atlanta, Georgia, 31 March - 4 April).

110. 'First comes the nation state, then a liberal constitution reinforced by a liberal political culture, and only then, if at all, democracy'. Michael Lind, 1994, 'In Defence of Liberal Nationalism', *Foreign Affairs* 73, (3), May/June: 95-7. This idea is not new and goes back to John Stuart Mill who argued that democracy would be feasible only in linguistically homogeneous states.

111. Ralf Dahrendorf, August 1991. 'Politik-Eine Kolumne: Europa der Regionen', *Merkur*, (509): 704.

112. Francis Fukuyama, 1994. 'Comments on Nationalism & Democracy', in Larry Diamond and Marc F. Plattner (eds.), *Nationalism, Ethnic Conflict, and Democracy*, Baltimore and London: The Johns Hopkins U.P.: 23.

113. 'In raising these questions, I mean to suggest that the idea of nationalism is impossible — indeed unthinkable — without the idea of democracy, and that democracy never exists without nationalism. The two are joined in a complicated marriage, unable to leave each other ... '. Ghia Nodia, 1994. 'Nationalism and Democracy', in Diamond and Plattner (eds.), *Nationalism, Ethnic Conflict, and Democracy*: 4.

114. Hans Binnendijk and Patrick Clawson, Spring 1995. 'New Strategic Priorities', *The Washington Quarterly* 18, (2): 117.

115. Isaiah Berlin, 1991. 'Two Concepts of Nationalism: An Interview with Isaiah Berlin', by Nathan Gardels, *The New York Review of Books* , 21 November: 19-23.

116. Ian M. Cuthbertson and Jane Leibowitz, 1993. 'Introduction', in Cuthbertson and Leibowitz (eds.), *Minorities: The New Europe's Old Issue*: 3.

117. Barry Buzan, 1993. 'Societal security, state security and internationalization', in Waever, Buzan, Kelstrup and Lemaitre, *Identity, Migration and the New Security Agenda in Europe*: 57. For the Third World see K.J. Holsti, 1993. 'Armed Conflicts in the Third World: Assessing Analytical Approaches and Anomalies', (Paper presented at the Annual Meeting of the International Studies Association, Acapulco, Mexico, 23 - 27 March).

118. Harold James observes that in German national historiography the term 'nation' has gradually been replaced by 'society' without changing the substance. 'Society' is considered to be less problematic. Harold James, 1993. *Vom Historikerstreit zum Historikerschweigen, Die Wiedergeburt des Nationalstaates*, Berlin: Siedler-Verlag.

119. On definitions of citizenship see Rainer Bauböck, 1994. 'Changing Boundaries of Citizenship: The Inclusion of Immigrants in Democratic Polities' (Paper prepared for the annual convention of the American Political Science Association, New York, 1-3 September.

120. Concerning the Hungarian example see Peter Hardi, 1994. 'Small State Security in Post Cold War Europe: The Case of East-Central Europe', (Paper presented at the Conference on Small State Security, Institute of International Relations, University of British Columbia, Vancouver, Canada, 24-25 March: 9).
121. Uri Raþanan makes this distinction. As examples of the first case he mentions among others the former Soviet Union and former Yugoslavia but also France; of the second case Hungary. Uri Raþanan, 1991, 'Nation und Staat: Ordnung aus dem Chaos', in Erich Fröschl, Maria Mesner and Uri Raþanan (eds.), *Staat und Nation in multi-ethnischen Gesellschaften*, Vienna: Passagen Verlag: 23-65.
122. Kedourie, *Nationalism*: 99-102.
123. László Kiss, 1994. 'Nationalstaat, Integration und Subregionalismen in Mittel und Osteuropa', *WeltTrends*, (2): 31.
124. As regards this debate compare Allen Buchanan, 1991. *Secession: The Morality of Political Divorce from Fort Sumter to Lithuania and Quebec*, Boulder: Westview Press.
125. Renée de Nevers, 1993. 'Democratization and Ethnic Conflict', in Brown (ed.), *Ethnic Conflict and International Security*: 61-78.
126. George Schöpflin, Summer 1991. 'Nationalism and National Minorities in East and Central Europe', *Journal of International Affairs*, 45, (1): 60.
127. Hannah Arendt, 1973. *The Origins of Totalitarianism*, New York: Harcourt Brace Jovanovich: 292.
128. For a general view about institutions and means of the protection of minority rights see Andreas Unterberger, 1994. 'Minderheitenschutz und Selbstbestimmung: Die große historische Aufgabe zur Jahrtausendwende', *Europäische Rundschau* 22, (3): 37-50.
129. Otto Bauer, 1907. *Die Nationalitätenfrage und die Sozialdemokratie*, Vienna. Second Edition, 'Marx-Studien', Vienna, 1924; Karl Renner, 1918. *Das Selbstbestimmungsrecht der Nationen in besonderer Anwendung auf Österreich*, Vol. 1, Nation und Staat, Vienna: Deuticke; Karl Renner, 1913. *Was ist die Nationale Autonomie? Was ist die Soziale Verwaltung? Einführung in die nationale Frage und Erläuterung der Grundsätze des nationalen Programms der Sozialdemokratie,* Vienna: Wiener Volksbuchhandlung; Karl Renner, 1899. *Staat und Nation: Zur österreichischen Nationalitätenfrage. Staatsrechtliche Untersuchung über die möglichen Principien einer Lösung und die juristischen Voraussetzungen eines Nationalitätengesetzes*, Vienna: Josef Dietl.
130. Renner's concept was also designed to save the Austrian-Hungarian monarchy from disintegration. Regarding the implementation of the concept see John Coakley, 1994. 'Approaches to the Resolution of Ethnic Conflict: The Strategy of Non-territorial Autonomy', *International Political Science Review* 15, (2): 299-301.
131. Franc Rozman, 1993. 'Etbin Kristan und seine Ideen der Personalautonomie', in Helmut Konrad (ed.), *Arbeiterbewegung und nationale Frage in den Nachfolgestaaten der Habsburgmonarchie*, Vienna: Europaverlag: 97-110. Ruggie's concept of 'unbundling' of territoriality with various functional regimes and political communities as an institutional negation of exclusive territoriality can be seen as a modern version of this concept not on the level of the nation but on the

level of state. John Gerald Ruggie, 1993. 'Territoriality and beyond: problematizing modernity in international relations', *International Organization*, 47, (1), Winter: 165.

132. Of course, some aspects of functional approaches are also related to the territory; for example, the opportunity to use and learn the mother tongue. Raimo Väyrynen, 1994. 'Towards a Theory of Ethnic Conflicts and their Resolution', (An Inaugural Lecture by John M. Regan, Jr., Director of the Joan B. Kroc Institute for International Peace Studies at the University of Notre Dame, delivered on 15 March: 28. Concerning the territorial approach see John Coakley, 1993. 'Introduction: The Territorial Management of Ethnic Conflict', in *The Territorial Management of Ethnic Conflict*, London: Frank Cass.

133. Functional approaches must not be confused with 'regional regimes', which require the 'deconstruction and rearrangement' of concepts of territorial borders and state sovereignty. Gidon Gottlieb, 1994. 'Nations without States', *Foreign Affairs* 73, (3), May/June: 100-12.

134. Karl Renner, quoted and interpreted in Gerald Stourzh, 1991. 'Probleme der Konfliktlösung in multi-ethnischen Staaten: Schlüsse aus der historischen Erfahrung Österreichs 1848 bis 1918', in Fröschl, Mesner and Ra'anan (eds.), *Staat und Nation*, 106. See also Cvetka Knapic-Krhen. 'Karl Renner und die nationale Frage in den Nachfolgestaaten der Monarchie. Was blieb vom Personalitätsprinzip?', in Konrad (ed.), *Arbeiterbewegung und nationale Frage*: 11-143.

135. The OSCE does not exclude personal and functional solutions. The CSCE Copenhagen Document of 1990 (paragraph 32) states: 'To belong to a national minority is a matter of a person's individual choice and no disadvantage may arise from the exercise of such choice'. Paragraph 35 speaks of 'the right of persons belonging to national minorities to effective participation in public affairs'. *Document of the Copenhagen Meeting of the Conference on the Human Dimension of the CSCE*, 29 June 1990. This formulation spilled over to the Declaration of the World Conference on Human Rights (June 1993). Vienna Declaration and Programme of Action, 25 June 1993, paragraph 10. Of course, the reason for this formula was mainly the fact that there was no consensus about the definition of national minorities. See also Arie Bloed, 1991, 'A New CSCE Human Rights *Catalogue*: The Copenhagen Meeting of the Conference on the Human Dimension of the CSCE', in A. Bloed and P. van Dijk (eds.), *The Human Dimension of the Helsinki Process: The Vienna Follow-up Meeting and its Aftermath*, Dordrecht: Martinus Nijhoff Publishers: 67-9. Koen Koch, 'The International Community and Forms of Intervention in the Field of Minority Rights Protection', in Cuthbertson and Leibowitz (eds.), *Minorities*: 257-62.

136. David Mitrany, 1966. *A Working Peace System*, Chicago: Quadrangle Books; Ernst B. Haas, 1958. *The Uniting of Europe*, Stanford: Stanford U.P.; Ernst B. Haas, 1964. *Beyond the Nation-State: Functionalism and International Organization*, Stanford: Stanford U.P.; and Ernst B. Haas, 1975. *The Obsolence of Regional Integration Theory*, Berkeley: Institute of International Studies, University of California.

137. This is already true of the Czech Republic which is having second thoughts about membership in the EU. Prime Minister Vaclav Klaus said that not only the Czech Republic but also the other former Communist states need 'to find their own identity and not to lose it straight away on their road to Europe'. Quoted in William Pfaff, 1994. 'Sifting Through the Past In Search of an Identity', *International Herald Tribune*, 26 May.

138. The argument has been put forward that the people of Luxemburg has not been absorbed during the integration process. But this assurance has more significance for the Germans or French, of course.

139. For Kenneth Waltz a united Europe might emerge as a third superpower, since for Waltz the only transformation which can take place within the structure is that the units move away from the anarchic structure they form to an hierarchic, highly centralized, and more powerful state. Waltz, *Theory of International Politics*, 180, p. 202. Despite the difficulties to form a single, effective political entity that controls foreign and military policies as well as economic ones, for Waltz the uneasiness over German power and the competition with Japan and America on even terms may enable Western Europe to achieve political unity. Kenneth N. Waltz, 1993, 'The Emerging Structure of International Politics', *International Security* 18, (2), Autumn: 69f.

140. Hedley Bull, 1977. *The Anarchical Society: A Study of Order in World Politics*, London: Macmillan: 254-55 and 264-76.

141. In the medieval period, the political units include civitates, principes, regni, gentes, respublicae. *Ibid.*, p. 29. See also John Gerard Ruggie, 1986. 'Continuity and Transformation in the World Polity: Towards a Neorealist Synthesis', in Robert O. Keohane (ed.), *Neorealism and its Critics*, New York: Columbia U.P.: 155.

142. Barry Buzan, 1993. 'From international system to international society: structural realism and regime theory meet the English school', *International Organization* 47, (3), Summer: 327-52.

143. Andrew Moravcsik, 1992. 'Liberalism and International Relations Theory', (Centre for International Affairs, Working Paper, No. 6), July: 10.

144. Mark W. Zacher, 1992. 'The Decaying Pillars of the Westphalian Temple: Implications for International Order and Governance', in James N. Rosenau and Ernst-Otto Czempiel (eds.), *Governance without government: order and change in world politics*, Cambridge: Cambridge U.P.: 100.

145. Kegley, Jr., 1993. 'Cold War Myths': 149ff.

146. James N. Rosenau, 1990. *Turbulence in World Politics: A Theory of Change and Continuity*, New York-London-Toronto-Sydney: Harvester-Wheatsheaf: 271.

147. *Ibid:* 250.

148. James N. Rosenau, 1994. 'Fragmegrative Dynamics: Notes on the Interaction of Globalizing and Localizing Processes' (Paper presented at the 35th International Studies Association Convention, Washington D.C., 28 March-1 April); James N. Rosenau, 1994,'New Dimensions of Security: The Interaction of Globalizing and Localizing Dynamics', *Security Dialog* 25, (3) September: 255-81.

149. Hans-Henrik Holm and Georg Sørensen, 1995. 'Whose World Order? Uneven Globalization and the End of the Cold War', Boulder: Westview Press.

150. In the context of the argument in this paper, Zürn means 'destate-ization'. Michael Zürn, 'The Challenge of Globalization and Individualization: A View from Europe', in Holm and Sørensen (eds.), *Uneven Globalization and the End of Cold War*: 137-65.

151. Robert W. Cox, 1992. 'Towards a post-hegemonic conceptualization of world order: reflections on the relevancy of Ibn Khaldun', in James N. Rosenau and Ernst-Otto Czempiel (eds.), *Governance without government: order and change in world politics*, Cambridge: Cambridge U.P.: 144.

152. See also Michael E. Brown, 1993. 'Causes and Implications of Ethnic Conflict', in Michael E. Brown (ed.), *Ethnic Conflict and International Security*, Princeton: Princeton U.P.: 8.

153. Van Evera, 1994. 'Hypotheses on Nationalism and War': 10-12, 33-39.

154. *la Repubblica*, 23 and 24 April, 1994.

155. Dahrendorf, 'Politik — Eine Kolumne'. See also Anton Pelinka, 1993. 'Europa der Regionen: Zur Unschärfe eines Begriffs', in Johann Burger and Elisabeth Morawek (eds.), *Mehr Europa? Zwischen Integration und Renationalisierung: Informationen zur politischen Bildung*, Vienna: Bundesministerium für Unterricht und Kunst: 43-46.

156. The chairman of the South Tyrolian Peoples Party (by far the biggest party in South Tyrol), Siegfried Brugger, complained in January 1995 that Austria's new government did not include the concept of an all-Tyrolian European region into their programme. Within the party there is a debate whether the South Tyrolian members of the European Parliament should vote with Austria and not with Italy.

157. South Tyrolian politicians always supported the idea of a Europe of the regions hoping to strengthen their ties to the German speaking North. When, in the summer of 1994, leaders of the two main Italian parties, the 'Lega Nord' and the 'Forza Italia' suggested an Italian federalism as the basis of a Europe of the regions, they protested strongly.

158. Famous are former Chancellor Bruno Kreisky's words: 'We have a national soccer team, a national library, a national bank — therefore we are a nation'.

159. The rest believes that Austria is 'not yet' or 'not at all' a nation. Ernst Bruckmüller, 1994. *Österreichbewuss-sein im Wandel: Identität und Selbstverständnis in den 90er Jahren*, Vienna: Signum Verlag: 15-18. See also Gabriele Holzer, 1995. *Verfreundete Nachbarn*, Vienna: Kremayr & Scheriau.

160. Egon Matzner sees the danger of Austria falling apart if Europe consisted of autonomous regions. Egon Matzner, 1993. 'Si disgrega anche l'Austria?', *Limes*, Rome, December: 219-23. More general, see Egon Matzner, 1993. 'Alternatives and Prospective for Europe 2020: On the making of a Socio-Economic Context for a Civilized Europe'. (Paper prepared for the Meeting of the Club of Rome + BBV Foundation in Lyon 29-30 September): 10f.

161. According to Robert Dahl, Hans Kohn and others, the state is the correct size for democracy and the legitimate form of political organization. See Bach, 'The Crisis of Democratic Discourse: Nationalism and Eastern Europe': 5.

162. Jackson and James (eds.), *States in a Changing World*, especially, 361-67. Hanspeter Neuhold, 1994. 'Weltpolitik zwischen Integration und Fragmentierung', in *Österreichisches Jahrbuch für Internationale Politik*, Wienand Köln and Weimar: Böhlau Verlag: 99-119.

163. Bull, *The Anarchical Society*: 278.

164. For definitions of sovereignty see among others Lynn H. Miller, 1994. *Global Order: Values and Power in International Politics*, Boulder: Westview Press: 24-29; and Joseph A. Camillieri and Jim Falk, 1992. *The End of Sovereignty? The Politics of a Shrinking and Fragmenting World*, Hants, England: Edward Elgar: 11-43.

165. Stephen D. Krasner, 1993. 'Westphalia and All That', in Judith Goldstein and Robert O. Keohane (eds.), *Ideas and Foreign Policy: Beliefs, Institutions, and Political Change*, Cornell University: Cornell U.P.: 235-38.

166. The debate on limitations of the sovereignty by law is based on the ideas of Hugo Grotius in the seventeenth century. He does not make general legal distinctions between different degrees of capacities for rights for different classes of states. In Grotius' view all sovereign states are equally bound by international law. Hidemi Suganami, 1992. 'Grotius and International Equality', in Hedley Bull, Benedict Kingsbury and Adam Roberts, (eds.), *Hugo Grotius and International Relations*, Oxford: Clarendon Press: 221-40.

167. Regarding different conceptions of sovereign authority see Bruce Cronin, 1994. 'Distinguishing Between a Domestic and an International Issue: The Changing Nature of Sovereignty and Obligation in International Relations' (Paper presented at the Annual Meeting of the American Political Science Association, Washington, DC, 1-4 September 1994).

168. Stephen D. Krasner denies that the Peace of Westphalia marks a turning point in history. Krasner, 'Westphalia and All That': 235-64.

169. Whether there is an analogy between feudal actors and modern states see Markus Fischer, 1993. 'Feudal Europe, 800-1300: communal discourse and conflictual practices', *International Organization* 46, (3), Spring: 427-78; and the criticism by Rodney Bruce Hall and Friedrich V. Kratochwil, 1993. 'Medieval tales: neorealist *science* and the abuse of history', *International Organization* 46, (3), Spring: 483-85.

170. Bull, *The Anarchical Society*: 20ff.

171. Urs W. Saxer, 1994. *Die Zukunft des Nationalstaates, Staaten zwischen Souveränitätsorientierung und Integrationsoffenheit in einem sich wandelnden internationalen System*, Basler Schriften zur europäischen Integration (6), Basel: Europainstitut an der Universität Basel: 34-36.

172. Bruce D. Porter, 1994. *War and the Rise of the State: The Military Foundations of Modern Politics*, New York: The Free Press; and Ekkehart Krippendorff, 1985. *Staat und Krieg*, Frankfurt: Suhrkamp.

173. Michael W. Doyle, Kant, 1983. 'Liberal Legacies, and Foreign Affairs', *Philosophy and Public Affairs* 12, (3 and 4): 205-35 and 323-53; and Bruce Russett, 1993. *Grasping the Democratic Peace: Principles for a Post-Cold War World*, Princeton: Princeton U.P. A good summary of the arguments of this hypothesis is given in Thomas Nielebock, 1993. 'Friede zwischen Demokratien: Ein empirisches Gesetz der Internationalen Beziehungen auf der Suche nach seiner Erklärung', *Österreichische Zeitschrift für Politikwissenschaft* 22, (2): 179-94.

174. Heinz Gärtner, 1993. 'Small States and Concepts of European Security', *European Security* 2, (2), Summer: 193.

175. See the brilliant essay on the phenomenon of future civil wars by Hans Magnus Enzensberger, 1993. *Aussichten auf den Bürgerkrieg*, Frankfurt: Suhrkamp.

176. Barry Posen, 1993. 'The Security Dilemma and Ethnic Conflict', *Survival* 35, (1), Spring, pp. 27-47; and in Brown (ed.), *Ethnic Conflict and International Security*: 103-24.

177. Michael C. Williams and Keith R. Krause, 1994. 'The Subject of Security: Foundations of Rethinking Security' (Unpublished paper, 7 April).

178. Van Evera, 1994. 'Hypotheses on Nationalism and War': 10-20.

179. Tony Judt, 'The New Old Nationalism': 47.

180. Norbert Ropers, 1994. 'Ziele, Ebenen und Aufgaben', in Jörg Calließ (ed.), *Auf dem Wege zur Weltinnenpolitik: Vom Prinzip der nationalen Souveränitat zur Notwendigkeit der Einmischung*, Rehburg-Loccum: Evangelische Akademie Loccum, 1994: 98; and Lind, 'In Defence of Liberal Nationalism': 92.

181. Alexis Heraclides sees four prerequisites as essential for accepting secessionist self-determination: 1) The existence of a distinct and sizeable self-defined community or society within a state; 2) constant and systematic discrimination, exploitation or domination against a sizeable self-defined collective on the part of the state or the dominant ethnic group; 3) cultural domination, and 4) the state's rejection of dialogue. Alexis Heraclides, September 1994. 'Secessionist Conflagration: What Is to Be Done?', *Security Dialogue* 25, (3): 289. The questions remain, however, how large 'distinct and sizeable' is (minorities usually do not want to be counted) and how to measure 'discrimination, exploitation or domination'.

182. Milica Z. Bookman, 1994. 'War and Peace: The Divergent Break-ups of Yugoslavia and Czechoslovakia', *Journal of Peace Research* 31, (2): 175-87.

183. Secession as a global concept is suggested by Christian P. Scherrer, 1994. *Ethno-Nationalismus als globales Phänomen: Zur Krise der Staaten in der Dritten Welt und der früheren UdSSR*, INEF-Report (6) Universität Duisburg Gesamthochschule: 56-66.

184. Kovrig, 'Hungarian Minorities in East-Central Europe': 18, and 22.

Bibliography

Acimovic, Ljubivoje 1987. 'The CSCE Process from a Yugoslav Viewpoint', in Hanspeter Neuhold (ed.), *CSCE: N+N Perspectives: The Process of the Conference on Security and Cooperation in Europe from the Viewpoint of the Neutral and Non-Aligned Participating States*. Vienna: Wilhelm Braumüller: 79-100.

Anderson, Benedict 1983. *Imagined Communities: Reflections on the Origin and Spread of Nationalism*. London: Verso.

Arendt, Hannah 1973. *The Origins of Totalitarianism*. New York: Harcourt Brace Jovanovich.

Bach, Jonathan P.G. 1993. 'The Crisis of Democratic Discourse: Nationalism and Eastern Europe'. Paper presented at the 34th Annual International Studies Association Conference, Acapulco, Mexico, 23-27 March.

Balogh, András 1993. 'Conventional Wisdoms on National Minorities and International Security'. *Defence Studies: Army and Security Policy in Hungary* 2. Budapest: Institute for Strategic Studies.

Bauböck, Rainer 1994. 'Changing Boundaries of Citizenship: The Inclusion of Immigrants in Democratic Polities'. Paper prepared for the annual convention of the American Political Science Association, New York, 1-3 September.

Bauer, Otto 1907. *Die Nationalitätenfrage und die Sozialdemokratie*. Vienna. 2nd ed. 'Marx-Studien' Vienna, 1924.

Bayer, Joszef. 1994. 'Nationalismen in Osteuropa: Sackgasse oder notwendiges Durchgangsstadium zur Demokratie?' In *Friedensbericht 1994: Krieg und gewaltfreie Konfliktlösungen*. Zürich: Verlag Rüegger.

Betts, Richard K. 1992. 'Systems for Peace or Causes of War? Collective Security, Arms Control, and the New Europe'. *International Security* 17 (1): 4-43.

Binnendijk, Hans and Patrick Clawson 1995. 'New Strategic Priorities'. *The Washington Quarterly* 18 (2).

Bloed, Arie 1991. 'A New CSCE Human Rights *Catalogue*: The Copenhagen Meeting of the Conference on the Human Dimension of the CSCE', in A. Bloed and P. van Dijk (eds.), *The Human Dimension of the Helsinki Process: The Vienna Follow-up Meeting and its Aftermath*. Dordrecht: Martinus Nijhoff.

Bookman, Milica Z. 1994. 'War and Peace: The Divergent Break-ups of Yugoslavia and Czechoslovakia'. *Journal of Peace Research* 31 (2): 175-87.

Breuilly, John 1982. *Nationalism and the State*. Manchester: Manchester U.P.

Brown, Michael E. 1993. 'Causes and Implications of Ethnic Conflict', in Michael E. Brown (ed.), *Ethnic Conflict and International Security*. Princeton, N.J.: Princeton U.P.

Bruckmüller, Ernst 1994. *Österreichbewuss-sein im Wandel: Identität und Selbstverständnis in den 90er Jahren*. Vienna: Signum Verlag.

Buchanan, Allen 1991. *Secession: The Morality of Political Divorce from Fort Sumter to Lithuania and Quebec*. Boulder: Westview.

Bull, Hedley 1977. *The Anarchical Society: A Study of Order in World Politics*. London: Macmillan.

Buzan, Barry, Charles Jones and Richard Little 1993. *The Logic of Anarchy: Neorealism to Structural Realism*. New York: Columbia U.P.

Buzan, Barry 1993. 'From international system to international society: structural realism and regime theory meet the English school'. *International Organization* 47 (3): 327-52.

Buzan, Barry 1993. 'Societal security, state security and internationalization', in Waever, Buzan, Kelstrup and Lemaitre, *Identity, Migration and the New Security Agenda in Europe*: 57.

Camillieri, Joseph A. and Jim Falk. 1992. *The End of Sovereignty? The Politics of a Shrinking and Fragmenting World*. Hants, England: Edward Elgar.

Cetinyan, Rupen 1994. 'The Institution of Ethnicity: The Political Economy of Ethnic Organization and Conflict'. Paper presented at the 1994 Annual Meeting of the American Political Science Association, New York, 1-4 September.

Claude, Inis R. 1966. *Power and International Relations*. New York: Random House.

Coakley, John 1993. 'Introduction: The Territorial Management of Ethnic Conflict', in *The Territorial Management of Ethnic Conflict*. London: Frank Cass.

Coakley, John 1994. 'Approaches to the Resolution of Ethnic Conflict: The Strategy of Non-territorial Autonomy'. *International Political Science Review* 15 (2).

Conference on Security and Cooperation in Europe. 1994. *Towards a Genuine Partnership in a New Era*. Budapest: CSCE.

Conference on Security and Cooperation in Europe. Fourth Meeting of the CSCE Council, Rome, 1993. *CSCE and the New Europe — Our Security is Indivisible*, Decisions II (3).

Conversi, Daniele 1995. 'Reassessing Current Theories of Nationalism: Nationalism as Boundary Maintenance and Creation'. *Nationalism & Ethnic Politics* 1 (1): 73-85.

Coulmas, Peter 1993. 'Das Problem des Selbstbestimmungsrechtes: Mikronationalismen, Anarchie und innere Schwäche der Staaten.' *Europa-Archiv* 48 (4): 85-92.

Cox, Robert W. 1992. 'Towards a post-hegemonic conceptualization of world order: reflections on the relevancy of Ibn Khaldun', in James N. Rosenau and Ernst-Otto Czempiel (eds.), *Governance without government: order and change in world politics*. Cambridge: Cambridge U.P.

Cronin, Bruce 1994. 'Distinguishing Between a Domestic and an International Issue: The Changing Nature of Sovereignty and Obligation in International Relations'. Paper presented at the Annual Meeting of the American Political Science Association, Washington, DC, 1-4 September.

Cuthbertson, Ian M. and Jane Leibowitz 1993. 'Introduction' in Cuthbertson and Leibowitz (eds.), *Minorities: The New Europe's Old Issue?*

Dahrendorf, Ralf 1991. 'Politik-Eine Kolumne: Europa der Regionen'. *Merkur* (509): 704.

Dann, Otto 1991. 'Begriffe und Typen des Nationalen in der frühen Neuzeit', in Bernhard Giesen (ed.), *Nationale und kulturelle Identität: Studien zur Entwicklung des kollektiven Bewußtseins in der Neuzeit*. Frankfurt: Suhrkamp.

de Nevers, Renée 1993. 'Democratization and Ethnic Conflict', in Brown, (ed.) *Ethnic Conflict and International Security*: 61-78.

Declaration on the Principles of Cooperation between the Republic of Hungary and Unkrainian Soviet Socialist Republic in the guaranteeing of Rights for National Minorities. Budapest, 31 May 1991.

Deutsch, Karl W. 1972. *Der Nationalismus und seine Alternativen*. München: Serie Piper: 41-68. (*Nationalism and Its Alternatives*). New York: Alfred A. Knopf, 1969.

Doyle, Michael W. 1983. 'Liberal Legacies, and Foreign Affairs'. *Philosophy and Public Affairs* 12 (3 and 4).

Elias, Norbert 1988. *Über den Prozeß der Zivilisation, Soziogenetische Untersuchungen*, Vol. 2, *Wandlungen der Gesellschaft: Entwurf zu einer Theorie der Zivilisation*. Frankfurt: Suhrkamp.

Enzensberger, Hans Magnus 1993. *Aussichten auf den Bürgerkrieg*. Frankfurt: Suhrkamp.

Eyal, Jonathan 1994. 'Liberating Europe From Nationalism Will Not Be Easy'. *International Herald Tribune*, 24 May.

Fischer, Markus 1993. 'Feudal Europe, 800-1300: communal discourse and conflictual practices'. *International Organization* 46 (3): 427-78.

Freedman, Lawrence (ed.) 1990. *Europe Transformed: Documents on the End of the Cold War, Key Treaties, Agreements, Statements and Speeches*. New York: St. Martin's Press.

Fukuyama, Francis 1994. 'Comments on Nationalism & Democracy', in Larry Diamond and Marc F. Plattner (eds.), *Nationalism, Ethnic Conflict, and Democracy*. Baltimore: Johns Hopkins U.P.

Gaddis, John Lewis 1992/93. 'International Relations Theory and the End of the Cold War'. *International Security* 17 (3): 5-58.

Gardels, Nathan 1991. 'Two Concepts of Nationalism: An Interview with Isaiah Berlin'. *The New York Review of Books*, 21 November: 19-23.

Gellner, Ernest 1991. 'Nationalism and politics in Eastern Europe'. *New Left Review* 189 (September/October): 127-34.

George, Bruce 1994. *After the NATO summit: Draft General Report*. Brussels: International Secretariat of NATO, May, II./10-17.

Giddens, Anthony 1987. *The Nation-State and Violence*, 2 vols. *A Contemporary Critique of Historical Materialism*, vol. 2. Berkeley: University of California Press.

Gottlieb, Gidon 1994. 'Nations without States'. *Foreign Affairs* 73 (3): 100-12.

Greenfeld, Liah. 1992. *Nationalism: Five Roads to Modernity*. Cambridge, MA.: Harvard U.P.

Gurr, Ted Robert 1994. 'Peoples Against States: Ethnopolitical Conflict and the Changing World System'. (1994 International Studies Association Presidential Address). *International Studies Quarterly* 38 (3): 362-63.

Gyurcsík, Iván 1993. 'New Legal Ramifications of the Question of National Minorities', in Ian M. Cuthbertson and Jane Leibowitz (eds.), *Minorities: The New Europe's Old Issue*. New York: Institute for East-West Studies: 20.

Gärtner, Heinz 1993. 'Small States and Concepts of European Security'. *European Security* 2 (2): 193.

Gärtner, Heinz 1992. *Wird Europa sicherer? Zwischen kollektiver und nationaler Sicherheit.* Vienna: Braumüller.

Hall, Rodney Bruce, and Friedrich V. Kratochwil 1993. 'Medieval tales: neorealist science and the abuse of history'. *International Organization* 46 (3): 483-85.

Hardi, Peter 1994. 'Small State Security in Post Cold War Europe: The Case of East-Central Europe'. Paper presented at the Conference on Small State Security, Institute of International Relations, University of British Columbia, Vancouver, Canada, 24-25 March.

Havlik, Peter, et al. 1994. *More solid recovery in Central and Eastern Europe, continuing decline elsewhere.* Research Report (207) Vienna: The Vienna Institute for Comparative Economic Studies.

Helsinki Document 1992, Decisions, II (3).

Heraclides, Alexis 1994. 'Secessionist Conflagration: What Is to Be Done?' *Security Dialogue* 25 (3).

Hobsbawm, Eric 1990. *Nations and Nationalism since 1780: Programme, Myth, Reality.* Cambridge: Cambridge U.P.

Holm, Hans-Henrik and Georg Sørensen. 1995. 'Whose World Order? Uneven Globalization and the End of the Cold War'. Boulder: Westview.

Holsti, K.J. 1993. 'Armed Conflicts in the Third World: Assessing Analytical Approaches and Anomalies'. Paper presented at the Annual Meeting of the International Studies Association, Acapulco, Mexico, 23-27 March.

Holzer, Gabriele 1995. *Verfreundete Nachbarn.* Vienna: Kremayr & Scheriau.

Honig, Jan Willem 1992. 'The Renationalization of Western European Defence'. *Security Studies* 2 (1): 122-38.

Hoynck, Wilhelm 1994. 'CSCE Works to Develop its Conflict Prevention Potential'. *NATO Review* 42 (2).

Hutchinson, John 1987. *The Dynamics of Cultural Nationalism.* London: Allen and Unwin.

Haas, Ernst B. 1958. *The Uniting of Europe.* Stanford: Stanford U.P.

Haas, Ernst B. 1975. *The Obsolence of Regional Integration Theory.* Berkeley: Institute of International Studies, University of California.

Haas, Ernst B. 1964. *Beyond the Nation-State: Functionalism and International Organization.* Stanford: Stanford U.P.

Inotai, András 1994. 'Die Visegrád-Länder: Eine Zwischenbilanz'. *Europäische Rundschau* 22 (1): 51-4.

Jackson, Robert H. and Alan James 1993. 'The Character of Independent Statehood', in Robert H. Jackson and Alan James (eds.), *States in a Changing World: A contemporary Analysis.* Oxford: Clarendon.

James, Harold 1993. *Vom Historikerstreit zum Historikerschweigen, Die Wiedergeburt des Nationalstaates.* Berlin: Siedler-Verlag.

Job, Brian L. and Don Munton 1991. 'Disentangling the Alliance: The Role of Small and Middle States in NATO'. Paper presented at the 33rd International Studies Association Convention, Atlanta, 30 March-4 April.

Joffe, Joseph 1992. 'Collective Security and the Future of Europe: Failed Dreams and Dead Ends'. *Survival*: 36-50.

Joseph Rothschild 1994. 'Nationalism and Democratization in East Central Europe: Lessons from the Past'. *Nationalities Papers* 22 (1).

Judt, Tony. 1994. 'The New Old Nationalism.' *The New York Review of Books*. 26 May: 46.

Kedourie, Elie 1960. *Nationalism*. London: Hutchinson: 71.

Kegley, Charles W. Jr. 1993. 'Cold War Myths and the New International Realities: Reconsidering Theoretical Premises'. *Österreichische Zeitschrift für Politikwissenschaft* 22 (2).

Kelleher, Catherine McArdle 1994. 'Cooperative Security in Europe', in Janne E. Nolan (ed.), *Global Engagement: Cooperation and Security in the 21st Century*. Washington, D.C.: The Brookings Institution: 321-22.

Keohane, Robert O., Joseph S. Nye and Stanley Hoffmann 1993. *After the Cold War: International Institutions and State Strategies in Europe: 1989-91*. Cambridge, MA.: Harvard U.P.

Keohane, Robert O. 1989. *International Institutions and State Power: Essays in International Relations Theory*. Boulder: Westview.

Keohane, Robert O. and Joseph S. Nye 1971. *Transnational Relations and World Politics*. London: Harvard U.P.

Kiss, László 1994. 'Nationalstaat, Integration und Subregionalismen in Mittel und Osteuropa'. *WeltTrends* 2.

Knapic-Krhen, Cvetka. 'Karl Renner und die nationale Frage in den Nachfolgestaaten der Monarchie. Was blieb vom Personalitätsprinzip?', in Konrad (ed.), *Arbeiterbewegung und nationale Frage*.

Koch, Koen 1993. 'The International Community and Forms of Intervention in the Field of Minority Rights Protection', in Cuthbertson and Leibowitz (eds.), *Minorities*: 257-62.

Kovrig, Bennett 1995. 'Hungarian Minorities in East-Central Europe'. The Atlantic Council of the United States: Occasional Paper, March.

Krasner, Stephen D. 1993. 'Westphalia and All That', in Judith Goldstein and Robert O. Keohane (eds.), *Ideas and Foreign Policy: Beliefs, Institutions, and Political Change*. Ithaca: Cornell U.P., 235-38.

Krippendorff, Ekkehart 1985. *Staat und Krieg*. Frankfurt: Suhrkamp.

Krizan, Mojmir 1995. 'Postkommunistische Wiedergeburt ethnischer Nationalismen und der Dritte Balkan-Krieg', *Osteuropa* 45 (3): 202.

Kupchan, Charles A. 1994. 'Strategic Visions', *World Policy Journal* 40 (3).

Kupchan, Charles A. (ed.) 1995. *Nationalism and Nationalities in the New Europe*. Ithaca: Cornell U.P.

la Repubblica, 23 and 24 April, 1994.

Lapid, Yosef 1993. 'Nationalism, Identity and Security: Global Threats and Theoretical Challenges'. Paper presented at the 34th International Studies Association Convention, Acapulco, 23–27 March.

Lind, Michael 1994. 'In Defense of Liberal Nationalism', *Foreign Affairs* 73 (3): 95-7.

Lunak, Petr 1994. 'Security for Eastern Europe: The European Option', *World Policy Journal* 40 (3).

Matzner, Egon 1993. 'Alternatives and Prospective for Europe 2020: On the making of a Socio-Economic Context for a Civilized Europe'. Paper prepared for the Meeting of the Club of Rome and BBV Foundation in Lyon 29-30 September.

Matzner, Egon 1993. 'Si disgrega anche l'Austria?' *Limes*, Rome, December: 219-23.

Mearsheimer, John J. 1990. 'Back to the Future: Instability in Europe after the Cold War', *International Security* 15 (1): 5-56.

Merritt, Giles 1993. 'A Charter For Peace In Europe', *International Herald Tribune*, 5 May.

Miller, Lynn H. 1994. *Global Order: Values and Power in International Politics*. Boulder: Westview.

Mitrany, David 1966. *A Working Peace System*. Chicago: Quadrangle Books.

Moravcsik, Andrew 1992. 'Liberalism and International Relations Theory'. Centre for International Affairs, Working Paper, No. 6, July.

Moynihan, Daniel Patrick 1993. *Pandaemonium: Ethnicity in International Politics*. New York: Oxford U.P.

Nelson, Daniel N. 1993. 'Great Powers and World Peace', *Österreichische Zeitschrift für Politikwissenschaft* 22 (2): 169-78.

Neuhold, Hanspeter (ed.), 1991. *The Pentagonal/Hexagonal Experiment: New Forms of Cooperation in a Changing Europe*. The Laxenburg Papers LP 10. Vienna: Wilhelm Braumüller.

Neuhold, Hanspeter 1994. 'Weltpolitik zwischen Integration und Fragmentierung', *Österreichisches Jahrbuch für Internationale Politik*. Vienna: Böhlau Verlag, 99-119.

Neuhold, Hanspeter. 1994. 'Conflicts and Conflict Management in a *new* Europe', *Austrian Journal of Public and International Law* 46: 109-29.

Nielebock, Thomas 1993. 'Friede zwischen Demokratien: Ein empirisches Gesetz der Internationalen Beziehungen auf der Suche nach seiner Erklärung', *Österreichische Zeitschrift für Politikwissenschaft* 22 (2): 179-94.

Nodia, Ghia 1994. 'Nationalism and Democracy', in Diamond and Plattner (eds.), *Nationalism, Ethnic Conflict, and Democracy*. Baltimore: Johns Hopkins U.P.

Office of the Secretary General. *CSCS Facts*. Vienna: 15 November 1993.

Office for National and Ethnic Minorities. *The principle of reciprocity in the policy towards national minorities*. Budapest, January 1992.

Olson, William C. and A.J.R. Groom 1991. *International Relations Then and Now: Origins and Trends in Interpretation*. London: Harper Collins Academic.

Organization for Cooperation and Security in Europe. *Document of the Copenhagen Meeting of the Conference on the Human Dimension of the CSCE*, 29 June 1990.

Pelinka, Anton. 1993. 'Europa der Regionen: Zur Unschärfe eines Begriffs', in Johann Burger and Elisabeth Morawek (eds.), *Mehr Europa? Zwischen Integration und Renationalisierung: Informationen zur politischen Bildung*. Vienna: Bundesministerium für Unterricht und Kunst.

Pfaff, William 1994. 'Sifting Through the Past In Search of an Identity'. *International Herald Tribune,* 26 May.

Pfaff, William 1994. 'East Europeans Have a Basic Adjustment to Make', *International Herald Tribune* 21-22 May: 4.

Pfaff, William 1993. *The Wrath of Nations.* New York: Simon & Schuster.

Pichler, Tibor 1994. 'Die Eigenständigkeit als Idee des Slowakischen sprach-begründeten Nationalismus', in Eva Schmidt-Hartmann, *Formen des nationalen Bewußtseins im Lichte zeitgenössischer Nationalismus-theorien.* München: R. Oldenbourg Verlag.

Porter, Bruce D. 1994. *War and the Rise of the State: The Military Foundations of Modern Politics.* New York: The Free Press.

Posen, Barry 1993. 'The Security Dilemma and Ethnic Conflict', *Survival* 35 (1): 27-47; and in Brown (ed.), *Ethnic Conflict and International Security*: 103-24.

Puhovski, Zarko 1994. 'Nationalismus und Demokratie im postkommunistischen Schlüssel', in Margit Pieber (ed.), (Österreichisches Studienzentrum für Frieden und Konfliktlösung). *Europa — Zukunft eines Kontinents: Friedenspolitik oder Rückfall in die Barbarei.* Münster: Agenda Verlag.

Rauchensteiner, Manfried 1994. *Der Tod des Doppeladlers: Österreich-Ungarn und der Erste Weltkrieg.* Graz: Styria.

Raþanan, Uri 1991. 'Nation und Staat: Ordnung aus dem Chaos', in Erich Fröschl, Maria Mesner and Uri Raþanan (eds.), *Staat und Nation in multi-ethnischen Gesellschafte.* Vienna: Passagen Verlag.

Renner, Karl 1899. *Staat und Nation: Zur österreichischen Nationalitätenfrage. Staatsrechtliche Untersuchung über die möglichen Principien einer Lösung und die juristischen Voraussetzungen eines Nationalitätengesetzes.* Vienna: Josef Dietl.

Renner, Karl 1913. *Was ist die Nationale Autonomie? Was ist die Soziale Verwaltung? Einführung in die nationale Frage und Erläuterung der Grundsätze des nationalen Programms der Sozialdemokratie.* Vienna: Wiener Volksbuchhandlung.

Renner, Karl 1918. *Das Selbstbestimmungsrecht der Nationen in besonderer Anwendung auf Österreich,* Vol. 1, Nation und Staat. Vienna: Deuticke.

Rittberger, Volker 1993. 'Research on International Regimes in Germany: The Adaptive Internalization of an American Social Science Concept', in *Regime Theory and International Relations.* Oxford: Clarendon.

Ropers, Norbert 1994. 'Ziele, Ebenen und Aufgaben', in Jörg Calließ (ed.), *Auf dem Wege zur Weltinnenpolitik: Vom Prinzip der nationalen Souveränitat zur Notwendigkeit der Einmischung.* Rehburg-Loccum: Evangelische Akademie Loccum.

Rosenau, James N. 1994. 'Fragmegrative Dynamics: Notes on the Interaction of Globalizing and Localizing Processes'. Paper presented at the 35th International Studies Association Convention, Washington D.C., 28 March-1 April.

Rosenau, James N. 1994. 'New Dimensions of Security: The Interaction of Globalizing and Localizing Dynamics', *Security Dialog* 25 (3): 255-81.

Rosenau, James N. 1990. *Turbulence in World Politics: A Theory of Change and Continuity.* New York: Harvester-Wheatsheaf.

Rozman, Franc 1993. 'Etbin Kristan und seine Ideen der Personalautonomie', in Helmut Konrad (ed.), *Arbeiterbewegung und nationale Frage in den Nachfolgestaaten der Habsburgmonarchie*. Vienna: Europaverlag: 97-110.

Ruggie, John Gerard 1986. 'Continuity and Transformation in the World Polity: Towards a Neorealist Synthesis', in Robert O. Keohane (ed.), *Neorealism and its Critics*. New York: Columbia U.P.

Ruggie, John Gerald 1993. 'Territoriality and beyond: problematizing modernity in international relations', *International Organization* 47 (1).

Rummel, Rudolph J. 1994. 'Power, Genocide and Mass Murder', *Journal of Peace Research* 31 (1): 1-10.

Ruperez, Javier 1994. *Democratization in Eastern Europe: an Interim Assessment*. Draft General Report, I and II, May, Brussels: International Secretariat of NATO.

Rupnik, Jacques 1990. 'Central Europe or Middle Europe?' *Daedalus* 119 (1) Winter: 249-78.

Russett, Bruce 1993. *Grasping the Democratic Peace: Principles for a Post-Cold War World*. Princeton: Princeton U.P.

Rutland, Peter. 1994. 'State Failure and State Building in Post-Socialist Europe: Implications for Theories of Nationalism'. Paper prepared for the annual convention of the American Political Science Association, New York, 1-3 September: 5-9.

Saxer, Urs W. 1994. *Die Zukunft des Nationalstaates, Staaten zwischen Souveränitätsorientierung und Integrationsoffenheit in einem sich wandelnden internationalen System*. Basler Schriften zur europäischen Integration (6). Basel: Europainstitut an der Universität Basel.

Scherrer, Christian P. 1994. *Ethno-Nationalismus als globales Phänomen: Zur Krise der Staaten in der Dritten Welt und der früheren UdSSR*, INEF-Report (6) Universität Duisburg Gesamthochschule: 56-66.

Schoch, Bruno 1992. *Nach Strassburg oder nach Sarajevo? Zum Nationalismus in postkommunisatischen Übergangsgesellschaften*. HSFK-Report (6). Frankfurt: HSFK.

Schoch, Bruno 1992. 'Der neu aufbrechende Nationalismus in Europa als Bedrohung für Stabilität und Frieden', in Achim Güssgen and Rüdiger Schlaga (eds.), *Chancen und Probleme einer zukünftigen europäischen Friedensordnung*. Frankfurt: Hessische Stiftung Friedens und Konfliktforschung.

Schöpflin, George 1991. 'Nationalism and National Minorities in East and Central Europe', *Journal of International Affairs* 45 (1).

Stourzh, Gerald 1991. 'Probleme der Konfliktlösung in multi-ethnischen Staaten: Schlüsse aus der historischen Erfahrung Österreichs 1848 bis 1918', in Fröschl, Mesner and Ra'anan (eds.), *Staat und Nation*.

Suganami, Hidemi 1992. 'Grotius and International Equality', in Hedley Bull, Benedict Kingsbury and Adam Roberts (eds.), *Hugo Grotius and International Relations*. Oxford: Clarendon Press, 221-40.

Tilly, Charles (ed.) 1975. *The Formation of National States in Western Europe*. Princeton: Princeton U.P.

Unterberger, Andreas 1994. 'Minderheitenschutz und Selbstbestimmung: Die große historische Aufgabe zur Jahrtausendwende', *Europäische Rundschau* 22 (3): 37-50.
Unterberger, Andreas 1994. 'Minderheitenschutz und Selbstbestimmung: Die große historische Aufgabe zur Jahrtausendwende.' *Europäische Rundschau* 22 (3): 37-50.
Van Evera, Stephen 1994. 'Hypotheses on Nationalism and War', *International Security* 18 (4): 10-12, 33-39.
Väyrynen, Raimo 1994. 'Towards a Theory of Ethnic Conflicts and their Resolution'. An Inaugural Lecture by John M. Regan, Jr., Director of the Joan B. Kroc Institute for International Peace Studies at the University of Notre Dame, delivered on 15 March.
Väyrynen, Raimo 1993. 'Territory, Nation State and Nationalism', in Jyrki Iivonen (ed.), The Finnish Institute of International Affairs, *The Future of the Nation State in Europe*. Aldershot: Edward Elgar: 159-78.
Waever, Ole, Barry Buzan, Morten Kelstrup and Pierre Lemaitre 1993. *Identity, Migration and the New Security Agenda in Europe*. London: Pinter.
Waever, Ole and Morten Kelstrup 199 . 'Europe and its nations: political and cultural identities', in Waever, Buzan, Kelstrup and Lemaitre, *Identity, Migration and the New Security Agenda in Europe*.
Walt, Stephen 1987. *The Origins of Alliances*. Ithaca: Cornell U.P.
Waltz, Kenneth N. 1979. *Theory of International Politics*. New York: McGraw-Hill.
Waltz, Kenneth N. 1993. 'The Emerging Structure of International Politics.' *International Security* 18 (2).
Warbrick, Colin 1992. 'Recognition of States: Recent European Practice'. Paper presented at the 33rd Annual Convention of the International Studies Association, Atlanta, Georgia, 31 March-4 April.
Weber, Max 1978. *Economy and Society*. Günther Roth and Claus Wittich (eds.). Berkeley: University of California Press.
Weber, Katja 1993. 'A New Era in Global Relations: A reassessment of Security Arrangements'. Paper presented at the 35th International Studies Association Convention, Washington, D.C., 28 March-1 April.
Weber, Max 1948. 'The Nation', in H.H. Gerth and C. Wright Mills (eds.), *From Max Weber: Essays in Sociology*. London: Routledge & Kegan Paul: 171-79.
Weitz, Richard 1993. 'Pursuing Military Security in Eastern Europe', in Keohane, Nye and Hoffmann (eds.), *After the Cold War*: 342-80.
Williams, Michael C., and Keith R. Krause 1994. 'The Subject of Security: Foundations of Rethinking Security'. Unpublished paper, 7 April.
Zacher, Mark W. 1992. 'The Decaying Pillars of the Westphalian Temple: Implications for International Order and Governance', in James N. Rosenau and Ernst-Otto Czempiel (eds.), *Governance without government: order and change in world politics*. Cambridge: Cambridge U.P.
Zürn, Michael 1995. 'The Challenge of Globalization and Individualization: A View from Europe', in Holm and Sørensen (eds.), *Uneven Globalization and the End of Cold War*: 137-65.

Post-1918 Austria: Long-Lasting Centre/Periphery Effects on a Political System

Gerhard Botz

It is actually quite surprising that the twin concepts of centre/periphery[1] — or more precisely centrality/peripherality — have traditionally been accorded such scant attention in historical research,[2] whereas, throughout many other fields of social sciences such as geography, economics, sociology and anthropology, and even in jurisprudence and philosophy,[3] territorial phenomena have been the focus of more or less intense consideration. This unwillingness on the part of history, and often of political science as well, to employ the categories of territory and centre/periphery is even more astonishing in light of Fernand Braudel's reflections on this matter: 'Territory as an interpretational point of departure influence all historical realities, all spatially-defined phenomena: states, societies, cultures and economies'.[4]

It should be kept in mind that thinking in terms of categories of centre/periphery indeed implies a hierarchial ordering of spatial relationships, be it in a horizontal respect (city-urban, metropolis-rural outskirts, 'motherland'-colony, urban centre-suburbs, etc.) or in a vertical respect (e.g. economic dominance, political supremacy, social differentiation, cultural hegemony). Thus, with regard to 'closed' economic (world) systems (économie-mondes), Fernand Braudel mentioned three essential characteristics which are relevant to our discussion of the topic of centre/periphery:

1) borders which circumscribe a zone, providing such a system of centrality/peripherality with its identity
2) a (single, in the normal case) centre which constitutes both a 'metropolis', to use a term from the theory of imperialism,[5] and a dominant market economy, and
3) a pronounced hierarchy existing, on the one hand, between a number of less prosperous, moderately advanced sub-economies on the periphery, and on the other, a more affluent economic system at the centre. From this hierarchy emerge the fundamental inequalities and tensions which divide such a system into two camps, the 'haves' and the 'have-nots', and which account for the changes which the system undergoes over the long term.[6]

Immanuel Wallerstein, *the* historian of centre/periphery models on a world-wide scale, emphasizes two additional aspects beyond these above-mentioned attributes which are significant for our discussion: a world system does not contain only peripheries and a centre, but rather semi-peripheries as well and these elements oppose one another in intensive reciprocal relationships and division of labour. Beyond these are fringe areas not yet integrated into the system.[7]

Primarily with reference to the regions and nation-states of Western Europe during the second half of the 20th century, the noted Norwegian political scientist, Stein Rokkan, (1921-1979) applied an analysis employing centre/periphery relationships to:

the endowment of resources [i.e., raw materials, capital, knowledge, symbolic capital, etc.,] distances and channels of communication. Typically, a centre controls the bulk of the transactions among the holders of resources across a territory; it tends to be closer than any alternative site to the resource-rich areas within the territory; and it is able to dominate the communication flow through the territorial diffusion of a standard language and through its control of a set of institutions for consultation and direction. By contrast, a periphery controls at best its own resources, tends to be isolated from other regions, and contributes little to the total communication flow within the territory.[8]

A centre is therefore frequently described as 'the nexus of the decision-making process, the command and control hub, the focal point of power,'[9] and, to the extent that it has achieved a certain magnitude, so to speak, the geographic embodiment of the political system. It is posited by social geographers that, in order to carry out these functions, a centre concentrates specialized personnel and organizations, bureacracies, cultural and military elites, religous hierarchies, commercial institutions, transportation facilities, etc. The usual statistical indicators of social conditions and trends used in historical studies are derived from such social geographic concepts.[10]

Centre/periphery concepts have achieved broad acceptance not only in social geography, in which locality models using these ideas have been developed since the 1930s and have become central concepts in quantitive research and urban planning.[11] They have also proved to be highly productive conceptual tools in other fields, above all in social scientific and historical research on mass-scale voting behaviour and national-level political parties. Centre/periphery concepts also became interesting for researchers, primarily in the 1960s, in some rather theoretical approaches to international economics, global politics, imperialism, dependence and similar subjects. At present, macro theories such as these, also seem to be in a position to provide scholars with one of the few unifying principles for a modern world history whose procedures go beyond the mere additive or anecdotal. Rokkan adapted this fundamental conceptual pattern into diverse formulations depending upon the respective object of his investigative interest, so that it is not possible to speak of 'the' or a single centre/periphery theory in Rokkan's work.

In the following sections, I will briefly outline three of Rokkan's macro-historical models[12] which seem to be very relevant to the history of Austria. However, it is clear that this 'inversion' of the process of constructing models in the social sciences — the application of theoretical models to an individual case for the purpose of an historical interpretation — is not unproblematic.[13]

The Geohistorical 'Reich' Paradox and Austria: Federalism and Central State

The objective of this approach, which derives its point of reference from an interpretational model developed in a later phase of Stein Rokkan's work, is to employ a comparative-macrohistorical perspective[14] in order to shed new light on the internal structure of the Austrian state, specifically with regard to federalism/centralism and the collapse of democracy in the 1930s in the context of Austria's geopolitical situation since the Middle Ages. This interpretational model, which the Norwegian political sociologist first began developing in the middle of the 1970s, proceeds from a conceptual map of Europe and contains eight chief points, which I will briefly summarize.[15]

1) A broad belt of trade routes and cities, from Northern Italy to the English Channel and the North Sea, particularly along the River Rhine, has stretched clear across Europe since the late Middle Ages and can, moreover, still be discerned on contemporary economic, social and transport maps of Europe.[16]

2) This 'city belt' was the chief area of influence of the Roman Catholic Church, with its closely knit network of cathedrals, monasteries and ecclesiastical principalities.

3) It was precisely this density of established urban and religious centres in this belt which made it difficult for any one of these centres to ascend to a position of dominance.

4) The establishment of the Holy Roman Empire likewise failed to bring about unification within this zone and its emperors remained weak; for this reason, a strong territorial state initially failed to emerge within this belt.

5) In contrast to these conditions, the formation of centres proved to be a simpler matter on both the western and eastern fringes of the urban belt of the old 'reich'. These centres were in a position not only to profit from the resources of the dense urban network's monetary economy, but also to achieve control over peripheral territories which lay far beyond the central belt of trade routes.

6) The earliest incidence of the formation of territorial states was, therefore, in the coastal plains of Western and Northern Europe (France, England, Scandinavia) and later in Spain.

7) Only during a second wave did centres and territorial states successfully emerge on the landward side: first under the Habsburgs in the core land of modern-day Austria, then in Sweden, and finally and decisively in Germany beginning in Prussia.

8) The economically strong but politically weak belt of cities and small states in the middle remained disunited and violently disputed. A portion of the western fringe was integrated into the Kingdom of France. In some regions of this zone, cities and other local political entities formed 'consociational'[17] alliances, of which the ultimately short-lived Hanseatic League, the confederation of Helvetia and the United Netherlands are the foremost examples. For a time, it appeared as though the Habsburgs would gain control over substantial territories within the belt. It was, however, from Berlin and Torino, centres located in the European semi-periphery, that Prussia and Piedmont finally succeeded in uniting Germany and Italy in the 19th century.[18]

Depicted in the form of a conceptual map of the 'state-economy dimension' in Western Europe during the early modern period, this configuration appeared as shown in the following map on Page 122.[19]

What I would like to refer to as the geohistorical *'Reich'* paradox lies in the fact that this central European zone, although socially and economically most highly developed, remained 'underdeveloped' with respect to the formation of a modern territorial state until the 19th century, so that urban and commercial centres were in a position to form strong centralized states only on the semi-periphery, with their spheres of control extending outward to the periphery. What consequences can be derived from this model for the process of state formation in Austria?

The provinces comprising the territory of modern-day Austria came into being not only as a result of noble families succeeding in the accumulation of

Gerhard Botz

possessions and titles. 'Rather, to a much greater extent, the emergence of new territories *and* the new social entities which accompanied them' were the result of a social-historical process connected to the increasing importance of commerce and the cities.[20]

Stein Rokkan's "Conceptual Map" of the States in Western Europe

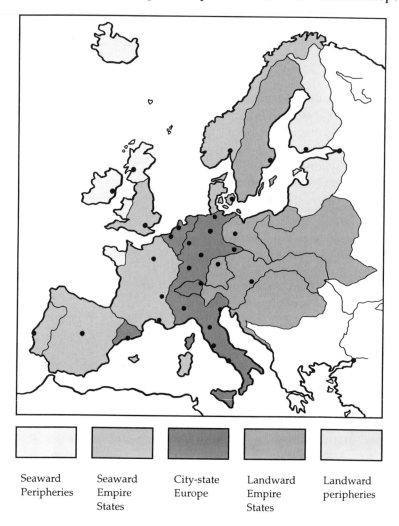

Seaward	Seaward	City-state	Landward	Landward
Peripheries	Empire	Europe	Empire	peripheries
	States		States	

This map has been outlined with reference to Stein Rokkan and Bernt Hagtvet (The Conditions of Fascist Victory, in: S.U. Larsen, *Who were the Fascists,* Bergen 1980, 139) by G. Botz.

The formation of provinces occurred at various times: earliest in Styria as well as in Salzburg and (Lower) Austria (from the middle of the 12th century to the first third of the 13th century respectively), followed by Tyrol and Carinthia (from the middle of the 13th and in the second third of the 14th century). Thus, this sequence tends to display an east-west gradient which, notwithstanding other explanations, could also conform to Rokkan's model: even the processes of province formation in Austria took place earlier — though certainly not independent of long-term social forces and factors related to European geography[21] — on the edges of the urban belt rather than in regions which were within or closer to it.[22] In this sense, though reversed, an Austrian province such as Salzburg, interpreted from a contemporary perspective, would thus be an example of an abortive state formation (as late as 1805/1815).

If we accept as true the widely held, though unproved, thesis advanced by numerous regional historians and province-level politicians, that federalism and *'Landesbewusstsein'* (regional consciousness) in 20th century Austria are, above all, historically rooted, then it must also be assumed that the structural factors which had already been determinative in the historical processes of province formation were not (completely) eradicated under the Habsburgs. In the Austrian state, in which the process of state formation reached a preliminary conclusion only as late as 1848,[23] they may certainly continue to be operative today. Furthermore, the hypothesis can also be proposed that the strength of *Landesbewusstsein*, separatism and federalism, increasing the further west one goes in Austria (particularly at the outset of the First Republic), is also consistent with Rokkan's model.[24] If this were true, it would likewise conform to a dividing line, seemingly running clear across Austria from north to south, approximately along the Pyhrn Pass line (Linz-Klagenfurt). This division, which is a more frequent subject of consideration for social geographers and folk-lorists than for sociologists and political scientists in Austria,[25] deserves further empirical research. This boundary also seems to find expression in certain distinctive features which have characterized the Austrian political landscape until the recent past: in the West, a rather integrative consensus orientation in which many characteristics of the *'ständisch'* (estate) society seem to have been conserved ('liberal conservatism'); a rather centralist-standardizing political culture, though displaying tendencies and structures leading to political polarization and populism (Socialist and Social Christian mass politics) in the East.[26]

Deferred Repercussions of the Failed Process of Empire Formation and Decline to the Semi-Periphery Level: Authoritarianism

The essential aim of the method of the conceptual map of European states is to explain the extremely diverse party systems in Europe and the highly divergent paths which the processes of democratization have taken there (apart from the area under communist domination prior to 1989). This of course includes, conversely, hypotheses addressing the subject of the violent interruptions of democratization — the collapse of democracies and the establishment of dictatorships.[27] Indeed, Rokkan has put forth a number of different solutions to these questions, which were rather peripheral to his work; and which deserve further testing through detailed research on Austria. The following factors, contained in a European political model employing Rokkan's concepts of centre/periphery, are relevant to the collapse of democracy:[28]

a) The fact that Austria has constituted a core component of the Catholic universalistic 'world', implicit in which is early state formation though late nation building, a weak mass mobilization for democracy and specific attempts at a (Catholic) mobilization 'from above'.

b) This also implies the strength of absolutism during the phase of social modernization and a deep-seeded and long-lasting breach of 'ständisch' traditions of self-determination, which persisted from the 17th to the early 20th century.

c) Furthermore, the Habsburg empire assumed the character of a 'crusader' state in opposition to the Turks.

d) In contrast to the democracies of Western and Northwestern Europe, in which a phase of parliamentary government typically preceded mass-level democratization, this sequence of decisive steps in the process of political modernization was exactly reversed. That is to say, the introduction of universal suffrage (for men) occurred prior to the establishment of an effective parliamentary form of government, whereby turn-of-the-century Austria proved to be following a 'Sonderweg' (special way) more similar to the German model.

It was only in the late 1970s that Rokkan, in collaboration with Bernt Hagtvet, made an explicit and extremely comprehensive attempt[29] to apply his model to the explanation of 'violent breakdown of competitive mass politics', thus to the establishment of fascist and authoritarian regimes, and to reformulate his previous models.[30] The essential points of this model variant are: All five cases of such dictatorships — Germany, Austria, Italy, Spain and Portugal — either lay within the urban belt or were historically closely linked to it. Despite the numerous highly divergent geoeconomic characteristics — which doubtless constitute one of the weaknesses of this model — these states display three common characteristics:

1) Persistent strength of an imperial heritage stemming from the land's geopolitical position (city-belt) and from failed ambitions towards empire formation in the respective phases of their histories;

2) Decline to the status of a semi-periphery as a result of the developmental process of a capitalist world economic system which had been underway since the 16th century and a series of hegemonic conflicts with the 'new' economic powers of NorthWest Europe, primarily England and the Netherlands, to a limited extent France as well;[31]

3) A sociopolitical alliance of state formational factors (ruler, military, and centralized bureaucracy) with aristocratic proprietors of large landed estates and a majority of the industrial bourgeoisie, in the manner of Bismarck's 'blood and iron';[32]

At least until 1939, therefore, 'the chances for the *survival* of competitive multiparty politics was greatest within the *core* of the world economy,' while conversely 'the likelihood of fascist-type victories was greatest in the semi-peripheralized territories of earlier city-studded empires.' And then, closely following the theories of Barrington Moore, Rokkan and Hagtved come to the conclusion that 'the probability of *communist-type* victories was greatest in the much more markedly *peripheral* areas of earlier empires of the 'agrarian bureaucracy' type, empires with poorly developed commercial-industrial bourgeoisies'.[33]

Indeed, this model could have achieved a higher degree of precision had it attributed increased significance to the decisive differentiation between 'Catholic' political cultures and those of a reformational Protestant character, a contrast otherwise given such strong emphasis by Rokkan in the processes of state formation and nation building. This would have made possible an explanation of essential characteristics and differences of regime typology, discriminating between the repressiveness of mass mobilization, nationalist-*völkisch* national socialism, and the more or less authoritarian, *Catholic-type* dictatorships which are often simply, and quite improperly, subsumed under the category of 'fascism'. As inadequate as this interpretational approach may be with respect to the Austrian 'Corporatist State', it clearly deserves further pursuit in connection with the Eastern and East Central European regimes of the interwar period.

Historical Roots of Patterns of Sociopolitical Coalitions: The Limited Capacity for Action of Democratic Government in the First Republic

Finally, an additional, 'early' variant of Rokkan's centre/periphery model is applicable to the political situation of the interwar era, and indeed to the constellations of governmental and political power during this eventful 20-year period of revolution, coalition and dictatorship.

Rokkan's chief interpretational objective in this theoretical variant was to once again have recourse to factors emerging from the distant historical past in order to explain the configuration of party and governmental systems in the nation-states west of the divide between the former communist and non-communist systems of 20th century Europe. Rokkan attempted to apply this theory to a comparative data base on a broad, international and national scale,[34] thereby achieving notoriety primarily among analysts of voting behaviour and political scientists. It is beyond the scope of this paper to sketch this model's wide-ranging theoretical foundations with respect to modernization and political systems.[35] Of sole significance in our present context is Rokkan's work in tracing party systems back to fundamental sociopolitical cleavages which have taken shape and been passed on during the multifarious process of modernization since the beginning of the modern period and are based upon even older sociohistorical (see above) and linguistic-cultural patterns. Rokkan sees the Reformation and Counter-Reformation, the 'democratic revolutions' occuring from the end of the 18th century, and the Industrial Revolution as decisive factors. His model differentiates among the following sociopolitical variables, represented by the following abbreviations in parentheses. Weak sociopolitical factors are placed in parentheses ( ). The symbol A, an expansion which I have introduced, is placed in brackets { }. Model variables which are not relevant for Austria are placed in brackets [ ].[36]

(N) The process begins with a hard core of 'nation-state formative elements' which control the essential elements of the emerging state machinery;

[C] A national church which establishes itself within the territory of a state during the course of the Reformation and assumes an important role in the formation of the national cultural character (not relevant for Austria as Protestantism was defeated during the Counter-Reformation period);

(R) The universally oriented Roman Catholic Church with its transnational hierarchy whose influence upon society was decisively fixed during the Counter-Reformation;

[D] A group of dissenting religious nonconformists. Again, in the case of Austria an immaterial consideration, or one that only comes into the picture in connection with crypto-Protestants and peripheral pockets of Protestant resistance;[37]

(L) A group of aristocratic proprietors of large landed estates cooperating with the nation-state formative elements;

(U) An urban bourgeoisie emerging during the course of the Industrial Revolution which controls the growing commercial and industrial sector and constitutes a powerful countervailing force to the landed aristocracy. (With regard to Central and East Europe, it appears to be a deficit of Rokkan's model that it does not take into account the existence of a Jewish bourgeoisie prior to 1939/44);

{A} A political entity representing the working class and opposing the class interests of the bourgeoisie.[38] This group, in turn, went through a process of splintering in certain countries after 1917;

(P) And finally, a social-political periphery factor which — by definition — attempts to resist the factors tending to subjugate it to the control of the centre.

From the preceding factors, the following Table can be derived from our investigation of sociopolitical coalitions in Austria:

Table: Sociopolitical Coalitions 1918-1938		
	Centrality/Peripherality of social political forces:	
Subperiod	central/ semi-central	:	semiperipheral/ peripheral
pre-1918	N + L + R + (U)	:	(U) + P + A
1918-20	A + (P) + (N) + (U)	:	R + L + (P)
1921-29/32	(N) + U + (R)	:	(A) + P + L
1933-38	N + L + R + (U)	:	(U) + P + A

Sociopolitical Coalitions 1918-1938

To express in words the meaning of this table: In the final phase of the Habsburg empire, the traditional formative elements of the Austrian nation-state-imperial court, bureaucracy and military — in cooperation with the major groups of (non-German speaking) landed aristocracy and the Catholic Church, as well as with segments of the liberal and German nationalist bourgeoisie (U), controlled the centre both with regard to political power and to the economy and social hierarchy. The non-German speaking bourgeois groups, the traditional rural populace and the labour movement were peripheral or tended to peripherality.

The consequence of the disintegration of the multi-ethnic Habsburg state was that the new Austrian state inherited the majority of the pre-existing social and political structures, in addition to new problems stemming from the collapse of its integrated commercial sphere. Not the least of these was that the centre, Vienna,[39] became even more dominant within the new territorial framework than it had been previously, which inevitably provoked intensified resistance from the periphery. In this situation, the 'Austrian Revolution' temporarily brought forth a new sociopolitical coalition at its centre: namely, the Social Democratic Worker's Party, which had been dominant for several months, and their Christian-Social coalition partners, representing the periphery and, above all, the provinces, both of whom had to rely to a certain extent upon the support of the traditional state bureaucracy and the urban bourgeoisie. The political as well as spatial periphery was now occupied by the Catholic clergy and the aristocratic proprietors of large landed estates who, along with other resistance elements, were not prepared to accept the new republican-democratic political conditions.[40]

With the end of the coalition government of the Social Democrats and the Social-Christians (1920) and the economic austerity measures resulting from the Geneva Protocols (1922) aimed at stabilizing the Austrian finances, there began a process of regrouping of the power combination in control of the centre. The state bureaucracy together with the urban bourgeoisie and centrist elements of the Christian-Social Party gained increased significance. The Catholic Church also won renewed importance. The province-level Social Christians were now once again rather peripheralized. In spite of their involvement in the *Heimwehr*, the rightist armed militia movement, large land owners were unable to advance to the centre of power. The Social Democratic labour movement declined to the level of an internal semi-periphery despite the fact that, considering its main point of geographical concentration, it was a central factor.

With the increasing concentration of power in the executive branch of government since the end of the 1920s and the establishment of the authoritarian 'Corporatist State' under Dollfuss and Schuschnigg,[41] the system of sociopolitical power was toppled once again. Elements of the state bureaucracy, the *Heimwehr*, the aristocracy, the Catholic clergy and segments of the bourgeoisie controlled the state in centralist-authoritarian fashion. Despite the promise of full integration of all classes and economic sectors in the 'corporatist state', the traditional rural populace on the spatial periphery, remained politically and socially marginalized. Exactly the same can be said about the 'Marxist' working class.

During the world economic crisis of the 1930s, a new — and with external support in March, 1938 — finally victorious factor of political power arose, though, within a substantial segment of the middle classes (in the broadest sense of the word) — National Socialism. It first gained mass support as a semi-peripherial phenomenon[42] before achieving a breakthrough into the centre of political power.

By comparing the sociopolitical coalition schema of the phase of the bourgeois coalition government (1921-1929/32) which I have developed here with that of the stable democracies of Western and Northern Europe found in Rokkan's work,[43] it is possible to advance the following hypothesis: contrary to an interpretational pattern widely accepted by scholars of modern Austrian history,[44] the power configuration of the 1920s in Austria had better chances to preserve democracy than the preceding power pattern of the grand coalition government of Social Democrats and Social Christians. This also implies that the breakup of this coalition did not automatically lead to civil war and dictatorial rule.

However, the historical preconditions, going back as far as the Counter-Reformation, for the development of such a combination were unfavourable. In the context of the prevailing symbiosis of Church and State, which had only been weakened or temporarily interrupted by the reforms of Joseph II, the formation of a secularized bourgeoisie which was not pan-German but rather oriented towards an Austrian nation would have been extremely difficult, to say the least. But only this could have lent support to a process of an Austrian nation building as early as in the interwar period. It must also be assumed then, that the 'revolutionary' constellation in Austria had likewise been too radical and unstable. And the 'corporatist state' would then in fact have been a type of attempted revival of the *ancien régime*.

Furthermore, it is interesting to note that all system-threatening fascist movements, as has also been confirmed by preliminary analyses of voting behaviour,[45] have emerged from the semi-periphery. Following their takeover of power, however, they have renounced their periphery-based interests in favour of a new and even more extremely dictatorial centralism.

Interpretational approaches such as these certainly permit an extension of their range of geographical application to the region of the post-Communist states. This would indeed raise completely new problems with respect to the adaptation and further development of Rokkan's macro models. It might also lead, if not to their falsification as general interpretational patterns, then to the elaboration of an extended centre/periphery grammar along the lines of Rokkan's work.[46]

Notes

1. This is a revised and shortened version of a paper presented at the Austrian Historians' Convention in 1993. Gerhard Botz, 1994, 'Zentrum/Peripherie in der Politik der Ersten Republik: drei Makro-Modelle Stein Rokkans', in *Bericht über den 19. Österreichhischen Historikertag in Graz*, Vienna: 150-60.

2. However, for Austria, compare Michael Mitterauer, 1971, 'Das Problem der zentralen Orte als sozial und wirtschaftshistorische Forschungsaufgabe', in *Vierteljahrschrift für Sozial — und Wirtschaftsgeschichte*, Vol. 58, also reprinted in Michael Mitterauer, 1980, *Markt und Stadt im Mittelalter*, Stuttgart: 22-51; Ernst Hanisch, 1981, 'Provinz und Metropole. Gesellschaftsgeschichtliche Perspektiven der Beziehungen des Bundeslandes Salzburg zu Wien (1918-1934)', in Eberhard Zwink (ed.), *Beiträge zur Föderalismusdiskussion*, Salzburg: 67ff.

3. Compare Henri Lefebvre, 1974, *La production de l'espace*. Paris; Denis Retaillé, 1992, 'Géographie universelle: une quête prématurée', in *Éspaces Temps. Le Journal*, (49/59): 110-14.

4. Fernand Braudel, 1979, *Civilization materiélle, économie et capitalism, XVe-XVIIIe siécle*, Vol. 3, Paris: 12.

5. Compare Johan Galtung, 1972, 'Eine Strukturelle Theorie des Imperialismus', in Dieter Senghas (ed.), *Imperialismus und strukturelle Gewalt*, Frankfurt: 29-104; and Francois Perroux, 1964, *L'economie de XXe siècle*, Paris.

6. Braudel, *op.cit.*: 16.

7. Immanuel Wallerstein, 1974. *The Modern World System*, Vol. 1, New York: 3ff.

8. Stein Rókkan and Derek W. Urvin, 1983. *Economy, Territory, Identity*, London: 14; compare also [Stein Rokkan], 'The Centre-Perihery Polarity', in Stein Rokkan and Derek W. Urwin, 1987, *Centre-Perihery-Structures in Europe. An ISSC Workbook in Comparative Analysis*, Frankfurt: 17ff.

9. Manfried Welan, 1984, 'Zentrum und Periherie', in Grete Klingenstein (ed.), *Krise der Fortschritts*, Vienna: 103-21; compare also, Tonino Bettanini, 1976, *Spazio e scienze umane*, Florence; and Francoise P. Levy and Marion Segaud, 1983, *Anthropologie de l'éspace*, Paris.

10. Stein Rokkan et al., 1971. 'Nation-Building. A review of Recent Comparative Research and a Select Bibliography of Analytical Studies', *Current Sociology*, Vol. 19, (3): 3.

11. Compare Peter Schöller (ed.), 1972. *Zentralitätsforschung*, Darmstadt. (This volume also includes a reprint of the innovative article, Walter Christaller, 1933, 'Das System der zentralen Orte': 3-22; and Hans Bobek and Maria Fesl, 1978, *Das System den zentralen Orte Österreichs*, Vienna.

12. There is a multitude of models by Rokkan which are neither homogeneous, nor without contradiction to each other, nor invariable over time, having been constantly modified by Rokkan himself. See, Stein Rokkan, 1980, 'Eine Familie von Modellen für die vergleichende Geschichte Europas', in *Zeitschrift für Soziologie*, Vol. 9, (2): 118-28. This is also the conclusion of Peter Flora, 1981, 'Stein Rokkans Makro-Modell der Politischen Entwicklung Europas: Ein

Rekonstruktionsversuch', in *Kölner Zeitschrift für Soziologie und Sozialpsychologie*, Vol. 33: 397-436.

13. From here onwards, I mainly follow my paper 'Staatsbildungsprozesse und Zentrum-Peripherie-Probleme in der Ersten Republik', presented 13 November, 1981, at the conference of the 'Wissenschaftliche Kommision...zur Erforshung der Jahre 1918 bis 1938 in Vienna', on 'Federalism in Austria 1918-1938'.

14. It should be self-evident that this macro model itself and, to an even greater extent, its application to Austria must necessarily be generalized and extremely simplified. I am fully cognizant of the numerous objections it is likely to raise on the part of historians who adhere to an *historistisch* paradigm. In general compare Peter Flora, *op.cit.*: 434; Charles Tilly, 1981, *Stein Rokkan's Conceptual Map of Europe*, Ann Arbor, Mich. (CRSO Working Papers no. 229): 2ff.

15. For the first elaboration in a cartographic form, see, Bernt Hagtvet and Stein Rokkan, 1980. 'The Conditions of Fascist Victory: Towards a Geoeconomic-Geopolitical Model for the Explanation of Violent Breakdown of Competitive Mass Politics', in Stein U. Larsen et al. (ed.), *Who were the Fascists: Social Roots of Fascism and Nazism in Europe*, Bergen: 139.

16. Éteinne Juillard and Henri Nonn, 1976. 'Éspaces et régions en Europe occident-ale', Paris. *Actions thématigues programmées, A.T.P.,* (10). Mainly: 22ff., and maps 2-8.

17. MacRae, 1969. *Consociational Democracy*, London; and Philippe Schmitter, 1986, *Corporatism in Europe*, Stanford.

18. With slight simplifications and some additions, I here mainly follow Rokkan's own words which he repeated on several different occasions. Stein Rokkan, 1973, 'Cities, States, Nations', in Samuel N. Eisenstadt and Stein Rokkan (ed.), *Building States and Nations*, Vol. 1, Beverly Hills, : 81; in general, Stein Rokkan, 1975, 'Dimensions of State Formation and Nation-Building', in Charles Tilly (ed.), *The formation of National States in Western Europe*, Princeton: 562-600.

19. Reprinted from Hagtvet and Rokkan, *op.cit.*: 139.

20. Ernst Bruckmüller, 1985. *Sozialgeschichte Österreichs*, Vienna: 104ff.

21. Compare Jenö Szücs, 1983. 'The Three Historical Regions of Europe', in *Acta Historica*, A.S.H., (29): 131-83. (German: Die Drei Historischen Regionen Europas, Frankfurt, 1990); for a recent overview see, Erich Landsteiner, 1993, 'Europas innere Grenzen', in *Österreichische Zeitschrift für Geschichtswissenschaften*, Vol. 4, (1): 8-43; compare also István Bibó, 1992, *Die Misere der Osteuropäischen Kleinstaaterei*, Frankfurt.

22. Compare Walter Jambor (ed.), 1971. *Der anteil der Bundesländer and der Nationswerdung Österreichs*, Vienna; and Friedrich Koja, 1976, *Entwick-lungstendenzen des österreichischen Föderalismus*, St. Pölten.

23. Ernst Bruckmüller, 1984. *Nation Österreich*, Vienna: 68.

24. See Stein Rokkan, 1980. 'Territories, Centres, and Peripheries: Towards a Geoethnic-Geoeconomic-Geopolitical Model of Differentiation within Western

Europe', in Jean Gottmann (ed.), *Centre and Periphery. Spatial Variation in Politics*, Beverly Hills: 163-204, mainly 187.

25. Compare Melany Sully, 1990. *Modern Politics in Austria*, London.

26. In contrast to Emmanuel Todd, 1990, *L'invention de L'Europe*, Paris: 433ff.; compare this against, Hans Bobek, *Österreichs Regionalstruktur im Spiegel des Atlas der Republik Österreich*, [ca. 1970].

27. Here, Rokkan draws similar conclusions, though starting from a different approach, like Barrington Moore, 1967, *Social Origins of Dictatorship and Democracy*, Harmondsworth.

28. Compare Gerhard Botz, 1987. '"Der 4 März 1933" als Konsequenz ständischer Strukturen, ökonomischer Krisen und autoritärer Tendenzen', in Gerhard Botz, *Krisenzonen einer Demokratie*, Frankfurt: 155-80; also, most recently Ernst Hanish, 1994, *Der lange Schatten des Staates: Österreichische Gesellschaftsgeschichte im 20. Jahrhundert*: 24ff.

29. Hagtvet and Rokkan, *op.cit.*: 131-52.

30. In doing so, he relied increasingly upon Wallerstein's concept, referred to above, of the semi-periphery and the decline into such a condition in a political-economic respect.

31. Cf. Immanuel Wallerstein, 1980. *The Modern World-System*, vol. 2, New York, 231ff.; now also Immanuel Wallerstein, 1989, *The Modern World-System*, Vol. 3, San Diego.

32. For a more detailed development, see also the unpublished manuscript, Bernt Hagtvet, 1978, 'Alliance Configurations in the Decisive Phase of Nation Building: Some Notes on Germany, Italy, Spain, and Austria for the Explanation of Violent Breakdown of Competitive Mass Politics', Bergen.

33. Rokkan and Hagtvet, *op.cit.*: 149 (italics by the authors).

34. Seymour M. Lipset and Stein Rokkan, 1967. 'Cleavage Structure, Party Systems and Voter Alignments: An Introduction', in Seymour M. Lipset and Stein Rokkan, *Party Systems and Voter Alignments: Cross-National Perspectives*, New York: 1-64, mainly 36ff.

35. For a well argued critique, see Charles Tilly, *Big Structures, Large Processes, Huge Comparisons*, New York, especially 125-43; compare also, Stefan Immerfall, 1991, 'Sozialer Wandel in der Moderne. Neuere Forschungsergebnisse zum Prozess gesellschaftlicher Modernisierung im 19. und 20, Jahrhundert', in *Neue Polititische Literatur*, Vol. 36: 5-48.

36. The variable "S" — secularization as an option of "N", has been completely omitted in the case of Austria.

37. Margarethe Haydter and Johann Mayr, 1984. 'Regionale Zusammenhänge zwischen Haubtwiderstansgebieten zur Zeit der Gegenreformation und den Julikämpfen 1934 in Oberösterreich', in *Bericht über den 15. österreichischen Historikertag 1982 in Salzburg*, Vienna: 406-21.

38. For reasons we do not know, Rokkan did not explicitly specify this group, whose existence can be clearly derived from lines of reasoning presented elsewhere in his model; in contrast to this, see Flora, *op.cit.*: 429.

39. Compare Hannes Hofbauer, 1992. 'Österreich zwischen Metropole und Peripherie. Ökonomische Integrationsprozesse seit der Ersten Republik', in *Österreich auf dem weg zur 3. Republik: Zwischen 'Deutschnationalismus' und 'Habsburger-Mythos'*, Vienna: 71-83.
40. Compare Gerhard Botz, 1983. *Gewalt in der Politik*, 2nd ed., Munich.
41. Compare Ulrich Kluge, 1983. *Der österreichische Ständestaat*, Vienna.
42. Franziska Schneeberger, 1988. *Sozialstruktur der Heimwehr in Österreich. Eine vergleichend-politische Sozialgeschichte der Heimwehrbewegung*, unpublished Ph.D. dissertation, University of Salzburg; Gerhard Botz, 1988, 'Quantitative Analyse der Sozial- und Altersstruktur der österreichischen NSDAP-Mitglieder (1926-1945)', in *Austriaca*, Cahiers universitaires d'information sur l'Autriche, (26): 63-72; see also Johannes Dressel, 1985, 'Sozialstruktur einer NS-Elite: die österreichischen Abgeordneten zum Grossdeutchen Reichstag 1938', in *Bericht über den 16. Historikertag 1984 in Krems/Donau*: 644-55.
43. Lipset and Rokkan, Cleavage Structure, *op.cit.*: 37.
44. For instance, Norbert Leser, 1985. *Zwischen Reformismus und Bolschewismus*, 2nd ed., Vienna.
45. See the contribution of Gerhard Botz and Albert Müller, 1994. 'Zentren un Peripherien im lichte der Wahlergebnisse der Ersten Republik', in *Bericht über den 19 österreichischen Historikertag in Graz*, Vienna: 545-59.
46. For their editorial assistance in the preparation of this paper as well as for substantive comments and suggestions, the author expresses his thanks to Dr. Albert Müller, Vienna, Univ.-Doz. Christian Fleck, Graz, and Dr. Gerald Sprengnagel, Salzburg. The author is also indebted to the Maison des Sciences de l'Homme in Paris for having provided an atmosphere conducive to scholarship in March, 1993, and likewise expresses his gratitude.

Bibliography

Bettanini, Tonino 1976. *Spazio e scienze umane*. Florence.
Bibó, István 1992. *Die Misere der Osteuropäischen Kleinstaaterei*. Frankfurt: Verlag neue Kritik.
Botz, Gerhard 1981. 'Staatsbildungsprozesse und Zentrum-Peripherie-Probleme in der Ersten Republik'. Paper presented 13 November at the conference of the 'Wissenschaftliche Kommision...zur Erforschung der Jahre 1918 bis 1938 in Vienna', on 'Federalism in Austria 1918-1938'.
Botz, Gerhard 1987. '"Der 4 März 1933" als Konsequenz ständischer Strukturen, ökonomischer Krisen und autoritärer Tendenzen', in Gerhard Botz, *Krisenzonen einer Demokratie*. Frankfurt: Campus Verlag, 155-80.
Botz, Gerhard 1983. *Gewalt in der Politik*, 2nd ed. Munich.
Botz, Gerhard 1994. 'Zentrum/Peripherie in der Politik der Ersten Republik: drei Makro-Modelle Stein Rokkans', in *Bericht über den 19. Österreichhischen Historikertag in Graz*. Vienna.
Botz, Gerhard 1988. 'Quantitative Analyse der Sozial- und Altersstruktur der öster-

reichischen NSDAP-Mitglieder (1926-1945)', in *Austriaca*, Cahiers universitaires d'information sur l'Autriche, (26): 63-72.

Botz, Gerhard and Albert Müller 1994. 'Zentren un Peripherien im lichte der Wahlergebnisse der Ersten Republik', in *Bericht über den 19 österreichischen Historikertag in Graz*, Vienna: 545-59.

Braudel, Fernand 1980. *Civilization materiélle, économie et capitalism, XVe-XVIIIe siécle*, Vol. 3. Paris: Armand Collin.

Bruckmüller, Ernst 1985. *Sozialgeschichte Österreichs*. Vienna.

Bruckmüller, Ernst 1984. *Nation Österreich*. Vienna.

Dressel, Johannes 1985. 'Sozialstruktur einer NS-Elite: die österreichischen Abgeordneten zum Grossdeutchen Reichstag 1938', in *Bericht über den 16. Historikertag 1984 in Krems/Donau*: 644-55.

Flora, Peter 1981. 'Stein Rokkans Makro-Modell der Politischen Entwicklung Europas: Ein Rekonstruktionsversuch', in *Kölner Zeitschrift für Soziologie und Sozialpsychologie*, 33: 397-436.

Galtung, Johan 1972. 'Eine Strukturelle Theorie des Imperialismus', in Dieter Senghas (ed.), *Imperialismus und strukturelle Gewalt*. Frankfurt.

Hagtvet, Bernt 1978. 'Alliance Configurations in the Decisive Phase of Nation Building: Some Notes on Germany, Italy, Spain, and Austria for the Explanation of Violent Breakdown of Competitive Mass Politics', unpublished manuscript. Bergen.

Hagtvet, Bernt and Stein Rokkan, 1980. 'The Conditions of Fascist Victory: Towards a Geoeconomic-Geopolitical Model for the Explanation of Violent Breakdown of Competitive Mass Politics', in Stein U. Larsen et al. (ed.), *Who were the Fascists: Social Roots of Fascism and Nazism in Europe*, Bergen: Universitetsforlaget: 139.

Hanisch, Ernst 1981. 'Provinz und Metropole. Gesellschaftsgeschichtliche Perspektiven der Beziehungen des Bundeslandes Salzburg zu Wien (1918-1934)', in Eberhard Zwink (ed.), *Beiträge zur Föderalismusdiskussion*. Salzburg.

Hanish, Ernst 1994. *Der lange Schatten des Staates: Österreichische Gesellschaftsgeschichte im 20. Jahrhundert*.

Haydter, Margarethe and Johann Mayr 1984. 'Regionale Zusammenhänge zwichen Haubtwiderstansgebieten zur Zeit der Gegenreformation und den Julikämpfen 1934 in Oberösterreich', in *Bericht über den 15. österreichischen Historikertag 1982 in Salzburg*. Vienna: 406-21.

Hofbauer, Hannes 1992. 'Österreich zwischen Metropole und Peripherie. Ökonomische Integrationsprozesse seit der Ersten Republik', in *Österreich auf dem weg zur 3. Republik: Zwischen "Deutschnationalismus" und "Habsburger-Mythos"*. Vienna: 71-83.

Immerfall, Stefan 1991. 'Sozialer Wandel in der Moderne. Neuere Forschungsergebnisse zum Prozess gesellschaftlicher Modernisierung im 19. und 20, Jahrhundert', in *Neue Polititische Literatur*, 36: 5-48.

Jambor, Walter (ed.), 1971. *Der anteil der Bundesländer and der Nationswerdung Österreichs*. Vienna.

Juillard, Éteinne and Henri Nonn 1976. 'Éspaces et régions en Europe occidentale', Paris.

Kluge, Ulrich 1983. *Der österreichische Ständestaat.* Vienna.

Kluge, Ulrich 1984. *Der österreichische Ständestaat, 1934-1938.* Entstehung und Sheitern. Munchen: Oldenburg.

Koja, Friedrich 1976. *Entwicklungstendenzen des österreichischen Föderalismus.* St. Pölten.

Landsteiner, Erich 1993. 'Europas innere Grenzen', in *Österreichische Zeitschrift für Geschichtswissenschaften,* 4, (1): 8-43.

Lefebvre, Henri 1974. *La production de l'espace.* Paris.

Leser, Norbert 1985. *Zwischen Reformismus und Bolsschewismus,* 2nd ed. Vienna.

Levy, Francoise P. and Segaud Marion 1983. *Anthropologie de l'éspace.* Paris.

Lipset, Seymour M. and Stein Rokkan 1967. 'Cleavage Structure, Party Systems and Voter Alignments: An Introduction', in Seymour M. Lipset and Stein Rokkan, *Party Systems and Voter Alignments: Cross-National Perspectives.* New York: Free Press, 1-64.

MacRae, 1969. *Consociational Democracy.* London.

Mitterauer, Michael 1971. 'Das Problem der zentralen Orte als sozial und wirtschafts-historische Forschungsaufgabe', in *Vierteljahrschrift für Sozial — und Wirtschaftsgeschichte* 58.

Mitterauer, Michael 1980. *Markt und Stadt im Mittelalter.* Stuttgart.: Anton Hirsemann..

Moore, Barrington 1967. *Social Origins of Dictatorship and Democracy.* Harmondsworth.

Perroux, Francois 1964. *L'economie de XXe siècle.* Paris.

Retaillé, Denis 1992. 'Géographie universelle: une quête prématurée', in *Éspaces Temps. Le Journal,* (49/59).

Rokkan, Stein 1975. 'Dimensions of State Formation and Nation-Building', in Charles Tilly (ed.), *The formation of National States in Western Europe.* Princeton: Princeton U.P.

Rokkan, Stein 1973. 'Cities, States, Nations', in Samuel N. Eisenstadt and Stein Rokkan (eds.), *Building States and Nations,* Vol. 1. Beverly Hills: Sage.

Rokkan, Stein et al., 1971. 'Nation-Building. A review of Recent Comparative Research and a Select Bibliography of Analytical Studies', *Current Sociology,* 19, (3): 3.

Rokkan, Stein 1980. 'Eine Familie von Modellen für die vergleichende Geschichte Europas', in *Zeitschrift für Soziologie,* 9, (2): 118-28.

Rokkan, Stein 1987. 'The Centre-Perihery Polarity', in Stein Rokkan and Derek W. Urwin, *Centre-Perihery-Structures in Europe.* An ISSC Workbook in Comparative Analysis. Frankfurt: Campus.

Rokkan, Stein and Derek W. Urvin 1983. *Economy, Territory, Identity.* London: Sage.

Rokkan, Stein 1980. 'Territories, Centres, and Peripheries: Towards a Geoethnic-Geoeconomic-Geopolitical Model of Differentiation within Western Europe', in Jean Gottmann (ed.), *Centre and Periphery. Spatial Variation in Politics.* Beverly Hills: Sage.

Schmitter, Philippe 1986. *Corporatism in Europe,* Stanford.

Schneeberger, Franziska 1988. 'Sozialstruktur der Heimwehr in Österreich. Eine vergleichend-politische Sozialgeschichte der Heimwehrbewegung'. Unpublished PhD dissertation, University of Salzburg.

Schöller, Peter (ed.), 1972. *Zentralitätsforschung.* Darmstadt.

Sully, Melany 1990. *Modern Politics in Austria*. London.

Szücs, Jenö 1983. 'The Three Historical Regions of Europe', in *Acta Historica*, A.S.H., (29): 131-83.

Tilly, Charles 1981, *Stein Rokkan's Conceptual Map of Europe*. (CRSO Working Papers No. 229), Ann Arbor, Mich.

Tilly, Charles *Big Structures, Large Processes, Huge Comparisons*. New York.

Todd, Emmanuel 1990. *L'invention de L'Europe*. Paris.

Wallerstein, Immanuel 1974. *The Modern World System*, Vol. 1. New York: Academic Press.

Wallerstein, Immanuel 1989. *The Modern World-System*, Vol. 3. San Diego.

Welan, Manfried 1984. 'Zentrum und Periherie', in Grete Klingenstein (ed.), *Krise der Fortschritts*. Vienna: 103-21.

The East Central European Party Systems: Linkages between Parties and Society

Attila Ágh

The social and political existence of parties

Parties have been defined in several ways: politically as organizations contesting elections, culturally as organizations promoting a set of values in their programmes. It is clear from all the definitions that parties have various forms of existence, one of which usually dominates conventional approaches. For an analysis of the East Central European (ECE) party systems, it is, however, particularly important to study parties as complex phenomena with several features, i.e. as having both social and political levels of existence, since the differentiation of these party systems from other social sub-systems is only in its initial stage. In short, parties are very strong politically and very weak socially in East Central Europe and we can analyse them properly only by carefully separating their different forms and levels of existence in their interrelationships.[1]

In my understanding, parties have distinct forms of social and political existence with characteristic cultural features in both spheres. At a closer look, even the social and political forms of existence have a further distinction within them, giving rise to four forms of party existence altogether. I think that this model is generally valid, and that it may be applied to all parties. I suggest, however, that this model is especially useful in analysing the ECE party systems since an unbalanced relationship between these forms is particularly characteristic of them.

Social existence of parties:

1) *Membership-party* — Empirically, these parties have an 'inner' party, a membership with social characteristics, and also an 'outer' party, a 'camp' of party supporters or voters, i.e., their constituency, which can also be characterized sociologically. The latter determines the social structure of a given party and the particular social dialogue and discourse which the party has with the whole of society, which has marked cultural characteristics at the grassroots level.

2) *Organization-party* — These parties have a national organization as well as regional and local levels of membership with structured and institutionalized activities. The internal organization of a given party, with its differentiation, hierarchy, efficiency and party democracy, is particularly important.

Political existence of parties:

3) *Programme-party* — These parties appear in politics the first time with their particular sets of values, formulated in specific political programmes, which are in fact special programme packages resulting from the articulation and aggregation of the demands of different interest groups. These parties have characteristic political actions and profiles and patterns of confrontation and cooperation with other parties. Their political discourse and style of behaviour can be described in politico-cultural terms, this time more from the point of macro-politics and the elite behaviour of those representing the parties at the national level.

4) *Power-party* — These parties take part in the institutionalized political power in pluralist democracy, and this concept also encompasses opposition parties to some extent and in special ways. This is the most visible form of the existence of parties to the general public but even political scientists tend to reduce the activities of parties to their special activities in the tough institutional structure of macro-politics. These include general elections, parliamentary-legislative work and exercising power in central and/or local governments, although this form or function can be theoreticized only in its interrelationship with the other forms or functions.[2]

Historical experience shows that (1) the special combination of these four forms of party existence is characteristic of a given region or country and (2) these forms develop very unevenly in the formation process of parties and party systems; therefore their particular combination can be the starting point for analysis. In the case of the ECE parties, we have the following series of hypotheses:

1. The hypothesis of 'hovering' party systems

The political existence of the ECE parties is much stronger than their social existence and it developed earlier. Parties exist in the ECE without a proper social base and popular support, as parties 'hovering' or 'floating' over social reality — i.e. over society's strata with their particular demands — because they appeared as premature catch-all parties.

2. The hypothesis of the 'upside-down' structure of parties

Both the social and political forms of existence of the ECE parties repeat the above-mentioned contradiction in themselves, and thus the whole party structure shows an 'upside-down' character as specified below:

(a) In its social forms of existence, the membership-party is much weaker than the organization-party. The membership-party is in fact the weakest form of party existence, i.e. the parties have only a very small membership, but the national organizations, no matter how undeveloped they are, are still relatively strong since they are organized and controlled from above. Furthermore, the voting and social support for the parties (the outer party) is also volatile and obscure.

(b) In its political form of existence, the programme-party is much weaker than the power-party. The parties seize political power with only very vague political profiles and programmes, but they are very assertive, even aggressive and arrogant, in exercising this power. This situation leads to a new kind of alienation from politics among the population and to a very low effectiveness of the parties' policy-making.

This four-level structure of the ECE parties can be characterized somewhat more precisely in the following way:

Membership-party — the party membership is rather small and it provides only a weak base for the whole party. The biggest parties have around 40,000 members (even in Poland which is a big country according to ECE standards!); the average parliamentary party has 20,000 members (like ODS, the Civic Democratic Party, the governing party in Czechia) but smaller parliamentary parties have only around 10,000 members. Most of the party members are rather old (and often markedly senile and frustrated since the younger and middle generations are too busy making a living). The parties are generally unpopular and lack attraction for potential members and voters. In addition, the whole 'upside down' structure described here discourages people from joining parties, since they feel that they cannot have a say in 'big' party politics.[3]

Organization-party — parties as organizations exist mainly from above, i.e., as some kind of national organization in the party headquarters but not as nation-wide organizations. They lack a meaningful set of regional and local party organizations. The party leadership at the top is separated from the membership because of these organizational weaknesses. Most parties, however, deliberately try to prevent party democracy because they fear their own overactive 'conservative' membership. Thus party meetings of a mostly rather aged membership are rather meaningless. Because of the lack of nation-wide organizations as channels to party members, the party leaders tend to communicate with their own members more through the national media than through personal or organizational contacts. The top party leaders stay in and act through parliament; the parliamentary faction thus becomes dominant over the entire party and 'overparticization' and 'overparliamentarization' emerge and converge.[4]

Programme party — even after five years of power transition, the party programmes are still reduced to sloganeering. They are too vague and general. It is not because the parties lack experts who can formulate concrete and specific programmes for them, but it is first of all due to the 'hovering' character of parties. The parties do not know the specific demands of the different social strata because the organized interests have not been developed sufficiently to articulate them meaningfully, precisely and adequately. What is more, even if they know them, the parties are not ready to accept and represent these demands in concerted national programmes because most of them claim to represent almost all social strata as catch-all parties. As 'national' parties, they subscribe to the deceptive idea that the national interest may exist directly, and that they represent it against all the other narrowly oriented parties (who advocate the same fallacy).[5]

Power-parties — the transitory political elites 'fell' into political power unexpectedly and were therefore inexperienced and unprepared. This political elite group had either a sense of historical mission or a moralistic-messianistic attitude, both of which placed them, in their own self-image, well above the average citizen. This arrogant behaviour has, however, backfired and most members of the transitory elite have already 'fallen out' of political life. Nevertheless, this top elite determined the top-down structure of parties for some years. Because of the structural weaknesses of parties, power politics is still dominant within the ECE parties, even within those in opposition, rather than the social 'conversion' functions which can secure their success in the long run. They want to keep and/or extend their present positions in the power structure at any price and this drive for power penetrates all party functions. Sometimes, however, the power positions of parties change drastically since a short-sighted power-eagerness makes their public support fade away quickly.[6]

The 'upside-down' structure of the ECE parties manifests itself clearly in their financial dependence on their power-party existence. The small membership-parties are unable financially to support themselves through membership fees; the membership fees are low and are not always paid regularly. Some parties do not even collect them. Consequently, the parties have to rely for their finances on the state budget which provides the major part of their income. Campaign contributions to party coffers from private persons or enterprises are usually regulated, and thus so far they have not been a major source of the parties' finances. Their income is derived mostly from state subsidies; these are based on the proportional electoral results and thus the state even supports some rather large non-parliamentary parties. The power-party domination of party finances is actually greater than this official procedure would suggest since the (partially or completely) state-run enterprises and banks have often been forced by the governing parties to finance their activities in many indirect ways, such as supporting the pro-government press and other publications.[7]

ECE citizens have no particular interest in joining parties unless they aim for a career in local or central public administration. On the local level, independents may be elected to local government posts in great numbers, but the larger the community, the more the parties dominate in a spoils system. It is again the power-party which controls the recruitment of members, and by this system the leading party bodies exert greater control over the office-holders at different levels than the rank-and-file party members. The regular elections inside the parties for the party leadership do, however, have a balancing and controlling effect, but the upside-down dependence is still the prevalent pattern. This is one of many reasons why the parties respond belatedly and weakly to social demands and to newly arising social issues. It explains why they have a rather low social sensitivity. Pressure concerning social issues cannot be formulated intensively enough through the party and its fragile national organization, and thus cannot be properly transmitted to the government and/or parliament. Usually social concerns reach the parties and party leadership through the media; local or small conflicts are, therefore, in most cases overpoliticized and not solved on the spot, but discussed and managed only at the higher levels of macro-politics.

This general description somewhat overstates the negative features of the emerging parties in order to make them more evident. These negative features have diminished lately as more mature parties have been formed. But this description is still generally valid. Furthermore, the analysis presented here in which the ECE parties are seen as 'upside-down' rests on the normative premise that parties should aggregate and transmit values and interests from the bottom up and that this is the normal state of affairs in Western party systems. I admit that this normative view cannot describe some Western parties accurately either. Nevertheless, this model is more or less generally valid for parties that have undergone an organic development. Not surprisingly, the newly and inorganically emerging parties in ECE have not yet developed a balanced relationship between their various forms of existence. This balanced relationship would be a solid pyramid model of existence with a large base in a membership-party, represented socially in the organization-party with many party activists. Furthermore, this 'balanced' party can appear on the political level first as a specific programme-party with a set of particular socio-political demands, and second, as a mature party with a solid base of all social attributes in its power-party existence.

The ECE parties are more like an empty shell having a leadership without a following, i.e. lacking a large and disciplined, devoted and active membership. Yet I call this formation process political 'overparticization', since these socially very weak parties have nevertheless become the major actors in the democratic transition. Indeed they are almost the only actors, and they try to monopolize their political position. The parallel process in parliament as the central site of democratic transition is 'overparliamentarization', because parliament has become the only forum of political life. Thus the first and model institution has also monopolized the entire political life of the country. These processes are transitory features and characteristic contradictions of the early democratic institutionalization process. The particular paradox of the formation of parties can be summarized in the following way: The weaker the parties are socially, the more they try to prevent the other social and political actors from entering the decision-making process. But the more the other actors are missing, the more the parties themselves are weakened, since it is only the organized meso-system (interest groups) and micro-system (civil society associations) that can give them a solid social background. So far the 'envious' ECE parties have been in a vicious circle reproducing their own social weakness. Even now they tend to compensate by overdoing or overstretching their political roles, which alienates the population from parties in particular and politics in general.

The Party Formation Process in ECE

I have identified four major stages of party formation in ECE. The first is when parties existed in the former system in an indirect way as party germs or embryonic parties, i.e., in the form of other social organizations (trade unions or civil society associations, etc. — as 'travestita' parties). In the second period, before the first democratic elections, some newly born or proto-parties existed first 'de facto' but not yet 'de jure'. Later on, as a result of the round-table negotiations, these new parties became legal, and mushroomed so much that a 'hundred-party-system' preceded the 'founding elections'. With these elections we entered the third period, that of parliamentarization. The first elections resulted in a cruel natural selection process between parliamentary and non-parliamentary parties. Only very few parties could survive outside parliament, but the parliamentary parties became the real embodiments of political power, together enjoying monopolistic positions. The fourth stage has just begun, and it is a stage involving new power bargaining between the parties and the other social and political actors. This is what I call the public policy period.

Obviously, the forms of social and political existence of the parties have changed drastically in these four periods. In the first period, the membership -parties were very small informal networks of friends, colleagues and sympathizers, more or less connected with the large, spontaneous and fluctuating social movements (as in Poland and Hungary). The party embryos were outside of power, but they had some influence, and their programmes were reduced to a more or less timid or brave confrontation with the former political system. The parties had their origins in the preceding 'tribalism', i.e. in the 'tribal' connections of polito-culturally or mentally close groups of intellectuals organized initially only as loose movement-parties. The entire further development of parties may be described as a transition from value- -based 'cultural' politics to interest-based 'political' politics and this process has not yet come to an end.[8]

The particular type of political organization which emerged here as a party is the so-called movement-party. Judy Batt (1991, 55-56) characterizes them in the following way:

The key characteristics of the movement-party are its broad coalitional form, its vague, non- or anti-ideological and strongly moralistic programme, and the informality of its internal organizational structure. Movement-parties first emerged as the representatives of 'civil society' in mass protest against totalitarian communist rule. (...) Subsequently, the organizational demands posed by the elections contributed to the first steps in their development as quasi-political parties, but, after the elections, when confronted with the new task of exercising power, internal strains have appeared both within the leaderships and among leaders in government, parliamentary deputies and grass-roots activists. The unmanageable variety of ideologies, interests, personalities and general political objectives that they embrace lies at the root of the instability of the movement-parties, and both external observers and the participants themselves accept the inevitability of reorganization and realignments in future.

The movement-parties entered the political scene in the first period and were transformed into quasi-political parties in the second. To some extent, they represented the 'original' and 'ideal' unity of society and party, even though they were fragile and transitory political phenomena, not yet suitable for the role of political parties in a competitive multiparty system. They had no stable or definite membership, just participants in their actions. A cult of spontaneity allowed them to overcome the division between everyday life and politics, making horizontal ties dominant over vertical ones. Leadership roles were based on personal authority and not on the elected posts of the party hierarchy. The programmes were vague, emotionally supported and directly connected with such actions as mass demonstrations. These movement-parties and their social movements played a big role in ECE right before and after the collapse of the former system, but they had to transform themselves step by step into real parties. This turning point came in Hungary in late 1989, in Poland and Czecho-Slovakia in late 1990, but has not yet been fully achieved in Slovakia, where the HZDS, as the largest party, has tried to preserve its emotional features, maintaining itself as a populist movement.[9]

In the second period, however, the parties attract some stable members, initially as networks and/or movement parties, and by this they take the first steps towards becoming national organizations with party programmes. Before the first founding elections, the early political organizations were under pressure to decide whether they would, or could, become real parties instead of the previous travestita parties. This was the honeymoon period for the newly emerging parties since the new legal regulations favoured parties over other organizations, e.g., over organized interests and civil society associations. Therefore many interest organizations opted for a party structure in order to be able to exert pressure in the political arena; since then the borderline between macro- and meso-systems, parties and organized interests, has remained blurred. Actually all important newly created parties had already won some power, or at least political influence, through negotiating mechanisms between the government and opposition, but their political strength was still unclear before the elections.

The overparticization process had already begun in the second period. The parties became the major actors in the political transformation, and during their formation process they used and abused all their available resources. This is why virtually all socio-political forces sought to be organized as parties, otherwise they would have been left out of politics. The parties were, however, more successful externally than internally, i.e. they succeeded in pushing out other actors from politics, but they were not very successful in organizing themselves. Their organizational deficit was clear even in this dynamic period. The ECE societies were activized and overpoliticized, but the parties' social existence remained minimal, since people did not join parties in great numbers and the national organizations remained weak. Therefore the biggest difficulty for the parties was how to transform themselves from movement-parties with loose organizations and spontaneous action (which had the broad support of the population) to organized parties with a disciplined membership, regular and formalized meetings, and an extended party bureaucracy and professional leadership. Even the most successful newly born parties were only elite parties led by a small group of intellectuals with a rather small and inactive membership.[10]

The crucial turning point for the parties came after the first elections through the transference of power and the initiation of the parliamentarization process. The overparticization was reinforced by the winners, the parliamentary parties, which acted aggressively in excluding both other non-party actors and the non-parliamentary parties from politics. Their justification was based upon the particularistic nature of other organizations compared to parties representing more general, if not national, interests. Exclusion was also presented as a means of protecting parliamentary democracy from 'corporative' organized interests which were, supposedly, delegitimized by their participation in the former political system. At the same time, the parliamentary parties concentrated all the resources available in political and public life on themselves, which made the 'entrance fee' into politics too high for the other parties. There was one historic occasion following the first elections when parties were given accommodation for their headquarters in large office buildings, along with many other privileges. The democratic institutionalization of macro-politics — parties, parliament and government — had to take place quickly and its actors asserted their rights definitively and aggressively.[11]

The biggest challenge to the parties' structure was certainly their participation in power with all its consequences. The parties were, even before the elections, organized from above by small groups of intellectual elites who took the initiative. Rather shockingly, after the elections, this top-down approach quickly became the absolute predominant pattern. Over-particization and over-parliamentarization have reinforced each other and politics has again become a realm remote from the people, but this time on a multiparty basis. The size of the party membership first increased quickly in the parliamentarization phase, then it began to decline slowly after a peak. The parliamentary parties remained relatively small. They still monopolize the public scene by having privileged access to the media. This sorting process among the parties produced by the first elections was both necessary and unavoidable, yet at the same time, it has been excessive and counter-productive. The selfishness of parliamentary parties and their eagerness to become the only actors in the political game backfired and isolated the parliamentary parties even more from society as a whole.

The political parties had to turn themselves inside out in order to organize themselves under the new, powerful pressure of parliamentarization. This occurred in two ways: in parliament as party factions with their leaderships and expert teams; and within the party as a relationship between the newly 'parliamentarized' leadership and the larger membership. For some time, the parties had very few leading personalities and an even smaller group of experts. The leadership of party and parliamentary factions merged, suddenly increasing the gap between the narrow party elite and rank-and-file members. The new organizational pressure appeared in the relationship between (a) the party elite and the basic party organizations, (b) the party and its original social movement, and (c) the party elite and the media.

The relationship to the media turned out to be vital for these new parliamentary parties in at least three respects:

1) The new party leaders were intellectuals with extreme sensitivity and vanity concerning the press, the opinions of their former colleagues and those of their own former socio-cultural milieu.
2) The new parties were engaged in a cultural war among themselves because of their vague and over-ideologized programmes and 'tribal', sub-cultural political profiles. In this cultural war, the media played an essential role.
3) Intensive media contacts helped the party leaders compensate for the party's organizational deficit and for the weakness of the national organization with its missing communication channels within the party. In fact, media messages became a substitute for regular party meetings.

The social vacuum in and around the new parties has been reinforced by overparticization in the parliamentarization stage. It has weakened their 'conversion' function. They have been largely unable to articulate and aggregate social demands into programme packages as political alternatives at the national level. The more they have attempted to create an independent political profile, the more similar and indistinguishable they have become on basic issues of social and economic policy. The genetic defect of the ECE party systems is that most parties claim to represent the whole nation directly and without any distinction between, or special preference for, the particular interests of some social strata or classes. It should be noted, however, that there is a small group of parties which are still 'travestita interest organizations'. They represent the very particularistic interests of some social strata directly and rigidly. But these organized interests, in the form of parties, are exceptions and the 'national' parties dominate on the political scene. 'The national' parties are exclusivist and overcompetitive, but as all premature or pseudo-catch parties, they are still faceless to the general population. The parties lack a solid party identity of their own. Consequently, party identification is also very weak among their voters. Since they are so weak in the social wilderness, the parties rely much on their privileged political power, which creates, by means of this vicious circle, more and more social alienation from politics.[12]

As this analysis shows, the ECE parties are not really fully developed parties yet. They are either above this level, claiming to be the only 'national' party (state-party complex), or below this level as barely concealed representatives of the specific organized interests (interest organization complex). With all these setbacks, the parties have developed significantly in the parliamentarization stage, first of all in an organizational-institutionalizational aspect. Considerable structural differentiation has occurred inside the parliamentary parties among various party institutions. This has taken the form of special departments in the party headquarters. Role differentiation along the lines of the Weberian division of labour between political leaders, party administrators and special expert teams has also progressed. The parties have been the major actors in the parliamentarization process, but they have also been the most important products of this process, although still unfinished with both institutional and cultural deficits.

In spite of this contradiction, the parties and party systems in ECE have to some extent entered the fourth stage of their emergence. The widening of politics has become a vital necessity for the parties, although they have only hesitantly given up their monopoly over political roles. Yet, the opening of the national political scene has begun, step by step, to organized interests and civil society associations in the pre-parliamentary stage of the decision-making process. The low level of organization of the political meso-systems (the missing middle) and its fragility has always been the weakest point in the ECE political systems, as has the missing link between the parties and the population been. There has been a lack of functional democracy which could provide macro-politics with interest articulation and aggregation. This unfortunate historical heritage must now be overcome. To examine this Central European negative tradition more closely, we must turn to the problems of the cultural over-determination (tribalization) of ECE political life, including the parties themselves. Finally, we analyse the present situation of the ECE party systems, giving a composite picture of the parties.

Culture versus Organizations: The Linz Thesis

Central Europe moves in long historical cycles of redemocratization. In this century, the present 'wave' constitutes the third attempt at democratization. Former attempts (after World War I and World War II) failed above all because of unfavourable international circumstances. In the present redemocratization process, after four decades of authoritarian rule, we have not in fact a party formation process, but a 're-formation' process, i.e., a re-emergence of the real multiparty system for the third time. What is manifest in this process is that generally it is not the same parties that re-emerge after a long time-span. The few historical parties which do re-surface are relatively weak and not dominant in the new party system. At the same time, it is not the 'hard' social factors such as the socio-economic structure, but evidently the 'soft' ones such as the cultural ('tribal') factors that are decisive in this party formation process. In short, we face the dilemma of institutional discontinuity and politico-cultural continuity.

As far as I know, this phenomenon was first described and theoretised by Juan Linz concerning the party formation process in Spain. Linz's thesis offers a key to explaining the same process in ECE. Linz stresses the contrast between institutional discontinuity and politico-cultural continuity in the redemo-cratization process, first of all during party formation following authoritarian rule. This may be the general situation, indeed, in all redemocratizations. As Maurizio Cotta points out, the longer the authoritarian rule has lasted, the less the chance of reviving the former organizational structures, or the less they are able to serve as an adequate institutional base for redemocratization. At the same time, somewhat surprisingly, the cultural patterns, the political sub-cultures or mentality types, models of political behaviour or attitudes, political discourses, and the like, persist for a long time. Even following long periods of authoritarian rule, they are the most active factors in democratic transitions and in the shaping of new institutions.[13]

Thus, the relatively autonomous cultural factors, which have persisted in a hidden way, are decisive in the first periods of redemocratization, since these are the only models to which people can return. The re-emerging multiparty systems in ECE are entirely newly organized, based mostly on parties without an organizational prehistory. The historical parties, those re-emerging within the old institutional framework, are much less important. The parties and their interrelationship reflect, however, the traditions of the various political sub-cultures including their beliefs and behaviours. The past determines the present, not so much through an institutional continuity as in advanced democracies where institutions persist without longer interruptions, but mainly through a politico-cultural continuity. The enduring and inherited cultural and/or mental structures recreate the multiparty system in the redemocratization process, not by reviving the same former parties but by forming new parties to represent and embody the same 'idea', the same political sub-culture.

It is very difficult to revive a political organization after forty years of dormancy and the original organization becomes outdated, less and less suitable to represent the same 'idea'. The most obvious obstacles to the reorganization of a former party are its surviving leaders and members, who are hopelessly aged, frustrated and outdated, but still aggressively fighting for personal compensation and leadership roles. They try to monopolize the 'brand-name' of the party on the political market for themselves and for their own renewed political career, and these efforts deter younger generations from participation in that party — which precludes the necessary modernization or adjustment, not to mention intergenerational reproduction. As this case of political suicide proves, the revival of cultural traditions is not at all always positive; negative traditions may also return with a vengeance. Still this cultural 'renaissance' is overwhelmingly positive. The ECE countries have their democratic traditions in the multiparty systems as well, and they revigorate them quickly and successfully, creating new parties instead of former ones in order to leave behind the rigid, 'archaic' structures and to produce new and flexible ones, adjusted to the present situation. The same political sub-culture organizes a new party for itself again and again. As the Linz Thesis suggests also for ECE, real continuity appears in the cultural factors, and the institutional continuity for redemocratization is only a secondary and derived one; primarily the cultural factors determine the party formation process.

This 'longue durée' view already indicates that the party formation process in ECE concerning the party-society relationship cannot be reduced to the problems of overcoming state socialism. It is also a question of much deeper and longer Central European traditions. Following the logic of redemocratization, parties always begin from a zero level, compared to any institutional existence in the former democratization period. New-old parties simply seem to reject the former model and try to overcome it completely while looking for a more modern form of organization. The actual party formation process is, however, much more complicated from the organizational perspective as well, since this process does not occur in an organizational vacuum; other organizational models and traditions can be found in ECE.

As is well known, traditional Central European political systems have been mixed regimes, mostly authoritarian types but with some democratic features varying in proportion from country to country, and from one particular historical period to another. When parties start to organize their institutional structures nowadays, they have actually two opposing models. First, the loose model of social movements as in their current prehistory, in which organization and action are in an early, undifferentiated unity; this has to be overcome to achieve real political existence in a competitive multiparty system. The second model is the traditional party model, which has survived the last century and was shaken only in the brief periods of redemocratization: the model of hegemonic or state-parties. This hegemonic or state party is a 'national' party, actually the only real power-party even in a multiparty system; because it is so dominant, it fuses with the state and public administration. Furthermore, it is based on an economic 'clientura' and it secures its re-election in the long term even in 'free and fair' democratic elections.

Consequently, the major contradiction of the ECE party formation process is that the newly emerging parties, with many difficulties, switched very quickly from loose movement-parties — representing some kind of unity of parties and society — to rigidly-organized power-parties — expressing the new separation of parties and society — approaching the traditional type of hegemonic parties. In order to analyze the revival of this type of party structure in ECE, it is now time to turn to the ECE party systems.

The Major Features of the ECE Party Systems

a) The Succession Process of Hegemonic Parties

The movement-party, functioning as an umbrella organization, was the dominant type of party in the early transition period in ECE. This typical model during political transition was represented first of all by the Polish Solidarity, followed by the Hungarian Democratic Forum; later on, these Forum-type parties were organized everywhere in ECE. This family of transitory parties, or pre-parties, suddenly declined after the power transition and finally disappeared everywhere. This has had two major consequences. The first is the legacy of the 'national' party, i.e., the alleged legitimacy and strong claim by one party to represent the whole nation, disqualifing all others as 'anti-national' or disturbing national unity. The second is the disintegration of the movement-parties causing frustration at the disappearance of the party-society closeness in the form of a high level of popular participation.

The other type of party determining the face of the ECE party systems is the hegemonic or state-party, which was well-known during the long 'pre-communist', authoritarian, or half-democratic periods. The whole present party system of the ECE countries reflects the contradictions of the path by which parliamentary parties turned from movement-parties to power-parties, as self-styled quasi-hegemonic parties. In the Central European tradition, the ruling hegemonic or state-parties had a rather large membership, actually almost the whole 'political class', united in one party. The members of the hegemonic parties offered their political loyalties to the party leadership in exchange for particular economic and social benefits. When a systemic change came, because of the transformation of the world system, most party members of the ruling party rapidly joined the newly emerging ruling party, even those from opposite political and ideological poles. This succession process has created an organizational as well as a cultural continuity for hegemonic parties across systemic changes, i.e., in organizational design and political culture.

The same succession process could be observed immediately after World War II when the members of the defeated right-wing parties rushed to the victoriously emerging communist parties. The same movement happened again in the late eighties in the opposite direction. Thus, the well-known succession process has taken place recently as well, since the former party members reappeared in large numbers in the newly emerging oppositional parties. One new umbrella organization, the Hungarian Democratic Forum, even allowed dual party membership in 1988-89. As a significant proportion of the MPs and party members from the new ruling parties after the first free elections came from the former ruling parties, it is no wonder that there has been so much continuity in organization and culture between the old and new parties, as evidenced by the top-down organizational rigidity and the arrogance of the new leaders. The commonsensical Western analysis is, therefore, completely mistaken in considering the 'post-communist' parties as the only successor-parties. Consequently, the gap or contrast between the post-communist and newly emerging parties has not been as great as the 'black and white' approach suggests, and as the leaders of the new parties claim. Actually, in most cases, even the opposite may be true, since after the first elections the new parties came to power and they inherited the mantle of the traditional hegemonic state-parties. History, of course, does not repeat itself completely, but without seeing the rebirth of the hegemonic parties as a tendency in ECE, we cannot understand the present widespread popular alienation from politics.

b) The Multidimensional Model of Party Systems

It is clear in the ECE party literature that a multidimensional model is needed to characterize the Central European party systems — at least, a model with two axes, e.g. that of Left-Right and Traditionalism-Modernism (or Provincial-ism-Europeanism). This multidimensional model in a simplified form with two axes is quite common in the Hungarian and Polish debates on party systems, sometimes in different formulations with the role of the state versus individual liberties as the second axis. As Olson notes:

The many parties of post-Communist countries do not easily fit into a left-right scale, conventional in Western Democracies. The very fluidity of leadership, structure, formation and programme precludes any orderly placement on a single dimension. Neither has public opinion coalesced into a single dimensional structure. (Olson, 1993: 631).

Some writers have identified three major dimensions, (1) economic issues, (2) secularism and (3) decommunization, or (1) statism-liberalism, (2) clericalismsecularism and (3) nationalism-Europeanism, but usually only two major political camps: national-Christian-rural and liberal-westernized-urban (see also Kitschelt, 1992 and Glaessner, 1994).

This dual view has been reinforced by the latest political developments. The particular party complex which can only be characterized as traditionalism-conservatism and nationalism-populism came to the fore first during the early democratic transition in the form of the new ruling parties. Consequently, in the East Central European party systems, new frontlines have emerged between Traditionalizers and Europeanizers, partially interwoven with the new-old contradictions of Left and Right. The rebirth of the old party-state in a new, milder and traditionalist-conservative form is still nowadays the biggest obstacle to Europeanization and modernization, as Adam Michnik has warned several times (see e.g. Michnik, 1991).

I suggest that there have been four major types of parties in ECE defined by their place in the party systems: the Europeanizer Left, the Europeanizer Right, the Traditionalizer Left and the Traditionalizer Right. First, in the parliamentarization phase, the victory of the single, broad and amorphous movement-party over the former ruling party, as in Poland, creates confusion. This large 'anti-communist' party proves to be many parties in one, and these sub-parties diverge immediately on all the other basic issues of traditionalism and modernism. As the Polish case between 1991-93 has clearly shown, it is impossible to form a stable coalition between the Europeanizer Right and the Traditionalizer Right. At the latest elections in the ECE countries, party fragmentation and polarization have somewhat decreased, although the Right in general and the Traditionalist Right, in particular, has remained very fragmented in Poland and Hungary, as has the re-emerging Left in the Czech and Slovak Republics. The Europeanizer parties, however, both left and right, have come to the fore (except in Slovakia) and this is why there is now a chance of achieving a more balanced and less over-ideologized relationship between the leading parties, thus allowing the consolidation process of parties and party systems to begin.

c) Consolidation of Party Systems

The Southern European and then ECE developments have shown that strongly organized parties opt for strong parliamentary government, while weakly organized parties in Latin America and Eastern Europe encourage presidential systems and personal leadership. This helps explain contrasts between the Latin American and South European developments, but our concern here is only to show the relative closeness of the ECE developments to Southern European democratization. The 'strong parties and strong parliamentarism' connection has increasingly dominated, however, in all four ECE countries, as the parties have become stronger and better organized in the Czech and Slovak Republics and in Poland as well. The tension between strong parliamentarism and presidential powers has also recently increased in these countries.

Democratic consolidation as the next step of the institutionalization process must be initiated and accomplished by the consolidation of the party systems through a 'rupture' with traditionalism and the promotion of Europeanization. In the case of party development, Europeanization means new types of linkages between parties and society, and a social dialogue, institutionalized via solid contacts between political parties and interest organizations. As G. Pridham (1991:37) emphasizes,

Consolidation through parties is characterized, above all, by the organization and expansion of the party structures and the party system as a whole, which is then able to control and, if need be, moderate and integrate all forms of participation. (...) Clear, long term alignments between parties and social groups are established. Identities and rules or internal competition among the party elites are formed.

Political party consolidation has at least two aspects. The first is the 'external' consolidation, i.e., through social contacts and the establishment of firm relationships between macro- and meso-politics, parties and organized interests. The second aspect is internal, through a further and 'final' institutionalization process of parties, 'incrementally through piecemeal changes', as Haggard and Kaufman (1994:15) suggest:

Party-system consolidation can be encouraged through a number of different institutional reforms (...) Party systems, of course, often reflect social and cultural cleavages that will persist even after the implementation of changes in electoral rules. Even so, such changes can make a considerable difference in reducing party-system instability.[14]

d) Conclusion: The Hypothesis of the Early Freezing of Parties in ECE

Altogether, the ECE party systems as well as the parties themselves have already reached an early 'freezing' as a first stage of maturation. Individual parties and the structure of party systems have become almost ready and quasi-consolidated. They have not yet reached by far the West European stability levels, but the ECE party systems will keep their regional particularities, just as the SE party systems have kept theirs after the first phase of Europeanization. Therefore, we can concur with Olson's statement based on the findings of ECE analysts:

Parties now developing in Central Europe may very well evolve their own distinctive traits, not closely resembling those currently known in western democracies. The range of possible structure and behavior is much wider in the new democracies simply because they are starting anew. While their leaders are acutely aware of at least some western democratic practices, and while many attempt to duplicate what they see, their new circumstances have the potential to lead to entirely new political structures and behaviors than currently known and which the participants themselves cannot currently foresee. We are perhaps witnessing the 'freezing moment' of the new party systems of post-communist countries. (Olson, 1993:620).[15]

This hypothesis might seem to contradict the mainstream argumentation of this paper about the social vacuum in and around these 'half-created' parties and party systems, but it does not. If we take two factors into account, we can see why this early freezing has occurred. The first one is rather obvious: the ECE parties can survive internationally and domestically only if they fit into the West European party systems, i.e. into the party Internationals. These Internationals established a mandatory framework for all the major types of ECE parties, they support and protect them, by forcing them through a political learning process. The shape of individual parties and the structure of the party system exist for the ECE parties in the EU as an expectation they have to meet in order to be accepted. Therefore there is actually not too much of a chance for late-comers or 'non-standard parties' (as the Slovak political scientists call the 'outsiders'), but there is a good chance for a further selection, fusion or disappearance of parties belonging to the same family of parties. Altogether, the party structures may be fragile. Some parties can still emerge and/or disappear, but the major actors are already on the political scene and future transformations (except for Slovakia) will be only marginal.

The second conditioning factor operates domestically and it is much less obvious than the international one but its impact is much more intense. The existing bigger parties have already represented the major political alternatives and occupied the political space. There is, therefore, little chance for a new party to speak for a large unrepresented constituency. Furthermore, nowadays, in the fourth stage of the party formation process, the social strata are reconquering the parties, making them more and more suitable to represent their views. Thus after the 'culturalization' phase the parties have now entered the 'socialization' phase, in which socio-economic constraints and pressures create closer linkages between some parties and their respective social bases. Both the individual parties and the party structures become more and more arranged according to the cleavages of the Lipset-Rokkan model. After at least two general elections, the parties have developed a greater capacity for social dialogue and particular preferences for the specific demands of social strata. While still a long way from the well-established 'Rokkanian' parties and party systems, the same parties and the same party systems have to go through the next phase of the maturation process (see Ágh and Ilonszki, 1996).

This argument suggests on the one hand that the ECE parties and party systems have been getting closer to the West European ones in their major features, although the overparticization as a transitory feature has also indicated some regional peculiarities. In 1984 Bartolini and Mair wrote in their 'Introduction' to Party Politics in Contemporary Western Europe that 'in Spain, as in Greece, the key question concerns whether existing typologies offer appropriate models for these new party systems' (Bartolini and Mair, 1984:3). In 1995 we are in a similar situation in Central Europe. The real problem is, indeed, whether the party system of the young ECE democracies is 'identifiable in terms of typologies devised for the more established party systems in Western Europe' (Bartolini and Mair, 1984:4). Obviously, the answer is negative, the West European models cannot be directly applied to ECE which has a specific process of party formation. At the same time the partial and cautious application of West European models and theories is necessary and unavoidable.

My closing hypothesis is that the specific feature of ECE parties, i.e. overparticization, has gradually turned into a new phenomenon of 'cartel parties'. As it is known, Katz and Mair have recently presented their ideas about the cartel parties as a new phase of the Western party development (Katz and Mair, 1995:16). The cartel party as a tendency means that the (bigger) parties have common interests and use the state for their purposes. I suggest that this Western tendency of the mature party systems has appeared as a 'premature senility' in the ECE parties and party systems, bringing along a new and 'consolidated' situation of the alienation of the population from politics. In these terms, the ECE parties and party systems have covered a party formation process from the original 'movement parties' to the newly emerging, relatively consolidated 'cartel parties'.

Notes

1. I have already tested this four-level model on the Hungarian Socialist Party (see Ágh, 1995a), which is 'socially' the most advanced party in the region, i.e. its social existence is at least as developed as its political existence. In this paper, I try to illustrate my theoretical findings concerning the Hungarian party system. Usually it is very difficult to obtain reliable data on the ECE parties since they are either not available or are very inflated due to the permanent campaign situation. But the situation in Hungary is much easier. Since 1988 my Department at the Budapest University of Economics has published the Political Yearbook of Hungary, so data, documentation and analyses on parties in Hungary are easily available in these volumes.

2. I have created (with László Szarvas) a 'matrix' of the programmes of eight Hungarian parties concerning 12 policy issues prior to the 1994 elections (published in Magyar Hirlap, a Budapest daily on 15 April 1994), which has shown that in most cases the programmes of parties differ only in small details. Their behaviour when in power and their actual policies, however, differ greatly.

3. The membership figures of the six Hungarian parliamentary parties are, approximatively, as follows: Hungarian Socialist Party (HSP), 45,000; Alliance of Free Democrats (AFD), 35,000; Hungarian Democratic Forum (HDF), 30,000; Independent Smallholders Party (ISP), 60,000 (a highly inflated figure); Christian Democratic People's Party (CDPP), 20,000; Alliance of Young Democrats (Fidesz) 15,000. The relative size of the party membership reflects rather closely the relative proportion of votes cast for that party at the 1994 election.

4. Hungary has about 3,000 settlements. The HSP has about 400 local organizations (and about 2,000 basic organizations), the other parties have at most 200-400 basic organizations, usually only in the rather big settlements. This means that while these parties have national headquarters and county level organizations, below them the network of local organizations is largely missing. Actual party life exists largely only in the capitals of the counties, otherwise it is rare and irregular.

5. The four 'national' parties in Hungary usually offer solutions in their programmes for all strata. The exceptions among the parliamentary parties are the two small historical parties, the ISP and the CDPP (in 1995 with 6.7 and 5.7 per cent of the seats, respectively). The ISP is an organized interest group for the traditional peasantry and the CDPP acts as the 'Church trade union'.

6. In parliamentary democracy, all parliamentary parties have some share in the power and decision-making, if not elsewhere then at least in standing committees. In Hungary, we have had a constitutional requirement of a two-third majority in the case of fundamental laws. So in the First Parliament (1990-94), the coalition needed the cooperation of the opposition to pass or amend these 'fundamental' laws.

7. In Hungary, the Act on Parties (October 1989) also regulated the party finances and state subsidies for parties. The Hungarian budget supported the parties with 700 million forints in 1991 and with 1,100 million forints in 1995 (7 million and 11 million dollars, respectively). Between 1990 and 1995, most of this financial support has been given to the six parliamentary parties, with a smaller portion going to the non-parliamentary parties (to those above one per cent in the latest election; altogether seven, after the 1994 election, four parties received some support in this category). The percentages of state finances in 1990 of the total budgets of the respective parties were: ISP (93.1), CDPP (88.0), Fidesz (83.8), AFD (57.9), HDF (44.8) and HSP (33.6). This shows that the historical parties are financially weak and state-dependent, while the HSP, with its large membership and regularly paid membership fees, is the least state-dependent.

8. In my paper (Ágh, 1994a), I have tried to analyze this cultural dimension closely by describing the five major types of political discourse in ECE and the three levels of the cultural manifestations (as 'customs', 'worldviews' and 'ideologies').

9. The HDF as a movement was formed in September 1987 at a meeting in Lakitelek, where a group of 'populist' writers, public figures and social scientists issued an organizing declaration. The AFD emerged as a group of urban intellectuals, based on the hard core of the 'democratic opposition'. Fidesz was originally a group of law students. The roots of the HSP were in the reform circles centred around the leading reformist intellectuals of the ruling party, who decisively were turned against the official line. As of November 1988, all of the four major parties had emerged on the scene as opposition movements; the two historical parties were re-activized much later, after much hesitation, and lacked a base in a social movement.

10. The most difficult issue for the new parties was the transformation from movements or networks to real parties with membership, leadership and discipline. The ruling party, the Hungarian Socialist Workers Party, passed a Central Committee resolution supporting a multiparty system on 11 February 1989 which first legalized the new parties. In March 1989, an Oppositional Round-table was formed, first with eight then with nine members. Five of the members of this Roundtable are now parliamentary parties (AFD, HDF, ISP, CDPP and Fidesz), two members failed to become parliamentary parties (Hungarian Socialdemocratic Party and Hungarian People's Party), and two other members were and remain purely social organizations (Society 'Bajcsy Zsilinszky' and League of Free Trade Unions). When the act on parties was passed by parliament in October 1989, most socio-political organizations were very far from being parties, but nevertheless decided to become parties because it was in many ways advantageous.

11. In Hungary at the end of 1989, there were about 120 parties, giving rise to what I call the 'hundred-party-system'. Out of the 120 parties, 66 registered for the first parliamentary elections and 12 were able to establish a national list. The 1990 elections caused a cruel 'natural selection'; only six organizations were able to become parliamentary parties and only a few parties survived outside parliament. The 1994 election reinforced the same six parliamentary parties, although with markedly different results. Thus, the party system has been relatively stable from its very beginning in 1988 with the same leading parties; this was because the party formation process in Hungary began very early and was gradual.

12. F. Plasser and P. Ulram point out in a recent comparative study (see their Table 6: Confidence in Institutions in East-Central Europe, 1994: 13) that political parties in six Central and East European countries usually have least confidence, in most cases less than the parliaments. These data are as follows with figures in percentages, first for parliaments and second for parties: East Germany (26-18), Czech Republic (32-24), Slovak Republic (22-6), Hungary (23-11), Poland

(24-8) and Russia (12-14). It is noteworthy that the prestige of parties is lowest in Hungary and Poland where the multiparty system was formed first.

13. I have found the first reference to the Linz Thesis in Pridham (1991: 8), quoting a paper by Linz in Spanish from 1987. The idea was further developed in Cotta (1991) dealing with the redemocratization in Southern and Central Europe. I have tried to apply the Linz Thesis to the ECE party systems in detail in several papers, initially in Ágh (1993).

14. In a recent book, Glaessner (1994) gives an in-depth analysis of all the actors of transition, including the parties as major actors in early consolidation processes. Glaessner also indicates that the main contradiction of the ECE party systems is between the 'Strukturkonservative' and 'Modernisierer' parties (Glaessner, 1994: 260).

15. Remington analyses the 'freezing' problem extensively in both the introductory and closing chapters of his book (Remington, 1994: 5-12 and 220-230).

Bibliography

Ágh, Attila 1993. 'The Emerging Party Systems in East Central Europe', *Aula*. Budapest, vol. 16, (3): 26-54.

Ágh, Attila 1994a. 'The invention of democratic tradition in Hungary', in Gy. Csepeli et al. (eds.), *From Subject to Citizen*. Budapest: Hungarian Centre for Political Education: 218-45.

Ágh, Attila 1994b. 'The Hungarian Party System and Party Theory in the Transition of Central Europe', in *Journal of Theoretical Politics*. vol. 6, (2), April 1994: 217-38.

Ágh, Attila 1994c (ed.), *The Emergence of East Central European Parliaments: The First Steps*. Budapest: Hungarian Centre for Democracy Studies.

Ágh, Attila 1995a. 'The partial consolidation of the East Central European Parties: The Case of the Hungarian Socialist Party', in *Party Politics*, 1 (4) 1995: 48-64.

Ágh, Attila 1995b, (ed. with Sándor Kurtán). *Democratization and Europeanization in Hungary: The First Parliament, 1990-1994*. Budapest: Hungarian Centre for Democracy Studies.

Ágh, Attila 1996, (ed. with Gabriella Ilonszki). *Parliaments and Organized Interests in Central Europe: The Second Steps*. Budapest: Hungarian Centre for Democracy Studies.

Batt, Judy 1991. *East Central Europe from Reform to Transformation*. London: Pinter.

Bartolini, Stefano and Peter Mair (eds.) 1984. *Party Politics in Contemporary Western Europe*. London: Frank Cass.

Butorová, Zora and Martin Bútora, 1994. 'Political Parties and Slovakia's Road to Independence', in *Csepeli* et al. (eds.): 319-39.

Cotta, Maurizio 1991. 'Transition to Democracy and the Building of New Party Systems: The East European Cases in Comparative Perspective', paper presented at the Joint Sessions of ECPR, Essex, 22-28 March 1991.

Cotta, Maurizio 1992. *New Party Systems after the Dictatorship*. Siena: University of Siena Press.

East, Roger 1992. *Revolutions in Eastern Europe.* London: Pinter.

Flores Juberias, Carlos 1994. 'The Transformation of Electoral Systems in Eastern Europe and its Political Consequences', paper presented at the 16th World Congress of the IPSA, 21-25 August 1994, Berlin.

Gebethner, Stanislaw 1993. 'Political Parties in Poland (1989-93)', in Gerd Meyer (ed.), *Die Politischen Parteien Ostmitteleuropas in Umbruch.* Tübingen: Francke Verlag.

Glaessner, Gert-Joachim 1994. *Demokratie nach dem Ende des Kommunismus.* Opladen: Westdeutscher Verlag.

Haggard, Stephan and Robert Kaufman, 1994. 'The Challenges of Consolidation', *Journal of Democracy.* vol. 5, (4), October 1994: 5-16.

Hofrichter, Jürgen and Inge Weller, 1993. *On the application of the left-right schema in Central and Eastern Eurobarometer Surveys.* Mannheim: Zeus.

Katz, Richard and Peter Mair, 1995. 'Changing Models of Party Organization and Party Democracy: The Emergence of the Cartel Party', in *Party Politics,* vol. 1, (1), January 1995: 5-28.

Katz, Richard and Peter Mair, 1994. *How Parties Organize.* London: Sage.

Kitschelt, Herbert 1992. 'The Formation of Party Systems in East Central Europe', in *Politics and Society,* (20): 7-50.

Kurtán, Sándor et al. (eds.) 1988-1994. *The Political Yearbook of Hungary.* Budapest: Hungarian Centre for Democracy Studies.

Linz, Juan 1987. 'Il sistema partitico spagnolo', in *Rivista Italiana di Scienza Politica,* (3).

Mangott, Gerhard 1992. 'Parteienbildung und Parteiensysteme in Ost-Mitteleuropa im Vergleich', in Peter Gerlich et al. (eds.), *Regimewechsel: Demokratisierung und politische Kultur in Ost-Mitteleuropa.* Vienna: Böhlau.

Michnik, Adam 1991. 'Zwei Visionen eines posttotalitaeren Europas', in Rainer Deppe et al. (eds.), *Demokratischer Umbruch in Osteuropa.* Frankfurt: Suhrkamp.

Olson, David 1993. 'Political Parties and Party Systems in Regime Transformation: Inner Transition in the New Democracies of Central Europe', in William Crotty (special editor), *Political Parties in a Changing Age,* a special issue of *The American Review of Politics,* vol. 14. Winter: 619-58.

Plasser, Fritz 1994. 'Measuring Political Culture in East-Central Europe', paper prepared for the conference on political culture in East-Central Europe, 14-16 September 1994, Vienna.

Plasser, Fritz and Peter Ulram, 1994. 'Monitoring Democratic Consolidation: Political Trust and System Support in East-Central Europe', paper prepared for the 16th World Congress of the IPSA, 21-25 August 1994, Berlin.

Pridham, Geoffrey (ed.), 1990. *Securing Democracy: Political Parties and Democratic Consolidation in Southern Europe.* London and New York: Routledge.

Pridham, Geoffrey 1991. 'Southern European Models of Democratic Transition and Inter-Regional Comparisons: A Precedent for Eastern Europe?', paper presented at the Joint Sessions of ECPR, Essex, 22-28 March 1991.

Remington, Thomas (ed.) 1994. 'Introduction' and 'Conclusion', *Parliaments in Transition.* Boulder: Westview Press.

Reschova, Jana and Jindriska Syllová, 1994. 'The Legislature in the Czech Republic: 1993', *Budapest Papers on Democratic Transition*, (103): 1-49.

Schmitter, Philippe C. and Terry Karl, 1992. 'The Types of Democracy Emerging in Southern and Eastern Europe and South and Central America', in Peter M.E. Volten (ed.), *Bound to Change: Consolidating Democracy in East Central Europe*. New York and Prague: Institute for East West Studies (distributed by Westview Press).

Szajkowski, Bogdan (ed.) 1991. *New Political Parties of Eastern Europe and the Soviet Union*. Harlow (Essex): Longman.

Wessels, Bernhard and Hans-Dieter Klingemann, 1994. *Democratic Transformation and the Prerequisites of Democratic Opposition in East and Central Europe*. Wissenschaftszentrum Berlin für Sozialforschung, (FS III 94-201): 1-37.

White, Stephen, Judy Batt, and Paul G. Lewis, 1993. *Developments in East European Politics*. Durham, N.C.: Duke University Press.

Whitefield, Stephen and Geoffrey Evans, 1994. 'The Ideological Bases of Political Competition in Eastern Europe', *APSA paper*, New York Annual Meeting: 1-19.

Democracy and Parliament in Czech Politics

Peter Bugge

In the euphoric days of 1989, many predicted Eastern Europe's *return to Europe*, after decades of Soviet hegemony, via a rapid transition from one-party rule and inefficient state-planning to democracy and market prosperity. Since then the transformations in the region have proven so problematic and conflict-ridden that the goals of 1989 seem to have disappeared from the agenda. The *civil war* (Enzensberger) and *clash of civilizations* (Huntington) have replaced *Europe without borders* as the dominant metaphors for today, and even the 'avantgarde' of the East, the Visegrad countries, is in danger of landing again on the wrong side of a Western drawn borderline between 'us' and 'them'.

In this situation, the Czech Republic has attained — or at least very eagerly claimed — an exceptional status as a paragon for the whole region. The Czech achievements *are* remarkable: political and social stability prevails, the ex-communists have made no political come-back, privatization has been a success, the economy is healthy, human rights are respected, a multi-party system and a free press has emerged. Václav Havel may thus (at least in the Czech case) be right when he demands that we stop calling his and other countries *post-communist* or *former members of the former Warsaw pact* and start respecting them instead for what they have become: almost normally functioning democracies (Havel 1994a: 2ff; 1994b: 3).

Liberal Democracy — a Czech Tradition!?

The Czech Republic's success has been attributed to its rather favourable economic and social starting position and its geo-political location, combined with the intelligent policies of its present leaders. But one often meets references also to an alleged strong *Czech liberal and democratic tradition* which promotes Czech commitment to, and understanding of, Western democratic principles. This tradition made it 'natural' for the Czechs to 'pick up' after 1989 where they 'left off' five and four decades earlier when Nazism and Communism intervened. In his first presidential New Year's speech, Václav Havel spoke of *the humanistic and democratic traditions* that 'slumbered somewhere in the subconscious of our nations and national minorities, and were discreetly transferred from generation to generation', only to reappear in 1989 (Havel 1990: 14), and recently he described the Czechoslovak state founded in 1918 as 'modern, democratic, liberal, based on values, which all democratic Europe today acknowledges and in which it sees its future.' (Havel 1995: 8).

One may also see present-day Czech developments explained in these terms in academic writings. Tony Judt mentions the Czech and Slovak *advantages of history — a strong liberal and democratic tradition...* (Judt 1992: 115), and according to the Czech sociologist Jiří Musil:

There can be no doubt that the event called 'the velvet revolution' was 'a rectifying revolution.' The Czech republic consciously endeavored to return to the evolutionary trajectory of its modern history, which laid great stress on liberal democracy. (Musil 1992: 179ff.)[1]

These views imply that a strong Czech liberal and democratic tradition may be historically identified, and that its inherent political norms and values have been capable of surviving forty years of Communist rule and of asserting themselves in the shaping of the new Czech political system after 1989.[2]

To test these assumptions we shall here examine the past and present role of parliament in Czech politics, since this institution (embedded in a proper constitutional framework) seems crucial to liberal democracy as commonly understood.

The Role of the Czech Parliament Today

A first striking feature is the low popular trust in the Czech parliament. Until December 1992, opinion polls spoke of a relatively stable level of trust at slightly above 50 per cent (the then significant Federal parliament, by contrast, experienced a rapid decline in trust as the Czech-Slovak constitutional crisis deepened), but as the Czech National Council became the sole existing parliament of the new Czech republic, respondents' trust has steadily declined until settling (since July 1993) at well below 30 per cent. At the same time, opinion polls do not reveal any general distrust of the political system as such, or major dissatisfaction with recent developments. Since July 1992, the government has in all polls enjoyed the trust of more than 50 per cent of the respondents and trust in president Havel is even higher. People also express satisfaction with their 'own' politicians, which makes their scepticism towards the forum in which these politicians work all the more remarkable.[3]

Several theories have been put forward to explain this fact. Journalists and others have claimed that most parties presented only second-rate politicians for the Czech National Council at the June 1992·elections, reserving their elite for the Federal Assembly, which was then, before the partition of Czechoslovakia, considered more important than the National Councils. Also, parliament's reluctance to pass a bill defining appropriate conduct in the event of a conflict of interests has created a public image of parliamentarians as self-interested individuals using their position for their own benefit only. The parliamentarians, obviously frustrated, have countered by attacking the press for conveying a biased image of their work. More substantially, they have complained about poor working conditions: a lack of equipment and secretarial help, and not having their own offices. Improvements have occurred — there is now one office for every two parliamentarians — and it awaits to be seen how this will affect the work of the House (Holub 1995: 10).

A more substantial obstacle to the effective functioning of parliament has been its standing orders, which — although amended four times — dated back to before 1989. Among other things, the standing orders granted the parliamentarians the right to bring amendments directly on the floor (Reschová, 1994, p. 68), which on several occasions led to confused and chaotic proceedings and to inconsistent legislation. Often, the government and the parliamentarians (even from the government coalition) have accused each other of presenting low quality draft bills. In April 1995, new standing orders were passed (coming into force on 1 August 1995) that aim at improving the legislative mechanism. Bills are only to be presented in paragraphed form, there will be three readings of each bill, and only written amendments are now allowed. The new standing orders also give extra financial support to oppositional 'clubs' (i.e. organized party factions), since the opposition cannot draw information from 'their' ministers. This is likely to strengthen parliament. At the same time, the number of parliamentarians required to form a club is raised from today's five to ten (*Lidové noviny*, 20 April 1995: 3). Since clubs are financially favoured and have exclusive access to seats in the standing committees, this amendment will inhibit dissenting factions and independents and increase the party discipline.[4]

The Czech Constitution itself leaves sufficient scope for the self-assertion of parliament, so a general assessment of parliament's position vis-a-vis the executive in the Czech political system must focus on more specific factors. David M. Olson, commenting upon the Federal Assembly, has noticed that 'if the opportunities for parliamentary activism are greatest in new democratic systems, their capacity to take advantage of those opportunities is the least' (Olson 1994: 37).

This holds true for the Czech parliament too, although its position is already considerably stabilized. Parliament still has a lot to say in the process of establishing procedures for its own and the government's work, and the lack of party discipline (although more widespread by far among opposition parties)[5] has often forced the government to take its parliamentary rank and file seriously. On the other hand, the strength of parliament in this respect is often of an 'obstructive' kind, since the above-mentioned lack of resources (especially as compared with the government) is a serious handicap. Also, unlike many of the present ministers, most parliamentarians lack experience — only 66 of the 200 parliamentarians elected in 1992 had a seat in the previous Czech National Assembly (Holub 1995: 11).

In one respect, parliament as an institution is severely crippled although, somewhat paradoxically, the present parliament may see this as an advantage: the Czech Constitution, passed with a large majority by the present parliament on 16 December, 1992, prescribes a bicameral parliament (Art. 15) with a House of Representatives (i.e., the former Czech National Council) elected by proportional vote and a Senate elected by majority vote (Art. 18). Yet the Senate has existed only on paper for nearly three years now, and neither the government, nor parliament has been able to see to its creation or, alternatively, to abandon it through a constitutional reform. It may be argued that legislation may proceed even without the Senate, that provisions exist for the rule of one chamber only (Art. 106, Section 2), and that the Senate has only limited powers (it has only a suspensive veto on legislation passed in the House of Representatives). But apart from showing disrespect for the letter of the law, the continual extension of this provisional arrangement may under special circumstances provoke a constitutional crisis since it deprives the President of the right to dissolve parliament and issue writs for new elections (Art 106, Section 3) (Gerloch 1994: 89f).[6]

The non-creation of the Senate is not the only example of contemporary neglect of constitutional provisions. Article 99 on territorial self-government insists that besides the local municipalities (*obce*), higher regional self-governing bodies in the shape of 'lands' or 'counties' (*země nebo kraje*) must be created. Yet here again this has not occurred. The ex-ODS parliamentarian Josef Ježek claims that the ODS (the Civic Democratic Party, by far the strongest government party) deliberately delays their formation to prevent a decentralization that would deprive the executive of much of its power over the elected officials. Ježek argues that parliament today would have great difficulty exerting control over the central branches of the executive (the ministries) and that parliament has no influence over the executive's regional branches whose leading officials are politically appointed, especially from the ranks of the ODS (Ježek 1994: 4). Ježek's accusations may be exaggerated, but a recent proposal to implement Art. 99, which enjoyed the support of three coalition parties and the Social Democrats, was again blocked by the ODS, whose leaders, including premier Klaus, have repeatedly stressed their lack of interest in seeing the present civil service 'burdened' with any further organs of public self-government.[7]

Eventually, however, the present policies on regional self-government and the Senate result in the consolidation of an attitude seeing no substantial problem in the continued infringement of the Constitution, while the publicly elected bodies (including the 'not yet elected' Senate and regional self-governmental institutions) are clearly handicapped in relation to the executive.

The Role of the Czech Parliament in the Past

Seen in a historical perspective, Krejčí has argued, such a postponement of the formation of higher self-governmental organs is by no means unique. Following each of the Czechoslovak revolutions in this century — in 1918, in 1948, and in 1989 — the new governments have soon held local elections, while the establishment of regional self-government has been deferred for years, to 1927, to 1954 (in what was mostly an administrative reform), and — at the least — to 1996 (Krejčí 1994: 306; Gerloch 1994: 140ff).

The role and status of parliament in Czech(-oslovak) politics also exhibit similar traditions or trends. Beginning with the birth of constitutionalism in Austria in 1848, Czech politics 'grew up' under the 1867 Constitution which, though predominantly liberal, had certain democratic deficiencies, including a limited and unequal curial franchise, which was removed only in 1907, and the absence of genuine parliamentarism. The cabinet was responsible only to the Emperor, who kept defense and foreign policy in his own domain. Furthermore, strong conservative forces sought to minimize popular influence over the decision-making process. The Czech attitude towards the Austrian *Reichsrat* was ambiguous. They saw this parliament as the outcome of Austrian-Hungarian Dualism, which ruined their hopes of Bohemian autonomy, so it was not until 1879 that they ended their boycott of it. Then they turned to pro-government politics until 1891, and after 1891 they oscillated between government support and opposition, turning even to obstruction and filibustering at times. In the mid-1890s, facing a weak and vulnerable parliament, the Czechs with some success launched a new strategy to gain influence in Austria. A 'long march through the institutions' was to secure them their share of posts in the government and the civil service, irrespective of their position in parliament (Bugge, 1994b: 203f).[8]

In sum, until the collapse of Austria-Hungary in 1918, the *Reichsrat* remained a weak institution enjoying little respect and affection from the Czechs.[9]

A Czechoslovak state was created in 1918 and its Constitution of 1920 definitely counts as democratic. The bicameral parliament was elected by a proportional vote with no limiting threshold; suffrage was equal and universal, and the government was responsible to parliament. However, strong centralism caused dissatisfaction among the national minorities (local self-government, which had served the Czechs so well in Austria, was strongly reduced; see Slapnicka 1975: 128ff), and many factors weakened parliament and prevented it from playing a constructive role in the political life of the republic.

First, contrary to the letter of the constitution, parliament seats effectively belonged to the party, not to the parliamentarian, a principle that made the parliament rank-and-file completely dependent on their party leaders. Also, the occasional changes between government responsibility and opposition inherent in representative democracy were effectively suspended in the First Republic. One group of Czech parties remained permanently in power (although granting some ministerial offices to Germans and Slovaks), and all policies were determined by the so-called *pětka* ('group of five'), an unofficial board of Czech party leaders, which cooperated closely with the un-elected 'castle' group (*hrad*) led by the President. Fear of communism and a Czech wish to keep the (mainly German and Slovak) opposition from power, dictated this union of socially highly heterogenous parties, but as conflicts were regulated and power and influence distributed in these forums, the political system possessed strongly corporative features. Parliament had very little authority — it has been called a mere 'voting machine' for decisions made elsewhere — and it was never used as a democratic instrument for conflict regulation. This has tempted Peter Heumos (whose excellent analysis has inspired this presentation) to wonder if the stability of Czechoslovak parliamentary democracy up until 1938 was facilitated by its never having been exposed to the burden of true responsibility (Heumos 1989: 68).[10]

This may explain why the Czechs in the 'Second Republic', created in October 1938 in what was left of Czechoslovakia after the German seizure of the Sudeten German borderlands, did not hesitate to abandon most of the pluralistic democratic principles of the First Republic. This resulted in a swift and radical break with the earlier parliamentary multi-party system: All pre-Munich Czech parties were replaced by two new ones, a *National Unity Party* containing the 'non-socialist' parties and a *National Labour Party* of Social Democrats and National Socialists. The Communist Party was forbidden. (In Slovakia, which obtained full autonomy, a fascist one-party system emerged). The National Labour Party served as loyal opposition to the National Unity Party in an arrangement of 'authoritarian democracy' that met with minimal popular protest. The interests of the state and the nation were now to take precedence over 'party egotism' (Prečan 1979: 535ff).

Party pluralism was thus (besides German and Slovak treason) singled out as the *cause* of the pre-war Czechoslovak political system's weakness. As President Beneš in his exile in London began to plan the reconstruction of

Czechoslovakia, neither he nor Gottwald's Communists in Moscow showed any veneration for the old system. Beneš sought to reduce the number of parties to two or three — a leftist, a rightist, and perhaps a centrist — and in December 1943 he and Gottwald agreed upon a scheme for post-war Czechoslovakia that outlawed all right-wing parties (including the Agrarians, the largest Czechoslovak pre-war party) and united the rest in a *National Front* exempted from outside control or challenges. As the 'rightist authoritarianism' of the Second Republic was thus replaced by an equally uncontrolled 'leftist authoritarianism' (ibid: 551), one can hardly speak of a restoration of Czecho-slovak democracy in 1945. In fact, Beneš and the government of the National Front long ruled by decree (passing vast amounts of highly important legislation) before the National Front in October 1945, without elections, set up a provisional Parliament (with one chamber only, although the Constitution of 1920 was still formally in force) (Slapnicka 1971: 272ff). From 1945 to 1948, the government was 'de facto' responsible to the National Front rather than to the weak parliament, and the elections held in May 1946 (again with a proportional vote, but with an explicit ban on opposition parties; Germans, Hungarians and 'collaborators' were prevented from voting) served more as an 'opinion poll' of factional strength within the National Front than as genuine free elections.

A liberal representative democracy was not on the Communist agenda from 1948 to 1989, so only a few features of the Communist regime's attitude towards parliament and the constitution need mentioning. One of the first acts of the Communist regime in 1948 was to arrest a number of opposition parliamentarians in a direct violation of their parliamentary immunity as guaranteed by the still valid Constitution of 1920. Later, Art. 3, Sec. 3 of the 1960 Constitution introduced the 'Leninist' principle that elected representatives at all levels, at any moment, could be recalled by their voters. This article was removed in February 1990 and the new Czech Constitution declares (also in contrast to the practice of the First Republic) that *'parliamentarians and senators perform their mandate personally ... unbound by any instructions'* (Art. 26).[11]

We may also observe that 'reformers' and 'normalizers' alike in the tumultous years of 1968-69 were ready to manipulate parliament and the Constitution to serve their interests. Parliamentary elections were to be held in the spring of 1968, but the reformers decided to extend the election period beyond the four years prescribed by the Constitution (prolonged in October 1968 to five). Later, the normalizers had pro-reform parliamentarians removed and replaced administratively (in another violation of the Constitution). Eventually, the parliament elected in 1964 had to wait until 1971 before new elections could be held.[12]

The constitutional reform of October 1968 called for a Constitutional Court (the Court of the 1920 Constitution had been abandoned in 1948), but it was never empanelled. The present rulers thus had plenty of local historical precedents for not establishing the Senate and other constitutionally prescribed institutions.

One may finally claim that the Czech(-oslovak) tradition of neglecting legality for the sake of efficiency, of which our historical survey has given ample evidence, was resumed even in the 'velvet revolution' of 1989. The revolution was to bring an end to the political abuse of parliament, the courts and other institutions, but to achieve this many Communist parliamentarians in the Federal Assembly were recalled in the winter of 1989-1990 and replaced administratively by members of the leading organizations of the democratic revolution, the Czech *Civic Forum* and the Slovak *Public Against Violence*. There were good reasons for doing so, and the June 1990 elections ensured that the anomaly was of only limited duration. Yet in sum, Czechoslovakia has no less than four times experienced a 'revolutionary', i.e. self-appointed, parliament assuming work without elections to decide upon its composition: in 1918, in 1945, in 1969, and in 1989-90 (Krejčí 1994: 306). From a strictly juridical perspective of democratic legitimacy, even the transformation of the Czech National Council (which was not elected as the highest representative organ of the Czech people) into the parliament of the new Czech state without new elections may be considered dubious.[13]

These remarks are not intended to downplay the profundity of the change in 1989 or the Czechoslovak and Czech governments' intent to introduce and buttress a western-like pluralistic political and economic system with constitutional guarantees of civic rights and mechanisms to distribute power between the legislature, the executive and the judiciary.[14]

Rather this analysis points to a historical heritage which — though disregarded in Czech political self-perception — in some respects still asserts itself today. This legacy includes:

1) accepting or even upholding a weak parliament, unable to function as a genuine popular control of the executive;
2) accepting the violation of constitutional provisions for reasons of political expediency;
3) accepting and upholding a political system which leaves the opposition impotent (or, from 1945 until 1989, criminalized) and with few prospects of coming to power; and
4) preferring strong, efficient government to any strict adherence to democratic norms and procedures.

All these points illustrate the relativity of the Czech claim to a special liberal democratic tradition.

Towards a Majoritarian Democracy?

Dvořáková and Kunc note that in 1989 the Czechoslovak reformers were faced with the dual, and in some ways incompatible, tasks of creating a new system of *political representation*, ideally representing the whole population as a state-nation, and a new form of *social representation*, integrating the interests and demands of the newly emerging social strata. Thus they had to create new, universal 'rules of the game' while simultaneously mediating social conflicts. Social relations and political strategies remained unclear, so the June 1990 elections became a referendum on the past, not a genuine choice between clear political alternatives. Therefore, as stressed by Havel and others, the primary task of the new Federal Assembly was to create a constitutional framework as a *precondition* for the democratic articulation and regulation of competing social interests. However, this 'universal' task was soon supplanted by a 'particular' assessment of the relative strength of different interest groups. This led to a change in decision-making from consensus-seeking to majority assertion, and to a devaluing of the principle of constitutionalism through a multitude of *ad hoc* constitutional amendments (Dvořáková and Kunc 1994: 130-38).[15]

This analysis largely confirms and supplements our earlier conclusions about the priority of efficiency before procedure in Czech politics. We may then ask how far the Czech political system (i.e., its formal institutions) 'fits' Czech political culture. All representative democracies must assert the unity and authority of the state while also absorbing and respecting the diversity of interests in society, but evidently political systems may gravitate towards one or the other pole. Using these extremes, Arendt Lijphardt distinguished between two ideal types of democracy:

Majoritarian democracy	Consociational democracy
- government by a single party	- broad coalition
- domination by the executive branch	- balance between the executive and the legislative branches
- two-party system	- multi-party system
- one-issue-dimension party system	- multi-issue-dimension party system
- voting system favouring majority rule	- proportional representation
- centralization	- decentralization
- single-chamber system	- two-chamber system
- unwritten constitution	- rigid constitution
	(from Avril, 1993, p. 216f).

Basically, in majoritarian democracy, there are no obstacles to majority domination, while consociational democracies establish limits to pure majoritarianism.

Lijphardt calls majoritarian democracy the *Westminster model* with reference to its obvious similarities with the British political system. Examples of consociational democracies are found in the Benelux countries and Scandinavia, while the German system may be placed somewhere in between.

As defined here, majoritarian democracy seems to fit Czech political culture better than consociational democracy, while the existing political system may be described as a mixture of both. The multi-party system and the coalition government suggest consociational democracy, but the domination of the executive and the continued centralization of power point in the other direction. Also, the Constitution is less rigid than those mostly found in Western European states since it may be changed by a qualified majority of 60 per cent in each chamber. The Constitution prescribes proportional representation for the House of Representatives (the most important of the two chambers), but the present election act circumscribes this provision somewhat by introducing a restrictive 5 per cent threshold.

The electoral system has been a controversial theme in Czech politics. The discussion gathered momentum when in late 1991 President Havel called for the introduction of majority voting.[16]

Havel did this less to promote a strong government than to secure that 'personalities', not 'party bureaucrats', were elected. Havel's distrust of political parties stems (apart from a then prevailing general aversion to the very notion of a party after forty years of Communist party rule) from a perception of 'true democracy' as the rule of 'the wise and the good'. In the tradition of Masaryk, Havel believes a good ruler to be a person capable of rising above particular interests in search of a genuinely universal solution, 'the common good', a view that makes the very idea of interest representation in politics preposterous.[17]

Others have been led to advocate majority voting by a wish to see the number of political parties in parliament reduced, though not to zero. In 1991, Jiří Kabele, in his recommendation of majority voting brought up the historical argument that a proportional system did not 'pay off' for the Czechs in 1935 and 1946. He argued that only majority voting creates political stability by forcing all political groups to join one of two parties, which would then gravitate towards the political centre. This would promote a problem-free change of government. History seemed to prove that 'open' parties defending the common good emerged only with majority voting (Kabele 1991a: 2, see also

1991b: 3, and 1992: 3). Martin Daneš too bolstered his argument with references to 'the Western experience'. To Daneš, strong and stable government is the essence of democracy, and in his defense of majority voting he gives a highly peculiar account of Western European history to create the image that proportional voting has destabilized nearly every country in the region and represents a grave danger to democracy (Daneš 1992: 3).[18]

Adherents of proportional voting have sought to refute the assertion that it produces instability, while emphasizing what has mostly been ignored by its opponents: the necessity of providing sufficient scope in the political system for a diversity of particular social interests and of creating mechanisms that favour compromise and consensus-building in order to minimize the risk of alienating large groups in society. 'Particular interests' are not seen as alien to democracy, but as a basic aspect of the social fabric (Barša 1991; Říchová 1991; Dvořáková and Kunc 1992; Kunc and Říchová 1992).

As mentioned, elections in 1990 and 1992 were based on proportional voting, but with a 5 per cent threshold to prevent a proliferation of small parties. In 1990, the argument that majority voting would increase the polarization between the Civic Forum/Public Against Violence and the old regime, and prevent other viewpoints from gaining representation, carried considerable weight. In 1992, then, the minor parties in parliament were not willing to give up all hopes of re-election, while others may simply have believed in the virtues of proportional voting. In the shaping of the Czech Constitution, finally, the legacy of the First Republic is also said to have played an important role (Gerloch 1994: 53).[19]

By contrast, opinion polls reveal that about 46 per cent of the population prefers majority voting and only about 27 per cent proportional voting (Krejčí 1994: 196).

There are indications that the present government is dissatisfied with even the limited scope for smaller parties afforded by the present system. In 1993 the Ministry of the Interior prepared a bill with the explicit purpose of reducing the number of parties running for elections. The bill would require all parties to pay 100,000 Czech crowns, (approximately $3200), to participate in the general elections. This security deposit would be returned only if the party obtained at least 5 per cent of the vote. For the moment, all such amendments to the law on parliamentary elections must await a compromise on the Senate issue. But Krejčí asserts that all government plans for changes in the election system introduced in 1994 aim at a reduction of the scope for smaller parties (Krejčí 1994: 206). The new law on elections to local assemblies points in the same direction (and makes it very difficult for independent candidates to register), as does an amendment to the Law on Political Parties of 29 April, 1994. State aid to the parties was increased, but simultaneously the threshold for receiving this aid was raised from 2 to 3 per cent of the vote (*Lidové noviny* 30 April 1994, 3 May 1994, 18 May 1994, 4 June 1994).

Conclusion

The correspondence between 'Czech' and 'democratic' may in an historical perspective appear to be less self-evident than claimed in Czech political self-perception. But still, the existence of such images plays a role in shaping political norms. The commitment to 'western democracy' is today generally accepted and constitutes a politically indisputable framework within which the unarticulated yet persistent tradition of seeking efficient leadership unfolds, even at the cost of a certain constitutional laxity. There are good arguments for promoting political efficiency in the enormously complicated transition process, and the present Czech government may be right in asserting that economic progress is a (though not *the*) prerequisite for a stable democracy and that its popular mandate is confirmed in every new opinion poll. The narrow focusing on efficiency in Czech political tradition does, however, contain the danger that democratic institutions and principles — in times of political crisis — are considered dispensible, not an end. And if a system of strict majoritarian democracy is introduced, too many groups in society may become politically alienated and the political system may prove incapable of providing peaceful methods of arbitration needed to preserve the social stability so hotly desired.[20]

Notes

1. One notices that Musil, though writing before the partition of Czechoslovakia, reserves the liberal democratic tradition solely for the Czechs. This opinion is well-established in Czech national self-perceptions, and especially in 1992 the Czech-Slovak constitutional antagonism was frequently explained — from the Czech side — as a clash between a 'civic', liberal Czech community and a nationalist, authoritarian Slovak one. This, obviously, tells more of Czech attitudes towards Slovaks than about existing patterns of political opinions in the two communities.
2. One empirically observable example of the deep-rootedness of old political habits may be found in the electoral behaviour of many Czech voters: there has

been a remarkable continuity in the regional distribution of strong and low support for the 'historical' Czech parties (the Communists, the Social Democrats, the People's Party, and the Socialist Party) from 1946 to 1990 and 1992. See Krejčí, 1994: 213ff; and Petráček, 1992: 4-5.

3. See Krejčí, 1994, 266ff, 273ff; and *Lidové noviny*, 16 August 1994, for recent figures. The weekly *Respekt* has recently brought a major feature on the problem (see Holub, 1995).

4. It has also been claimed that parliament is handicapped by an informal, but effective ban on interpellations from the ranks of the government parties to their ministers (see *Lidové noviny*, 18 May 1994: 1). Brokl and Mansfeldová, 1995: 29, commenting upon this fact, have suggested that this ban renders the coalition parliamentarians 'invisible' to the public, which sees in parliament only a vociferous opposition.

5. See Bugge, 1994a, for an account of the Czech party system.

6. The present parliament benefits from the lack of competition from another elected body, while the government profits from not having its legislation delayed by its additional reading in a second chamber. Quiring, 1995, offers a competent discussion of the problem from a legal as well as a political point of view.

7. See *Mladá Fronta Dnes*, 27 June 1995 and 30 June 1995; and Klaus 1994: 95ff.

8. Jan Křen, noticing the intense factional strife in Czech politics in the 1890s, comments: 'This is one of the great deficiencies of Czech political culture until today: the Czechs have never had much success with political alternatives'. (Křen 1986: 247). So far, developments since 1989 have not seriously invalidated this observation.

9. Bugge, 1994b: 268, concludes: 'Austrian parliamentary politics was caught in a vicious circle: the less political influence, the greater the incitement to prove one's importance to the voters with spectacular manifestations of national zeal; and the more the 'Reichsrat' was exposed to obstructions and fights, the harder it was to argue for the virtues of a democratic approach' (ibid: 316).

10. Also, the Constitutional Court introduced in the Constitution of 1920 had very limited competences (Heumos 1989: 69). One may compare Heumos's account with that of Věra Olivová (1992), who neglects all structural weaknesses of the inter-war Czechoslovak political system and puts the whole blame for its eventual collapse on foreign powers and the '*disloyal opposition*'. Significantly, Olivová stresses T.G. Masaryk's wisdom and democratic mind as a main guarantee of democracy in the First Republic. Masaryk's concept of democracy, which emphasized ethics and social responsibility rather than formal institutional procedures, has played a vital role in Czech political thought and may be met today in Václav Havel's ideas.

11. Interestingly, in May 1992 a full 82 per cent of the Czech respondents declared that they preferred the old system of recallable deputies. Only 7 per cent supported the western system of unbound deputies (Krejčí 1994: 187). Krejčí too

argues that the public control with the political process would be increased if deputies were recallable (ibid: 307).

12. See Skilling 1976: 345; and Kusin 1978: 53, 91ff.
13. In the autumn of 1992, the Federal Assembly was virtually forced by the — nominally subordinate — governments of the Czech and Slovak National Councils to dissolve itself. See Kipke and Vodička 1993, on this and other aspects of the division of Czechoslovakia.
14. We are aware of a certain one-sidedness in our line of argument, which focuses on some specific, re-occurring traits in Czech political behaviour, while disregarding the general political settings and the profound differences between these at different times. A substantial treatment of the problem in all its major aspects would, however, far exceed the scope of this paper, which aspires only to illuminate some neglected aspects of Czech political traditions.
15. Also, several politicians contributed to discrediting parliament's authority by appealing to the people to 'mobilize' against the 'incompetent' parliament: in 1991, Havel asked the public to force parliament to end the deadlock in the Czech-Slovak constitutional negotiations, while before the 1992 elections Klaus and others evoked a 'leftist threat' to Czechoslovakia's new democratic system, which — in case the 'leftist' Slovaks and the Czech left wing got a majority in the Federal Assembly — would 'force' the Czech right to dissolve Czechoslovakia in order to save democracy and reform in the Czech half of the country.
16. Havel's proposal was very complicated and has been presented as a combination of majority and proportional voting (Kabele, 1992: 3). By contrast, Kunc and Říchová claim that it would eventually only increase the preferential treatment of big parties inherent in majority voting (Kunc and Říchová 1992: 10-11).
17. The 'anti-party' and 'strong personalities' argument was also brought up by others (Calda 1992: 8).
18. Notice also how Brokl and Mansfeldová (though not recommending any particular electoral system) use the authority of Masaryk and Beneš (eventually in an historically inaccurate way) to present the reduction of the number of parties as superior: 'Das nie realisierte Ideal der Gründer der Tschechoslowakei zwischen den beiden Weltkriegen war ein System von nur drei Parteien. Die Meinungspräferenzen des ersten Jahres der ČR haben sich diesem Ideal angenähert'. (Brokl and Mansfeldová 1995: 12).
19. The legacy of the First Republic may also have inspired the adherents of the Senate to include it in the new Czech Constitution. The Senate was also to serve as a guarantee against rash decision-making in the House of Representatives (in the spirit of 'consociational democracy'), while majority voting was introduced to make the composition of the two chambers differ. As suggested above, the establishing of the Senate has become a farce: Its adherents (especially in the small Civic Democratic Alliance (ODA)) try to avoid the principle of majority voting, while to the Civic Democratic Party, which would benefit from this, the Senate is an obstacle to political efficiency. Critics have argued (and some

provisions in the Constitution seem to confirm this) that the Senate was thought mostly as a forum for the 'dispossessed' members of the Federal Assembly. See Kunc 1994, for a sharp critique of the institution.

20. Krejčí claims that majority voting might today prevent up to two-thirds of the Czech voters from accurately expressing their preferences (Krejčí 1994: 198); see also Avril 1994: 217, and the interview with Lijphardt in *Přítomnost* 1, 1992: 8.

Bibliography

Avril, Pierre 1993. 'The democratic institutions of European countries', in Gérard Duprat et al. (eds), *European Democratic Culture*. Milton Keynes: Open University Press: 211-33.

Barša, Pavel 1991. 'Jakou demokracii pro Československo', in *Přítomnost* 7, 1991: 3.

Brokl, Lubomír & Zdenka Mansfeldová, 1995. *Bilanz der tschechischen Innenpolitik im Jahre 1993*. Berichte des Bundesinstituts für ostwissenschaftliche und internationale Studien, Köln, No. 8.

Bugge, Peter 1994a. 'The Czech Republic', in Szajkowski, Bogdan (ed.), *New Political Parties of Eastern Europe, Russia and the Successor States*. London: Longman: 149-74.

Bugge, Peter 1994b. 'Czech Nation-Building, National Self-Perception and Politics 1780-1914'. PhD Dissertation, Aarhus.

Calda, Miloš 1992. 'Bez zpětné vazby to nejde', in *Přítomnost* 1: 8.

Daneš, Martin 1992. 'Všechno je jinak — Obhájci poměrného systému hájí nestabilitu', in *Respekt* 3: 2.

Dvořáková, Vladimíra & Jiří Kunc, 1992. 'Strany, straníci, konsensus', in *Přítomnost* 5: 3-6.

Dvořáková, Vladimíra & Jiří Kunc, 1994. *O přechodech k demokracii*. Praha: Slon.

Enzensberger, Hans Magnus 1993. *Aussichten auf den Bürgerkrieg*. Frankfurt: Suhrkamp.

Gerloch, Aleš et al., 1994. *Ústavní systém České Republiky*. Praha: Prospektrum.

Havel, Václav 1990. 'Projev k občanům na Nový rok', in Václav Havel, *Projevy*, Praha: Vyšehrad: 11-19

Havel, Václav 1994a. 'A Call for Sacrifice', in *Foreign Affairs*, Vol. 73, (2): 2-7.

Havel, Václav 1994b. 'Nejsme post-komunistickým světem', (interview), *Literární noviny* (3): 3.

Havel, Václav 1995. 'Češi a Němci na cestě k dobrému sousedství', in *Lidové noviny*, 18 February.

Heumos, Peter 1989. 'Konfliktregelung und soziale Integration — Zur Struktur der ersten Tschechoslowakischen Republik', in *Bohemia* 30: 52-70.

Holub, Petr 1995. 'Svobodu ano, parlament ne — Český sněm hladá důvěru demo-kratů', in *Respekt* 28: 9-11.

Huntington, Samuel P. 1993. 'The Clash of Civilizations?', in *Foreign Affairs*. Summer: 22-49.

Ježek, Josef 1994. 'Persona non grata: opozice jsem já', (interview), *Literární noviny/Přítomnost*, 27: 4.

Judt, Tony R. 1992. 'Metamorphosis: The Democratic Revolution in Czechoslovakia', in Ivo Banac (ed.), *Eastern Europe in Revolution*. Ithaca, N.Y. and London: Cornell University Press: 96-116.

Kabele, Jiří 1991a. 'Většinový volební systém', in *Respekt* 21: 2.

Kabele, Jiří 1991b. 'Boj o voliče — Volební systém a politická síla', in *Respekt* 48: 3.

Kabele, Jiří 1992. 'Volební zákon — Prezident navrhuje většinový systém. Poslanci zatím proti', in *Respekt* 1: 3.

Kipke, Rüdiger & Karel Vodička, (eds.) 1993. *Rozloučení s Československem — příčiny a důsledky česko-slovenského rozchodu*. Praha: Český spisovatel.

Klaus, Václav 1994. *Česká cesta*. Prague: Profile.

Krejčí, Oskar 1994. *Kniha o volbách*. Prague: Victoria Publishing.

Křen, Jan 1986/1990 edn. *Konfliktní společenství — Češi a Němci 1780-1918*. Prague.

Kunc, Jiří 1994. 'Senát: jaká auctoritas?', in *Literární noviny/Přítomnost* 22: 4-5.

Kunc, Jiří & Blanka Říchová, 1992. 'K nepřijatému návrhu volebního zákona', in *Přítomnost* 2: 10-11.

Kusin, Vladimir V. 1978. *From Dubček to Charter 77*. New York: St. Martin's Press.

Lijphardt, Arend 1992. 'Atraktivní model demokracie' (interview), in *Přítomnost* 1: 8.

Musil, Jiří 1992. 'Czechoslovakia in the Middle of Transition', in Stephen R. Graubard (ed.), *Exit from Communism — Augmented Version of Daedalus*. Spring 1992, New Brunswick: 175-95.

Olivová, Véra 1992. 'The Czechoslovak Government and its 'disloyal' opposition 1918-1938', in John Morison (ed.), *The Czech and Slovak Experience*. New York: 89-101.

Olson, David M. 1994. 'The New Parliaments of the New Democracies: the Experience of the Federal Assembly of the Czech and Slovak Federal Republic', in Attila Ágh (ed.), *The Emergence of East European Parliaments: The First Steps*. Budapest: Hungarian Centre of Democracy Studies: 35-47.

Petráček, Zbyněk 1992. 'Spojité nádoby extrémů — Nová politická mapa Československa II', in *Respekt* 25: 4-5.

Prečan, Vilém 1979. 'Probleme des tschechischen Parteiensystems zwischen München 1938 und dem Mai 1945', in Karl Bosl (ed.), *Die Erste Tschechoslowakische Republik als multinationaler Parteienstaat*. München: Oldenbourg, 529-52.

Quiring, Christian 1995. *Die Einrichtung des tschechischen Senats — Chronik eines angekündigten Todes?*, Magisterarbeit im Fach Politikwissenschaft, Universität zu Köln.

Reschová, Jana 1994. 'Parliaments and Constitutional Change: the Czechoslovak Experience', in Attila Ágh (ed.), *The Emergence of East European Parliaments: The First Steps*. Budapest: Hungarian Centre of Democracy Studies: 55-68.

Říchová, Blanka 1991. 'Čas a prostor pro konsensus', in *Přítomnost* 10: 22-23.

Skilling, H. Gordon 1976. *Czechoslovakia's Interrupted Revolution*. Princeton: Princeton University Press.

Slapnicka, Helmut 1975. 'Der neue Staat und die bürokratische Kontinuität, die Entwicklung der Verwaltung 1918-1938', in Karl Bosl (Ed.), *Die demokratisch-parlamentarische Struktur der Ersten Tschechoslowakischen Republik*. München and Wien: Oldenbourg, 121-47.

Slapnicka, Helmut 1971. 'Verfassungsprobleme der Tschechoslowakei im Jahre 1945', in Karl Bosl (Ed.), *Das Jahr 1945 in der Tschechoslowakei*. München and Wien: Oldenbourg, 259-85.

Do the Expelled Sudeten Germans Hold the Key to the Czech Future?

Eva Hahn

Introduction

At first glance, the question formulated in the title seems suspiciously exaggerated. The roughly 700,000 citizens of the Federal Republic of Germany and the few thousand other former Czechoslovak citizens of German nationality in other countries (Austria, Great Britain, Sweden and in Latin America) could hardly have sufficient influence to determine the future of the Czech Republic. Furthermore, they must all now be over fifty years old to have been expelled from Czechoslovakia at the end of the Second World War.

Still, one frequently encounters those among the Czech, as well as the German public, who would answer this question in the affirmative, although often only indirectly implied by the views which they hold. Hence, it is these views in particular with which I will concern myself. My comments concern the discourse on the so-called 'Sudeten German problem' since the fall of communism. I have chosen to examine the modes of argumentation that interpret present political developments with the aid of supposed knowledge of the past, as well as those which predict the future based upon the past. I therefore take the theme of 'Forward to the Past' as a stimulus for the analysis of the ways of thinking that draw their orientational framework from the past in striving to solve the so-called Sudeten German problem of the present.

To anticipate my conclusions, in my opinion a Sudeten German problem does indeed exist today, although not in the forms in which it is usually perceived and interpreted. The current formulations of this problem on both sides of the Czech-German border to a large extent correspond to a position that could be called a 'Forward to the Past' mentality. Today few notice that the problem lies not with the expulsion of the Germans from Czechoslovakia itself, but rather with the historical consequences of the deprivation of rights of, and forced resettlement of, roughly three million people from the territory of today's Czech Republic a half-century ago.[1]

What Is the Sudeten German Problem?

Immediately after the Second World War, around three million Czechoslovak citizens of German nationality were stripped of their civil rights and most were packed in freight trains and shipped across the border.[2] Germans were not the only victims of the so-called Retribution Decrees — these also affected Magyars, as well as Czechs and Slovaks designated 'traitors and collaborators'. However, Germans constituted the largest group among those expelled. Not all of these 'collectively punished' Germans considered themselves Sudeten Germans. Among those expelled were a few German-speaking Jews who had survived the Holocaust, German emigrants and resistance fighters,[3] and members of the Bohemian nobility and upper classes who only in rare cases thought of themselves as Sudeten Germans.[4]

The designation 'Sudeten German' as a collective term denoting the German inhabitants of the Bohemian lands emerged in general usage at the beginning of the twentieth century. The feeling of collectively belonging together spread among Bohemian and Moravian Germans outside of the prominent, nationally conscious German circles for the first time after 1918, when they all became Czechoslovak citizens of German nationality, i.e., members of the German minority. Only in the 1930s was the so-called 'Sudeten German Unity Movement' (*Sudetendeutsche Einheitsbewegung*) able to win greater popularity. By 1938, around two-thirds — not the ninety per cent that is often maintained today — of the Germans in former Czechoslovakia had declared themselves followers.[5]

As a commonly shared traumatic experience, the 1945 expulsion bound its victims together, above all in West Germany (especially in Bavaria where around one million of them settled). A Sudeten German associational structure was gradually built there, achieving recognition as the so-called Sudeten German ethnic group by German politicians.[6]

The most important of these organizations, the *Sudetendeutsche Landsmannschaft* (SL), today demands recognition by the Czech Republic as the representative of the Sudeten German ethnic group (or of the so-called Sudeten German tribe (*Volksstamm*)). From the statements of individual spokespersons it often appears that they would be prepared to compromise if the Czech government would engage in a 'dialogue' — as it is called in today's terminology. The extensive goals of the Sudetendeutsche Landsmannschaft are, however, firmly established in its statute, in its successive and continually cited proclamations and in the statements of its numerous officials. Accordingly, the SL demands that members of this ethnic group (which, according to official SL figures number almost four million people)[7] be granted Czech citizenship, that property once owned by members of this group in the Bohemian lands be returned or that its owners or heirs be compensated and that the SL as the representative of the Sudeten Germans, be granted consultative rights (*Mitspracherecht*) in the Czech Republic. These demands are commonly collected under the rubric of 'Ethnic Homeland and Self-Determination Rights' (*Heimat- und Selbstbestimmung der Volksgruppe*). Yet, it is unclear exactly what the various Sudeten German expellee organizations in Germany really expect from the Czech Republic. That this ambiguity has not led to a more concrete discussion of their demands is in itself both an illustration and a consequence of the present form of discourse, one which revolves around the past rather than the present.

German politicians support the demands of the Sudeten German organizations to varying degrees. The Bavarian Christian Social Union supports the SL's objectives, vague as they are. The current Federal Government has called for the recognition of the SL as the 'representative of the ethnic group' by the Czech government. It has also linked settlement of the property question to compensation for the Czech victims of Nazism. The Social Democratic opposition demanded the recognition of the SL and a dialogue between the SL and the Czech government.[8] It is no wonder, therefore, that the Czech mass media continue to be occupied with this theme. In the Czech Republic, however, the discussion has focused more on the support given by a large part of the Sudeten German population to National Socialism in 1938 and thereafter, the Second World War, the millennium-long Czech-Sudeten German cohabitation in the Bohemian lands and, the German 'Drang nach Osten', rather than demands of contemporary Sudeten German organizations. Here we certainly have an example of how the past co-shapes the political present in the Czech Republic.

While Germany stands at the centre of my discussion, all the countries in the region are, to a lesser extent however, confronted with this problem:

1) A number of Sudeten German and Austrian politicians — among others, the former foreign minister Alois Mock and President Thomas Klestil — are pressuring the Czech government to search for a compromise with the expelled former Czechoslovak citizens.

2) The Hungarians in Czechoslovakia were deprived of their rights after the Second World War, just as the Germans were, although they were not expelled to the same extent or in the same way. Hungarian politicians make no secret of the fact that they consider the relationship of the two Czechoslovak successor states to these events and their consequences, to be an unresolved issue.

3) The Slovaks not only took part in the expulsion, but today they must redress injustice suffered by their Magyar co-citizens (though they have maintained good relations with the organizations of Germans expelled from Slovakia).

For these reasons, it is surprising that the so-called Sudeten German problem has not obtained any attention outside the Czech Republic. Latent national animosities in the form of unsolved historical conflicts always turn into open ones as soon as real conflict situations arise. They hold the potential for emotional conflict and the mobilization of broader segments of the population. Therefore, allowing the Sudeten German problem to remain unresolved can lead to serious consequences for Czech-German relations. One explanation why it is so difficult today for the Czech public to come to terms rationally with this problem is provided by Tony Judt's brilliant analysis of political myth in postwar Europe; however, this knowledge alone cannot solve the current German-Czech problem — or, as the case may be, the Czech and the German domestic political problems — arising as a result of the forced resettlement of three million Germans out of Czechoslovakia after the Second World War.[9]

The analysis which follows examines how various modes of argumentation in the present discourse concerning the so-called Sudeten German problem make use of the past as a vehicle in the search for the future. I present four models of argumentation to demonstrate these features of the current discourse on the Sudeten German problem.

Four models of argumentation

1. The Czech Variant: 'Forward to the Past', but not Entirely

In contrast to Austria, Hungary and Slovakia, a nearly uncontested Czech consensus holds that the past provides the best orientational framework for fashioning the future. The 'return to Europe', 'democracy', 'humanism', and 'prosperity' are as a rule understood as the features of pre-communist Czechoslovakia (i.e., the first Czechoslovak Republic of the interwar period). The Czechoslovakia of that time is recalled as a social order that was destroyed by the German National Socialist regime in 1938. Ten years later (after its reinstatement), the Czech social order was destroyed by the expansionist communist regime of the Soviet Union. This consensus advocated that as far as possible the pre-war Czechoslovakian political system should be imitated today. The First Republic embodied many of the aspirations of today's Czech society and, in the eyes of many, addressed so-called nationally specific and historically anchored aspirations of the Czech people. In this respect, the slogan

'Forward to the Past' probably better describes the mood in the Czech Republic than anywhere else: the Czech past seems to prove that the Czech Republic is predestined to realize this generally popular conceptual goal. Only a few individuals question this commonly held view.

However, from the perspective of the so-called Sudeten German problem, it turns out that precisely the loudest protagonists of the 'Forward to the Past' formula in Czech society are not so terribly interested in a possibly faithful imitation or even restoration of the political culture of pre-war Czechoslovakia. According to them, not only has the multicultural national mix of the interwar republic been destroyed (i.e., it no longer exists), but moreover this aspect of pre-war culture should rather not be included in descriptions of the past. Consequently, among those who steadfastly defend the First Republic against all its critics and deeper questioning, we find precisely those who adamantly reject any discussion with or about the expelled Sudeten Germans. For them the Sudeten German question is a product of traditional German expansionism.[10]

The expelled Sudeten Germans are portrayed as lackeys of German power in this scenario. Because this picture of the past proceeds from the traditional concept of German 'Drang nach dem Osten', the key to the future belongs to the Germans. Just as the German citizens of Czechoslovakia were held responsible for the destruction of the country in 1938, so they also seem — with their 'brothers of conviction' in Germany — to pose a threat to Czech political independence and cultural autonomy today. The 'Forward to the Past' position, expressed by the mythologizing of the First Czechoslovak Republic, rejects a complex critical examination of the problem of the past and indirectly stirs up fears of the Sudeten Germans and of Germans in general, and implicitly accepts the expelled Sudeten Germans as the custodians of the future of Czech society.

2. The Sudeten German Variant: 'Forward to the Past', but not Entirely

The second perspective in the wider discourse on the so-called Sudeten German question is advocated by the Sudetendeutsche Landsmannschaft, which supports the demand for the restoration of the right to a homeland, (*Heimatrecht*), in the Czech Republic for the expelled Sudeten Germans. This position looks back a half-century to a distant past as a vision of the future.

The right of return for the expelled Sudeten Germans and the restitution of their property is asserted by Sudeten Germans who, like many Czechs, are disinclined to see the past as a whole or to allow an unhindered critical discourse on the actual events of the half-century. They also orient their political demands and their vision of the future towards the past, although not the entire past.

These groups demand their *Heimatrecht* as a historically based right, but in contrast to the thousand-year tradition of the Bohemian lands, they demand the *Heimatrecht* for themselves as a 'collective right' (*Gruppenrecht*). Thus, they are not concerned with whether individual expellees are allowed to return, but rather with the collective representation by the Landsmannschaft to the consultative rights enjoyed by Czech citizen groups. At the same time, they wish to retain their present residency and their German citizenship.

The Sudetendeutsche Landsmannschaft presents itself not as the representative of the interests of the expelled former Czechoslovak citizens, but rather as the spokesperson of an ethnic group, a tribe of people that first constituted itself in exile in Germany after the Second World War.

The history of the Sudeten German organization in West Germany after 1945 offers a vivid example of the nation-building process that we know from all over Europe. Particular groups of former German residents of the Bohemian lands acquired particular traditions (i.e., those of Konrad Henlein's Sudeten German Unity Movement from the interwar period), and out of the historical multiplicity of the Bohemian past created their own historical picture, a territory (within the borders defined by the Munich Accords of 1938), a coat of arms, a flag, and a political 'ethnic representation', i.e., the Sudetendeutsche Landsmannschaft.[11]

The SL poses demands on behalf of this ethnic group as part of a reconstruction of the past of the Bohemian lands, although — similar to the case of the Czech protagonists in their reconstruction of the past — one that would be a little different than before. In their political comments, they always stressed that without a 'solution to the Sudeten German question' no peace or security in Europe is conceivable, and that the Czechs themselves have no hope for a better future without the Sudeten Germans. Thus, here we also meet a 'Forward to the Past' mentality.

3. Third Model: Reshaping the Past

Various versions of the 'Forward to the Past' position can be found among the numerous Sudeten Germans and Czechs who are engaged in a more complex examination of the past than provided by the two scenarios already discussed. They seek an historical understanding which claims for the future the logical conclusions flowing from their own self-understanding of the past.

One demonstration of this conceptual model comes from Rudolf Hilf, a prominent critic of the Sudetendeutsche Landsmannschaft in Munich and one of the 'favourite Sudeten Germans' of the Czech public because of his criticism of the Landsmannschaft. Hilf proceeds from the historical necessity of a 're-ordering of the Czech-German relationship'. The word 're-ordering', of course, also implies that the past is a constituent element of the future, but it emphasizes not reconstruction but rather a refashioning in the future:

> Peace will only arise when both sides attempt together to find a new beginning that in principle calls neither the rights of the expelled Germans nor the rights of the Czechs in this region into question. 'Homeland' — that is, protection in peace, in security and under law — will for both arise when they are conscious that from history it is their common home and neither any longer wants to drive the other out.[12]

By demanding that the Czech Republic recognize the historical rights of the expelled Sudeten Germans, coupled with the assertion that only in this way will peace be achieved, Hilf also places himself in a position in which the future of Czech society is dependent on the Sudeten Germans. Thus, the Sudeten Germans appear to hold the key to the Czech future in their hands. In contrast to the Landsmannschaft, Hilf does not try to construct the restoration of the historical rights of the expelled Sudeten Germans without taking the present Czech society into consideration. Instead he stresses that the present situation must be taken into consideration in righting the injustice done to the Sudeten Germans. His model clears the way for a Czech-Sudeten German dialogue — this time the past should be 'reshaped'.

In a weakened form and in different variations we meet fundamentally the same position on the Sudeten German question among numerous German politicians.[13] They have placed the Czech government under open and massive pressure from 'Bonn, Munich and Vienna' — as, for example, the *Frankfurter Allgemeine Zeitung* puts it — to 'enter into a dialogue with the Sudeten Germans'.[14] The Federal Finance Minister Theo Waigel calls upon the Czech Republic to rescind — as he calls it — 'President Beneš' expulsion decree', and Federal Minister of the Interior Manfred Kanther assures the Sudeten Germans that the Federal Government will support the recognition of the homeland right. Waigel furthermore maintains that the Christian Social Union stands openly opposed to Czech aspirations for membership in the European Union until the rights of the Sudeten Germans are recognized: 'Prague will have to accept the European house rules'. As Waigel explains, this means that 'the Czech government must distance itself officially from the expulsion of the Sudeten Germans from their ancestral homeland and declare the Beneš decrees invalid'.[15] A similar demand is made by Bavarian Minister President Edmund Stoiber, with the slogan 'The only road to Brussels leads through Munich.' The double meaning of 'Munich' has not been lost on the Czech public.

The German politicians discussed here do not demand a restoration of the past, but they also make the German-Czech relationship dependent on the position of the Czech government regarding past events. Since high-ranking German politicians demand such clear decisions with such weighty consequences for their neighbouring state, the Sudeten German theme is far from 'uninteresting' for the German public. It is much more than the 'non-problem' many German politicians, including the former Federal President Walter Scheel, have claimed.[16]

Scheel, of course, is right when he asserts that the German public is not terribly interested in this theme. Nevertheless, one of the sources of the present difficulty lies hidden here: the suggestion that something that does not interest the German public has no meaning or consequence, that it therefore is not a problem. The present political structures of the Sudeten German organizations developed over the course of a half-century within the Federal Republic of Germany, and therefore an intra-German discourse over these demands would have to take place before the German government can put pressure on its Czech neighbour. The popular complaisance with the widespread German disinterest in the organizational structure and political goal-setting of the expelled Sudeten Germans is based on a problematic point of view.

4. Fourth Model: The 'Bottom Line' Model

This 'bottom line' perspective finds widespread support not only among a German public that refuses to consider the Sudeten German problem; it is also an extremely popular position among the Czech population. Czech historians came out in support of it in their 1991 public statement on the Sudeten German problem, writing that it is necessary in 'the near future to put a full stop after the most recent era of our relationship and begin to build the future on entirely different, humanitarian and democratic principles'.[17]

At first glance, this position hardly corresponds to the 'Forward to the Past' formula; rather it points to the one way into the future that is unburdened by the past. This approach offers a vision of a 'new' future, one that distinguishes itself from the past, breaks with it, stands out clearly against it through its new value conception. And yet, the statement of the Czech historians demonstrates extremely clearly that the 'bottom line' model also implies that attitudes and beliefs from the past continue to influence the present and that past conflicts are brought to expression in the perception of the past, leaving their stamp on historical consciousness.

The history of the Bohemian lands is interpreted in a backward projection from the Czech-German conflict. The collectively grasped history of the 'two peoples of Bohemia' allows for no recognition of the conscious process of modern nation-building or the development of liberal legal understandings. Any discussion about the expulsion, or a dialogue with the expelled Sudeten Germans, is viewed as a 'resuscitation of old animosities' and a reproduction of the allegedly dangerous opinions held during the pre-war period.

The 'bottom line' position is based on a conception of history as a stream — a stream that flows from the past through the present and into the future. This stream must be halted through a conscious decision to erect a barrier that breaks the course of history by an act of will. The conception of a 'bottom line' reflects both the desire and the attempt to break the 'Forward to the Past' stream that many assume to be a historically immanent tendency.

In political life, the 'bottom line model' leads to a marginalization of all those whose demands perpetrate the memory of the past. This model provides no room for a discursive process that can critically assess the past and no platform for an argument with the positions and demands seemingly handed down by the past. In this particular concrete case, this approach forces the Sudeten German organizations to the margins of political life, stylizing them as 'those who live in the past'. Advocates of the fourth model are then free to react irrationally in any confrontation with those who disagree. By rejecting the possibility of a discursive conflict over the past, the 'bottom line' position constitutes a general prescription for all such 'Forward-to-the-Past Conflicts'.

Conclusions

What then comes from our consideration of these various models of relating to the past in the case of the Sudeten German problem?

'Forward to the Past' positions may generally be regarded as a blinding by the past. In the case of the Sudeten German problem, it is clearly shown how much the 'past' can hinder a more nuanced perception of the present, i.e., only occasionally is the problem perceived in its current form. A real problem does exist that one could call a 'Sudeten German problem', and it is about the following:

— The fact that half a century ago almost three million people were resettled from one side of the Bohemian-German border to the other does not permit the consequences of such a deep intervention into the social, cultural and political structures of both countries to remain unconsidered, denied, or suppressed.

— Half a century ago in Czechoslovakia, almost three million people were stripped of all their civil rights in the name of the victory over the criminal National Socialist regime. It is unrealistic to expect today that none of them will seek moral and legal satisfaction.

— Given that the present Czech society understands itself as the executor of the historical inheritance of the Bohemian lands, it is unrealistic to expect that those who seek an historically adequate interpretation of Bohemian history and protest the narrowing of the Czech past to the history of ethnic Czechs — those who are not satisfied with eradicating the Bohemian Germans and their expulsion from historical memory — will disappear.

For these three reasons, I consider the Sudeten German problem to be a weighty problem inside present-day Czech society as well as for German-Czech relations. In addition, I think that it is not only a Czech-German problem, as genera"ˎ considered today, but for the reasons presented above, it is a problem that also concerns neighbours of the Czech Republic — Austria, Hungary and Slovakia. It is not a problem that must necessarily spawn mutual antagonism among the societies concerned. Rather it must be seen as their common problem, for they are all confronted today with the consequences of the forced resettlements of that time.

Formulated in this way, the Sudeten German problem appears differently than it is as a rule perceived today. In my view, it is not primarily about the guilt or innocence of the expelled Sudeten Germans, nor is it about the normative legal (*völkerrechtliche*) legitimacy or illegality of the expulsion or property law sophistries. In short, it actually is not so much about what happened 'then', it is more about what is a problem 'today'.

If today, in harmony with our legal understanding, we call forced re-settlement an injustice, we must recognize those victims living among us as victims of an injustice, independent of the historical circumstances under which this injustice was perpetrated against them. The conflict over the historical circumstances surrounding the decisions and actions of that time belongs to the past, while the judgment of what is just and what is unjust is an expression of the present legal sensitivities.

However, just because we today unconditionally recognize the expulsion as an injustice, we cannot derive the demands for the restoration of the past from this recognition. If we understand justice as a power in itself giving order to the human community, we must abandon the conception of collective historical rights which prepares us to march into battle with individual aspects of the past as a political strategy whenever and for whomever it seems opportune. Historians acting as ammunition suppliers for politicians have a different conception of their profession than historians who attempt a discursive, analytical examination of the past. Since the aim of historical writing is neither to represent interests nor to clarify legal questions, no political demands can be derived from the recognition of a past injustice.[18]

The Czech-German discourse about the expulsion and about the expelled Sudeten Germans has led into a cul-de-sac because it has focused on the past instead of the present. As I have tried to show in the conceptual models I have sketched, the Sudeten Germans are assigned a role in which they hold the key to the Czech future. This condition will last for as long as the 'Forward to the Past' formula determines the perception of the Czech-Sudeten German relationship.

The past will cease to co-determine the present and future only when it is recognized as 'past', i.e., when the present is freed from its slavery to memory and we self-consciously understand the present and future as an independent world of free and self-determining people. A detached examination of the past, one in which 'then' is divided from 'now', can follow only from a past understood in this way. Such an examination can, for the first time, turn to the *entire* past, and, as such investigation into the past lives no more from past fears, it does not justify either one or the other historical actor, and judges all by the same standard and with its own sensitivity to justice.

In contrast to the perception of the Sudeten German problem sketched above, a 'From-Now-Back-to-the-Past' interpretation offers a different picture of the expelled Sudeten Germans: as people with traumatic experiences and with a special relationship to the Bohemian lands (i.e., the Czech Republic). Many have fully integrated into their new environment, others could only put down roots in Germany because they could rebuild the social networks they brought with them from Bohemia and Moravia, and finally there are others who will remain embittered and marked by their traumatic experiences until the end of their lives. Seen in this way, the expelled Sudeten Germans appear as a diverse group of people coming from the Bohemian lands. They were expelled from their homes and deserve our sympathy because they no longer belong in the country where they felt they belonged because of their socialization, and out of whose history and culture they had created their collective identity. Far removed from it, hardly able to co-fashion the future of that country, the expelled Sudeten Germans certainly do not hold the key to the Czech future.

Seen in this way, the Sudeten German problem provides a vivid example of how present-day political life in the Czech Republic, where profound changes have taken place, is also still stamped to a considerable extent by the past. The Sudeten Germans were expelled a half-century ago, but in spite of that they are perceived by many Czechs in the same image as before. The continuity in how the Sudeten German problem is perceived stands in stunning contrast to a changed reality that in this case cannot be overlooked. The discussions strongly resemble those of the interwar period; many Czechs and many Sudeten Germans serve up the same old arguments. The same mentalities still determine the Czech-German discourse today.

It is worth mentioning that precisely the conceptual models that search in the past for arguments for their visions of the future are 'not so terribly' interested in the past itself. Behind the supposed 'Forward to the Past' position, a 'Back to the Future' position makes itself notably clear: the future cannot be understood any differently than as a repetition of past conflicts, as a permanent, continual battle over historically constant problems in the face of all real historical changes.

In reality, it is also an example of continuing mental conditions that prohibit those involved from seeing the past differently than it was perceived 'then', or from perceiving the differences between the past and the present. The Sudeten Germans were expelled a half-century ago and they still are perceived as they were before their expulsion: as a homogenous minority, as lackeys of a supposedly traditional German 'Drang nach Böhmen', as the source of a feared threat. The question of 'Continuity and Change in Political Development' in the Czech Republic can hardly find a more vivid example than this in the analytical search for its answer.

Notes

1. For the precursors to this essay cf. Eva Schmidt-Hartmann, 1993. 'Tschechen und Sudetendeutsche: Ein mühsamer Abschied von der Vergangenheit'. (Czechs and Sudeten Germans: A Laborious Parting from History), in 'Vergangenheitsbewältigung: Was kann die Geschichtswissenschaft beitragen?' (The Overcoming of the Past: What Can Historical Scholarship Offer?) Special issue of the journal *Bohemia* 34, (2): 421-33. This volume offers other relevant studies for the question under consideration here. The author has dealt extensively with the Sudeten German problem in her *Sudetoněmecký problém: obtížné loučení s minulostí* (The Sudeten German Problem: The tiresome farewell from the past). Prague 1996.

2. The literature on the course of the expulsion is extensive. Most works come from authors standing close to the Sudeten German organizations and are therefore committed to one-sided conceptual schemata and pose no discursive-analytical questions. Czech publications of recent vintage are discussed in Jaroslav Kučera, 1994, 'Česká historigrafie a odsun Němců'. (Czech Historiography and the Transfer of the Germans), in *Soudobé dějiny* 1, (2-3): 365-73. For a view of the Czech discussion of the expulsion in the late 1970s and early 1980s, see Eva Schmidt-Hartmann, 1985, 'Menschen oder Nationen? Die Vertreibung der Deutschen aus tschechischer Sicht'. (People or Nations? The Expulsion of the Germans in the Czech View), in *Die Vertreibung der Deutschen aus dem Osten*. (The Expulsion of the Germans from the East). Wolfgang Benz (ed.), Frankfurt: 178-98.

3. According to the most recent Czech research, 189 resistance groups were identified in which Czechs and Germans fought together. See Pavel Škorpil, 1993, 'K problematice počtu československých obětí nacionálně socialistického Německa v letech 1938-1945'. (On the Problem of the Number of Czechoslovak Victims of National Socialist Germany, 1938-1945), in *Terezínské listy 21:* 60-79, here 67.

4. On the contemporary reception of this problematic, see Eva Schmidt-Hartmann, 1993. '"My" a "oni": hledání české národní identity na stránkách Dneška z roku 1946'. ('We' and 'They': The Search for the Czech National Identity in the Pages of Dnešek in 1946), in *Stránkami soudobých dějin, Sborník statí k pětašedesátinám historika Karla Kaplana.* (Though the Pages of Contemporary History. Essays In Honor of the Sixty-Fifth Birthday of the Historian Karel Kaplan). Karel Jech (ed.), Prague: 93-109.

5. The most recent survey consideration of the history of the Czech-German co-habitation in the Czech lands is Ferdinand Seibt, 1992, *Deutschland und die Tschechen. Geschichte einer Nachbarschaft in der Mitte Europas.* (Germany and the Czechs. The History of Two Neighbours in the Centre of Europe). München.

6. The ambivalent function of the recognition of a 'Sudeten German ethnic group' by German politicians — for example in the form of recognizing the Sudeten Germans as the 'fourth tribe' of Bavaria, which was originally meant to contribute to the 'integration' of the Sudeten Germans but which a half-century later has served for a group of political functionaries as a means for 'setting apart' the Sudeten Germans as a special 'minority' with special claims and demands — is seldom perceived in its historical context. Much earlier, the recognition of membership in the Sudeten German minority was felt by independent observers to be only an expression of the memory of the 'evil' past of Konrad Henlein's Sudeten German Unity Movement in the 1930s, as an attempt to permit the past to collaborate in the fashioning of the future. So here, also, the paradoxical dislike of historicizing history reveals itself in precisely those conceptions that project the past as a source of future threats. Cf. Eva Hahn. 'Wer sind die Sudetendeutschen am Ende des 20. Jahrhunderts und warum sind sie ein Problem?' (Who Are the Sudeten Germans at the End of the Twentieth Century and Why are They a Problem?), in *Nationale Minderheiten in Ostmitteleuropa.* (National Minorities in East-Central Europe). Hans Henning Hahn (ed.), Publication forthcoming.

7. Although only about 3,000,000 Sudeten Germans were expelled after the Second World War — so a half-century ago — today the number of Sudeten Germans is given as 3,800,000. Strictly viewed, this does not mean that the Sudeten Germans have increased so much in number in a biological way; much more importantly, not only descendents but also married 'Reichsdeutschen' are counted, just as Germans who are 'considered Sudeten Germans' or 'equated with Sudeten Germans' according to the statute of the Landsmannschaft. In Paragraph 4 of the statute of the Sudetendeutsche Landsmannschaft, the criteria

for an uncommonly extensive interpretation of the concept of ethnicity are laid out:

'(1)   A Sudeten German is a German who was born in, or has right of homeland in, a community in the lands of Bohemia, Moravia, or Silesia.

(2)   A German who has at least one parent or grandparent who is a Sudeten German, or has a spouse who is a Sudeten German or who is considered a Sudeten German, is considered a Sudeten German.

(3)   A German who for an extended period lived in a community in the lands of Bohemia, Moravia or Silesia and expresses his ties to the Sudeten German ethnic group is also considered a Sudeten German.

(4)   A German who approves of the purpose of the Sudetendeutsche Landsmannschaft (Paragraph 3) and expresses his ties to the Sudeten German minority through the acquisition of membership in the Sudetendeutsche Landsmannschaft is also equated with a Sudeten German.'

8. A survey of the positions of the individual parties of the German Bundestag appears in the weekly *Das Parlament*, Vol. 24, 24-31 March 1995.
9. Tony Judt, 1993. 'Die Vergangenheit ist ein anderes Land'. (The Past is Another Country), in *Transit 6*: 87-120.
10. The Czech fears of the expelled Sudeten Germans, popular today in retrospect, were formulated already in 1946. For example, in the journal Dnešek the following questions were posed: 'Since the Sudeten Germans had already not liked us — even when they had no reason, since we had not harmed them — what will they likely do in the future? Will they possibly inflame all of German politics against us and in this sense influence it?' Cf. my analysis of the journal Dnešek, cited in note 4.
11. The most informative example of the present form of the collective identity of the Sudeten German minority is presented in *Die Sudetendeutschen. Eine Volksgruppe im Herzen Europas*. (The Sudeten Germans. An Ethnic Group in the Heart of Europe). Oskar Böse and Rolf-Josef Eibicht (eds.), Catalogue of the Exhibition assembled by the Sudetendeutscher Rat. München, 1989.
12. From Rudolf Hilf's numerous statements, cf. for example 'Poznámky k "českému problému". (Notes on the 'Czech Problem'), in *Soudobé dějiny* 1 (2-3), 1994: 252-55 and his 'Thesen und Vorschlag Grundkonsens', (Theses and Proposal for a Basic Consensus), presented for discussion at the second Schwarzenberg Meeting in Scheinfeld in 1993.
13. The following is based on various press reports from German newspapers in 1994 and 1995.
14. *Frankfurter Allgemeine Zeitung*, 24 May 1994. All the following quoted material was also taken from this issue.

15. The 'Beneš Decrees' is the name popularly given today to the Czechoslovak legislation of the immediate postwar period, which carried out the deprivation of the rights of the Germans as well as an extensive constitutional reform.
16. Walter Scheel, 1993, in *Rudé právo*. 2 October 1993.
17. *Národní osvobození*, 13 August 1991.
18. Hans Henning Hahn formulated and developed these ideas in his contribution to the discussion in '"Unsere Geschichte": Tschechisch-deutsche Vergangenheit als Interpretationsproblem'. (Our History: The Czech-German Past as a Problem of Interpretation), in *Bohemia* 35, (2), 1994: 429-34.

Bibliography

Benz, Wolfgang (ed.), 1985. *Die Vertreibung der Deutschen aus dem Osten*. (The Expulsion of the Germans from the East). Frankfurt/M.: Fischer Taschenbuch.

Böse, Oskar and Rolf-Josef Eibicht, (eds.) 1989. *Die Sudetendeutschen. Eine Volkgsgruppe im Herzen Europas*. (The Sudeten Germans. An Ethnic Group in the Heart of Europe). Catalogue of the Exhibition assembled by the Sudetendeutscher Rat. München: Sudetendeutscher Rat.

Das Parlament, vol. 24, 24-31 March 1995.

Frankfurter Allgemeine Zeitung, 24 May 1994.

Hahn, Eva 'Wer sind die Sudetendeutschen am Ende des 20. Jahrhunderts und warum sind sie ein Problem?' (Who Are the Sudeten Germans at the End of the Twentieth Century and Why are They a Problem?), in *Nationale Minderheiten in Ostmitteleuropa*. (National Minorities in East-Central Europe). Hans Henning Hahn (ed.), Publication forthcoming.

Hahn, Hans Henning 1994. 'Unsere Geschichte': Tschechisch-deutsche Vergangenheit als Interpretationsproblem', (Our History: The Czech-German Past as a Problem of Interpretation), in *Bohemia*, 35: 2.

Hahnová, Eva 1996. *Sudetoněmecký problém: obtížné loučení s minulostí* (The Sudeten German Problem: The tiresome farewell from the past). Prague: Prago Media.

Hilf, Rudolf 1994. 'Poznámky k českému problému'. (Notes on the 'Czech Problem'), in *Soudobé dějiny*, 1: 2-3.

Jech, Karel (ed.) 1993. *Stránkami soudobých dějin, Sborník statí k pětašedesátinám historika Karla Kaplana*. (Through the Pages of Contemporary History. Essays In Honour of the Sixty-Fifth Birthday of the Historian, Karel Kaplan). Prague: ÚSD.

Judt, Tony 1993. 'Die Vergangenheit ist ein anderes Land', (The Past is Another Country), in *Transit 6*.

Kučera, Jaroslav 1994. 'Česká historigrafie a odsun Němců'. Czech Historiography and the Transfer of the Germans, in *Soudobé dějiny*, 1: 2-3.

Národní osvobození, 13 August 1991.

Rudé právo, 2 October 1993.

Schmidt-Hartmann, Eva 1993. 'Tschechen und Sudetendeutsche: Ein mühsamer Abschied von der Vergangenheit', (Czechs and Sudeten Germans: A Laborious Parting from History), in *Bohemia*, 34: 2.

Seibt, Ferdinand 1992. *Deutschland und die Tschechen. Geschichte einer Nachbarschaft in der Mitte Europas.* (Germany and the Czechs. The History of Two Neighbours in the Centre of Europe). München: Piper.

Škorpil, Pavel 1993. 'K problematice počtu československých obětí nacionálné socialistického Německa v letech 1938-1945'. (On the Problem of the Number of Czechoslovak Victims of National Socialist Germany, 1938-1945), in *Terezínské listy* 21.

Forward to a New Past? The Czech Historical Debate since 1989[1]

Christiane Brenner

Karel Kučera, a Czech historian who died in 1990, described the radical transformation of academic judgement as one of the main characteristics of the Czech historical discourse. Each generation of historians, Kučera asserted, instinctively rejects everything the preceding generation has thought and written on history. According to Kučera, this lack of intellectual continuity is a result of the belated and rapid development of the Czech society, which has often led the historical debate into a dead-end of political polemics while the concern for genuine historical knowledge declined.[2]

Indeed, discussions of history play a different role within the Czech society than in countries where a continual development of historical consciousness and academic life has taken place. In Germany, we have had several very emotional and politically charged debates on the recent national past since the sixties, but they were still less passionate than the Czech example.

If we agree with Kučera's hypothesis, the political change of the year 1989 is likely to become the starting point for a new radical change in academic judgement and — as a result of this — in public opinion concerning the past.

Certainly, the end of the socialist regime has brought about a radical break in historical research, historiography and historical discussion that can hardly be over-estimated. In spite of this outward impression, there is considerable continuity in historical thinking and debate, in some spheres even more continuity than change.

The continuity of the basics of Czech historiography paradigms is the most obvious of these. The basic paradigms lack a theoretical background and at the same time exhibit a strong tendency towards historical philosophy.[2] History is comprehended predominantly through a religious dichotomy, dividing Czech history into a Catholic and a Protestant line of interpretation, with opposite implications. Moreover, Czech historiography identifies itself strongly with the nation. Furthermore, there has been almost no change in the way history is written and told or the topics that attract historical interest. Nor have historians sought a different definition of their position in society.

The second reason not to emphasize 1989 too much as a watershed year for historiography is the slow development of historical interest and consciousness during the last two decades. In my opinion, the 'return of history,' euphorically welcomed in 1989, started in the early eighties. Throughout Europe, history and nation became more important again, and this trend was not hindered by the iron curtain. The birth of an independent historiography formed part of this European development, although it can be argued that *samizdat* historiography reached only a relatively small circle of readers and remained an isolated phenomenon until the end of the socialist system. But even in Czech society as a whole, interest in history was growing, especially the national history of the last two centuries. The socialist state reacted to this interest in history and tradition with a great number of publications, from merely academic works to more popular and purely folkloristic titles.[3]

The political transformation of 1989 lent a new quality and dimension to this 'return of history' even though the discussion was not inspired by new data. The end of the state monopoly over information and the interpretation of history — even if it might not have been very effective during the last years of communism — made it possible to study what had been suppressed for a long time. A huge number of articles on historical topics in newspapers and journals along with (at least in the beginning) great public interest in classic works of Czech philosophy and historiography and in the former samizdat-authors all indicated a genuine desire to make up for lost time.

But this process also brought about new conflicts in Czech society. By opening the debate on history, many difficult themes and problematic questions concerning the recent past have also surfaced, which had been taboo for a long time. This taboo meant relief and reassurance for a certain part of the Czech population, especially for the generation who took part in the events at the end of World War II. Different groups in Czech society apply different meanings to the decisive points in their national history, depending on their social status, ethnic affiliation and political convictions. Individual memories and the way one interprets historical events often form a counterhistory to the history told by others. As the discussion of the past draws nearer to the present, the more it becomes connected to the biographies of individuals. Consider the impassioned reactions to President Václav Havel's apology for the expulsion of the Germans[4] as well as the strenuous efforts to remove the remains of communist rule and to eradicate the memory of past experiences so completely that it was as if they had never existed.

This historical discourse is a struggle about identities in the broadest sense. Both society and the new state are legitimated by the break with the recent past, as well as by historical traditions. But whose history and what kind of history can Czech society accept as their own today? The past has become one of the crucial problems of the present.

Czech historiography has always been closely tied to the nation. Since its emergence in the 19th century — with the active help of historians — the nation has always stood at the centre of historical interest. Many Czech historians do not regard the interdependence of historical research and the nation as a disadvantage. Dušan Třeštík, for instance, defends the connection between history and nation against demands for distance and the integration of Czech history into European history. In his view, the mutual relationship is a basic condition for historical work.[5]

His argument is not very convincing because the very concentration on the national past limits the scope of vision. It tends to regard phenomena as unique to one's own national history, ignoring that other societies went through similar developments, and it leads to an underestimation of foreign influences on the history of individual countries.

Nevertheless, both popular and academic understandings of who belongs to the nation and what forms part of the national history have obviously changed over the last few years. Since the 19th century, there has been a strong tendency in the central European societies to seek to eliminate pluralism. In the Czech debate today, the contribution of the Germans and the Jews is increasingly acknowledged and the variety of influences that have effected the history of the Czech lands are appreciated.[6] Many authors regard the capacity of the Bohemian society to integrate alien and new influences as a special quality.[7]

While searching for answers to the eternal question of 'jáci jsme' — 'how are we', it might be very instructive to take into account the discussion of the administrative separation of the Czechs and Slovaks. Here we are almost exclusively dependent on newspaper articles and other popular texts. Despite more than 70 years of a common Czechoslovak state, Slovak history has never lost its character of an appendix to the history of the Czech lands, either in written accounts or in the historical consciousness of the Czechs. It is treated with comparative carelessness in both official publications of the last decades as well as in the samizdat publications of the eighties. Even the latest works on the history of Czechoslovakia which have appeared in the bookstalls since 1989 have downplayed the role of Slovak society.[8]

The present discussion of Czechs and Slovaks often gives the impression that the standards of Czech self-definition are still tied to the paradigms of the romantic era and the so-called 'national rebirth'. The negative stereotype of Slovak inferiority and backwardness, often used to explain the alleged tendency of the Slovaks towards authoritarian systems and their supposed inability to implement democracy, still circulates even in serious publications. Alternatively, the romantic vision of the complementarity of Czechs and Slovaks, with a slightly more favourable view of Slovakian society, has lost little of its popularity. Those who support this view regard the Slovaks as an emotional, spontaneous and unpredictable 'childish' nation compared to the more logical, rational, democratic and 'grown-up' Czechs. These contrasting stereotypes of 'national-characters' are often reinforced by characterizing them as 'Eastern' and 'Western' types of nations.[9]

Indeed, one gets the impression that the Czechs had already moved a bit towards the West before they divorced their Slovak partners. In the Czech historical debate, the geographical position of Bohemia and Moravia 'in the heart of Europe' was often interpreted as proof of a special historical mission for the Czech nation. This 'paradigm of the centre' has sometimes been slavophile and sometimes directed against Russia and the East. In other contexts, the Czechs regarded it as their duty to mediate between East and West; sometimes they saw their nation as an outpost of one of the two worlds. In the discussion about 'Central-Europe' (Střední Evropa) during the eighties, driven largely by writers and historians, the idea of the Czech nation as a bridge between East and West was abandoned in favour of an unambiguous classification of Czech culture as a part of the West.[10] This tendency has clearly continued since 1989 in politics as well as in public discourse about the past and the future of the Czech nation.

Jiří Rak, for example, presents the European and the Central-European options as two ideas in Czech history of unequal value. Rak argues that flirting with the role as mediator between East and West has always led to a dead end. His examples range from Havlíček Borovský, who was cured of his Slavophilism by a longer sojourn in Russia; to Palacký, who discovered the East when he was old and senile and heavily disappointed by the Vienna government and the Kaiser; to the last chapter of the Central-European option, the experiment with a 'third way' in 1968. In contrast to these 'Central European dreams,' he clearly sides with the West:

What does it mean in the Czech case, to identify oneself with Europe ... ? The European orientation is completely obvious, it does not mean joining the continent, but its Western part, the principles of Western civilization.[11]

Historians in particular have adopted this orientation towards the West with great vigour. Their preoccupation with their Eastern and Central European neighbours, whose fate the Czech have shared more or less voluntarily during the last decades, has nearly disappeared. No attempts have been made to examine the socialist experience in cooperation with historians from other ex-socialist states, even though this would lead to a more systematic and general understanding of socialist systems and societies.

The Czech self-identification as a Western nation reveals their conviction that the Czech nation has always been democratic. This image of a special Czech talent for democracy was first expounded by Palacký, later modernized by the first Czechoslovak President, T.G. Masaryk, and became a kind of 'national education programme' in the Czechoslovak Republic (ČSR) between the wars. Today, the Czech Republic draws on the tradition of the Czecho-slovak state between 1918 and 1938. This state was the most successful in the region after World War I. While all other Central European states mutated into more or less authoritarian regimes, the ČSR stayed democratic until it was destroyed by fascist Germany. In the social and economic realm, the Czechoslovakian state offered more to its inhabitants than did the governments of most of its neighbours. Not surprising then, communist historiography, when discussing the First Republic and its protagonists, for a long time came to a very negative judgement. This did not change until the late eighties when the communist rulers tried to base their claim to power on a broader historical base and rediscovered the First Czechoslovak Republic as a part of the nation's tradition.

Thus, Czech historians today tend to stylize the history of the First Republic as a success story.[12] Věra Olivová, for example, demands that the younger generation in particular, having grown up under an authoritarian system, should study the history of the ČSR to learn about democracy. But why should they not study the problems of this state as well? They learn little about these problems in either Olivová's text-book for secondary schools or her writings on Czechoslovakian history between the two World Wars prepared for university students.[13]

In another work by the same author, one learns that the tradition of the First Republic was revived during the years from 1945 to 1948, as well as in 1968, and again today.[14] But what exactly does that mean? The brief period between the end of World War II and February 1948 can surely be interpreted as a revival of the pre-war traditions, if our discussion is limited to the mere existence of a Czechoslovak state and a sort of multi-party system. But if we concede the democratic tradition to cover more than these two formal characteristics — obviously Olivová has more in mind because she talks about Masaryk's 'Civil Society' and the democratic political culture of the First Republic — then the early postwar years and 'socialism with a human face' can hardly be identified with the interwar period.

Masaryk deserves special mention. In many of the innumerable books and articles on the first Czechoslovak president which have been published since 1989, his era is presented with almost no historical distance as a precursor of the modern civil society and a democratic unified Europe in the sense of the European Community.[15] Masaryk was certainly one of the most impressive personalities in Czech history and his works are still relevant today. But we must also acknowledge that he was influenced by his time, and so was his political thinking.

One of the most emotional and most controversial debates in Czech historical self-definition concerns a tragic chapter of Czech history: the years of the Second World War and the events immediately after the war. In my opinion, no topic is better suited to demonstrate how historical consciousness has been changing during the last decades than the discussion on the expulsion of the Germans from the Czech lands in 1945-46. One of the symptoms of this evolution is the lack of a uniform opinion in contemporary Czech society on the expulsion. One can assume that in the years after the war, a great majority of Czechs approved of — or at least tolerated — this measure as an act of justified revenge against the Germans and a step towards greater ethnic homogeneity following the unhappy experience of the multinational First Republic.

The first attempts at a critical discussion on the expulsion of the Sudeten Germans (i.e., the Bohemian Germans) came in the sixties, but they were suppressed by the socialist rulers immediately after the autumn of 1968. The controversy of the sixties became public only after 1989,[16] at the same time as the debate in *samizdat* journals. In connection with political events — President Havel's apology for the expulsion of the Sudeten-Germans from Czechoslovak territory, the Sudeten Germans' demand for compensation of their material losses, and the discussion of the treaty between Czechoslovakia and the Federal Republic of Germany — these publications led to a heated controversy that continues today.[17]

Without elaborating on individual arguments in the discussion, let me offer some observations on the general character of the debate.

1) Critical distance to the past or accepting it in all its dimensions. This polarization is a very important aspect of the debate. In Czech society, fear is growing that the material claims of the 'Sudetendeutsche Landsmannschaft'[18] would be supported if one accepted history in all its parts. This makes open discussion even more difficult and threatens to lead to its stagnation. The 'Landsmannschaft' demands compensation for their groups' expulsion by the Czech State and their claims have been supported by the Bavarian administration and by certain parts of the German government. The unfortunate and cynical offer of compensation to Czech victims of Nazi terror, in exchange for compensation of the Sudeten Germans by the Czech state, antagonizes even those in Czech society who had been prepared to

engage in a real dialogue. At the same time, the position of the 'Landsmannschaft' reinforces the perception by many that even after fifty years, German revanchism is alive as well; and for them, German policy represents the interests of the 'Landsmannschaft'.

2) By the end of the sixties, the first critical debates concerning the expulsion had raised several problems with the history of the German occupation. Some historians questioned the behaviour of the majority of the Czech population in the so-called 'protectorate' and at the end of World War II. Among the most powerful post-war myths in Czechoslovakia was the neat division of victims and culprits. Challenging this legend today — and with it the justification of the expulsion — is not only morally explosive, but challenges the biographies of an entire generation. Not astonishingly, Czechs react with indignation, anger and aversion if this topic is broached.

3) Even more surprisingly, many historians call for an end to the debate on this 'terrible story'.[19] The idea of making a fresh start in history without critically reappraising the past, as more than 300 Czech historians demanded in a paper published in 1991, flies in the face of the historian's duty. Furthermore, this position is at best illusionary because the history of the war and postwar period engages the last decades as well as those of the present. This leads to my fourth and last point.

4) The story of the expulsion raises not only questions concerning its origin, i.e., the general brutalization of political culture and the destruction of the Czech elite, but also demands investigation into the long-term effects of this 'dehumanization'.[20] According to historian Tomaš Staněk, the expulsion led to a deterioration in the ethnic and political relations of the country. It was a step towards dictatorship in domestic policy and it helped unite political blocs in foreign policy.[21] Taking into account the historical origins and results of the expulsion, the breaks of 1945 and 1948 are less decisive than conventional wisdom would suggest.

Having referred so frequently to the search for tradition and identity, let me return to the basic paradigms of Czech historiography. After 1989, Czech historians complained that the reputation of historical research and of historians in general had suffered lasting damage during the previous decades.[22] Considering this, it is even more astonishing how self-confident some Czech historians are when characterizing their social duty today. More so than their colleagues in the West, they feel competent to offer an unambiguous social identity to the country.

This is not only specific for the Czech case. From the 19th century on, in all nations without a national state, the imagination of a glorious past replaced real political force in the present. Already Frantisek Palacký, the founder of modern Czech historiography in the 19th century, understood the creation of historical consciousness as his political task, and developed patterns for interpreting Czech history. This political programme — characterizing the Czechs as a democratic and liberal nation between warlike and authoritarian Germany and Russia — endured for many generations.

During the past few decades, the discourse on the past — especially in samizdat publications — served as a substitute for an authentic public debate on the present that was not feasible at the time. The conditions and function of discussions about historical interpretation have changed, but the historical debate is still largely dominated by its relevance for the present. That the discussion is highly politicized is neither accidental nor unintended. Jan Křen, for example, characterizes the work of the historian as that of a bridge-builder to create a common historical identity that leads the nation into the future.[23] Dušan Třeštík sees the historian's 'burden of responsibility' as that of orienting and strengthening a new self-confidence in Czech society, which still lacks a consensus on the goals and 'idea of the Czech state.' 'Not until they have completed this task', argues Dušan Třeštík, 'can they follow the recipe of their colleagues in the West, that means, to retreat into a purely academic sphere.'[24]

The debate on the book *Podiven*, which appeared in bookstalls at the end of 1991, leads the outside observer to conclude that the moment of retreat is still far off. *Podiven*, a work on modern Czech history, was written by the psychiatrist Petr Příhoda, the lawyer and political scientist Petr Pithart (who was Prime Minister at the time) and the historian Milan Otáhal. Its contents can certainly be criticized in some respects, but this is not my point here. The form and content of the public debate that the book roused are more important in this context. Věra Olivová, for example, characterizes the authors' negation of positive Czech traditions as a continuation of the 'falsification' of history in the service of two totalitarian systems since 1938 and as a threat to the democratization of Czech society.[25] Aleš Haman argues similarly that it is irresponsible to weaken the nation by criticizing it, given the present situation. The national consciousness, having been treated with the universal slogans of proletarian internationalism for forty years — in Haman's view — finds itself completely paralyzed. For that reason, a criticism like the one *Podiven* expounds implies the danger that the already strong inferiority complexes of the Czech society and the indifference towards the national culture are intensified. Haman calls for an affirmative approach to Czech history to strengthen collected forces in order to mobilize the mental potentials of the nation.[26]

Josef Hanzal continues this line of criticism by asking two of the authors of *Podiven*: 'How can you, Pan Pithart and Pan Příhoda, represent and defend a nation you do not value and even despise?'[27]

Of course this is an extreme view and not all Czech historians support it. In my opinion, attributing a meaning to past and present in this way as well as supplying a political orientation would prevent any critical perspective on history. I have concentrated on the unpleasant tendencies in Czech historiography, but many good and interesting historical works have appeared in the last five years. The future also depends on whether various aspects of the communist system — e.g., its genesis, its functioning and the conditions of 'normality' for the people living with it — are critically analyzed and assessed. Another important question is whether the communist era will be accepted as a part — however inconvenient — of the Czech past, or whether it will be regarded as something alien to the national tradition, an interpretation that would delegate responsibility for the last fifty years to 'others'. Last, but not least, it remains to be seen whether a new myth will be created, one that denies that the wheels of history in 1989 were once again moved from the outside. And all these questions will surely provoke many debates among historians.

The events in the autumn of 1989 are often portrayed as the end of the age of ideologies, and as the close of an epoch in which we searched for global explanations and a general motive in history. Historians in particular are welcoming the beginning of an era of rationality, the end of superstition and historical myths, and a chance for an objective interpretation of history.[28] However, reflections on the problems of 'historical truth' and 'objectivity,' on the dependence of historical research on the politics of the recent past and of the present, have not yet really started among Czech historians.[29] But this is not the only reason why I view the proclamation of the post-ideological age with some reservations. Historiography comes closer to objectivity, not only by searching for the 'one and only truth', but by regarding itself as a product of its time and accepting other standpoints and interpretations. The political system can supply (and destroy) the conditions for historical work and debate — but it cannot guarantee its success in seeking objectivity. History is a permanent dialogue between past and present, and it is mainly a discourse among people. The debate on the past should be a permanent process, starting again and again with new questions. Historians everywhere, not only in the former socialist countries, are challenged by the responsibility of keeping this dialogue alive and not suffocating it by asserting 'absolute truth'.

Notes

1. This article is based on a lecture held in Autumn 1994. In the meantime many of the discussions mentioned here have changed considerably. For recent developments refer to: Christiane Brenner, 'Last der Geschichte oder Wegweiser in die Zukunft? Vergangenheitsbewältigung in der tschechischen und der slowakischen Gesellschaft', in Herwig Roggemann, and Holm Sundhaussen (ed.), *Ost- und Südosteuropa zwischen Tradition und Aufbruch. Aspekte und Dimensionen der Umgestaltungsprozesse in den postsozialistischen Ländern.* Wiesbaden 1996: 53-74.
2. Jaroslav Marek, 1994. 'Místo teorie a teorií v dějepisectví přítomnosti', in *Soudobé dějiny* 2-3: 193f.
3. Eva Schmidt-Hartmann, 1988. 'Forty Years of Historiography under Socialism in Czechoslovakia', in *Bohemia* 29, (302): 300-24.
4. In November 1989, a few days before the democratic revolution in Czechoslovakia started, Václav Havel wrote in a letter to the German 'Bundespräsident' Richard von Weizsäcker: 'I personally — just as a lot of my friends — condemn the expulsion of the Germans ... I always considered it as an act of deep immorality, that caused harm ... not only to Germans but, perhaps in an even larger extend to the Czechs.' A few weeks later when Havel was elected President and on his first official visit to Germany, he repeated this statement. *Dokumentation Ostmitteleuropa.* Vol. 5 (6), Marburg: Lahn 1991, 298.
5. Dušan Třeštík, 1991. 'Co čeká české dějepisectví?', in *Přítomnost* 3: 30.
6. Jan Křen, 1993. *Historické proměny češství*, Praha: 22. For a bad example see, Jaroslav Krejčír et al., 1993, *Dějiny české. Chronologický přehled*, Prague. The authors of this book 'forgot' to mention the minority of more than three million German inhabitants in the chapter about the First Czechoslovakian Republic.
7. Jaroslav Marek, 1991. 'Konturen des zeitgenösssischen Nchdenkens über die Geschichte', in *Bohemia* 32: 311.
8. For example, Jaroslav Marek (ed.), 1991. *České a československé dějiny*, vol. 2, Prague; Eduard Kubů (with M. Rampouchová), 1993, 'Der Tschechoslowakismus und die Entwicklung der tschechisch-slowakischen Beziehungen', in *Ethnos-Nation. Eine Europäische Zeitschrift*, 1: 7-21.
9. Petr Příhoda, 1993. 'Sociálně-psychologické aspekty soužití Čechů a Slováků', in Rüdiger Kipke, Karel Vodička (ed.), *Rozloučení s Československem*. Praha: 33-39, 34-35.
10. Martin Schulze Wessel, 1988. 'Die Mitte liegt westwärts. Mitteleuropa in tschechischer Diskussion', in *Bohemia* 29: 325-44.
11. Jiří Rak, 1992. 'České (středo)evropanství', in *Tvar 6*, (1-5): 5.
12. See also, Peter Heumos, 1993. 'Probleme des Neuanfangs. Bemerkungen zu Konzeptionen und Methoden der tschechischen zeitgeschichtlichen Forschung nach 1989', in *Bohemia* 34: 359-80.
13. Věra Olivová, 1994. *Dějepis. Nová Doba 2. Československá republika v letech 1918-1938*, Prague; and Věra Olivová, 1991, *Československé dějiny 1914-1939*, 2 Vol., Prague.

14. Věra Olivová, 1993. 'Manipulace s dějinami první republiky', in *ČČH*, (3): 442-59.
15. Masaryková idea československé státnosti ve světle kritiky dějin. (Sborník příspěvků z konference konané ve dnech 24. a 25. září 1992 v aule Obchodné akademie v Hodoníně) Prague 1993; and, Masaryk a myšlenka evropské jednoty. (Sborník příspěvků z konference konané ve dnech 13. a 14. cervna 1991 na univerzitě v Praze) Prague 1992.
16. Bohumil Černý, Jan Křen, Václav Kural, Milan Otáhal (ed.), 1990. *Češi - Němci - odsun. Diskuse nezávislých historiků*, Prague.
17. For a survey on this discussion see, Manfred Alexander, 1993, 'Die tschechische Diskussion um die Vertreibung und deren Folgen', in *Bohemia*, 34, Vol. 2: 390-409; 'Die Diskussion über die Vertreibung der Deutschen in der ČSFR' (bearbeitet von Reiner Beushausen). *Dokumentation Ostmitteleuropa*, December 1991, Vol. 5 (6); and Karel Kaplan, 1990, *Pravda o Československu*. Prague: 137.
18. The *Sudetendeutsche Landsmannschaft* is a strongly conservative political organization that claims to represent not only those Germans who were expelled from the Czech Lands, but also their children and grandchildren. Even though most Sudeten Germans are neither members of the *Landsmannschaft* nor identify with its activities, the *Landsmannschaft* has successfully claimed to be the only spokesman of the Sudeten Germans in the public debate in Germany as well as in the Czech Republic.
19. 'Sudetští Němci a my Stanovisko českých historiků', in *Komu sluší omluva. Češi a sudetští němci*. Prague: 212-14. One of the first books on Czech history that came out after 1989 was particularly disappointing on this score, Vojtěch Mencl, Miloš Hájek, Milan Otáhal, Erika Kadlecová, 1990, *Křizovatky 20. století. Světlo na bílá místa v nejnovějších dějinách*. Prague.
20. *Právo Lidu*, 1980, (1), Zürich.
21. Tomáš Staněk, 1991. *Odsun Němců z Československa* 1945-94. Prague: 522f.
22. Dušan Třeštík, 1991. 'Die tschechische Geschichte und die tschechischen Historiker', in *Bohemia 32*: 281.
23. Jan Křen, 1990. *Bílá místa v našich dějinach*, Prague: 10ff.
24. Dušan Třeštík, 1991. *Die tschechische Geschichte und die tschechischen Historiker*, in *Bohemia* 32: 281.
25. Věra Olivová, 1993, 'manipulace s dějinami první republiky', in *ČČH* 91.
26. Aleš Haman, 30 January 1992. 'Provokativní kniha', in *Literární noviny,*
27. Josef Hanzal, 5 February 1992, 'Podivný Podiven', in *Literární noviny* 30.
28. Jaroslav Marek, 1991. 'Konturen des zeitgenössischen Nachdenkens über die Geschichte', in *Bohemia* 32: 297ff.; Dušan Třeštík, 1991, 'Die tschechische Geschichte und die tschechischen Historiker', in *Bohemia* 32: 277 and 280.
29. Robert Luft, 1994. 'Als die Wachsamkeit des Regimes nachließ, Zur Beschäftigung mit der Vergangenheit des eigenen Faches in der tschechischen Geschichtswissenschaft nach 1989', in *Bohemia* 35: 105-21.

Bibliography

Brenner, Christiane 1996. 'Last der Geschichte oder Wegweiser in die Zukunft? Vergangenheitsbewältigung in der tschechischen und der slowakischen Gesellschaft', in Herwig Roggemann and Holm Sundhaussen (eds.), *Ost- und Südosteuropa zwischen Tradition und Aufbruch. Aspekte und Dimensionen der Umgestaltungsprozesse in den postsozialistischen Ländern*. Wiesbaden: Harrasowitz, 53-74.

Černy, Bohumil, Jan Křen, Václav Kural, Milan Otáhal (eds.) 1990. *Češi - Němci - odsun. Diskuse nezávislých historiků*. Prague: Academia.

Dokumentation Ostmitteleuropa, 1991. Vol. 5 (6). Marburg/Lahn, 298.

Haman, Aleš 1992. 'Provokativní kniha', in *Literární noviny* 30, 5 February: 7.

Hanzal, Josef 1992. 'Podivný Podiven', in *Literární noviny* 30, 5 February: 9.

Heumos, Peter 1993. 'Probleme des Neuanfangs. Bemerkungen zu Konzeptionen und Methoden der tschechischen zeitgeschichtlichen Forschung nach 1989', in *Bohemia* 34: 359-80.

Kaplan, Karel 1990. *Pravda o Československu*. Prague: Panorama, 137.

Krejčír, Jaroslav, et al. 1993. *Dějiny české. Chronologický přehled*. Prague: INFOA.

Křen, Jan 1990. *Bilá místa v našich dějinach*. Prague: Knihovna lidových novin.

Křen, Jan 1993. *Historické proměny češství*. Prague.: Karolinum..

Kubů, Eduard & M. Rampouchová 1993. 'Der Tschechoslowakismus und die Entwicklung der tschechisch-slowakischen Beziehungen', in *Ethnos-Nation. Eine Europäische Zeitschrift*, 1: 7-21.

Kučera, Karel 1992. 'O výklad našich nějnovějších dějin' (first in *Samizdat* 1988) in *Historie a Historici*. Prague, (219): 219-33.

Luft, Robert 1994. 'Als die Wachsamkeit des Regimes nachließ, Zur Beschäftigung mit der Vergangenheit des eigenen Faches in der tschechischen Geschichtswissenschaft nach 1989', in *Bohemia* 35: 105-21.

Manfred, Alexander 1993. 'Die tschechische Diskussion um die Vertreibung und deren Folgen', in *Bohemia*, 34, Vol 2: 390-409.

Marek, Jaroslav 1991. 'Konturen des zeitgenössischen Nachdenkens über die Geschichte', in *Bohemia* 32: 297ff, 311.

Marek, JKaroslav, (ed.), 1991. *České a československé dějiny*, vol. 2. Prague: Melantrich.

Mencl, Vojtěch, Miloš Hájek, Milan Otáhal, & Erika Kadlecová, 1990. *Křižovatky 20. století. Světlo na bílá místa v nejnovějších dějinách*. Prague: Naše Vojsko.

Olivová, Věra 1993. 'Manipulace s dějinami první republiky', in *ČČH 91*.

Olivová, Věra 1994. *Dějepis. Nová Doba 2. Československá republika v letech 1918-1938*. Prague: Univerzita Karlova.

Olivová, Věra 1993. 'Manipulace s dějinami první republiky', in *ČČH*, (3): 442-59.

Olivová, Věra 1991. *Československé dějiny 1914-1939*, 2 Vol. Prague: Univerzita Karlova.

Právo Lidu, 1980. (1), Zürich: 8.

Příhoda, Petr 1993. 'Sociálně-psychologické aspekty soužití Čechů a Slováků, in Rüdiger Kipke, Karel Vodička (ed.), *Rozloučení s Československem*. Prague: Český Spisovatel: 33-39, 34-35.

Rak, Jiři 1992. 'České (středo) evropanství', in *Tvar* 6, (1-5): 5.

Schmidt-Hartmann, Eva 1988. 'Forty Years of Historiography under Socialism in Czechoslovakia', in *Bohemia* 29, (302): 300-24.

Staněk, Tomáš 1991. *Odsun Němců z Československa 1945-47*. Prague: Academia/Naše Vojsko: 522f.

'Sudetští Němci a my Stanovisko českých historiků', 1992, in *Komu sluší omluva. Češi a sudetští němci*. Prague: Erika, 212-14.

Třeštík, Dušan 1991. 'Die tschechische Geschichte und die tschechischen Historiker', in *Bohemia* 32: 277 and 280.

Třeštík, Dušan 1991. 'Co čeká české dějepisectví?', in *Přítomnost* 3: 30.

Třeštík, Dušan 1991. 'Die tschechische Geschichte und die tschechischen Historiker', in *Bohemia* 32: 281.

Wessel, Martin Schulze 1988. 'Die Mitte liegt westwärts. Mitteleuropa in tschechischer Diskussion', in *Bohemia* 29: 325-44.

Past and Present in Slovak Politics

Tibor Pichler

Slovakia offers a provocative case study for examining the impact of the past on the post-communist situation. Indeed, exploring the dimensions of continuity and change begs the question of how we design a study of a newly emerging state that has no viable historical antecedent. The tentative answer offered here focuses on the cultural dimensions of continuity and change, including traditions in political thought as well as the ideas, habits, life strategies and behavioural patterns that constitute a particular culture. Our examination here concentrates on developmental tendencies during the 19th century, a formative period in the emergence of an independent Slovak consciousness.

Compared therefore to other post-communist countries in Central Europe, Slovakia represents an altogether different set of circumstances. While other societies face a transformation process that involves building stable democratic institutions and the conversion to a market economy, Slovakia must in addition confront the challenges of building an independent and autonomous state. Thus Slovakia today faces the simultaneous tasks of democratization, economic liberalization, and state-building in the context of an, as yet, not fully completed process of nation-building. Without a modern Slovak state tradition to transform, one must be invented. Thus the question of the relationship of present-day politics to the past can be translated in the Slovak case to an analysis of whether the state will be constructed largely on the basis of contemporary factors, or rather defined in terms of a historicist view that emphasizes the past. What are the chances of constitutional patriotism?[1]

The collapse of communism and the subsequent introduction of democratic institutions triggered not only a period of economic and political transition, but also a redrawing of the political map of Europe. While in Germany this meant the unification of two previously autonomous states, in Central Europe composite states disintegrated into their smaller, constitutive states. In the Yugoslav case, this resulted in violent conflict. In Czechoslovakia, it produced two separate states. The Slovak Republic is a newcomer not only on the political map, but also in international relations. Its national identity and international image reflect this novel situation. Identity has elements of both continuity and change, based in part on past experience but also defined in important ways by shared goals and visions of the future.

Identity includes both descriptive and evaluative elements: what we are and what we want to become.[2] Until 1918, Slovakia was more an idea than a real entity. Slovakia was the unofficial designation of territory in the northern part of historic Hungary, an area inhabited by Slovaks. This designation was used mostly by the Slovak nation-building elite in the literature of the time.[3] Before the establishment of the Czechoslovak Republic, Slovakia did not exist as a territory with defined borders, nor did it have any officially recognized status. Rather it was an integral part of the historic Kingdom of Hungary, known as *Hungaria Superior* since the 16th and 17th centuries.[4] This area was populated by ethnic Slovaks whose elites engaged in political and cultural initiatives to shape the population into a fully-fledged modern nation during the period of nationalism. Slovakia as a distinct territory with defined borders was the product of the peace treaties ending World War I and officially designated part of Czechoslovakia.

Thus Slovak nationalism emerged without a concomitant process of state-building. The idea of the nation surfaced in a non-institutionalized and non-formalized context. This aspect of Slovak nation-building makes it a particularly interesting case because it involves the development of an ethnic population in a compact territorial zone without any formal legal status.[5] The Slovak historian Daniel Rapant has referred to the Slovak case as one of pure ethnocultural nationalism.[6] Nevertheless, the Slovak elite participated in the modernization effort within the Hapsburg territories which took the form of various nationalist groups fighting over claims for the loyalty of, and sovereignty over, the available population. The elite constituted the nation in the sense that it was the intelligentsia that developed a national sentiment, consciousness and ideology. The project of building a modern nation belonged almost entirely to the elite. In the phrase of Svetozár Hurban Vajanský, the elite constituted the nation *pars pro toto*.[7]

As Ernest Gellner has argued, the particular content of the nationalist 'sentiment' was highly contingent, varying considerably from one group (nationality) to the next. However, nationalism as a 'principle', i.e., that nationalism should play a role in the process of creating a modern society in Central Europe, was unavoidable and non-contingent. This seems to be borne out in the Slovak case even though nationalism emerged as a phenomenon largely limited to the social elites.

The Hapsburg Empire was a culturally, historically, and politically hetero-geneous construction. Attempts from the dynastic centre to bring about cultural homogeneity and political centralization of authority generally failed. In the wake of these efforts, the empire's leadership faced divisive, if not disruptive, nation-building processes based on language. At first the competition for authority was based principally on cultural movements, but later these became political movements launched by local modernization elites in order to build independent nations. In Seton-Watson's terminology, an *official nationalism* seeking to engineer an Austrian or Hungarian nation-state failed.[8]

In the revolution of 1848-49, the inhabitants of the dynastic Hapsburg state did not constitute a nation, but rather several nations. Freedom was defined by local national modernization elites largely within ethno-national frameworks.[9] The revolution marked the end of the traditional estate society based on privilege, and the gradual 'invitation into history' of strata of the population that had previously lacked political rights. Thus the process of extending the franchise was protracted. A long march towards civil society, democracy and conscious citizenship had begun, but not yet ended.

The abolition of estates, therefore, did not automatically mean a smooth road towards modernity. Modernization in East Central Europe was coupled with nation-building. The establishment of modern standard national cultures and their successive politicization questioned and eventually threatened the territorial integrity of the dynastic Hapsburg state. Its break-up in 1918 started a wave of nation-state making which was not the last one in the region. To some extent this development was anticipated in 1848-49 when liberalization in the territory of the monarchy clashed with ethnic nationalization. It became increasingly clear that liberalization and democratization implied nation-building. Nation-building required territorial reorganization. The revolution of 1848-49 was not a revolution of the people, but of peoples. The Slovaks were one of these. During these years, the Slovak national elite headed by Ľudovít Štúr (1815-56) engaged in nation-building, entering the political arena with the intent of influencing policy. The time was favourable, but the forces of the Slovak national elite were inadequate. Štúr conceded that in the Slovak National Newspaper: 'What had been awaited only in a long span of time, what had been expected in 20, 30, 40 years, is already here, it came as if through the night'. But he also added, 'time has caught us unprepared'.[10] That he nevertheless entered the field of political action 'unprepared', feeling the compulsion of the revolutionary *kairos* as well as a kind of moral pressure, was a *Kraftakt* characteristic of romantic thinking and idealism. Romanticism fuelled the political imagination driving advocates to create a culturally and politically institutionalized nation — a fully-fledged nation — in one concentrated effort. The dominant role of Romanticism in Slovak politics is one important continuity between the past and the present.

The Slovak political programme presented in Liptovský Mikuláš in May 1848 was called *The Demands of the Slovak Nation in Hungary*.[11] These demands vindicated the instantaneous and full cultural and political institutionalization of the Slovak nation in historic Hungary and implied federalization along ethnic lines. The Slovak demands are interesting not only because of their substance, but also in relation to the barely begun process of Slovak nation-building. They cast an interesting light on the mentality of the authors and their perception of the relationship between theory and practice in politics. Ideal claims supported by natural rights arguments were not backed up by material forces and the necessary organizational infrastructure.

The 'external' time line of the revolutionary situation in Europe and the 'internal' time frame of the Slovak nation-building effort were out of synchronization. This wide discrepancy during the calm pre-revolutionary setting of Slovak national development is outlined by Ľudovít Štúr in the editorials of the *Slovenské národné noviny (Slovak National Newspaper)* in the years from 1845 to 1848. His observations proved him a critical, realistic and farsighted judge of the transformation of the Slovak ethnic group into a fully-fledged modern nation. But this realistic approach to Slovak nation-building was disrupted by the sudden arrival of a revolutionary situation. Thus the programme for constructing a nation was conditioned by the historical situation, the imperative to act. Seton-Watson (Scotus Viator) described the programme as 'curiously mixed'. Along with demands for universal suffrage, freedom of the press, and freedom of association, came national goals. Given the material situation of Slovak politics, these latter goals were 'visionary and extravagant', reflecting the 'hysteria of the moment in clear defiance of practical considerations.'[12] As Michal Chorváth wrote in his intriguing booklet *The Romantic Face of Slovakia*, published in Prague in 1939:

the Slovaks set themselves, unrelated to their forces, great immediate political goals. In 1848 they demanded the federalization of Hungary; in 1861 autonomy, although it is evident that their forces did not suffice.[13]

The development of the Slovak national sentiment occurred among the national elite, the *intelligentsia*, who were relatively inexperienced politically. Their approach took the form of subnationalism, that is, Slovak nationalism had to compete with other nationalisms within the same territory. But Slovak nationalism also occupied a weaker position because it lacked any legal status that might be reflected in public law or administration. Slovak nationalism had no institutional support to back it up, nor could it draw on a viable state tradition with relevance for the contemporary situation. Attempts to invoke the pre-Hungarian Great Moravian tradition drew on a lost memory to create a rallying effect. Thus Slovak nationalism acquired an 'emergent' quality. This emergent Slovak national identity took as its point of departure the individualizing force of the 'natural given' of language; the 'spirit' of Slovak nationalism was derived from the Herderian theory of natural community. The other current in Slovak national thought was based on the Hegelian principle that only politically present communities matter in history since it is these communities that participate in the game. The uneasy forging of Slovak individuality and identity using the 'givens' of an amorphous 'ethnographical' existence as building blocks of a national project, was led by Štúr, Jozef Miloslav Hurban and Michal Miloslav Hodža. They defined Slovak identity, to use Daniel Rapant's phrase, in opposition to the 'covering complexes' of territorial and political Hungarism and linguistic and cultural slavism.[14] Slovakism (slovenstvo) emerged using cultural slavism against linguistically Magyarasing Hungarism. The cultural Czecho-Slovak slavism was contrasted with the Slovak presence in historic Hungary.[15] Slovakism was defined by a kind of negative historicism, emphasizing the present moment and the role of future-oriented intellectualism and practical action. 'Slovaks had nothing, solely the idea and hope in their future'.[16] Negative historicism was reflected in the viewpoints of Štúr and Hurban in the sense that they referred to the Slovaks as having 'endured' history after the fall of Great Moravia. They did not make their own history and therefore lost recognition as a nation. This realization was to serve as the motivating force in an attempt to 'enter' history as a self-willed collectivity. In 1848, the theory of Slovak national identity was formulated and what remained was to put it into action, as Peter Brock argues in *The Slovak Awakening*. An evolutionary scenario would have been the more natural route to a Slovak nation. But the revolutionary fervour of 1848 presented a 'propitious moment' dictating another course of action. The urgency of the moment undoubtedly played into the general tendencies of romanticism, revolutionary zeal, and idealism. The great leap had to be attempted — and this was not the only occasion in the course of modern Slovak history when nation-building took this route.

The central characteristic of Slovak nationalism and Slovak political thought has been romanticism. All ethnic nationalisms rely to some extent on romantic arguments: language as the medium of a unique 'spirit of the nation'. Most emphasize the unique 'organic individuality' of a collectivity in the development of history. Thus this definition of romanticism is the theoretical point of departure for certain nationalist ideologies. But in a second sense, romanticism is also connected to the 'practice' or means of building a nation. Romanticism provides the basis for political imagination as well as decisions about how to handle the political process — the process of creating and managing political institutions. In Slovak history, the strong romantic undercurrent contributed to the tendency to create new realities at a moment's notice, to engage in wishful thinking, and to be impatient with respect to the systematic work that goes into development and sustaining a national movement, especially when faced with the demands of a revolutionary situation. Therefore Slovak nationalism has been characterized by a certain unsteadiness, of trying things out, applying different and sometimes contradictory solutions to problems, of taking risks in response to a real or perceived time pressure. Risk taking is spurred on by a remarkable confidence that things will work out, that Slovak nationalism will prevail. Thus Slovak nationalism lived on as a vehicle for change, fuelled by romantic notions. Romanticism, therefore, should not be entirely dismissed as an unrealistic and irrelevant cultural current since it provided a kind of 'fantastic realism' to sustain the dream of a recognized Slovak nation.

Thus Slovak history is romantic in the sense that romanticism helped drive the excited activity that intended to produce a fully-fledged nation via a coup. Disillusionment that comes from failed attempts does not necessarily result in realism, but rather the creation of a new illusion: that historical *imbroglio* will offer salvation at a later date. This idea is reflected in Štúr's *Slavism and the World of the Future*.[17] But Štúr was not alone in this view.

During the 19th century, the Slovak national elite developed the cultural tools needed for modern national development, but they did not succeed in institutionalizing the nation. Among the possible reasons, we should consider the peculiar circumstances in which they found themselves as well as the mentality of the Slovak nation-building elite and their maximalist strategy. This was the opinion of Samuel Štefanovič who wrote in 1886 that Slovak politics of 1848-49 ended unsuccessfully because they were fuelled by 'idealistic-fatalistic thought'.[18] Second, the contact between the Slovak peasant population and the nation-building elite was relatively limited. They lived in two separate worlds: the peasants struggled to survive on subsistence farming while the elite embraced a kind of romantic folk idealism and claimed to speak on behalf of the people. This is hinted at by Chorváth who assumed two Slovak worlds of thought, one belonging to the intellectuals and the other to the peasants. This aspect of failed Slovak nation-building, i.e., the relationship between the leadership and the mobilization of the people and the interactions between these two groups, remains an interesting and underdeveloped field of investigation.

Slovak nationalism did not lead to the development and growth of a national identity based on the cumulation of tradition and experience. Instead, sudden evolutionary boosts came as a result of circumstances largely beyond the control or influence of the nation-building elite. Circumstances unleashed the latent potential for nation-building. These unexpected spurts were not always matched by adequate resources among the elite and the population in order to realize the ultimate goal of a 'recognized nation'.

With 1918 came the establishment of Czechoslovakia and the first time that Slovakia acquired a territorial definition. According to Chorváth, the creation of Czechoslovakia came as a surprise to the peasant population who were neither prepared for, nor aware of its coming. Thus the broad Slovak population had a somewhat mechanical relationship to the idea of Czechoslovakia which they might have sought to change had they had more time to sort out the problems associated with the form it took after 1918.[19] Nevertheless, the creation of Czechoslovakia signaled the start of the modern politics of Slovakia. The introduction of universal suffrage for the adult population offered the first real possibility for mass participation in the political process for most inhabitants of Slovakia.

The problem of Slovak collective identity remained. The discrepancy between the proclaimed Czechoslovak democratic nationalism in rhetoric and practice sustained Slovak dreams of autonomy. Czechoslovak democratic nationalism laid claim not only to a political nation, but also to an ethnic identity which clashed with the political spectre of Slovak national identity and earlier attempts at its political institutionalization. Slovakia did not enter Czechoslovakia with a clearly formed national identity and symbols to inspire popular support. Nor was Slovakia represented by an uncontested national elite experienced in the art of modern politics. Slovakia had hardly emerged — it lacked a coherent identity. The tradition of the will and desire to be a nation had not yet produced a set of institutions, symbols, and practices that mobilized society in a common purpose. Slovak nationalism was an ideal whose bearers had undertaken several unsuccessful attempts to demonstrate its potential for development under favourable circumstances. But the social structure of the nation had not yet taken shape. This happened first in the context of Czechoslovakia, within which Slovak politics championing Slovak national identity surfaced with the kind of emergent properties reminiscent of similar attempts in historic Hungary. The problem was that an undeniable Slovak identity and Slovak individuality was emerging, but it had not yet crystallized. Slovak national identity lacked formal institutions to sustain it. The centre of Slovak politics was unclear: should it be in Prague or in Slovakia? The uncertainty in conducting politics was also reflected in the bifurcation of the Slovak political elite. Ivan Dérer discerned two Slovak nationalisms, the Slovak nationalism of 'Czechoslovak orientation' and the Slovak nationalism of 'political autonomy'.[20] This was also a split between conservatives and modernists. In the relatively underdeveloped context of Slovak politics due to the non-institutionalized origins of Slovak political thought and its peripheral situation, classification along standard dimensions does not make sense. Milan Hodža, prime minister of Czechoslovakia from 1935 to 1938, pointed out the inaccuracies of referring to the political ideologies of liberalism, conservatism, and socialism in Slovakia prior to World War I because Slovak politics centred around the top priority of how to institutionalize national identity.[21] This insight remained true for a long time to come.

Nor did Czechoslovakia have an uncontested state tradition. Its officially promulgated identity, used to create a state tradition, relied too heavily on historically derived elements. The state was justified on the basis of history, especially Czech history, rather than on the uniqueness of the creation of the state as a new chapter in the history of Central Europe. Sociologist Anton Štefánek understood the Czechoslovakia created in 1918 not as an achieved reality, but as a 'promise', a 'task' awaiting fulfilment. To him the differences between the Czech lands and Slovakia, especially with respect to social development, intellectual and material civilization, as well as the hard need to define qualities of individual psychology, represented major challenges for the new nation to address.[22]

Thus the question of Slovak national identity centres largely around the questions of continuity and change, especially the specific political choices about how to address continuity and change within the context of statecraft. Building a nation-state requires leaders who can choose and create an appropriate state tradition and manage issues related to continuity and change. This challenge has not yet been fully resolved in Central Europe. As Shmuel N. Eisenstadt put it, nation-state building requires the creation of a unit capable of absorbing change and of self-sustaining growth.[23] Seen from this perspective, the situation in Central Europe is problematic because modernization produced deep disjunctures in the evolutionary flow of history and the formation of a modern consciousness. Modernization produced multiple nation-building efforts, the dissolution of a dynastic state, and the creation of successor nation-states with significant national minorities. History thus became a burden rather than an asset. The inner weakness of the region made it vulnerable to outside influence and conquest. All these factors played an important role in the formation of collective national identities. Thus one of the continuities of Central European history is the recurrence of historical disjunctures, or discontinuity. In Central Europe we can see both the positive and negative effects of continuity: the lack of a strong and unambiguous tradition of either state or nation upon which to draw at critical historical moments when an independent state might have been established. Furthermore, the processes related to the formation of collective identities in this region never reached fruition, resulting in incompletely constituted identities, unevenly developed across regions, classes, and linguistic groups.

This incomplete transformation of collective identities thus left the question open to resolution by the workings of the international state system. Slovakia represents an extreme case since its identity as a nation represented a rather free-floating aspiration, a quest for a particular identity in the context of multinational states. Even today, although Slovakia exists as an independent nation-state, it encompasses significant national minorities and ethnic groups. This means that the new nation of Slovakia will have to develop a new interpretation of its collective identity and build a new tradition. This will require a critical assessment of the role of continuity and a determination to modify traditions in order to bring about change and consolidate a workable national identity that corresponds to the boundaries of the state.

The Slovak modernization effort started by the national elite during the 19th century consisted of nation-building of a pure ethnonational character (Rapant) with a discontinuous beginning and various ruptures as well as a considerable amount of outside influence (interference). In the words of Štúr's colleague, Jozef M. Hurban, the Slovaks have managed to persist, even though the endeavor to create a nation requires a new start, which is built on an ethnic base. He shares the negative historicist view that the Slovaks' cultural contribution to historic Hungary was 'nationally unidentified'. The Slovaks have become an historical subject, and thus a subject of history in their modern efforts to create a forward-looking nation, and not one that draws its identity from looking back into the past. This represented in Central Europe an initiative to constitute a collectivity with the aim of national status propelled forward by a 'self-creative and self-sustaining' process of development.[24] The 19th century nationbuilders sought to invent a new continuity. Their main concern, therefore, was what kind of continuity to create, and they chose one of 'being on the way to something else', a continuity of aspiration and not one of established institutional frameworks recognized by a functioning collectivity. Assuming that the nation-state of the Slovak Republic would be the end point of such nation-building endeavours, the question of tradition still plagues the new state because the establishment of the republic constitutes an 'arrival' in the context of this strategy of aspiring towards its realization. Thus, having now established the nation-state, its consolidation and institutionalization requires a new strategy, a fresh start for creating a new sense of continuity and a new national tradition.

As this brief exploration of the history of nation-building and institutional development in the Slovak region demonstrates, these efforts, as well as the national narratives connected with them, do not offer an unproblematic tradition on which to base current efforts. Instead contemporary nation-builders should invent a new tradition by critically reflecting and publicly assessing earlier attempts. For example, the new republic has little to gain from the monumentalized folkloristic traditionalism so closely tied to ethnicity. The cult of rural ethnicity reinforces tendencies towards isolationism and privileges a particular social group in a state encompassing significant minorities. Building a democratic society in a new state requires forging both a political and a social system from several national minorities and ethnic groups. This cannot be accomplished by using the national narrative style of the 19th century. The goal of social integration will not be accomplished by referring to old traditions as if there were no disjunctures in the historical evolution of the Slovak nation. The humanities and social sciences have an unusual opportunity to contribute to the process of Slovak modernization and nation-building by constructing a theoretical explanation and understanding of this unique historical experience. The idea of Slovakia is a project not only for historians, but also for social scientists. Social research can generate insights to stimulate political debate and thereby contribute to the development of a new style of Slovak politics. Thus there is both an ideological as well as a cultural dimension to the transformation of society, to help build an integrated and consolidated democratic nation-state in Slovakia.

Interpretations and national narratives help shape life strategies, behaviour, and culture understood as an anthropological, non-normative description of the ideas and habits developed by societies to deal with their surrounding environment. Culture in this sense is 'the distinctive style of conduct and communication of a given community'.[25] Culture can influence the speed and form of postcommunist transformation in Slovakia, as elsewhere.

Given this meaning of culture, what is the cultural background to the transition in Slovakia?[26] Culture defined as collective social habits encompasses the ideas, rules and strategies acquired in the day-to-day business of dealing with the world around us. The culture of Slovakia has been predominantly undemocratic and totalitarian except for the relatively short period of twenty years of democracy in pre-Munich Czechoslovakia. Communist culture was melded with pre-industrial traditionalism and these conditions were not favourable for producing a self-conscious citizenry or respect for the rule of law. Nor did this culture support trust in the written word of public ordinances and proclamations.[27] The population never developed trust in institutions as a form of representation or legitimate authority. Thus, it has had difficulty developing a modern political community and the institutions that go along with it. Public institutions appear as the enemy, an alien power outside or above the community of 'us'. Under these undemocratic hierarchical conditions, the population developed a high degree of cynicism and cunning, evidenced in an ability to circumvent authority through deceit and cunning in order to secure the material conditions for survival — and even a relatively comfortable existence — despite the circumstances. This cultural-behavioural tradition, typical of all post-communist Central European states, is stronger in Slovakia because of its peripheral location which strengthened provincialism and the tradition of indifference towards public culture.[28]

Soviet-enforced socialism made an ambiguous contribution to modernization. Apart from producing a level of welfare enjoyed by the rural population in particular, Soviet socialism led to misdevelopment, disproportional industrialization, artificial urbanization, etc. Soviet socialism fostered hierarchy and unauthentic communication between the government, party and population in both directions. Milan Šimečka rightly identified in both the 'restored order' after 1968 as well as during the 1950s, a public tendency towards 'lying' and 'adaptation' to the unfree conditions of life, but he may be mistaken in assuming that these tendencies did not penetrate the realm of private life and personal morality.[29] In practice, the private realm could not be protected from the contagion of the common practice of lying in the public sphere.

Socialism was a system of deceitful communication. During the socialist era, party officials lied *ex officio* and the average citizen lied in self defense. The real question is how deeply this behavioural adaptation penetrated the behavioural attitudes and mores of the population. Undoubtedly, this has seriously damaged public morality and produced *damaged societies*.[30]

Another important negative legacy of socialism is the misuse of language and semantic dishonesty. The habit of lying has lowered the cultural as well as the operational standards of language, undermining the kind of effective communication necessary for a modern society to function. Effective communication will require innovation both linguistically and terminologically. Democratic transformation will be possible only if contemporary nationbuilders can establish new terms to express authentic meanings with respect to public institutions, authority, and community — meanings considered legitimate and trustworthy by the citizenry. Today's leaders will have to change the rhetoric of public authority and demonstrate that their words also have substantive meanings that are reliable and not merely 'sound cover' for actions of dubious connotation. While no society has total communicative competence or authenticity, democratic societies have generally accepted and institutionalized rules that constitute a standard of conduct in public life.

During its modern history, Slovakia has had only limited opportunities to pursue a process of civic cultural modernization with any degree of continuity. The twenty-year history of democratic Czechoslovakia was insufficient to form the basis of the current transformation and even this period was marked by vacillation between home-made cultural conservatism and externally-oriented cultural modernism. This produced a deep rift in Slovak intellectual and political elites. The cultural polarization of Slovak intellectual and political elites which is still visible in today's Slovakia is the product of the Slovak process of modernization. An unquestioned Slovak urban tradition was never fully established, so that the clash between majority traditionalists who use rural symbolism and minority urbanists persists. As long as 'Slovakness' is constituted as something traditional and oriented towards the past, there is no room for a modern urban notion of the nation.

Forty years of socialist planned modernization has not solved the problem of the urban-rural cleavage. If anything, the communist era complicated the problem by attempting to negate the differences between city and village in trying to produce a rural-urban social type, which in its make-up was neither. In a social system based on a hierarchical top-down communication pattern, pre-modernist attitudes and habits were reinforced. Socialist modernizers may have occupied the top of the social order, but the results of their policies were hybrids of traditional and modern elements. Their approach to modernization relied on a process that was artificially accelerated, preconceived, and imposed from above rather than organic and evolutionary. Thus modernization did not emerge as the result of initiatives and activities undertaken by the population at large. Instead, political elites attempted to prescribe, enforce, and administer modernization from the top down. This kind of modernization neglects the importance of the cultural sphere, in particular the transformation of the dominant style of thinking and the political culture into those compatible with modern social relations. Modernity and prosperity cannot be called or ordered into existence. Both are the result of interactions among individuals, groups, and institutions. Modernization challenges the creativity and abilities of both the intellectual and political elites as well as the population at large. The development of a modern functioning state with a strong autonomous civil society has most frequently come about as the product of a process of dynamic interaction between elites and the broader population.

As I have argued above, Slovak elites in the 20th century have not established a pattern of self-sustained growth and continuity. Rather, their history is one of discontinuity brought on by regime changes and reinforced by Slovakia's peripheral status which the elite at times criticized and sought to overcome, and at other historical moments, revered and exalted to a cultural ideal.

Furthermore, forty years of socialist modernization have further inhibited the development of a political culture that can sustain democratic institutions and practices. Slovak society must overcome the culture of mistrust and indifference that pervades society, especially in non-urban areas. A significant part of the population focus their loyalty on prominent personalities rather than issues or policies. Charisma and traditionalism are the vestiges of pre-modern attitudes. Michal Chorváth rightly points out that Slovak politics have for too long been preoccupied with the relationship between the individual and the nation, rather than the relationship between the individual and the state. Romantically-oriented nationalism should be separated from the humanistic universalism of democratic politics.[31] Both citizens and politicians should be socialized into the practices associated with democracy as the institutional foundations of a legitimate democratic order are established. This is why I think Slovakia needs more politicians who lack charisma so that these values and practices can take hold without the distraction of personality politics. With less flamboyant personalities, people can focus their attention on what politicians do rather than who they are. The population can develop an admiration for those who demonstrate a sense of duty and thereby instill confidence in the institutions they are helping to establish. This is more conducive to a stable democratic order than the demagoguery associated with charis⸱ ⸱ic leadership.

In the beginning of this chapter, I posed the question whether a new tradition must be invented in response to the challenges of establishing a democratic order. In 1989, a chance was offered to make the transition to a stable democracy. To achieve this, Slovakia will also have to undergo the process of modernization that was never fully completed under the previous regimes. This will require the development of a self-sustaining society capable of producing sustained economic growth during a period of rapid institutional and cultural change.

To build a modern nation-state, romanticist political thinking and a national narrative based on traditionalism should be reappraised and preference given to a new concept similar to the 'constitutional patriotism' described by Habermas.[32] A new tradition based on constitutional patriotism emphasizes pride in the establishment of a constitutional order based on the rule of law, the protection of individual freedoms, democracy, and a liberal political culture. The constitution becomes the most venerable object of public loyalty. Constitutional patriotism does not require the rejection of historical experience, nor the imposition of a new set of values by an external power. Rather this new tradition emerges from the historical experiences of inadequate earlier attempts at the establishment of an independent democratic order and the unique processes that have given rise to the particularly Slovak national identity which is now fused with a set of universal abstract ideals. Thus the adoption of these abstract principles is the decision of a particular collectivity based on its own concrete experiences. The Slovak Republic is a state with significant national minorities and in need of an urban, cosmopolitan tradition. By emphasizing constitutional patriotism, the political community can demonstrate their overarching respect for civility and republicanism, rather than basing democracy on a narrower ethnic definition of the nation-state. Each society reaches its own solution to the problem of constituting a modern nation-state and establishing or selecting the appropriate motivational basis for loyalty and legitimacy. In the Slovak case, this basis must be selected and affirmed through a social process which both acknowledges and yet rejects historical attempts to define 'the nation' since these previous attempts were unsuccessful in completing the transformation of society into a modern political culture capable of sustaining a democratic political system and a productive growth-oriented economy. This is one of the first and most pressing problems that the Slovak republic must solve and one which will lay a solid foundation for the challenges which lie ahead.

Thus Slovak politics has originated in the challenges of nation and state building. It has emerged out of a non-formalized, and uninstitutionalized setting, historically conditioned by a context dominated by multinational states and various 'complexes' of official nationalisms. Slovak nationhood has been defined by the national elite or intelligentsia which usually relied on romantic notions of national identity as a means of rallying support and loyalty. Slovak elites tried to claim a kind of traditional continuity despite their tendency towards abrupt courses of action and shifting ideological commitments. Romanticism has been the most persistent feature of Slovak politics, probably because of the lack of institutional boundaries and the extra-institutional origins of political ideas. The romanticist tradition has prevailed because of the special situation of Slovakia and the historical origins of nationalism. The continuity of this Romanticist tradition can hardly be considered advantageous for Slovakia today. The demands of establishing a new state require a new tradition that can be developed only by taking a critical stance towards the legacy of the past with a determination to commit to a democratic future.

Notes

1. These questions also apply to other Central European states with stronger state histories and traditions. But the Slovakian case, as indicated, is more complex. In almost all Central European states we can, however, discern a clear tendency to draw on the symbols of the past for legitimacy and identity. One interesting manifestation can be seen in the state emblems. Almost all the newly declared republics use feudal symbols, especially crowns, in their coats of arms.

2. Jürgen Habermas, 1990. *Die nachholende Revolution. Kleine politische Schriften VII.* Frankfurt: Suhrkamp, 151.

3. A. Pražák, 1922. *Dějiny spisovné slovenštiny po dobu Štúrovu* (The History of Literary Slovak until Štúr's Time). Prague: Nákladem Gustava Voleského: 20.

4. *Ibid*: 22.

5. Ľ. Lipták, 1968. *Slovensko v 20. storoči* (Slovakia in the 20th Century). Bratislava: Vydavateľstvo politikej literatúry: 40.

6. Daniel Rapant, 1937. *Slovenské povstanie 1848-49. Diel I. Slovenská jar 1848,* (Slovak Uprising 1848-49. Vol. 1. The Slovak Spring 1848). Turčiansky: Sv. Martin: 88-89.

7. Svetozár Hurban Vajanský, 1897. *Nálady a výhľady* (Moods and Prospects). Turčiansky: Sv. Martin: 12.

8. Hugh Seton-Watson, 1977. *Nations and States. An Inguiry into the Origins of Nations and the Politics of Nationalism.* London: Methuen, 148

9. George Schöpflin describes the 'striking quality' of politics in Central and Eastern Europe: 'ethnic and civic agendas of politics were consistently confused and collective and individual freedoms were combined and sometimes confounded.' Schöpflin, 1993, 'Culture and Identity in Post-Communist Europe', in Stephen White, Judy Batt, and Paul G. Lewis (eds.), *Developments in East European Politics.* London: Macmillan, 18.

10. Ľ. Štùr, 1954. *Dielo v piatich zväzkoch* (Works in five volumes), Vol. 1, Bratislava: Slovenské vydavatelstvo krásnej literatúry: 358, 361.

11. Cf. *Dokumenty k slovenskému národnému hnutiu v rokoch 1848-1914. I. 1848-1867.* (Documents of the Slovak national movement...), František Bokes (ed.), 1962, Bratislava: Vydavatelstvo Slovenskej akadémie vied, 23-26; Michal M. Hodza, 1848, *Der Slowak.* Prague: Expedition der slawischen Centralblatter: 73-77.

12. Scotus Viator, 1908. *Racial Problems in Hungary.* London: Constable, 96-97.

13. Michal Chorváth, 1939. *Romantická tvár Slovenska.* (The Romantic Face of Slovakia), Prague: Maly Petr, 25.

14. Cultural Slavism is a conception based on the idea that there is a Slav nation formed by tribes with common cultural pre-dispositions and potential, not yet adequately developed. Slovak national ideologues were pioneers in this area and Ján Kollár was one of those who elaborated a very influential doctrine of cultural Slav solidarity during this era.

15. Rapant, *op.cit*: 89-90.

16. Cf. Dohnány: 18.

17. Ľudovit Štúr, 1931. *Das Slawenthum und die Welt der Zukunft*, (G.Jirdsek, ed.), Bratislava.

18. Mikuláš Dohnány and Samuel Štefanovič, 1988. *Slovenské povstanie z roku 1848-49.* Bratislava: Tatran, 221.

19. Chorváth, *op.cit*: 27.

20. Ivan Dérer, 1935. *Ceskoslovenská otázka*, (The Czechoslovak Question). Prague: Orbis, 18.

21. Cf. K. Kollár, 1994. *Milan Hodža.* Bratislava: Infopress, 25-26.

22. Anton Štefánek, 1922. 'Slovenská a československá otázka', (The Slovak and Czechoslovak Question), in *Prúdy* Vol. 1, (1): 23-24.

23. Shmuel N. Eisenstadt, 1979. *Kultur, Tradition und Wandel.* Frankfurt: Suhrkamp, 38, 59.

24. Štúr, *op.cit*: 177.

25. E. Gellner, 1983. *Nations and Nationalism*, Ithaca: Cornell U.P., 92.

26. Ľubomír Falťan and Soňa Szomolányi (eds.), 1993. *Slovensko. Kroky k Európskej únii*, (Slovakia: Steps to the European Union). Bratislava: Sociologický ústav SAV; Ľubomír Falťán, Soňa Szomolányi, K. Pekník, and E. Šarmír (eds.), 1994. *Slovensko a jeho perspektivy zaciatkom 90. rokov*, (Slovakia and its perspectives at the start of the 1990s). Bratislava: Sociologický ústav SAV.

27. M. Šimečka, 1990. *Obnovenie poriadku*, (The Restoration of Order). Bratislava: Archa: 133.
28. In his posthumously edited and published, *Soliloqous Considerations*, Marian Váross stated that institutional 'asymmetry' in the Czechoslovak socialist federation contributed to or strengthened provincialism and peripherality, rather than overcoming these. See *Úvahy v samote*, Bratislava: Bradlo, 1991: 171.
29. Šimečka, *op.cit*: 138-60, 162-71.
30. Cf. N. Ascherson, '1989 in Eastern Europe', in John Dunn (ed.), 1993. *Democracy: The Unfinished Journey, 508 BC to AD 1993*. Oxford: Oxford U.P., 234-35.
31. Cf. P.F. Drucker, *The New Realities*. New York: Harper and Row: 106-12.
32. Habermas, *op.cit*: 149-56.

Bibliography

Ascherson, N. 1993. '1989 in Eastern Europe', in John Dunn (ed.), *Democracy: The Unfinished Journey, 508 BC to AD 1993*. Oxford: Oxford U.P., 234-35.

Chorváth, Michal 1939. *Romantická tvár Slovenska*, (The Romantic Face of Slovakia). Prague: Maly Petr.

Dérer, Ivan 1935. *Ceskoslovenská otázka*, (The Czechoslovak Question). Prague: Orbis.

Dohnány Mikuláš and Samuel Štefanovič, 1988. *Slovenské povstanie z roku 1848-49*. Bratislava: Tatran.

Dokumenty k slovenskému národnému hnutiu v rokoch 1848-1914. I. 1848-1867. (Documents of the Slovak national movement...), František Bokes (ed.), 1962. Bratislava: Vydavatelstvo Slovenskej akadémie vied.

Drucker, P.F. *The New Realities*. New York: Harper and Row.

Eisenstadt, Shmuel N. 1979. *Kultur, Tradition und Wandel*. Frankfurt: Suhrkamp.

Faltán, Ľubomír, Soňa Szomolányi, K. Pekník, and E. Šarmír (eds.), 1994. *Slovensko a jeho perspektivy zaciatkom 90. rokov*, (Slovakia and its perspectives at the start of the 1990s). Bratislava: Sociologický ústav SAV.

Falťan, Ľubomír, and Soňa Szomolányi (eds.), 1993. *Slovensko. Kroky k Európskej únii*, (Slovakia: Steps to the European Union). Bratislava: Sociologický ústav SAV.

Gellner, E. 1983. *Nations and Nationalism*. Ithaca: Cornell U.P.

Habermas, Jürgen 1990. *Die nachholende Revolution. Kleine politische Schriften VII*, Frankfurt: Suhrkamp.

Hodza, Michal M. 1848. *Der Slowak*. Prague: Expedition der slawischen Centralblatter: 73-77.

Kollár, K. 1994. *Milan Hodža*. Bratislava: Infopress.

Lipták, Ľ. 1968. *Slovensko v 20. storoči* (Slovakia in the 20th Century). Bratislava: Vydavateľstvo politikej literatúry.

Pražák, A. 1922. *Dějiny spisovné slovenštiny po dobu Štúrovu* (The History of Literary Slovak until Štúr's Time). Prague: Nákladem Gustava Voleského.

Rapant, Daniel 1937. *Slovenské povstanie 1848-49. Diel I. Slovenská jar 1848*, (Slovak Uprising 1848-49. Vol. 1. The Slovak Spring 1848). Turčiansky: Sv. Martin.

Schöpflin, George 1993, 'Culture and Identity in Post-Communist Europe', in Stephen White, Judy Batt, and Paul G. Lewis (eds.), *Developments in East European Politics*. London: Macmillan.

Seton-Watson, Hugh 1977. *Nations and States. An Inguiry into the Origins of Nations and the Politics of Nationalism*. London: Methuen.

Šimečka, M. 1990. *Obnovenie poriadku*, (The Restoration of Order). Bratislava: Archa.

Štefánek, Anton 1922. 'Slovenská a československá otázka', (The Slovak and Czechoslovak Question), in *Prúdy* Vol. 1, (1): 23-24.

Štúr, Ľudovit, 1931. *Das Slawenthum und die Welt der Zukunft*, (G.Jirdsek, ed.). Bratislava.

Štùr, Ľ. 1954. *Dielo v piatich zväzkoch* (Works in five volumes), Vol. 1. Bratislava: Slovenské vydavatelstvo krásnej literatury.

Vajanský, Svetozár Hurban 1897. *Nálady a výhľady* (Moods and Prospects). Turčiansky: Sv. Martin.

Viator, Scotus 1908. *Racial Problems in Hungary*. London: Constable.

The Political Anthropology of Regime Changes in Hungary

László Kürti

Introduction

Over the past seventy years, Hungarians have been subjected to no less than six distinct political systems (Horthy, Rákosi, Nagy, Kádár-Grosz-Németh, Antall-Boross, Horn). Adapting culturally to the new climate — collapsing and prospering — may be one of the nation's excellent, if underrated, characteristics. Since 1990, Hungarians have controlled the destiny of their nation by popular rule. Parliamentary democracy and political freedom are by now taken for granted. Hungary, it seems, has an ability to re-invent itself at each political transformation. This chapter addresses the question of the fragile nature and future development of democracy in Hungary. I argue that we cannot understand what democratic developments are possible, unless we analyze in some detail the political formation of Hungary's educated elite, a group capable of exerting tremendous influence on the outcome of the country's political situation. At the same time, we must understand the inherent and acquired cultural, inegalitarian characteristics which may ignite popular dissatisfaction and which may, in turn, explain the political behaviour of the population at large. To understand regime changes, we must consider the cultural context of what prompted them and what followed them. In order to embark upon this enterprise, we start first with a brief critical examination of political anthropology and its application to the Hungarian case and then, secondly, we highlight the cultural tapestry in which to situate political changes in their proper localized contexts.

Political Anthropology

To engage political anthropology is similar to opening a can of worms of anthropological (cross-cultural) data and political science theories and *vice versa*. In general, we can trace its origins back to Lewis Henry Morgan's pioneering study of the political and kinship rules of the Iroquois indians of upstate New York in the middle of the nineteenth century.[1] For present purposes, however, we may discard the important historical milestones here; the names of Karl

Polanyi, Marcel Mauss, E.E. Evans-Pritchard, Max Gluckman and Edmund Leach will suffice to remind readers of the general developments in the comparative and cross-cultural 'study of political institutions'. In this endeavour, the general questions are: who rules? how is power distributed? how are decisions made and conflicts negotiated? Furthermore, coinciding with the approach of contemporary anthropologists, including Abner Cohen and Maurice Godelier, we may investigate how powerful symbols are fundamentally interconnected with the ways in which political actors manipulate them, and make sense of their environments.[2]

More specifically, we must focus our attention here on the questions of power relations and the inegalitarian nature of power politics as they are embedded in a specific cultural context. In political anthropology, societies have been described variously as 'primitive', 'pre-literate', or 'simple societies' sometimes collectively referred to as pre-state societies. In contrast to state-level societies, these societies have been entirely non-industrial, a characteristic feature which has been eroding rapidly since the beginning of the twentieth century. One of their distinct attributes is that they are relatively small (though Luxembourg or Monaco, or the Vatican are the smallest (nation-)states, and some tribes, such as the Navajos, number roughly one million). More important than size, however, is the fact that societies without the presence of the state — be they egalitarian bands, ranked groups, tribes, or chiefdoms — possess political institutions in which positions of power are numerous, flexible and function with built-in safety-valves.

Leaders and specialists with power, variously referred to as chiefs, big men, and shamans, may or may not inherit their distinguished positions in society. Yet many are able to maintain prestige and power only through ritual practices and through what Max Weber called 'charisma'. At the same time, and this may be more important in certain societies than others, the distribution of scarce resources is practiced through the institutions of reciprocity, redistribution and the market.[3]

In contrast to pre-state social formations, complex societies differ fundamentally by the very presence of the state: by definition, a hierarchical power centre governing through a specialized bureaucracy, army, police, tax system, and a centralized religion. Such state societies have been described as profoundly inegalitarian with respect to the relations of social groups and their access to power. There are royal, elite and distinct lineages throughout the power positions arranged hierarchically and systematically.[4] In such groups, close-knit by all means, both power and social divisions may be strictly inherited and the degree of, and access to, power becomes fixed by heredity. Politics here serves to create solutions to the problems of social integration, allowing a sizeable population to live as a unit (via bureaucracy, centralization, nationalism, etc). State ritual and religion play an ever-increasingly important role in managing conflict and maintaining the status quo. In fact, many modern nation-states in Europe, Asia and the Americas were able to emerge because of the full support of the clergy and religious doctrines.

One of the most important distinctions between non-state and complex societies is in the legitimation of violence and force (which is Max Weber's classic definition of the state). Yet, as Lucy Mair cogently writes:

> There are no societies where rules are automatically obeyed, and every society has some means of securing obedience as well as of dealing with offenders.[5]

Thus, we may assume that simply because a state exists with the law and justice system and its invisible hands — and the Hobbesian civil society in which authority is surrendered to a sovereign ruler — in our civilized European world we automatically obey all rules. This would mean that because we live in a Western nation-state all our actions are rule-based, lawful and rationalized, all in all we are more rational and logical than people living in tribal and pre-state social formations. This, however, as pointed out by many anthropologists, is a fallacy which harkens back to the ethnocentric imagination of the Enlightenment concerning the superiority of Europeans and their world.[6]

Anthropologists have shown that many contemporary states are notoriously weak and bureaucratic, full of loopholes and indifference, characteristics familiar to non-state societies as well.[7] In order to be successful and to combat the system, individuals must rely on informal networks, extended and ritualistic relationships, and specific cultural practices.[8] Thus, the phrase 'political culture' used by political scientists is not a novelty but a *given* to anthropologists accustomed to viewing culture simply as politics in disguise.

To provide a political anthropological case-study in inegalitarianism, it will suffice to recall the Ceausescu clan's nepotistic rule which was based on the simple extension of kinship ties into political office, a primordial power distribution existing for thousands of years in human history. The situation of the mafia in Italy is a classic example of the patron-client relationship well-known in Mediterranean and Middle Eastern societies (what the anthropologist Jeremy Boissevain characteristically referred to as 'the friend of a friend' symptom).[9] In fact, this is what may accompany the change of guard after governmental mutations occur and disparate policies follow in their wake.

Elite Formation and Nepotism

What follows below is a brief outline of twentieth century Hungarian politics in which emphasis is placed on the reproduction of inequality and the cultural construction of elites. With the collapse of the Dual Monarchy and the rise of Regent Miklós Horthy in 1920, we can trace how this happened.

After the Peace Treaty of Trianon in 1920, Hungary lost important coal and mining resources; the northern territory, to the newly created Czechoslovakia; the eastern parts were ceded to Romania; and the southern regions of Bacska and Banat to the newly created nation-state, Yugoslavia. The country actually benefitted from the partition sanctioned by the Trianon Treaty: its territory became smaller, more manageable, its population ethnically more homogeneous and, as refugees from the successor states flooded the urban and industrial centres of post-Trianon Hungary, its economy was on the upswing. Peasants from the extraordinarily poverty-stricken underdeveloped northern and western counties — so beautifully rendered by Hungary's foremost populist writer, Gyula Illyés, in his autobiographical novel *People of the Puszta* — also travelled to the newly emerging factory towns. To them, the booming industrial towns seemed a logical choice, a potential salvation from the miseries of landed estates. The communist poet Aladár Komját (1891-1937) captured this mood in his poem 'Hungary's Proletariat Marches' in 1937:

> The shop-floors are impregnated by us
> They feed us and we feed them...
> In the South, West, East and North,
> The determined peasantry moves forth.

As it can be ascertained from this text, both home-grown trade unionism and socialism, as well as populism (*népi mozgalom*), sprouted from the post-Trianon re-organizations of Horthy's Hungary. Furthermore, these cultural movements sprung up from the same source in unison: the country's economic backwardness and political weaknesses.

With the territorial losses, the Hungarians also experienced a collective group suffering. Mourning was marked in rituals fostered by the extreme right, aristocratic and religious circles. The populist and leftist intelligentsia emerged quite on its own from below, while the Hungarian political elite has in general been selected largely through the 'informal' networks maintained and manipulated by those in power. This was institutionalized by the fundamentalist clergy and the political right through various religious, military and economic channels. Among these, the manipulation of the large land holdings of the clergy, offering noble titles and the 'knighthood' (*vitéz*) to the aspiring middle class, and the militarization of industry, were all means of solidifying the 'patron-client' relationship necessary for the Horthy regime to stay in power against challenges from both the peasantry-oriented populist and the leftist elite circles.

All this corresponded with Hungary's position *vis-à-vis* the Third Reich which was ambiguous, to say the least, particularly in its early months. Apart from the brief periods of the Teleki (1939-41), Kállay (1942-44) and Lakatos (September 1944-October 1944) governments which attempted to maintain a detached or nonaligned status, the governments of Regent Horthy were pro-Nazi: they supported Hitlerism wholeheartedly. Economically there was little doubt that Hungary had joined forces with Nazi Germany when the administration of Premier Gyula Gömbös (1932-36) took office. Their close alliance could be found in the dynamic growth of metallurgy, the production of agricultural and electrical equipment, and especially aluminum processing. Despite the industrial upswing, the working classes lived in dismal conditions. As Hungary's tragic working class poet, Attila József, wrote, 'Poverty is our national sickness'.[10] He and his populist counterparts powerfully captured the gloom of a desolate working-class existence, and it was not without justification that an interwar Hungary of nine million had been labelled 'the country of three million beggars'.

In tandem with the growing social malaise and social atomization of the masses, there were nevertheless signs on the horizon that neo-fascist and extreme rightist religious circles were firmly in power. Moreover, governmental and clerical socialization assisted the emergence of extremism, racism and xenophobia. United in ultra-nationalist, anti-semitic and racist organizations such as the EME (Union of Awakening Hungarians), the MFP (Party of the Defenders of the Magyar Race), the MOVE (Hungarian National Defense League), and the MNYSZ (Hungarian Arrow Cross Party), and parading under the mantle of semi-liberalist national socialism, these groups reflected the fact that the ruling political tapestry was indeed quite monochrome in composition.

As a result of this rightward turn, strong Christian and para-military youth organizations sprang up around the country, reflecting the dominant trend of 'divide and conquer'. Most important among them were the *Cserkészet, Levente*, and *Hubások* groups, paralleling those of the *Wandervogel* and Boy Scouts in the West. These entities attempted to create a specific *generatio aequivoca* (equivocal birth) to unite the youth under an extremist Christian-fundamentalist ideological banner to serve the interests of the state. Perhaps most widespread among the male population between 12 and 21, the *Levente's* principal function consisted of providing a kind of compulsory pre-military Christian training. The Catholic Young Men's Organization (KALOT), the Catholic Agrarian Girls' Organization (KALÁSZ), and the Protestant Christian Youth League (KIE) were important political organizations that further factionalized the nation's youth according to religion and gender. This parochial education assured the reproduction and selection of committed Christian and right-wing youth for the government. In fact, this was the period of continual feudalization of Hungarians en masse.

This social engineering proved successful at the national elections in 1939, when two parties gained enormous popularity: the Hungarian Revival Party (MEP) and the Arrow Cross (*Nyilaskeresztes Párt*), both signalling Hungary's commitment to the ideals of the Third Reich and that Hungarian nationalism could piggy-back on the official ideology of *Mein Kampf*. A few persons in concert with a small military elite organized under the Hungarian Independence Movement (*Magyar Függetlenségi Mozgalom*) attempted in vain to sign a last minute armistice with Moscow on 11 October, 1944.[11] On 15 October, after the arrest of the Regent, the country came under the terror of the Arrow Cross and the *Hungarista* (Hungarist) commandos led by the extreme reactionary Ferenc Szalasi. Jews, communists, and leftist sympathizers were rounded up and taken away and Hungary lost the war as an ally of Nazi Germany. World War II did, however, not end the dichotomous political fragmentation of the Hungarian elite for much of the second half of the twentieth century political culture has been determined by the leftist, liberal and the conservative, populist tone of discourse.

On 4 November 1945, the country went to the polls in its first free elections after the war with astounding results: the Smallholders Party won 57 per cent and the Soviet-backed Communist Party 17 per cent of the votes. The populist alternative of moving towards a third road — not the capitalist west and not the communist Soviet Union — briefly gained popularity and confidence among the country's peasantry. For the time being, it seemed as if Hungary, despite occupation by the Soviet army, would be allowed to establish a truly democratic multi-party system while maintaining its relative independence. This was, however, not a likely future for the country.

During this brief post-war period, Stalin and his *apparatchik* (party bureaucrats) made their move to construct Bolshevik-style and Soviet satellite states in East-Central Europe. Between May 1945 and December 1947, the Communist Party increased its membership from 150,000 to 864,000, constituting a massive show of support and a popular base for its legitimacy. After two years of struggle, political and religious factions were eliminated and the newly created communist Hungarian Workers' Party (*Magyar Dolgozók Pártja* or MDP) became the country's only party.[12] The official ideology of the MDP aimed at eradicating any remnants of the bourgeois past, and its religious ideology was replaced by a communist consciousness based on a new division of youth into a politically correct age-set.[13]

Between 1945 and 1949, young people — those under 24, nearly three million out of a population of nine-and-a-half million in Hungary — were courted by competing party interests in dozens of youth organizations.[14]

Despite the high numbers, only about an eighth of those under 24 were card-carrying members of these parties, divided among four affiliations: religion, trade union, social democrats, and leftist parties. Gender was an added feature, for several youth groups — interestingly enough, not only the religious but the trade union groups as well — consisted of separate girls' and boys' organizations.

However, it soon became clear that the communists were not about to allow the proliferation of youth organizations and, following the Soviet model of the *Komsomol*, a single entity was to be created. The young János Kádár — Hungary's powerful future leader — appeared on the scene in a speech at the Csepel Works with a radical proposition to eliminate 'reactionary' and 'rightist' factions by propagating a single-party system. Consequently, in March 1950, all youth organizations became illegal, and were henceforth fused into a single youth group: the Workers' Youth Association (*Dolgozó Ifjúsági Szövetség*, or DISZ).[15] In tandem with this political reorganization, industrial enterprises, private businesses, banks, railroads, and schools were nationalized; large landed estates were removed from ownership by aristocrats, to be redistributed among peasants.

Following the brief period of experimentation between 1945 and 1948, Stalinism was implemented throughout Eastern Europe and 'clientelism' took an overtly political and ideological shape. From 1949 on, when the First Five-Year Plan was introduced, Stalinism and state control had been fully established throughout the economy and society. The communist party and the Muscovite 'gang of four' worked out a legitimizing political ideology to consolidate the centralized state. In order to eliminate the 'feudal' and 'bourgeois' heritage, its first and most important element was the creation of the inner circle of cadres in politics, industry, education, and the arts. The second element was terror, and later, the extension of fear into all parts of society. Even with the collapse of Stalinism and the creation of Kádárist rule in the 1960s and 1970s, some of these mechanisms seemed to defy cultural change. Clientelism and the creation of special offices to support governmental policies have continued well into the 1980s and beyond.

I do not wish to deal with the whole progression of Hungarian political history from the 1950s to the 1980s here. Much has been said about it: from Stakhanovism to the 1956 revolution, from Kádárism to goulash communism, and from the New Economic Mechanism of 1968 to the economy of shortage. The phrases of peasant-worker, the second economy, 'hobby-gardens', the 'black train commuters', labour hoarding, and the legitimacy crisis of Kádárism are well known to specialists in Hungarian socialism. All of these features have been analyzed in their historical, literary, political, economic and cultural dimensions in a scholarly fashion.[16]

Our particular concern here focuses on the ways in which Hungarian society acclimatized to these changes: it seemed that bowing to pressures from above there was a consensus among the populace not to hold elections between 1948 and 1990; to nationalize all landholdings; to fight against American imperialism and to save Cuba and Vietnam; to implement 'fraternal' internationalist cooperations through militarization of industry and trade (COMECOM, Warsaw Pact); and to make political education a prerequisite for progress and advancement in one's life and career. Yet, as Chris Hann suggests, one dimension which may explain the longevity and influence of socialism may be the 'moral endorsement' by which citizens 'legitimated' the regimes.[17] Combined with this was opportunism, a significant aspect of Eastern and Central European socialism.[18]

After the collapse of communism in the East Bloc, most scholars asked the same question: how could it happen so fast and so late? One important aspect of moral endorsement had to do with the creation of a socially conscious proletariat and intelligentsia, a reason why education was of primary importance. Contemporary newsreels and official photos reveal heads of state — whether Mao Zedong, Fidel Castro, Leonid Brezhnev, Nicolae Ceausescu or János Kádár — honoured by respectful young pioneers as symbolic patriarchs amidst a profusion of bouquets of red carnations.[19] The ideological spirit of state socialism placed youthful adherents on a pedestal to serve as its mouthpiece. All the while, the Kádár government was clearly apprehensive of the growing generational power of this youthful cohort, the uprising of 1956 clearly demonstrating what they were capable of. The reproduction of 'vanguard youth' — as Lenin had envisioned them in the task of building communism — was viewed as indispensable to the promotion of socialist relations. The 1971 Youth Constitution was unambiguous on the matter:

Society expects youth to be a worthy heir of the Hungarian People's revolutionary traditions, to work generously in building socialist society, and to participate in realizing socialism and communism.[20]

In the minds of the party leaders, then, no institution could exist without a systematic plan, an ideological charge to recruit, educate, and retain youth according to its needs.[21] The creation of a 'new society' was in full swing. The Rakosi government realized that the 'bourgeois and highly selective system of education' had to be replaced with a new educational system which favoured working-class and peasant children and youth; by 1953, their ratio in high school was 65 per cent, and in university, an impressive 55 per cent. Yet the new 'socialist' elite was factionalized beyond the ordinary, a point which may be clearly observed from the disparate affiliation of elite groups during the free elections of 1990 and 1994. This anti-government elite was, however, a key actor in the 1980s turmoil, a period which saw the emergence of political opposition to the regime and the giving up of single-party rule and central planning by both the reform communist and the democratic opposition elites.

However, interpretations of the velocity of social change which have characterized the 'Springtime of the Peoples', as the 1989-1990 years have been named, must be evaluated in relation to more gradual modifications that were already underway. From the beginning of the 1980s, the Kádár government consented to several major reform policies such as the legitimization of the right to form independent working units, the VGMK, and permission for citizens to engage in official (legal) 'second economies'.[22] The relatively seamless surface functioning of this reform-centreed system was ensured by a form of 'social contract', i.e., what the American political scientist J.F. Brown has ironically termed the Kádárist 'social compact'.[23]

This agreement was, to be sure, a bargain between the state (the *nomen-klatura*) and its citizens in which the latter were allowed to pursue private material interests in exchange for withdrawal from political life and state administrative responsibilities. At the same time, personal liberty and the right to form independent associations were tolerated, if not supported.

Nevertheless, the significant successes should be highlighted as well. It should be pointed out that in the arts, sciences, and education, socialism managed to gain international acclaim. Film-makers, artists, scholars and, lest we forget, gymnasts, have had success and fame beyond the borders of their nation-states. In the arts, humanities and sciences, and especially in literature, the local elite played a sensitive and alert game: on the one hand, they served the masters, while on the other they produced both required (passable) and outstanding works. Despite the plethora of works, the roles of the artist/intelligentsia during the times of crisis, is not yet fully understood in Eastern and Central Europe, a region where a playwright, an historian and a factory worker can all become presidents of their respective countries.

I would like to note in this context that Vaclav Havel's grassroots 'velvet revolution' and the 'revolutionary' changes, in Timothy Garton Ash's formulation, were instituted with the agreement of party bureaucrats and an elite opposition in most countries of the former Soviet Bloc.[24]

In fact, until the mid-1980s there was a single minor political opposition in Hungary known as the 'democratic opposition', a loose coalition of two factions often identified as including the 'urbanists' and the 'populists'. The clash between the two has been referred to by the political scientist, Attila Ágh, as the Long Culture War.[25] As described briefly above, this intellectual disparity, dating back to the 1930s, refers to the tension between a more conservative political stance with regard to Hungary's external relations, and a more liberal one. For their part, the populists have stressed the importance of the country's history and culture as a mobilizing force and advocated a more gradual integration into a privatized, Western-style market economy. The 'urbanites' (the Free democrats, the Young Democrats and the social democrats), on the other hand, have advocated a liberal, Western orientation that emphasizes civil liberties, stronger political and cultural ties to the West, and complete free-market liberalization. Gábor Demszky, elected mayor of Budapest in 1990, has summarized the way in which the opposition recognized the waning of communists' power as part of this 'urbanist agenda':

The question of the very survival of communism increasingly brought Kierkegaard's *Either-Or* to mind. We discovered, in other words, that there was no such thing as the 'social market economy': there was either socialism or market economy. Likewise, there was no 'socialist democracy': there was either socialism or democracy.[26]

Although both 'populists' and 'urbanites' have concerned themselves with questions of 'democracy' and a liberalized economic structure, the urbanists' emphasis has clearly focussed on these issues rather than on notions of 'Hungarianness' (*magyarság*) or 'Hungarian culture' (*magyar kultúra*) as elements of political unity and power.

After 1987, when the historic Democratic Forum summit took place at Lakitelek, the critical issues on the political agenda centred around ecological disasters, poverty, police brutality, illegally stationed Soviet troops, lack of funding for health and education, and especially the plight of the Hungarian diaspora in neighbouring states; issues wholly avoided by the MSZMP and the KISZ, its youthful alter ego. It was indeed by virtue of the latter that the opposition was able to gain the confidence and support of both the national and the international public.[27]

By mid-1988, when Hungary was experiencing an influx of Hungarian refugees from neighbouring Romania, Hungarian popular attention turned favourably towards the oppositional force emerging as the 'Democratic Forum' that championed the plight of ethnic Hungarians outside Hungary. The language of this newly emerging political discourse was anti-state and overtly populist. It openly addressed what it considered to be the devastating impact of 35 years of communist rule upon Hungarian citizens. By debunking communist slogans ('Eight hours work...' and 'Forward to building a socialist internationalism', incantations often heard at May Day parades) and con-fidently claiming the perpetuation of grave human rights violations in Romania and Czechoslovakia, this intellectual movement became an accepted political force by 1988, when one of the first (and largest) peaceful demonstrations took place in Budapest on 27 June, 1988.[28]

This solidarity march, condemning Nicolae Ceausescu's genocidal plan for the destruction of thousands of German, Hungarian, and Romanian villages in the Transylvanian region of Romania, was tantamount to a victory procession for the opposition and, at the same time, a funeral dirge for communism. This prompted Ferenc Fehér to state:

In Eastern Europe, there is no need for hesitation in discussing the demise of communism ... [for] the successor parties of, till recently, ruling communism never polled above 20 percent in the first, free elections, and often much lower.[29]

As it may be seen from the results of the 1994 election, this educated forecast was not supported by the recent socialist victory not only in Hungary, but Lithuania, Romania and Poland as well.

In the months following the more relaxed political atmosphere of the short-lived Grosz government after Kádár's dismissal, churches took up the cause of the welfare of Transylvanian refugees and their families who stayed behind, thereby emerging, in the words of a church-leader, as a 'radical anti-state force capable of uniting along these lines'. Catholic and Protestant, Evangelical and Baptist churches in Hungary thereby spoke with one voice to re-radicalize grass-root religious communities, marginalized during much of the preceding three decades, only to re-emerge with great vehemence. This would certainly lend credence to the Dutch anthropologist Mart Bax's observation concerning the significance of religion in state-formation. The newly emerging state (non-communist and religious) relied heavily on the symbols and power derived from Catholic and Protestant icons and ideology, a transformation that was abundantly evident during John Paul II's visits to Poland.[30]

One event in these developments deserves special mention because of its symbolic power to generate powerful popular support: the reinterment on 16 June, 1989, of Imre Nagy, the executed Prime Minister of the 1956 revolutionary government, in a nationally televised state funeral comparable in size and importance to the 1988 Transylvanian demonstration, except that this time the whole nation was mobilized.[31] According to surveys, millions watched while Nagy and his executed colleagues received a heroes' funeral; the nation mourned its revolutionary martyrs and celebrated its current victory over the previous regime.[32] This event and the revolution in Romania during the Christmas of 1989, were significant in gathering a political momentum for the MDF, a point which should be taken into account when discussing its phenomenal success during the spring 1990 elections. As the historian George Barany has observed: 'Hungarians could certainly be proud of what they had accomplished at the end of the 1980s'.[33] This general mood of optimism and euphoria would surely be in the air in 1990.

A law delegitimizing the presence of political parties in the workplace was put into effect at the beginning of 1990. This was an indispensable step towards the waning of the party state in Hungary. The result of the elections of 1990 are well-known: For the first time in its history Hungary established a multi-party parliament and devised a new constitution. The nationalist, Christian and conservative policies of the ruling MDF did not, however, help keep the party from falling apart. Cracks started to show: the taxi strike in October 1990 and the formation of the Democratic Charta in 1991 were signs on the horizon that popular discontent was growing.[34] Internally, the party also experienced crises when important figures began to leave the party and form their own political factions (Imre Pozsgay, Zoltán Biró, and István Csurka). Yet, this political fission also meant that the party was only marginally successful in shedding its right-wing and nationalistic image.[35]

In 1990 and immediately after, trustworthy people (no more reference to 'cadres'), mostly of 'anti-communist', 'conservative' and 'Christian' leanings, were elevated into governmental and cultural offices by the ruling MDF.[36] The elimination of certain industrial enterprises — many thought to be the fortress of communists — or support for companies, schools, and foundations which the government deemed fit, also followed the government take-over. However, more radical steps were also taken: most important perhaps was the Law of Reparation (*Kárpótlási törvény*) and the (re)distribution of land belonging to former state and local farming cooperatives. This obviously reflected the MDF's desire to reach out to the rural masses to win them over wholeheartedly. Yet, as the 1994 election figures illustrate, the MDF proved short-sighted in its assessment of rural voters.[37] Similarly, the educated also felt the MDF policies were distorted and one-sided. Since the foundation of the Duna TV (Hungary's third official channel), the elite has been systematically manipulated; some have become completely disillusioned, others simply turned away, and many opted for jobs outside the country. The semi-state re-burial of Regent Horthy, the foundation of supportive organizations such as the MUK (Hungarian Reporters' Association) and the Christian Doctors' Association, plus the media war in Hungary in the beginning of 1994 when the client system was openly being cemented by the regime — an act turning thousands of intelligent minds away from the propaganda of the MDF, all point to the MDF's failure to manipulate the public.[38] In light of what has been said above concerning the schooling of the new elite, it is not surprising that in 1992 the MDF instituted a more relaxed policy of higher education admission quotas which would raise the number of students by thirty per cent. Yet, this 'new' elite, national Christian-centre, was not created in time and in sufficient mass to back up the MDF.

Following the rise to power of the Horn government, clientelism can be detected from the personnel changes from 'previous-regime-clients' to 'experienced' and 'trustworthy' people. Yet this may be entrenched in what Adam Michnik has aptly termed 'velvet restoration', a phrase summarizing the conformist attitude of old-regime bureaucrats.[39] In rather stark contrast to the MDF's education policy, the policy of the socialist government may be characterized as 'university unfriendly'; hundreds of millions of forints were cut from the education budget by the end of 1995, including six to ten per cent cuts in faculty and staff.[40] While it is certain that education is not very high on the agenda of the Horn government, a similar selection programme to recruit 'clients' into the power hierarchy is underway in the media, finance, arts and industry.[41]

Such salient features of preference given to one group and favouring a specific segment of society — often associated with tribal, non-state and peripheral societies — may, it seems, also characterize contemporary governments in all societies. For both the MDF and the socialist governments, this policy of exclusion has been an immanent feature of securing their rule of law and of attaining the social consensus needed for a peaceful society. In this sense, it is rather ironic but not wholly surprising that both governments followed in the footsteps of the Kádár regime, a rule often criticized for its extreme clientelism and nepotistic power structure. Such a policy of preference, as it was clear in the Kádár era, will hamper social equality by its very standards of justice, availability and distribution of goods, services and benefits, as well as its policies concerning elite selection — including higher education.[42] The university and college tuition structure introduced in 1995 will certainly influence the nature of university enrolment for the coming years. Thus, as the implementation of educational and cultural policies indicates, inequality and an inegalitarian system may just be a regular feature of contemporary states, whether the leaders wish it or not, a point which cannot be stressed enough with reference to the Hungarian data at hand. We now turn to the specific features of how inegalitarianism has been continuing in contemporary Hungary.

Inequality

As the Hungarian economy struggles through transition to a 'free market', widening income differentials have re-aligned the social structure, dropping the middle-class downward, creating a small but visible class of *nouveaux riches* and triggering, not unexpectedly, widespread popular dissatisfaction.[43] Reneging on democracy's promise of equality of opportunity, government policies are creating a permanently segmented minority as a result of the process of 're-feudalization of society' (a phrase coined by the sociologist Zsuzsa Ferge). This situation has arisen because of the poor progress being made as former state enterprises are privatized (not without major mistakes and scandals) and because some mega-companies have been eliminated (mainly from the heavy industries of steel, mining and machine tools). Concurrently, the rising external debt and unemployment appear as the most serious side-effects.[44] Since the fall of 1994, a negative trend has been continuing with slightly more than eleven per cent of the work force unemployed, a pattern showing no signs of improvement.[45]

To combat these trends the government has reintroduced unemployment benefits, welfare and training programmes. However, extended benefits create a vicious circle: poverty increases as those collecting unemployment benefits rely more and more on social services. Lack of training and experience — not to mention welfare's stigmatizing effects on individuals — prevent individuals from re-entering the job market.[46] Coupled with the rising rate of inflation (especially for basic goods and necessities such as transportation, heating, water and electricity), the unemployed may feel doubly left out of the social redistribution system by the rising marketization of social services that were once free and subsidized (schools, hospitalization, medicine, and housing). Social peripherialization, the feeling of helplessness and complete abandonment result in increasing social segregation. Income differentials are far from trivial. Hungary's disenfranchised, enlarged and re-emerging lower classes are justified in blaming the previous, as well as the present Horn, government.

In contrast, when Hungary turned to a capitalist-market economy, a new breed of entrepreneurs seized the opportunity to make a 'quick forint' (even hard currency) on everything from 'bio-worms' to stock speculation to automobile promotion. Of course, some of the risk-takers were old-régime directors and party officials determined to invest both their savings and intellectual capital (connections, know-how) wisely.[47] It remains to be proven by statistics, but for the most part these dynamic new 'middle-class' entrepreneurs were unrelated to both the former bourgeoisie and the rehabilitated aristocracy. How many rags-to-riches stories exist in contemporary Hungary is difficult to ascertain. In 1991, only 0.28 per cent of the population officially reported incomes of one million forint (USD 14,000) or more. In 1993, this figure was still well under one per cent. Furthermore, a staggering number of small shopkeepers and business people report no income whatsoever, and many others only report a modest income (profit) of about 1,000 USD per year. Since income tax declarations are blurred by loopholes, shelters, and evasions, it is difficult to measure actual income and define wealth. This may be one of the reasons why the socialist government of Gyula Horn may be considering making a declaration of wealth by individuals mandatory.

Such a policy is based on the fact that this spirit of unbridled capitalism invites entrepreneurs to engage in conspicuous consumption instead of reinvesting in their businesses. In today's Hungary, as in many former Soviet Bloc countries, possessing the trappings of wealth seems almost as important as possessing wealth itself. Part of the reason may be the current hunger for consumer goods and conveniences — CDs, VCRs, cellular telephones, western cars, swimming pools, saunas — which were denied to citizens relegated to seeing such items in western films. As one friend complained after travelling in Austria with his Trabant: 'I will not be the laughing-stock of Austria again'. Before 1989, most Hungarians could only stare at an Opel Astra or Suzuki.

Today, both cars are manufactured in Hungary. In addition, during the last months of 1990, thousands of second-hand western cars were imported, a time known as the Great Mercedes Migration. These are signs of how things have moved on in the Hungarian economy. As the Hungarians became owners of former luxury items, they realized immediately that image and status symbol go hand-in-hand. The new rich are engaging in cultural consumption patterns which, according to their ideas, must be followed during an economic upswing: going to concerts, buying expensive paintings, visiting museums and galleries of international repute. This noticeable cultural consumerism is rejected by many, not least by those who have no chance of purchasing such goods and enjoying such cultural amenities.

Such a rearrangement of social and cultural relations affects the country's poor and marginalized as well. Organizations such as the SZETA, church-based help groups, the Red Cross, the AA, and shelters for battered women and the poor (now lacking or competing for governmental aid) have seen an unprecedented upswing in demand over the past few years. Not only is the degree of poverty increasing, the client profile is shifting considerably. While earlier, traditionally impoverished classes — unskilled workers, rural retirees, and youth — used the services of the state and independent social service organizations, since 1990 some middle-class families experiencing the effects of inflation, unemployment and increasing social peripherialization, have turned to them. Hungary's troubled minority, the Gypsies (*Roma*), together with refugees from the Balkan war, are also targets of racist and xenophobic outbursts as social tensions continue to rise.[48] While it is true that poverty levels are escalating, so is the problem's visibility. Beggars and homeless (many resulting from the country's new tenant eviction policies) are regular sights in the streets, metro stations and parks.

While there is much discussion about creating a middle class as a pre-condition of Hungary's Europeanization in the future, the economic scene provides a harsher yet realistic picture: this middle class is far from being created. More than sixty per cent of the country's wage-earners receive less than the average income needed to maintain a family of four; a large portion of the middle class is collapsing into poverty. Since 1992, at least fifty per cent of the population of 10 million lives at or below today's demarcation of the poverty line, or minimum subsistance level. Of these, more than two million fell into poverty, many as the result of the last four years of transformation. As the English sociologist Tom Bottomore sees it, the new regimes of the former East Bloc are attempting to implement a market economy and integrate into the European Union and the world market and, at the same time, a new class system and politics comparable to that of Western Europe may be emerging.[49]

While Gyula Horn's 'state-of-the-nation' address at the end of September 1994 did not manage to adequately summarize the real difficulties that lay ahead, and the way in which the government planned to act throughout much of 1995, the prospects for Hungary at present are grim and not without the possibility of social upheaval. Together with the formation of a new elite and power re-distribution, general social inequality is further exacerbated by both inherited as well as newly acquired difficulties in the economy, education, and welfare. Consequently, as the population at large is becoming poorer than ever before, and as a large section of the middle class recedes into poverty, an increasingly skeptical public questions the success of the Horn government and the promises made by the Socialist-Liberal coalition.[50]

At the moment, public opinion may be best characterized as a 'wait-and-see tactic', a period of relative 'tolerance' of the new government and its policies. Surveying the grim economic and social vistas, however, many feel that democracy and market economy was perhaps over-hyped political demagogy.[51] So, too, was the constant reference to a 'return to Europe' and 'Europeanization'. One of the fundamental components of public skepticism and discontent is that some of the 'old-timers' are still articulating the new political philosophy, and that the old regime democrats are parading under the mantle of liberalism and social democracy.[52] Another factor is the perceived lack of governmental empathy. Consequently, for the first time since the Horn government took office, there is growing social malaise among the public in general.[53]

Conclusions

In the foregoing analysis, I have argued that what is specific to Hungary is, in fact, characteristic of most contemporary states: social atomization and inegalitarianism. Perhaps the phrase 're-feudalization' best characterizes Hungarian society and this process may indeed be observed in all spheres of life. Thus, re-feudalization refers not only to the disempowerment of social groups and individuals but, at the same time, also entails the re-definition of symbolic kinship ties characteristic of power holders in high office. Trustworthy individuals, called 'experts', justifiably and rightfully take their positions from those who were given their place by the previous government. As mentioned above, this seems to be part of the re-bureaucratization of the state, this time from the vantage point of the socialist government, the second freely elected government after the ousting of the communists from power. Inequality, thus, trickles down from the top of the pyramid. As one Hungarian colloquialism aptly summarizes it, 'the fish always begins to stink from its head.' This, too, is part of the ironic view which forms the basis of the individual survival mechanism to cope with injustices and inequality built into the bureaucratic state machinery.

A further point of departure which should be taken into account when discussing Hungary's political future is the external relations of the country, particularly with its Slovak, Romanian and Serbian neighbours, not to mention the larger issues which connect the country to Germany, and the West in general.[54] Pressures from the IMF, the World Bank and private investors will be central in pressing for privatization, anti-inflationary measures and a reduction in the growing trade deficit. Repercussions will undoubtly follow: i.e. rising unemployment, price increases for basic goods and growing atomization of social groups contending for resources.

An added destabilizing feature will be the growing Hungarian national consciousness. The concept of national identity and unity is pivotal to an understanding of Hungary's future relations. Resurgent nationalism, though much discussed and little understood during the Christian-nationalist rule between 1990 and 1994, has been at the centre of the dramatic events which have characterized Hungary since 1989. The continuation of an acute sense of national awareness will linger on for many years to come (in France, Great Britain, and Denmark we may witness similar cultural movements).[55] This is not the result of nationalism going haywire or the revival of primordial symbols and true resuscitation of the collective identity of a nation. Hungary's incorporation into the global 'ethnoscape' (Arjun Appadurai), and 'ecumene' (Ulf Hannerz), will be enhanced considerably by the end of this century. In light of the increasing hostilities emanating from neighbouring countries, the growing social disenchantment and the emergence of trans-national identities, failing to take this seriously may mean that the country's present leaders will have missed one of the important lessons of the past four years: the idea that democracy must be constantly re-evaluated and re-negotiated if it is to remain safe and sound. This entails an unprecedented degree of self-criticism and the willingness on the part of those in power to engage in social dialogue. Surely, the order of the day is to act so as not to lose the trust and support of the citizens of Hungary.

Notes

1. See, for example, the classic works in anthropology, M.H. Fried, *The Evolution of Political Society*. New York: Random House; and L.A. White (1959), *The Evolution of Culture*. New York: McGraw-Hill.
2. Abner Cohen 1993, *Masquarade Politics: Explorations in the Structure of Urban Cultural Movements*. Berkeley: University of California Press; and Maurice Godelier (1988), *The Mental and the Material*. London: Verso.
3. This is, of course, Karl Polanyi's model. See Karl Polanyi 1957, *The Great Transformation*. Boston: Beacon Press.
4. See Elman Service, 'Political Power and the Origin of Social complexity', in J.S. Henderson and P.J. Netherly (eds.), 1993, *Configurations of Power: Holistic Anthropology in Theory and Practice*. Ithaca: Cornell U.P.: 112-36.
5. *Primitive Government*, 1970. Harmondsworth: Penguin Books: 18.
6. Michael Herzfeld, 1992. *The Social Production of Indifference*. Chicago: University of Chicago Press: 18-19.
7. Herzfeld, for instance, argues that when people assume that 'the bureaucratically regulated state societies of 'the west' are more rational — or less 'symbolic' — than those of the rest of the world ... (it) has all the marks of a religious doctrine'; see Herzfeld, *The Social Production of Indifference*: 17.
8. See, for example, the monographs on Portugal, Brian Juan O'Neill, 1987. *Social Inequality in a Portuguese Hamlet: Land, late marriage, and bastardy, 1870-1978*. Cambridge: Cambridge U.P.; and the restructured kinship relations in the two Berlins in the second-half of the twentieth century, John Borneman 1992, *Belonging in the Two Berlins: Kin, State, Nation*. Cambridge: Cambridge U.P.
9. See, Anton Blok, 1974. *The mafia of a Sicilian village*. Oxford: Basil Blackwell; and Diego Gambetta, 1993. *The Sicilian Mafia: The Business of Private Protection*. Cambridge: Harvard U.P.
10. Attila József was a true working-class poet, neither mystifying nor romanticizing the life styles of its members. Although he never openly identified himself with the dogmatism of the Communist Party, Attila József's poetry provided perhaps the most scathing criticism of the inter-war period.
11. István Szent-Miklossy 1988. *With the Hungarian Independence Movement, 1943-1947*. New York: Praeger, 89-93.
12. The secret political police (AVH) was one of the most important factors in assisting the establishment of Stalinist order in Hungary, a fact similar to those of other East European countries where the *Stasi* in East Germany, the *Cheka* or later the *KGB* in the Soviet Union, the *Securitate* in Romania, supported the establishment of totalitarian rule. They infiltrated all major institutions — schools, municipal administrations, factories, radio, television, newspapers, and

political parties — and began a reign of terror over the population. On 27 February 1947, the so-called 'conspiracy trials' began during which more than 200 people were sentenced before the 'People's Court'. See Charles Gati 1986, *Hungary and the Soviet Bloc.* Durham N.C.: Duke U.P.

13. In this study, I do not analyze the culture of the Hungarian children's organizations, namely the Young Pioneers' League (*Úttörő Szövetség*) and the 'Little Drummer' (*Kisdobos*). While there are excellent studies of similar organizations in the West, few have been published about the East Bloc and the Soviet Union; they should, I believe, constitute a separate study, and warrant serious scholarly attention as formal state institutions monitoring the lives of millions of children since the 1950s.

14. The growing interest in the youth can be illustrated by the number of political youth organizations between 1945-1949; most were, however, eliminated by the communists in 1948 and 1950. For the history of these see, Lajos Gál and Lászlóné Szarvas, *A magyar ifjusagi mozgalom tortenete 1945-1950* (History of Hungarian Youth Movement, 1945-1950). Budapest: Ifjúsági Lapkiadó Vállalat, 1981. The list of the youth organizations is impressive nevertheless:
Democratic World Federation of Youth (DIVSZ) 1947-
Working Girls' National Association (DLOSZ)
Workers' College National Association (DOKOSZ) 1947-49
'Emericana', Saint Emeric Friendship Society
United Peasant Youth National Association (EPOSZ)
Independent Youth Federation (FISZ)
Catholic Agrarian Youth Girls' Association (KALASZ)
Catholic Agrarian Youth Boys' Association (KALOT)
Catholic Working Girls' National Association (KDLSZ)
Hungarian Communist Working Youth's League (KIMSZ)
Catholic Merchant Youth National League (KIOE)
Hungarian Democratic Youth Association (MADISZ)
League of Hungarian University-College Associations (MEFESZ)
Hungarian People's Youth League (MINSZ) - 1948 -1950
Hungarian Youth National Council (MIOT) - 1950
Hungarian Scout Association (MCSSZ) - +1948
Hungarian Pioneers' Association (MUSZ) - 1946 -
National Association of People's Colleges (NEKOSZ)
Peoples' Youth Federation (NISZ)
National Youth Committee (OIB)
Guardians of the Heart (Sziv Garda) -1948
Socialdemocratic Youth Movement (SZIM)
Trade Union and Youth, and Apprentice Movement (SZIT)
National Organization of Apprentices and Youth Hostels (TIOSZ).

15. The Workers' Youth Association, DISZ (Dolgozi Ifjusagi Szovetseg), was founded on 16 June 1950. Its purpose was defined as follows: The Workers' Youth Association is a non-party mass organization uniting the widest spectrum of

working youth into a revolutionary association. It is the vanguard of the Hungarian working-class and the people, led indirectly by the Hungarian Workers'Party. All activities of the DISZ is determined by the victorious world-view of the working class, Marxism-Leninism; see Gyorgy Petrus (1984), *A magyar ifjusági mozgalom története (1950-1956)* (History of the Hungarian Youth Movement 1950-1956). Budapest: Ifjúsági Lap és Könyvkiadó: 41.

16. For instance, Michael Burawoy and János Lukács, 1992. *The Radiant Past: Ideology and Reality in Hungary's Road to Capitalism*. Chicago: The University of Chicago Press; János Kornai, 1990. *Vision and Reality, Market and State*. New York: Routledge; Nigel Swain, 1992. *Hungary: The Rise and Fall of Feasible Socialism*. London: Verso; and Ivan Szelenyi, 1988, *Socialist Entrepreneurs: Embourgeoisement in Rural Hungary*. Madison: The University of Wisconsin Press.

17. Chris Hann, 1993. 'Introduction: Social Anthropology and Socialism', in *Socialism, Ideals, Ideologies and Local Practice*. London: Routledge, 13.

18. Maybe this is what the writer-turned-politician Miklós Haraszti refers to when he writes about the 'velvet prison' in which 'Censorship is no longer a matter of simple state intervention. A new aesthetic culture has emerged in which censors and artists alike are entangled in a mutual embrace ... The state is able to domesticate the artist because the artist has already made the state his home'; see *The Velvet Prison: Artists Under State Socialism*. New York: Basic Books, 1987: 5.

19. One of the most insightful analyses of the cult of Kádár is Andrew Felkay, 1989. *Hungary and the USSR, 1956-1988: Kádár's Political Leadership*. New York: Greenwood Press; see especially 162-78.

20. An English version of the 1971 Youth Constitution, or Law on Youth, was published by the State Committee on Youth, a national body attached to the Council of Ministers.

21. The Stalinist politicization of age is evident from the 'Twelve Points of the Trade Union Youth Organization, SZIT':

 1. Members of the SZIT love their people and country — but hate its enemies;
 2. They are conscious fighters for proletarian internationalism, ready in the spirit of war or liberation to fight for peace;
 3. Through work, they make certain that the socialist Plan will be victorious;
 4. Their skills and education are for the benefit of the people;
 5. Through systematic study of Marxism and Leninism they develop a clear political vision;
 6. They are brave and joyous, conscientuous and orderly;
 7. They are ready to sacrifice in building socialism; are not discouraged by difficulties;
 8. They are comrades-in-arms with democratic youth around the world and follow their ideal, the heroic Soviet youth;
 9. They build the unity of Hungarian youth and reinforce the alliance of peasant and working youth;

10. Through healthy recreation, a pleasant manner, and physical culture, they prepare to meet challenges;

11. They protect and defend the Hungarian People's Republic and its wealth;

12. The honorable goal of members of the youth organization is to earn the privilege of joining the vanguard of the Hungarian working class through its organization, the Hungarian Socialist Workers' Party.

22. See László, Kürti, 1989. 'Red Csepel: Working Youth in a Socialist Firm', *East European Quarterly*, 23: 445-68; 'Hierarchy and Workers' Power in a Csepel Factory', *The Journal of Communist Studies* 6/2, 1990: 61-84; and Lajos Héthy and Csaba Makó, 1987. *Patterns of Workers' Behavior and the Business Enterprise.* Budapest: Institute of Sociology.

23. J.F. Brown, 1991. *Surge to Freedom: The End of Communist Rule in Eastern Europe.* Durham N.C.: Duke U.P.: 98-99.

24. The nature and the mixture of this opposition is not difficult to decipher from the variety of studies ranging from the collection in Sabrina P. Ramet (ed.) 1993, *Rocking the State: Rock Music and Politics in Eastern Europe and Russia.* Boulder: Westview Press, to the specific case study of Michael H. Bernhard (1993), *The Origins of Democratization in Poland.* New York: Columbia U.P.

25. See, *Basic Democratic Values and Political Realities in East Central Europe.* Budapest Papers on Democratic Transition No. 70, Budapest: Department of Political Science, Budapest University of Economics, 1993: 12-13.

26. Gábor Demszky, 1991. 'Building a Market Economy in Hungary', *Uncaptive Mind*, 4/2: 46.

27. For critical insights see István Schlett 1990, *Az opportunizmus dicsérete.* Budapest: Magvető; and Mihály Vajda 1992, *A történelem vége?.* Budapest: Századvég.

28. Endre Sik, 1990. 'Erdélyi menekültek Magyarországon', in Rudolf Andorka, Tamás Kolosi, és György Vukovich (eds.), *Társadalmi Riport 1990.* Budapest: Tárki: 516-533; and Péter Róbert and Endre Sik, 1993. 'Occupation attainment of Transylvanian refugees in Hungary', in *Proceedings Workshop Transformation Proceses in Eastern Europe.* The Hague: 19-49.

29. Ferenc Fehér, 1990. 'The Left after Communism', *Thesis Eleven* 27: 21.

30. Mart Bax, 'Religious Regimes and State-Formation: Towards a Research Perspective', in Eric Wolf (ed.), *Religious Regimes and State-Formation: Perspectives from European Ethnology.* Albany: State University of New York Press: 7-8.

31. László Kürti, 1990. 'People vs the State: Political rituals in contemporary Hungary'. *Anthropology Today* 6/2: 5-9.

32. Reburial and sacrifice of leaders and heroes are, of course, rituals which characterize both state and non-state societies equally; see the classic study of A.M. Hocart, 1970. *Kings and Councillors: An Essay in the Comparative Anatomy of Human Society.* Chicago: The University of Chicago Press.

33. 'Epilogue, 1985-1990', in Peter F. Sugar, Péter Hanák, and Tibor Frank (eds.) 1990. *A History of Hungary.* Bloomington: Indiana U.P., 404.

34. See, for example, István Schlett, 1992. 'Nacionalizmus és demokrácia a posztszocialista Magyarországon', *Sodrásban* I/1: 52-59.

35. See, Ivan T. Berend, 1993. 'Jobbra Át (Right Face). Right-Wing Trends in Post-Communist Hungary', in J. Held (ed.), *Democracy and Right-Wing Politics in Eastern Europe in the 1990s*. Boulder: East European Monographs: 105-134.

36. As Herzfeld writes: 'Both bureaucratic interaction and personality hospitality are deeply concerned with defining lines of exclusion and belonging;' see *The social production of indifference*: 170.

37. For the MDF's failure to win over the country-side with its land reform see, Vásáry Ildikó, 1995. 'Labyrinths of Freedom: An Agricultural Community in Post-Socialist Hungary', in David A. Kideckel (ed.), *East European Communities: The Struggle for Balance in Turbulent Times*. Boulder: Westview Press, 9-24.

38. For an analysis of this see Attila Ágh, 1993. *The Invention of Democratic Tradition in Hungary*. Budapest Papers on Democratic Transition No. 65. Budapest: Department of Political Science, Budapest University of Economics: 13-15.

39. See, Adam Michnik, 'A bársonyos restauráció', *Népszabadság*, 1 October 1994: 17.

40. This is certainly one hundred and eighty degree turn from the MSZP's original promises: 'We socialists are seeking a democratic many-sided educational system...non-interference of the government in cultural life, but, on the contrary, the government is responsible for the upkeep of national institutions and to provide the bases for their operations;' see the political advertisement, 'A Magyar Szocialist Párt A Modern Magyarországért', *Magyar Hirlap*, 27 August 1993: 6.

41. It is necessary of course that every government establishes its own system of power distribution and hierarchy. Yet, it is not without irony that after much debate (or self-flagellation) Lajos Csepi, Executive Director of the ÁVÜ (National Capital Agency), was released from his position; Miklós Mátrai replaced the MDF, appointed Katalin Botos as Director of ÁBF (Állami Bankfelügyelet, National Bank Supervisory Board); directors of the Hungarian Electric Corporation (Magyar Villamos Művek) and the Tisza Chemical Corporation were dismissed; and dozens of writer-reporters kicked-out of the Hungarian Radio and television already in the months following the coming to power of the Horn government in 1994. This was followed by newer implementation of the patron-client relationship in 1995 when museum directors and heads of hospitals were relieved of their posts.

42. That this is a real 'dilemma' may be seen from an interview with György Jánosi, political undersecretary in the Ministry of Culture. In an interview Jánosi openly admits that the eleven-twelve per cent of the voters with university diplomas who voted for the MSZP is not 'quite adequate.' A creation of an educated elite is of primary importance to the socialist government, an area of future development which will have to incorporate a systematic schooling policy; see, 'Az értelmiséget is be kell vonni a társadalom átalakitásában', *Népszabadság*, 17 September 1994: 13.

43. Róbert Kovács, 1992. 'Települési egyenlőtlenségek — területi feszültségek', in Rudolf Andorka, Tamás Kolosi, and György Vukovich (eds.), *Társadalmi Riport 1992*. Budapest: Tárki: 222-58.

44. According to figures released by the Economic Research Institute (*Gazdaságkutató Rt.*), Hungary's external debt increased to 26.5 billion USD by the end of July 1994 (*Népszabadság*, 27 September 1994: 12).

45. To describe in more detail the nature and complexities of Hungarian unemployment the following should suffice: According to figures released by the *Országos Munkaügyi Központ* as of 31 August 1994, the total number of registered unemployed was 551,000, which is slightly lower than that of July, (546,000). Out of this number 74,000 are looking for their first jobs; Budapest is, for the first time, leading in the number of unemployed; 33.4 per cent are reapplications; less than 10 per cent are participating in retraining programmes; 34 per cent have received unemployment benefits; 201,000 receive welfare and social assistance; and 162,000 have not been provided with any kind of benefits (*Népszabadság*, 24 September 1994: 5). By the end of September, the total number of unemployed further decreased to 545,868. (*Magyar Hirlap*, 6 October 1994: 5). Other figures released by independent organizations, such as the Koping-Datorg and Szonda-Ipsos, put unemployment as high as 16 per cent. Hungary's Minister of Labour, however, mentions that 'actual' or 'existing' unemployment may be as high as one million!

46. In a recent interview, the Minister of Labour, Kósáné Magda Kovács, expressed hope that with the help of the trade unions and the newly implemented social welfare, the government is expecting a positive outcome by the end of 1995; see 'Teljesen átalakul a munkanélküliség ellátórendszere', *Magyar Hirlap*, 26 August 1995: 7.

47. While it is fashionable to report on corruption, and mafia businesses together with rags-to-riches stories from the former Soviet Bloc, it needs to be mentioned that white-collar crime is also on the rise. The Hungarian daily, *Magyar Hirlap*, reported recently that one of the most prestigious private banks, Budapest Bank, was able to obtain illegally large land-holdings set aside originally for land redistribution to people with reparation tickets; see 'Per a Budapest bank ellen', *Magyar Hirlap*, 26 August 1995: 1.

48. I do not want to speak of a specific Hungarian Gypsy problem per se, for it has been misused so often in the past; for recent accounts on the Gypsies see D. Zoltán Barany, 1994. 'Living on the Edge: The East European Roma in Postcommunist Politics and Societies', *Slavic Review* 53 (2): 321-44; and the special issue of the Hungarian periodical *Replika*, Vols.17-18, June 1995.

49. *Classes in Modern Society*. London: Harper Collins, 1991: 80.

50. It should be mentioned here that one may detect cracks within the power structure itself as four of the original advisory team to the Horn cabinet decided to quit (Mária Petchnig Zita, Csaba Gombár, László Lengyel, and András Bródy); see, *Népszabadság*, 5 October 1994: 5. Ferenc Baja, Minister of Environment and Vice President of the MSZP, summarizes this aptly when he characterizes the mood within the party as 'vacuous' and 'insecure'; see *Népszabadság*, 5 October 1994: 6.

51. As an example I want to call attention to the interview with Prime Minister Gyula Horn when he noted, somewhat ironically, that '*Zárójelben megjegyzem, hogy én is nép-nemzetinek érzem magam*', (Parenthetically, I want to note that I, too, am a populist), *Magyar Nemzet*, 7 October 1994: 7.

52. On the negative value people attach to elites and politicians see György Csepeli and Antal Örkény, 1993. 'Az elitpercepció kognitiv és társadalmi meghatározói a mai Magyarországon', *Valóság* 12: 47-58.

53. However, according to a survey conducted by Szonda-Ipsos after the Horn government took office, the percentage of those undecided about voting for any party, should elections be held again rose to seventeen per cent among low-skilled and unskilled workers. On the contrary, among urban university educated, the decision to vote for the same parties they supported during the spring election increased slightly (See, *Népszabadság*, 27 September 1994: 7). What this really means is that for the first time since the election of the Hungarian Socialist Party to power, there is wide dissatisfaction among the populace, and trust in the government of Gyula Horn has been slowly eroding. As a natural consequence the number of committed voters in both the Free Democrats (SZDSZ) and the Socialist (MSZP) camps is also decreasing. This growing malaise has manifested itself in internal governmental uneasiness as the Horn government has considered cabinet level changes in the fall of 1995; see 'A kormányátalakitás ügye jövő héten kerül a kabinet elé', *Magyar Nemzet*, 26 August 1995: 1.

54. Although the Horn government managed to sign a basic agreement with the Meciar government of Slovakia, this agreement, while looked at with disdain by the elites of both countries, is not binding at all; for the text see 'A magyar-szlovák alapszerződés', *Magyar Nemzet*, 20 March 1995: 4. The Hungarian and Romanian contract is yet to be made but there are no signs on the horizon that the two governments are willing to work out the details especially related to the sensitive issues concerning the fate of the two million Hungarian minorities living in Romania.

55. See, for example, Thomas M. Wilson and estellie M. Smith, (eds.) 1993. *Cultural Change and the New Europe: Perspectives on the European Community*. Boulder: Westview Press; and Sharon Macdonald (ed.) 1993. *Inside European Identities*. Providence: Berg.

Bibliography

Ágh, Attila 1993. *Basic Democratic Values and Political Realities in East Central Europe*. Budapest Papers on Democratic Transition No. 70, Budapest: Department of Political Science, Budapest University of Economics.

Ágh, Attila 1993. *The Invention of Democratic Tradition in Hungary*. Budapest Papers on Democratic Transition No. 65, Budapest: Department of Political Science, Budapest University of Economics: 13-15.

Barany, D. Zoltán 1994. 'Living on the Edge: The East European Roma in Post-communist Politics and Societies', *Slavic Review* 53 (2): 321-44.

Bax, Mart 1991. 'Religious Regimes and State-Formation: Towards a Research Perspective', in Eric Wolf (ed.), *Religious Regimes and State-Formation: Perspectives from European Ethnology*. Albany: State University of New York Press: 7-8.

Berend, Ivan T. 1993. 'Jobbra Át (Right Face). Right-Wing Trends in Post-Communist Hungary', in J. Held (ed.), *Democracy and Right-Wing Politics in Eastern Europe in the 1990s*. Boulder: East European Monographs: 105-134.

Blok, Anton 1974. *The mafia of a Sicilian village*. Oxford: Basil Blackwell.

Borneman, John 1992. *Belonging in the Two Berlins: Kin, State, Nation*. Cambridge: Cambridge U.P.

Bottomore, Tom 1991. *Classes in Modern Society*. London: Harper Collins.

Brown, J.F. 1991. *Surge to Freedom: The End of Communist Rule in Eastern Europe*. Durham N.C.: Duke U.P.

Burawoy, Michael and János Lukács 1992. *The Radiant Past: Ideology and Reality in Hungary's Road to Capitalism*. Chicago: The University of Chicago Press.

Cohen, Abner1 1993. *Masquarade Politics: Explorations in the Structure of Urban Cultural Movements*. Berkeley: University of California Press.

Csepeli, György and Antal Örkény 1993. 'Az elitpercepció kognitiv és társadalmi meghatározói a mai Magyarországon', *Valóság* 12: 47-58.

Demszky, Gábor 1991. 'Building a Market Economy in Hungary', *Uncaptive Mind*, 4/2: 46.

Fehér, Ferenc 1990. 'The Left after Communism', *Thesis Eleven* 27: 21.

Felkay, Andrew 1989. *Hungary and the USSR, 1956-1988: Kádár's Political Leadership*. New York: Greenwood Press.

Fried, H.M. 1967. *The Evolution of Political Society*. New York: Random House.

Gál, Lajosand and Lászlóné Szarvas 1981. *A magyar ifjusagi mozgalom tortenete 1945-1950* (History of Hungarian Youth Movement, 1945-1950). Budapest: Ifjúsági Lapkiadó Vállalat.

Gambetta, Diego 1993. *The Sicilian Mafia: The Business of Private Protection*. Cambridge: Harvard U.P.

Gati Charles 1986, *Hungary and the Soviet Bloc*. Durham N.C.: Duke U.P.

Godelier, Maurice 1988. *The Mental and the Material*. London: Verso.

Hann, Chris 1993. 'Introduction: Social Anthropology and Socialism', in *Socialism, Ideals, Ideologies and Local Practice*. London: Routledge: 13.

Haraszti, Miklós 1987. *The Velvet Prison: Artists Under State Socialism*. New York: Basic Books.

Herzfeld, Michael and H. Bernhard 1993. *The Origins of Democratization in Poland*. New York: Columbia U.P.

Herzfeld, Michael 1992. *The Social Production of Indifference*. Chicago: University of Chicago Press.

Héthy, Lajos and Csaba Makó 1987. *Patterns of Workers' Behavior and the Business Enterprise*. Budapest: Institute of Sociology.

Hocart, A.M. 1970. *Kings and Councillors: An Essay in the Comparative Anatomy of Human Society*. Chicago: The University of Chicago Press.
Ildikó, Vásáry 1995. 'Labyrinths of Freedom: An Agricultural Community in Post-Socialist Hungary', in David A. Kideckel (ed.), *East European Communities: The Struggle for Balance in Turbulent Times*. Boulder: Westview Press, 9-24.
Kornai, János 1990. *Vision and Reality, Market and State*. New York: Routledge.
Kovács, Róbert 1992. 'Települési egyenlőtlenségek — területi feszültségek', in Rudolf Andorka, Tamás Kolosi, and György Vukovich (eds.), *Társadalmi Riport 1992*, Budapest: Tárki: 222-58.
Kürti, László 1989. 'Red Csepel: Working Youth in a Socialist Firm', *East European Quarterly*, 23: 445-68.
Kürti, László 1990. 'Hierarchy and Workers' Power in a Csepel Factory', *The Journal of Communist Studies* 6/2, : 61-84.
Kürti, László 1990. 'People vs the State: Political rituals in contemporary Hungary', *Anthropology Today* 6/2: 5-9.
Macdonald, Sharon (ed.), 1993. *Inside European Identities*, Providence: Berg.
Magyar Hirlap, 6 October 1994: 5.
Magyar Hirlap, 26 August 1995: 7.
Magyar Nemzet, 20 March 1995: 4.
Magyar Nemzet, 26 August 1995: 1.
Magyar Nemzet, 7 October 1994: 7.
Magyar Hirlap, 27 August 1993: 6.
Mair, Lucy 1970. *Primitive Government*. Harmondsworth: Penguin Books..
O'Neill, Brian Juan 1987. *Social Inequality in a Portuguese Hamlet: Land, late marriage, and bastardy, 1870-1978*. Cambridge: Cambridge U.P.
Michnik, Adam 1994. 'A bársonyos restauráció', *Népszabadság*. 1 October : 17.
Miklossy, István Szent 1988. *With the Hungarian Independence Movement, 1943-1947*. New York: Praeger.
Népszabadság, 27 September 1994: 7.
Népszabadság, 5 October 1994: 5.
Népszabadság, 27 September 1994: 12.
Népszabadság, 17 September 1994: 13.
Népszabadság, 24 September 1994: 5
Petrus, Gyorgy 1984., *A magyar ifjúsági mozgalom története (1950-1956)*, (History of the Hungarian Youth Movement 1950-1956). Budapest: Ifjúsági Lap és Könyvkiadó.
Polanyi, Karl 1957. *The Great Transformation*. Boston: Beacon Press.
Ramet Sabrina P. (ed.), 1993. *Rocking the State: Rock Music and Politics in Eastern Europe and Russia*. Boulder: Westview Press.
Replika, Vols.17-18, June 1995.
Róbert, Péter and Endre Sik 1993. 'Occupation attainment of Transylvanian refugees in Hungary', in *Proceedings Workshop Transformation Processes in Eastern Europe*. The Hague: 19-49.
Schlett, István 1990. *Az opportunizmus dicsérete*. Budapest: Magvető.

Schlett, István 1992. 'Nacionalizmus és demokrácia a poszt-szocialista Magyaror-szágon', *Sodrásban* I/1: 52-59.

Service, Elman 1993. 'Political Power and the Origin of Social complexity', in J.S. Henderson and P.J. Netherly (eds.) , *Configurations of Power: Holistic Anthropology in Theory and Practice.* Ithaca: Cornell U.P.: 112-36.

Sik, Endre 1990. 'Erdélyi menekültek Magyarországon', in Rudolf Andorka, Tamás Kolosi, és György Vukovich (eds.), *Társadalmi Riport 1990.* Budapest: Tárki: 516-33.

Sugar, Peter F., Péter Hanák and Tibor Frank (eds.) 1990. *A History of Hungary.* Bloomington: Indiana U.P.

Swain, Nigel 1992. *Hungary: The Rise and Fall of Feasible Socialism.* London: Verso.

Szelenyi, Ivan 1988. *Socialist Entrepreneurs: Embourgeoisement in Rural Hungary.* Madison: The University of Wisconsin Press.

Vajda, Mihály 1992. *A történelem vége?* Budapest: Századvég.

White, L.A. 1959. *The Evolution of Culture.* New York: McGraw-Hill.

Wilson, Thomas M. and Estellie M. Smith, (eds.) 1993. *Cultural Change and the New Europe: Perspectives on the European Community.* Boulder: Westview Press.

Hungary: The Transition to Democratic Politics

Bill Lomax

The first and most obvious lesson to be learned from the collapse of communism in the autumn of 1989 is that the disappearance of the communist regimes did not in itself ensure the emergence of democratic political systems. There were in fact many grounds for believing that the previous authoritarian structures would not necessarily disappear with the passing of communism, but would rather be reproduced in new forms with different ideological colouring. Cultural attitudes and patterns of behaviour do not simply vanish overnight. The fundamental question to which this article addresses itself is how, in such a situation, it may be possible for a fully democratic system of political parties to develop.[1]

A second, perhaps less obvious, lesson is the need to avoid the mistake of seeking to understand the changes in East-Central and Eastern Europe since the fall of communism in terms of political models developed on the basis of North American and West European experiences. The temptation to describe the new in terms of the old, to theorize the unknown in terms of the known, can lead the observer to miss that which is truly novel and unique, spontaneous and innovative, in social change.[2] Communist societies were unique social systems that required analysis in their own terms, and the same is true of the post-communist social systems currently in the process of formation.

The key concepts of political democracy are, nevertheless, common to both the established democracies of North America and Western Europe and to the new, fledgling democracies of the former communist states of East-Central and Eastern Europe. The latter societies are undergoing a transition from a one-party system, in which the ruling party totally dominated the state and all political life, to a multi-party system in which the new parties are subject to the restraints of constitutional checks and balances, political opposition, a free press, public criticism and an independent judiciary. Crucial to the success of this transition, however, is not just institutional change but the development of a pluralistic political culture and of democratic political attitudes and behaviour patterns.

This article confines itself to the emergence of Hungary's new party system, which it will be suggested displays greater consolidation and stability than is to be found in any of the other post-communist countries of East-Central and

Eastern Europe. Hungary's first democratically elected parliament ran its full course without any change of government for four years from 1990 to 1994. Moreover, only six parties were elected to the parliament in 1990, and the very same six parties were again those elected in 1994, representing a stability not found elsewhere. Nevertheless, these parties were not quite like those we are accustomed to in Western Europe, and they did not always appear to act in particularly democratic ways.[3]

The key question to which this article addresses itself is, thus, not simply that of the transition from a one-party system to a multi-party system, but that of whether and how the latter can be developed into a fully democratic multi-party system.

The Politics of Cultural Identity

The distinguishing feature of most Hungarian political parties is that their self-identity has so far been based in large part on cultural or historical values, symbols and traditions, rather than on any commitment to common interests or structured political programmes. They are very much elite parties, with a high proportion of intellectuals amongst their leaders, and with little implantation in society at large. It has been suggested that they are 'cultural milieu groupings', more like 'tribes' than parties, or even clubs of often long-standing personal friends rooted in Budapest's intellectual sub-culture.[4]

This 'tribal' nature of the parties means that (in their origins and in many respects still today) to the extent that the more conventional political cleavages are to be found in Hungarian political life, these are not congruent with the divisions between the parties. The Hungarian political spectrum is divided by many cleavages, not separating the parties from one another, but rather cutting through each equally. Each party has its left and right, its populists and nationalists, its centrists and liberals, social democrats and authoritarians.[5]

The self-identities of the parties are thus rooted in emotive commitments rather than rational policy positions. The political identities and cleavages they represent are based neither on social interests, nor political programmes, nor structured belief systems, but on cultural, emotional or even spiritual identifications through which their members come to belong to socio-cultural camps with common life styles and common attitudes that, in turn, provide the basis for common political styles and common behaviour patterns. Such political styles are very good at identifying enemies and scapegoats, but they are highly detrimental to the processes of bargaining and the pursuit of compromises that are the very essence of a pluralist democracy.[6]

Such political styles and behaviour patterns certainly appeared to characterize most of the parties, and particularly those of the government coalition, through the four-year term of Hungary's first democratically elected parliament. At the same time, this seems to have been one factor in the defeat of the government coalition in the elections of May 1994. The Hungarian electorate appears to have been less than enthusiastic about the politics of cultural identity, the more extreme versions of which (represented by the populist, racist and neo-Nazi right) were even more decisively rejected by the voters. The lesson seems to have been learned by the politicians, too; following the elections more moderate and pragmatic styles have been adopted by the leaders of the defeated parties, too.

Types of Parties

It is clearly too much of an oversimplification to characterize all the parties equally as 'cultural milieux parties'. One way of differentiating between them is on the basis of their origins.

None of Hungary's six major parliamentary parties today is a completely 'new' party in the sense of one having been formed after the fall of communism. All of them have a history going back to an existence under earlier regimes, but they can be most simply categorized into three types. First, those whose history goes back to before the communist assumption of power after World War II are often referred to as the 'historic' parties. Second, there are those that originate from opposition movements against the communist regime in the 1980s. In the third group are the parties whose origins lie in the former ruling party of the one-party state.

The most successful of the 'historic' parties has been the Independent Smallholders Party (FKGP). As the largest party in 1945, it won an overall parliamentary majority but then fell victim to the communist takeover of power. Lacking any clear policies other than a radical anti-communism and the demand for a land reform to return land to those who owned it in 1947, the Smallholders Party appeals to the sectional interests of the older peasants in the countryside who have been left behind by the change of regime. Interestingly, the real 'historical' leaders of the party have been ousted by the more demagogic radical populists led by the lawyer József Torgyán.

The Christian Democratic Peoples Party (KDNP) also has its origins in the post-1945 period of opposition to the communists. The most ideological and doctrinal of the right-wing parties, it nevertheless encompasses not only primitive clerical anti-communists, but also more modern and progressive, Europe-oriented, Christian democrats and even some Christian socialists.

The 'grand failure' of the 'historic' parties is the Social Democratic Party that had a long history of opposition to both the Horthy regime and the communists. From the time when they were re-launched in 1988, however, the

Social Democrats were plagued by generational, factional and personal conflicts. They failed to enter the parliament in 1990, and thereafter splintered into ever smaller quarrelling sects.

The Hungarian Democratic Forum (MDF) is perhaps the best example of a 'cultural milieu party'. It was formed at Lakitelek in September 1987 by a group of writers, poets, historians, sociologists, and other intellectuals representing a wide range of political views encompassing both socialists and conservatives as well as populists and radical nationalists. Initially they favoured cooperating with the 'populist left' of the ruling party to move gradually towards a democratization of the regime. The Forum's first leader, Zoltán Biró, was a former member of the ruling party and a close colleague of the communist reformer Imre Pozsgay. Later, under the leadership of József Antall, the party would move to the right and abandon its earlier alliance with the reformists and populists of the ruling party.

The Alliance of Free Democrats (SZDSZ) was formed in 1988 by former activists of the democratic opposition who had published *samizdat* journals and books and organized 'flying universities' throughout the 1980s. Unlike the Forum, the Free Democrats were definitely neither nationalists nor populists, but radical democrats committed to the rule of law and human rights. More than a few of them were former marxists, but by the late 1980s they had become champions of private property and capitalist development and in a more unrestrained manner than the Forum. They also represented a distinct 'intellectual milieu', but one that was clearly very different from that of the Forum, though their commitment to the values of liberalism and Western democracy was in some ways equally abstract and symbolic.

The Alliance of Young Democrats (FIDESZ) was the newest and, not surprisingly, the youngest of the new party formations. Set up by 37 young students in March 1988 as the first independent organization to challenge openly and successfully the communist monopoly on political organization, its members resolutely rejected both ideological approaches and 'cultural milieu' politics, advocating a pragmatic, technocratic political practice. They opposed the Forum and the Free Democrats for representing the traditional cultural division between populists and urbanists, and argued that their generation rejected such ways of thinking. At the same time, the political style of the Young Democrats was in no way less symbolic than that of the other parties.

It would be a mistake to see the Hungarian Socialist Party (MSZP) as a simple 'successor' party to the former ruling party, the Hungarian Socialist Workers' Party. The demands for change and political democracy in the latter half of the 1980s had been just as strong within the ruling party itself as within the country at large. 'Left populists', 'reform communists', democratic socialists, social democrats and 'new leftists' all campaigned within the party against one-party rule and the party-state. The years 1988-89 saw the growth of a nationwide movement of reform circles that, but for the caution of its leader Imre Pozsgay, would probably have replaced the old party even earlier. When the old party was finally dissolved in October 1989, and the new Hungarian Socialist Party launched, the break was not as clean as many had hoped. Even so, the bulk of the new party was made up of those who had sought to change the old one. Following its defeat in the 1990 election, the party adopted an explicitly social democratic programme, sought membership in the Socialist International, and began gradually to build up its popular support.[7]

A Tri-Polar Party System

Several commentators have argued that it is inappropriate to try to apply the traditional left-right dimensionality to post-communist societies because these societies have neither the same political traditions nor the property relations on which such traditions have arisen in the capitalist West. Another reason, however, for rejecting any bi-polar typology is that, as already explained above, the political cleavages in these societies are not congruent with one another. Some form of multi-dimensional model is required to understand them.

One proposal to deal with this problem in the case of the Hungarian party system has been advanced by the political scientist Mihály Bihari who has put forward a tri-polar model. He posits three poles around which the party system takes shape, each of which in turn serves as a centre around which multiple parties cluster.[8]

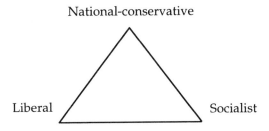

The three poles are as follows.

1) The *national-conservative*, Christian Democratic political centre, around which gather the Hungarian Democratic Forum, the Independent Small-holders Party, the Christian Democratic People's Party, and the radical right-wing populist groups such as István Csurka's Hungarian Justice and Life Party.

2) The *liberal*, social-liberal centre around which the Alliance of Free Democrats and the Alliance of Young Democrats are to be found, together with a number of smaller liberal parties such as the Agrarian Alliance, the Entrepreneurs Party and the Republic Party.

3) The *socialist*, left-wing, Social Democratic centre, around which are grouped the Hungarian Socialist Party, the various splinter social-democratic parties, and the old-style communist Workers Party.

While the parties tend to gather around the poles of the system, separate party factions or platforms and individual politicians, as well as party activists, supporters and voters, are more likely to be found somewhere along the sides of the triangle linking up the three poles, or sometimes even floating free inside or outside the triangle.

It should also be clearly understood that the tri-polar system does not mean a three-party system. The model is fully consistent with the continuation of the present Hungarian six-party parliamentary system or some variant of that. In fact this approach can reflect changes in the overall balance of power between the six parties within the wider context of a tri-polar structure. In the 1990 elections, the pendulum swung heavily in favour of the nationalist right and against the socialists, leading some to suggest that the main division in Hungarian politics was between nationalists and liberals. In 1994, the pendulum swung the other way, suggesting that a traditional left-right cleavage was now back on the agenda. More likely the tri-party system will continue, with different cleavages and bi-polarities becoming marked at different times but without any one coming to dominate the system in the long term.

The Parties and Society

The tri-polar model of the Hungarian party system says nothing about that system's relationship to the wider society. In fact most commentators argue that the party system is not at all firmly rooted in the social structure. Mihály Bihari has described it as a 'suspended' party system 'floating' above society.[9] This is, however, a comment on society just as much as on the parties. Not only do parties fail to represent specific interest groups, but organized and articulate interest groups are hard to find.

A good example of this is provided by the fate of the ecological movement that brought thousands onto the streets in 1988-89 in protest against the construction of the hydro-electric dam at Gabcivo-Nagymáros. Not only has that social movement vanished from sight, but the Hungarian Green Party was taken over in 1993 by a neo-Nazi group that actually supported the dam and campaigned in the 1994 elections on the slogan 'democrats — you're finished too!'

The situation is not very different with the trade unions. They are no more representative organizations of the workers than they were under the communist regime. They are bureaucratic organizations claiming to speak on behalf of the workers, but they are no more rooted in society than are the parties themselves. This is as true of the free or independent trade unions, and of the workers' councils, as it is of the 'successor' unions. Nor have they any form of institutional representation within either the Socialist or any other party.

Party membership also underlines the elite nature of the parties and their lack of any substantial social base. The Hungarian Democratic Forum and the Alliance of Free Democrats each claim membership figures in excess of 30,000, though other commentators suggest the real figures are well below 10,000. The Christian Democrats claim almost 30,000 members, though this figure is probably greatly exaggerated too. The Socialist Party's figure of 40,000 members could be fairly reliable; after all, the former ruling party had 800,000 members and the new party inherited most of the old structures. The Smallholders Party has also claimed high membership figures, in the region of 50,000 or more, and although these figures are highly unreliable, the nature of its support suggests that membership probably is high. Finally, the Young Democrats undoubtedly have the lowest membership of all, particularly since they abandoned their former radical and alternative policies in 1993. Personally I would be surprised if the total active party membership in Hungary were to be as high as 100,000 or 1 per cent of the population.

Some Hungarian politicians have sought to make a virtue out of this situation, arguing that the age of mass parties is over, and that modern people's parties and professional electoral machines no longer require a mass membership.[10] That observation might carry some weight in consolidated Western democracies, but at a time of democratic transition when millions of citizens are experiencing for the first time the practices and principles of democracy, the lack of popular involvement and participation in the newly emergent political process must surely be a cause for concern.

The Parliamentary Elections of March and April 1990

When, early in 1989, the Central Committee of the Hungarian Socialist Workers' Party voted to abandon the leading role of the party and introduce a multi-party system, paving the way to free elections for a democratic parliament, the party's leaders believed that by sharing power in this way they could avoid losing it altogether. They certainly did not foresee that within little more than a year they would find themselves displaced from government.

In the summer of 1989, after the rehabilitation and ceremonial reburial of Imre Nagy and other martyrs of the 1956 revolution, the party was still registering a respectable 30 per cent or more in the opinion polls, though this meant they were losing parliamentary by-elections to the Forum. The Forum's future leader József Antall, however, declared that he could not envisage a government without the participation of the socialists, and there appeared to be an unwritten understanding on a future coalition in which the Forum would provide the Prime Minister, while the reform communist, Imre Pozsgay, would become President of the republic to ensure stability and continuity in the transition.

All this changed in the autumn of 1989 when, with communist regimes crumbling all around, the Free Democrats launched a strident campaign against the socialists' attempts to hang on to their powers and privileges. They successfully torpedoed Pozsgay's presidential ambitions and sabotaged the notion of a Forum-Socialist Party coalition. In so doing, they established themselves as one of the most radical forces for change and as a leading contender for power. For many Hungarians, however, their style was too aggressive and overly self-confident.

The elections were held in March and April 1990, under a complex electoral system that combined voting for party lists at county level with two rounds of voting in single member constituencies. All votes cast are taken into account, and approximately half of the representatives are elected by each method.[11]

1990 Parliamentary Elections

	Party Lists	Individual Constituencies		Parliamentary Seats
		Round 1	Round 2	
MDF	24.73 %	23.93 %	41.54 %	165
FKGP	11.73 %	10.67 %	10.41 %	44
KDNP	6.46 %	5.84 %	3.53 %	21
SZDSZ	21.39 %	22.12 %	31.62 %	94
FIDESZ	8.95 %	4.97 %	1.91 %	22
MSZP	10.89 %	10.20 %	6.35 %	33
			(Independents	7)
Total				386

The result was a landslide for the right and the formation of a government coalition led by the Hungarian Democratic Forum. Together with the Forum's 'natural allies', as Antall described the Smallholders and the Christian Democrats, the right polled 42.92 per cent on the party lists, and 55.48 per cent in individual constituencies in the second round, giving them an overall majority of 229 of the 386 parliamentary seats.

The liberal parties, nevertheless, performed respectably well, polling over a third of the votes on both party lists and in individual constituencies in the second round (if the votes cast for the Free Democrats are combined with those for the Young Democrats, the Agrarian Alliance and the Entrepreneurs' Party). Contrary to some interpretations, the Free Democrats did not lose votes to the Forum between the two rounds; the improvement in the latter's performance was due to picking up many of the supporters of those other parties that did not get through to the second round.

Finally, the defeat of the socialists was not as disastrous as it appeared to many at the time. The Hungarian Socialist Party polled over 10 per cent both on the party lists and in the first round of voting for individual constituencies. Though their poll declined in the second round, they generally held their vote in those constituencies where their candidates were able to stand again.

Moreover, if the votes cast on the party lists for the Socialist Party are combined with those for the re-constituted Hungarian Socialist Workers Party, the two social democratic parties and the Patriotic Electoral Coalition, the total comes to just over 20 per cent (though some of these latter voters clearly supported the Forum in the second round). This would seem to refute the argument advanced by the sociologist Iván Szelényi, amongst others, that the relatively low turnout in the elections (65.1 per cent in the first round; 45.54 per cent in the second) belied an unrepresented or excluded 'social democratic constituency.'[12] On the contrary, a vote of 20 per cent for parties of the left in East-Central Europe, less than six months after the fall of the Berlin Wall, is a significant achievement.

In the voting for party lists, 15.75 per cent of the votes were cast for smaller parties, none of which secured the minimum 4 per cent required to enter parliament. Only 3.68 per cent of the votes were cast for the re-constituted Hungarian Socialist Workers Party, 3.55 per cent for the Hungarian Social Democratic Party, 3.13 per cent for the Agrarian Alliance, 1.89 per cent for the Entrepreneurs Party, and 1.87 per cent for the Patriotic Electoral Coalition. A further eight parties each secured less than 1 per cent of the votes.

Finally, the 1990 election results can be seen to support the notion of a tri-party system, if that is understood as a system in which there will always be a changing balance between its three poles. The nationalist-conservative pole clearly emerged strongest from the elections, giving the parties gathered around it a workable and overall majority in the parliament. The liberal and socialist poles, however, were also well represented (if less so in the parliament than amongst the electorate), and the parties gathered around them clearly had a viable future.

The 1990 election results also established the dominance of the six major parties that succeeded in gaining election to the parliament and that have continued to play the commanding roles in Hungarian politics ever since. This led several commentators to speak of a six-party system that was not likely to see any significant change, except in the relative strength of the six parties, in the foreseeable future.[13]

In the following sections of this article, I propose to examine the development of the six parties in the four years leading up to the second free elections in 1994.

The Nationalist-Conservative Parties

The Hungarian Democratic Forum started out as a radical, even left-wing movement in the spirit of Hungarian populism, cultural nationalism and radical democracy. The Forum identified with the notion of a 'third road' of development, one which was neither capitalist nor state socialist. Over the years, it changed into a more ideologically right-wing nationalist party, and one that has at times appeared to be seeking to establish itself as a new state-party.

The first step in this direction came with Zoltán Biró's replacement as party leader in October 1989 by the more right-wing conservative József Antall, and the Forum's abandonment of its earlier flirtation with the reform communists. Following the party's election victory in 1990, the coalition government formed under Antall's premiership pursued an increasingly ideological course in which right-wing Christian values and reactionary national traditions came increasingly to the fore. Government ministers suggested that opposition politicians were not loyal to the Hungarian nation or even to the values of European Christianity, and that it was undemocratic to oppose the democratically elected government. The ceremonial reburial of Hungary's inter-war dictator, Admiral Horthy, in 1993 indicated that the government was set on a very different course from that foreseen at the time of the reburial of the 1956 martyr, Imre Nagy, four years earlier.

At one point it even appeared that the Forum was on the verge of becoming an explicitly fascist or neo-Nazi party, when in August 1992 its vice-president, the playwright István Csurka, published a virulently anti-communist and openly anti-semitic tract in which he claimed that there had been no real change of regime and that the country continued to be dominated by foreign and alien interests. Eventually, however, Csurka was expelled from the Forum and he set up his own Hungarian Justice and Life Party. At the same time, two further ultra-right groups broke away to form the protectionist Market Party and the neo-Nazi Hungarian Interest Party.

The second party of the governing coalition, the Independent Smallholders Party, was also ridden with internal conflicts that were dominated by the personality of the controversial lawyer József Torgyán. After reconstitution in 1988, the party's leading posts were filled by an 'old guard' of politicians who had been active in the 1945-47 period, but Torgyán was elected as parliamentary group leader after the 1990 elections and used this position to build up his support throughout the party. In June 1991, he was elected party president, and at the beginning of 1992, the party adopted a new constitution vesting exceptional powers in the President and institutionalizing what was essentially a 'personal dictatorship' over the party.[14]

In February 1992, Torgyán announced his party's withdrawal from the coalition, but only eleven of the party's MPs accompanied him into opposition, the other 33 remaining loyal to the government. The split resulted in two separate Smallholder groups in the parliament: Torgyán's faction claiming to be the legitimate party, and the 'group of 33' that itself included several smaller Smallholder factions. Although in a minority in the parliament, Torgyán enjoyed overwhelming support in the party and the countryside, as was later proved when the two groups stood as separate parties in the 1994 elections.

The smallest of the coalition parties, the Christian Democratic People's Party, although not bedevilled by conflicts on the same scale as those that have beset the Forum and the Smallholders, is also a party that comprises a significant range of political tendencies. Although the Christian Democrats have not seen the emergence of separate platforms or party splits, there have nevertheless been significant differences between the more ideologically right-wing anti-communists and anti-socialists on the one hand, and the more pragmatic and European-oriented Christian Democrats and Christian Socialists on the other. While the party leader, László Surján, has represented the more moderate, centrist forces within the party, the more right-wing elements have gained increasing prominence in promoting its public image.

The Liberal Parties

Like the right-wing parties, the liberal parties have also had their share of internal conflicts though these have rarely gone so far as to result in party splits, and they have more often revolved around personalities than around ideological or policy differences.

Like the Forum, the Alliance of Free Democrats also arose as a large umbrella organization representing a broad spectrum of political opinion ranging from radical democrats and liberals to libertarian conservatives. Its support was equally varied, comprising both some of the poorest sectors of society and the aspiring new property owners and entrepreneurs. It is in many ways remarkable that the party has stayed together at all.

The party's first president, János Kis, the leading figure of the democratic opposition throughout the 1980s, resigned in October 1991, and was replaced by the more conservative Péter Tölgyessy, who had no background in the opposition but represented the more pragmatic, business-oriented sectors of the party. A year later, however, Tölgyessy was replaced in turn by Iván Petö representing the party's so-called 'hard core' originating from the former opposition. These internal conflicts resulted in the party's falling popularity in the opinion polls, but did not lead to any significant party splits or desertions.

The Free Democrats have faced the same problem as other centre parties: in which direction to look for allies. While the Alliance of Young Democrats prided themselves in their anti-socialism, and the Tölgyessy wing of the Free Democrats, would have preferred an alliance with the more moderate sections of the Forum, the party's more experienced leaders increasingly came to recognise that cooperation with the socialists would be, in the long term, a more realistic option. Even so, in the lead-up to the 1994 elections, the party finally settled on a Liberal Bloc with the Young Democrats, the Agrarian Alliance and the Entrepreneurs Party, declaring their aim to win over 50% of the votes and a parliamentary majority.

The Alliance of Young Democrats has been transformed more than any other party in the course of its short history. Originally a radical, alternative youth movement, its unexpected success in entering parliament in the 1990 elections combined with some exceedingly talented young leaders resulted in over-confident and over-ambitious political behaviour that eventually led to its downfall. In 1992, just when it was leading the opinion polls with 30 per cent or more support, the party's leaders decided to change their image, adopt a more conservative and nationalist political stance, and create a more centralized party. They also came out firmly against any collaboration with the socialists.

The change in the entire ethos of the party led to an open conflict between the party leader Viktor Orbán, representing the conservative and centralist trend, and the party's most popular politician, Gábor Fodor, representing alternative values and human rights. Fodor eventually resigned from the party at the end of 1993, and moved over to the Free Democrats, followed by many of his supporters.

It is perhaps also significant to note that in the case of the liberal parties, in contrast to the situation in the right-wing parties, internal conflicts and splits have not led to the formation of independent new parties.

The Socialist Parties

The Hungarian Socialist Party's defeat in the 1990 elections was a set-back from which it was to recover more rapidly than most commentators at the time expected. First, however, it needed to define its self-image more clearly and make a more obvious break with the past than it had achieved at its founding congress in 1989.[15]

The former general secretary of the old Hungarian Socialist Workers Party, Károly Grósz, had refused to join the new party in October 1989, while the former Prime Minister, Miklós Németh, resigned from the party to sit as an independent MP immediately after the elections. In May, at the new party's second congress, Rezsö Nyers stood down as Party President to be replaced by the former Foreign Minister, Gyula Horn. Finally, in November 1990, the reform communist, Imre Pozsgay, also left the party. By the end of the year, the party had an almost entirely new leadership.

Another prominent figure in the party has been the chairman of its national council, Iván Vitányi, who successfully campaigned for it to adopt a social democratic programme and for a closer relationship with the Free Democrats. At the same time, a new generation of politicians, coming from the reform circles movement of the late 1980s, has entered the leadership in the persons of the three young Vice-Presidents Imre Szekeres, György Jánosi and Ferenc Baja.

The changing fortunes of the socialists were first evidenced at the time of the local government elections in the autumn of 1990 when many former socialist councillors were re-elected as independents. When the Free Democrat, Gábor Demszky, stood down from parliament after being elected Mayor of Budapest, the socialist candidate successfully won the by-election held in April 1991, and the party had a similar by-election victory a year later. Meanwhile, the party's support in the opinion polls was steadily growing until, by the end of 1993, they had overtaken the Young Democrats and moved into first place.

The good fortune of the Hungarian Socialist Party was not shared by the other socialist parties. It would seem that the former's success has weakened the appeal of the latter. Despite an attempt to re-unite the various social-democratic groupings into a new party under the leadership of the former independent MP, Zoltán Király, the continual squabbling of the various social-democratic factions seems to have fatally undermined the social democrats' credibility. At the same time, the reconstituted, old-style communist, Hungarian Socialist Workers' Party, that re-named itself the Workers' Party in 1993, continues to maintain its basic support but has not made any significant gains or advances.

The Parliamentary Elections of May 1994

The 1994 elections saw the victory with an overall majority of the Hungarian Socialist Party and the formation of a coalition government by the Socialist Party with the Free Democrats. The result was an even bigger landslide than that of 1990, though this time in the opposite direction, but even so it did not call into question the tri-polar system.

It did, however, strengthen the position of the already dominant six major parties. With a significantly higher turnout than in 1990 (68.92 per cent in the first round; 55.11 per cent in the second), a greater number of candidates and more parties presenting county and national lists, the percentage of voters supporting the smaller parties actually fell. Only two individual candidates from smaller parties were elected, one for the Agrarian Alliance who joined the parliamentary group of the Free Democrats, and one for the Entrepreneurs' Party, the only MP to sit as an independent though supporting the Free Democrats.

Despite the defeat of the right-wing coalition government, the total votes cast in the voting for party lists for the nationalist-conservative parties was just over 30 per cent (if the votes cast for the break-away Hungarian Justice and Life Party and the Market Party are included). This fell to below 25 per cent in the second round, when some voters of the smaller right-wing parties, particularly the Smallholders, appear to have voted for the Socialist Party rather than for the Forum.

The liberal parties also polled well, only dropping back marginally on their performance in 1990. They secured almost a third of the votes cast for party lists and held their vote at 30 per cent in the second round.

The Hungarian Socialist Party trebled its 1990 score to gain a third of the votes cast for party lists, or over 37 per cent when taken together with the other socialist and social democratic parties. In the second round, their vote rose to 45.34 per cent, actually up by over 7 per cent on the combined votes of all left-wing parties in the first round, as many former voters for smaller parties, including the Smallholders, appear to have given them their second preference.

Although these figures translated into a greater disproportion of parliamentary seats, the socialist landslide certainly did not call into question the tri-polar party system. The liberal and nationalist-conservative poles have clearly retained their substantial bases of support in society, each representing between a quarter and a third of the voters.

1994 Parliamentary Elections

	Party Lists	Individual Constituencies		Parliamentary Seats
		Round 1	Round 2	
MDF	11.74 %	12.03 %	14.93 %	38
FKGP	8.82 %	7.88 %	5.89 %	26
KDNP	7.03 %	7.37 %	2.95 %	22
SZDSZ	19.74 %	18.62 %	28.49 %	70
FIDESZ	7.02 %	7.70 %	0.69 %	20
MSZP	32.99 %	31.27 %	45.34 %	209
			(Independents	1)
Total				386

The election, nevertheless, did result in certain differences from 1990, both as regards relations between the parties and relations within them. These could represent some significant trends for the future.

The most significant change to affect any one party was the overwhelming rout of the opponents of József Torgyán in the Smallholders Party. While Torgyán and his supporters, standing as the Independent Smallholders Party, polled a few per cent less than the party had won in 1990, their opponents, standing as the United Smallholders Party polled less than one per cent. This not only confirms Torgyán as the unquestioned leader of the Smallholders, but also places him in a position to claim to be one of the main leaders of the opposition in parliament.

One of the biggest shocks of the election was the setback for the Young Democrats, who a year before had been leading the polls. It is now difficult to see them having a future as an independent party, and their leaders have moved so far to the right that there seems little reason for them not to seek some form of rapprochement with the more moderate forces in the Forum and the Christian Democrats. The Forum's liberals have themselves come to the fore after the elections, with the election of the moderate and pragmatic former Finance Minister, Iván Szabó, as the party's parliamentary group leader, while the ideological right-wingers in the Christian Democrats have taken a back seat after their party's failure to make more significant gains in the elections. A possible realignment of forces on the right could thus lead to the emergence of the sort of modern conservative party that Hungary so clearly lacks at the moment, leaving Torgyán and the Smallholders to represent the radical right.

Not so much the election result, as the decision of the Socialist Party and the Free Democrats to enter into a government coalition, could have long term consequences for the development of these two parties. The strongest opposition within the Free Democrats to entering the coalition came from Péter Tölgyessy and his supporters, and it is not inconceivable that they might leave at some point to join up with Fidesz and other moderate conservatives. A wider question is whether the Free Democrats will be able to maintain their identity as a distinct liberal party if the coalition is a lasting one.

Opposition to the coalition was much weaker within the Socialist Party, but there was a faction there too (the former populist left) that, as in 1989-90, would have preferred an alliance with the Forum rather than with the Free Democrats. It is not impossible that this group might take its leave of the party, but in so-doing would be unlikely to have any significant consequences for the socialists.

The End of the Politics of Cultural Identity

The clearest and healthiest lesson of the 1994 elections was provided by the total failure of the small, and particularly the extremist, parties. The Workers' Party's vote was down on 1990 at 3.19 per cent, while the liberal Republic Party and the Agrarian Alliance polled 2.55 per cent and 2.10 per cent respectively, and István Csurka's Hungarian Justice and Life Party scored a mere 1.59 per cent. No other party polled above 1 per cent. This was despite the fact that there was a greater number of parties and individual candidates standing in the election than in 1990. This experience should lead to a reduction in the number of politicians changing parties (50 MPs did so at least once in the 1990-94 parliament) and of forming break-away and splinter parties.

The election also demonstrated the total lack of any popular base for the extremist parties of the far right. In previous years, some Hungarian intellectuals had expressed fears of a popular upsurge of support for extremist demagogues that might sweep away the new democracy, but the main support for István Csurka's party did not come from the depressed urban and rural areas of the country but from the middle-class villa districts on the Buda hills![16]

It was not, however, only the extremist ultra-right that was rejected by the Hungarian voters in the 1994 election. The entire political style of demagogic and ideological politics that had characterised the politics of the coalition government which had ruled Hungary for the preceding four years was abandoned. This was most evident in regard to the 'media war' that dominated Hungarian politics for most of the first parliament's term. Eventually, in 1993, the direction of the state radio and television fell into the hands of the far-right, resulting in programmes and news broadcasts of a style not witnessed in Hungary since the Stalinist era, and a political purge of journalists considered to be unsympathetic to the government. The propaganda, however, was counter-productive. Many voters gave this as a reason for their voting against the government in the elections.

The Socialist Party's success was due in large part not to some nostalgia for the communist past, but to the fact that it campaigned in a completely different way, avoiding ideological slogans or attacks on its opponents, and even limiting its publicity when compared to that of the other parties. The Socialists had been surprised at the start of the campaign by the strength of their support throughout the country, but the course of the campaign showed that they had a better understanding of the country than any of the other parties did.

The lesson of the need for a change of style seems to have been drawn by many other politicians in the aftermath of the elections. This is evidenced by the changes in the party and parliamentary leadership of both the Forum and the Christian Democrats, where ideologues and political demagogues like the Forum's former executive Vice-President, Sándor Lezsák, or the former Christian Democrat State Secretary for Religious Affairs, Miklós Pálos, have stepped down and been replaced by politicians in the more moderate and pragmatic style of the Forum's Iván Szabó. There have even been some changes within the leadership of the Young Democrats, with the party's new parliamentary group leader, József Szajer, who occupies a centrist position within the party, coming to play a more prominent role.

All this suggests that the politics of cultural identity which so dominated Hungarian political life between 1990 and 1994 may well have been an aberration rather than a fundamental characteristic of Hungarian politics. Should that be the case, it would represent a stage in the development of democratic politics and in the development of a democratic party system, rather than an obstacle or impediment to it. This would, however, suggest that contrary to much accepted opinion, it has not been the Hungarian people who have needed time to learn the practices of democracy but rather the politicians.

Conclusion: Parties and Party Systems

At first sight, it might appear that the 1994 election results confirm the view that Hungary's six-party system is here to stay, as the very same six parties, and only those six parties, that were elected in 1990 were elected again in 1994.[17] Indeed, the six major parties are even more dominant after the 1994 elections than they were in the 1990-94 parliament. Such an observation, however, is more than a little superficial. The conclusion which can be more safely drawn is that no new parties, other than these six (or transformations of them), are likely to enter the mainstream of Hungarian politics in the foreseeable future. There could, however, be realignments between the parties, or even a reduction in the number of parties, such as would occur in the event of the establishment of a modern conservative party.

One of the most interesting modern transitions to democracy, with which Hungary is often compared, is that of post-Franco Spain. In Spain as in Hungary, the previous regime was a 'soft dictatorship' and the transition to democracy was a gradual, bloodless and negotiated one. In Spain, the first party to come to power, the Centre Democratic Union, led by Adolfo Suárez, was a coalition of different if not divergent tendencies not dissimilar to the Hungarian Democratic Forum, representing the moderate centre-right that favoured change as long as it was not too radical. Nevertheless, after a period of four years in government, the Centre Democratic Union lost its electoral base and fell apart, and in the historic elections of 1982 the Spanish socialists were swept into power. Thereafter the Centre Democratic Union simply ceased to exist. It would not be surprising if a similar fate were to befall the first party to come to power in Hungary after the fall of the old regime, the Hungarian Democratic Forum, which, some commentators would argue, is unlikely to continue in its present form.[18]

The prospects of the liberal parties after the 1994 elections are no easier to assess. Compared to West European centre or liberal parties they have actually been remarkably successful, securing and holding virtually a third of the votes in two successive elections. Whether they will be able to hold this level of support in the long term, and whether the Free Democrats' entry into government coalition with the socialists will improve or damage their prospects, is difficult to predict. This is also complicated by the drift of the Young Democrats away from the liberal pole towards the nationalist right.

One thing is certain: if the Free Democrats continue to play a significant role in Hungarian politics, it will be as a very different political force from that which emerged from the democratic opposition in the late 1980s. The key intellectual dissidents of the 1980s — János Kis, Miklós Haraszti, Ottilia Solt, Tamás Gáspár Miklós — have all stepped down from the central political stage. They have been replaced by politicians of a different breed, often former company managers like Gábor Kuncze, the Free Democrats' Prime Minister Designate in the 1994 elections and Deputy Prime Minister in the new coalition government, or the Transport Minister, Károly Lotz. It could well be said that by their very success the former dissidents have brought about their own eclipse.[19]

The future of the socialists is an even more intriguing question. The very political force that initially sought to reform the old regime from within, and then played a crucial role in engineering its defeat, but was then itself ousted from power, has come back to occupy the centre of politics in Hungary today. It could be wrong, however, to see this merely as part of an overall East European trend seeing the return of the former communists throughout the former Soviet bloc. The eclipse of reformist political forces in revolutionary periods that they have themselves done much to bring about, and their return after disillusionment with the protagonists of more radical change, is not a new phenomenon. One interesting comparison is with the transition to democracy in Portugal, where a group of reformists within the old regime eventually returned to power after the revolutionary euphoria of the 1974-75 period had died out.[20]

In conclusion, there is every reason to expect that the tri-polar system of several parties revolving around conservative, liberal and socialist poles is likely to continue well into the twenty-first century. Whether the present six-party system will also survive is a matter of greater contention, but the likelihood is that it will be through transformations, splits or amalgamations of the present six parties that change will come about, rather than through the emergence of any new political forces.

Notes

1. I have discussed these problems at greater length in 'Obstacles to the Development of Democratic Politics', in Terry Cox and Andy Furlong (eds.), 1995, *Hungary: The Politics of Transition*, London: Frank Cass; and 'Impediments to Democratization in Post-Communist East-Central Europe: The Hungarian Case in Comparative Perspective', in Gordon Wightman (ed.), 1994, *Party Formation in East-Central Europe: Post-Communist Politics in Czechoslovakia, Hungary, Poland and Bulgaria*, London: Edward Elgar. See also: Ágnes Horváth and Árpád Szakolczai, 1992, *The Dissolution of Communist Power: the Case of Hungary*, London: Routledge.

2. This argument against traditional ways of thinking and systems of analysis has been put most consistently by Edward de Bono. See, most recently, his *Parallel Thinking*, London: Viking, 1994.

3. For two recent analyses of Hungary's party system after two free elections, see Attila Ágh, 1994, 'A régi-uj pártrendszer Magyarországon' (The old-new party system in Hungary), *Mozgó Világ*, (8): 3-12; and László Kéri, 1994, 'Pártok - két választás után' (Parties - after two elections), *Társadalmi Szemle*, (8-9).

4. György G. Markus, 1994. 'Parties, Camps and Cleavages in Post-Communist Hungary', in Bruno Coppieters, Kris Deschouwer and Michael Waller (eds.), *Social-Democracy in a Post-Communist Europe*, London: Frank Cass.

5. The Hungarian political sociologist László Kéri has suggested that the present Hungarian party system is like an unsolved Rubic cube, with the six different

colours mixed up on each of the six sides of the cube. See László Kéri and Ádám Levendel, 1994, 'The multi-party system in Hungary — from three years' perspective', in Gordon Wightman (ed.), *Party Formation in East-Central Europe: Post-Communist Politics in Czechoslovakia, Hungary, Poland and Bulgaria*, London: Edward Elgar.

6. George Schöpflin, 1993. 'The Condition of Post-Communism', in George Schöpflin, *Politics in Eastern Europe*, London: Blackwell.

7. Bill Lomax, 1991. 'Hungary from Kádárism to democracy: the successful failure of reform communism', in D.W. Spring (ed.), *The Impact of Gorbachev*, London: Pinter.

8. Mihály Bihari, 1991. 'Rendszerváltás és hatalomváltás Magyarországon: 1989-1990' (System change and regime change in Hungary: 1989-1990), in Kurtán Sándor, Péter Sándor and László Vass, *Magyarország Politikai Évkönyve 1991* (Hungarian Political Yearbook 1991), Budapest: Ökonómia Alapítvány — Economix Rt.

9. *Ibid.*

10. Bálint Magyar, 1992. 'A Liberális Paradoxon' (The Liberal Paradox), in A Liberális Koalíció elöadássorozata, *A Szabad Demokraták Jövöje* (The Future of the Free Democrats), Budapest.

11. Judy Batt, October, 1990. 'Political Reform in Hungary', *Parliamentary Affairs*, Vol. 43, (4).

12. Tamás Kolosi, Iván Szelényi, Sonja Szelényi, and Bruce Western, August, 1990. 'The Making of Political Fields in Post-Communist Transition: Dynamics of Class and Party in Hungarian Politics: 1989-1990', *Working Papers on Transitions from State Socialism*, Centre for International Studies, Cornell University.

13. László Kéri, 1991. *Összeomlás Után* (After the Collapse), Budapest: Kossuth.

14. Tamás Fricz, 1994. *A magyarországi pártrendszer kialakulásáról és jellemzöiröl: 1987-1992* (On the formation and characteristics of the Hungarian party system), candidate's thesis, Budapest: Hungarian Academy of Sciences, 185.

15. László Andor, 1994. 'The Hungarian Socialist Party', in *Labour Focus on Eastern Europe*, Summer, (48).

16. Such fears had been expressed by György Csepeli and György Péter, in 'Ne várjuk Kalibánt' (Don't wait for Caliban), *Népszabadság*, 24 August 1991; and 'Ködképek egy párt láthatárán' (Hazy scenes on the horizon of a party), *Népszabadság*, 9 November 1991.

17. The six parties referred to as gaining entry to the parliament are those that won over 5 per cent of the votes in the first round of voting for county lists enabling them to win list seats. Parties with less than 5 per cent of the votes that nevertheless won seats in individual constituencies (e.g, the Agrarian Alliance and the Entrepreneurs Party in 1994) are not counted as parliamentary parties.

18. András Bozóki and Bill Lomax, 'The Revenge of History: The Portuguese, Spanish and Hungarian Transitions — Some Comparisons', in Geoffrey Pridham and Paul Lewis (eds.), *The Emergence of New Party Systems and Transitions to*

Democracy: *Inter-regional Comparisons between Eastern and Southern Europe*, London: Routledge, forthcoming.

19. Federigo Argentieri, 1993. *From Opposition to Opposition: the Successful Failure of Former Dissidents in East-Central Europe*, paper presented to the conference on Transition, Indiana Memorial Union, Bloomington, 26-28 September 1993.

20. Lomax and Bozóki, *op.cit.*

Bibliography

Ágh, Attila 1994. 'A régi-uj pártrendszer Magyarországon' (The old-new party system in Hungary), *Mozgó Világ*, (8): 3-12.

Andor, László 1994. 'The Hungarian Socialist Party', in *Labour Focus on Eastern Europe*. Summer, (48).

Argentieri, Federigo 1993. *From Opposition to Opposition: the Successful Failure of Former Dissidents in East-Central Europe*. Paper presented to the conference on Transition, Indiana Memorial Union, Bloomington, 26-28 September 1993.

Batt, Judy 1990. 'Political Reform in Hungary', *Parliamentary Affairs*, Vol. 43, (4).

Bihari, Mihály 1991. 'Rendszerváltás és hatalomváltás Magyarországon: 1989-1990' (System change and regime change in Hungary: 1989-1990), in Sándor Kurtán, Péter Sándor and László Vass, *Magyarország Politikai Évkönyve 1991* (Hungarian Political Yearbook 1991). Budapest: Ökonómia Alapítvány — Economix Rt.

Bono, Edward de. 1994. *Parallel Thinking*. London: Viking.

Bozóki, András and Bill Lomax 1996. 'The Revenge of History: The Portuguese, Spanish and Hungarian Transitions — Some Comparisons', in Geoffrey Pridham and Paul Lewis (eds.), *Stabilising fragile democracies: Comparing new party systems in Southern and Eastern Europe*. London & New York: Routledge.

Fricz, Tamás 1994. *A magyarországi pártrendszer kialakulásáról és jellemzöiröl: 1987-1992*, (On the formation and characteristics of the Hungarian party system). Candidate's thesis. Budapest: Hungarian Academy of Sciences.

Horváth, Ágnes and Árpád Szakolczai 1992. *The Dissolution of Communist Power: the Case of Hungary*. London: Routledge.

Kéri, László 1991. *Összeomlás Után* (After the Collapse). Budapest: Kossuth.

Kéri, László 1994. 'Pártok — két választás után' (Parties — after two elections), *Társadalmi Szemle*, (8-9).

Kéri, László and Ádám Levendel 1994. 'The multi-party system in Hungary — from three years' perspective', in Gordon Wightman (ed.), *Party Formation in East-Central Europe: Post-Communist Politics in Czechoslovakia, Hungary, Poland and Bulgaria*. London: Edward Elgar.

Kolosi, Tamás Iván Szelényi, Sonja Szelényi, and Bruce Western, 1990. 'The Making of Political Fields in Post-Communist Transition: Dynamics of Class and Party in Hungarian Politics: 1989-1990', *Working Papers on Transitions from State Socialism*. Centre for International Studies, Cornell University, August.

Lomax, Bill 1991. 'Hungary from Kádárism to democracy: the successful failure of reform communism', in D.W. Spring (ed.), *The Impact of Gorbachev*. London: Pinter.

Lomax, Bill 1994. 'Impediments to Democratization in Post-Communist East-Central Europe: The Hungarian Case in Comparative Perspective', in Gordon Wightman (ed.), 1994, *Party Formation in East-Central Europe: Post-Communist Politics in Czechoslovakia, Hungary, Poland and Bulgaria*. London: Edward Elgar.

Lomax, Bill 1995. 'Obstacles to the Development of Democratic Politics', in Terry Cox and Andy Furlong (eds.), *Hungary: The Politics of Transition*. London: Frank Cass.

Magyar, Bálint 1992. 'A Liberális Paradoxon' (The Liberal Paradox), in A Liberális Koalíció elöadássorozata, *A Szabad Demokraták Jövöje* (The Future of the Free Democrats). Budapest.

Markus, György G. 1994. 'Parties, Camps and Cleavages in Post-Communist Hungary', in Bruno Coppieters, Kris Deschouwer and Michael Waller (eds.), *Social-Democracy in a Post-Communist Europe*. London: Frank Cass.

Népszabadság, 24 August 1991

Népszabadság, 9 November 1991.

Schöpflin, George 1993. *Politics in Eastern Europe*. London: Blackwell.

The Second Step: Democratic Inclusion, Interest Representation and Conflict Arbitration in Hungary

Lene Bøgh Sørensen

Introduction

The parties and leading politicians that emerged during the transition period in Hungary (1987-1990) have been criticized for their tendency to monopolize political decision-making and their reluctance to acknowledge and consult with social partners in vital matters linked to the economic reform process. Some critics claim that the conservative coalition government (1990-94), as well as the socialist-liberal coalition government (1994) have not engaged in a broad social dialogue on economic policy despite their declared intentions.[1] Two types of explanations have been offered for this phenomenon.

Some allege that Hungary has experienced a kind of 'entry into politics crisis'[2] as a direct result of a conscious government strategy to prevent interest groups from gaining a voice in key political decisions on socio-economic issues. Because the new Hungarian political elites are committed to implementing neo-liberal economic policies in order to meet IMF demands for structural adjustment, they have obstructed the development of a genuine social dialogue.

Another perspective emphasizes the slow development during the transition years of a parallel sphere of new social organization. The newly established parties and the governments formed on the basis of parliamentary politics have quickly gained legitimacy through the mechanism of competitive elections. Having established a stronghold in the Hungarian democracy, their identity is fairly secure. On the other hand, other social actors, including trade unions in particular, have had to wrestle with serious problems of identity, representativity and legitimacy. The emergence of autonomous labour interest organizations was marked by internal strife between new and reformed trade unions. This produced a pattern of fragmented and decentralized represen-tation.[3] Among newly emergent employers' organizations, a similar tendency towards pluralization and fragmentation can also be discerned.[4] From this general perspective, confusion about the organizational formation and the policy orientation of new labour and business interest organizations inhibited the early development of a 'social partnership'. Thus the development of a type of macro-level neo-corporatist structure of interest mediation characterized by a close relationship between the government, organized labour and organized business has emerged slowly.[5] Consequently, the source of the 'entry into politics crisis' lies not solely in a calculated choice made by omnipotent governments to inhibit participation, but also in the initial weakness and ambiguity surrounding the role and legitimacy of the social partners themselves.

By characterizing the current situation as critical, we also imply that the exclusion of particular interests in public policy choices and the absence of a genuine social dialogue will be detrimental to the consolidation of the new democratic regime. This author shares the view that democratic politics are inherently politics of negotiation and that the development of an intermediate sphere of autonomous mass-based interest organizations, as well as the creation of institutions to promote peaceful conflict resolution, are crucial to the consolidation of new democracies.

From this perspective, then, a central concern during the 'second step', that is, the period of democratic consolidation, is the particular relationship that develops between the state and organized interests in Hungary's new democracy. During the present period of economic transformation in Hungary, the establishment of an industrial relations system to regulate labour and employers interests is important. Such a system is essential to the peaceful settlement of conflicts. Also, negotiations leading to social pacts can distribute the heavy burdens of economic transition in a more socially acceptable way. The ideology behind a social pact can be described in simple terms as:

the ability of major partners to reach compromises through an 'open-minded' bargaining process concerning vital social and economic issues. Such a pact can ease tensions in society and contribute both to economic performance and to social justice.

The idea of a social pact, while appealing, involves many uncertainties, as the recent Hungarian experience reveals. Several East Central European countries have recently attempted to establish a form of neo-corporatist interest mediation. These efforts have involved 'tripartite' models of macro-level bargaining between the state, labour and business. However, far-reaching results such as a general social and economic pact have been difficult to attain.

In this chapter I argue that the long historical legacy of authoritarianism in Hungary, including the absence of genuine democratic popular mobilization and participation, reduce the probability that fully developed neo-corporatist arrangements can succeed within a short time span. Structural pre-conditions for corporate interest mediation that have contributed to the · success of corporatist institutional arrangements elsewhere (e.g., Austria and Scandinavia) are absent in Hungary. These include among other preconditions, the existence of a strong social democratic party, a well-organized, strong, autonomous and unified trade union movement and close ties between parliamentary parties, associations and social classes.[6] It is also a commonly held view that the deterioration of these structural supports has contributed to the decline of corporatist arrangements in Western Europe as well.[7] Such entrenched organizational structures do not exist in the new democracies in East Central Europe and are unlikely to develop overnight. Mihaly Bihary asserts that the new Hungarian democracy has developed in such a way that the new parties are 'floating' above the society.[8] Coinciding with the observation of Bihary, B. Lomax asserts that a political superstructure has evolved in Hungary which has no supporting beams within the structure of society.[9] According to Lomax, neither the parties nor the trade unions have firm roots in society.[10]

But, to borrow Schmitter's phrase, history does not dictate which particular 'type of democracy' will eventually be consolidated.[11] The institutionalization of a system of interest representation is the result of a long learning process involving struggles between social actors. This process is in its first stages in Hungary. It is still too early to predict with certainty what type of relationship between the state, labour and business will evolve. Throughout East-Central Europe, however, economic stress brought about by the introduction of a capitalist market economy runs the danger of producing debilitating social conflicts. This risk constitutes an important incentive for collaboration and for governments to pursue a more inclusive approach to politics.

Most studies to date focusing on the newly established democracies in East Central Europe have dealt with the formation, character, and identities of the new parties and party elites, including the social and geographical bases.[12] Empirical evidence and case studies that address the emergence and role of social actors are relatively few. This chapter attempts to remedy part of that lack by examining the trade union side of the equation, and to look at the role labour organizations are playing in the emergent institutional framework of conflict resolution.

The history of authoritarianism

The breakdown of the Austrian-Hungarian Dual Monarchy in 1918 was followed by a period of turbulent social and political development in Hungary. Between 1918 and 1945, Hungary experienced an extraordinarily large number of regime ruptures and transitions.[13] The 'failed revolutions' of 1918-1919 (the liberal democratic republic of Mihail Karolyi, November 1918-March 1919, and Bela Kun's Council Republic from March 1919-August 1919), were followed by the radical rightist white terror of the counter-revolutionary period (1919-21) under the military leadership of Admiral Horthy, Hungary's regent from 1920 to 1944.

The rightist authoritarian political regimes of the interwar period rested upon the political exclusion of the social and political groups that had helped establish and sustain the brief revolutionary socialist, as well as the liberal democratic experiments. Thus, following the revolutions of 1918-19 and the counterrevolution, liberal and democratic bourgeois groups and parties were weak and isolated. The Communist Party was banned and the potential political influence of working class organizations, including the Social Democratic Party and the trade unions, was curtailed.

In 1922, under Count Istvan Bethlen's more moderate conservative authoritarian rule (1921-32), the relatively wide Friedrich suffrage of 1919 was abolished.[14] A new, more restrictive electoral system was introduced which limited the electorate to between 27 and 29% of the adult population and the system of secret voting was eliminated in the countryside. In order to give the system a tinge of democratic legitimacy, secret voting was maintained in the major towns. Bethlen also negotiated an agreement with the leaders of the Social Democratic Party and trade union leaders in an attempt to incorporate the industrial workers into his right authoritarian corporatist political model.[15]

The Bethlen-Peyer Pact of December 1921, granted political amnesty to the Social Democratic Party, the trade unions and the workers cooperatives and returned their confiscated property. The Social Democratic Party and the industrial workers' unions enjoyed freedom of speech and association. In return, the Social Democratic and trade union leaders refrained from organizing farm labourers and certain other categories of workers.[16] Peasants and agricultural workers were severely repressed by this system in an attempt to integrate the magnates, the church, Jews, the bureaucracy, the army and the industrial workers into Bethlen's political machine.[17]

In general, there was no universal suffrage. Elections were manipulated and police repression and harassment were common especially in the countryside.[18] Pluralism was strictly limited in a system that served the interests of the wealthy and the powerful, i.e., the political and bureaucratic elite and the social and economic upper classes. But the system was not totalitarian.[19] Firstly, the corporatist element secured a certain elite pluralism. Secondly, the Bethlen regime tolerated some oppositional elements. Even if the elections were rigged so that the 'Government Party' always won, there were several constituencies — mainly in the major towns — which regularly returned opposition candidates. Thirdly, some freedom of the press existed. Finally, the Bethlen regime never tried to mobilize the masses, a defining element of genuine totalitarian regimes.[20]

Hungary's Bethlen regime could be described in Linz's terminology as a mix of two subsystems of authoritarian regimes, 'Bureaucratic-Military Authoritarianism' and 'Organic Statism'.[21] Linz defines authoritarian regimes in general as those with limited pluralism, without a comprehensive state supported ideology and without political mobilization.[22] Contrary to totalitarian regimes with their monolithic character, their state supported ideology and their mass mobilization,[23] authoritarian regimes are not as oppressive with respect to the private sphere. The specific features of the 'Bureaucratic-Military' sub-type of authoritarianism are the roles played by army officers and/or civilian bureaucrats while excluding the masses — especially 'workers, farm labourers and underprivileged peasants' — from political participation and interest articulation.[24] The central feature of the 'Organic Statism' sub-type is its corporatist structure aimed at eliminating class conflicts and securing organized interest representation within an authoritarian framework.[25]

The economic crisis of the 1930s had severe social consequences and was accompanied by rightist authoritarian radicalization in Hungary. Bethlen, who had belonged to the traditional conservative rightist 'aristocratic' Vienna group,[26] increasingly attacked by the new right radical and fascist groups (the Szeged groups), resigned in 1931. The period from 1931 to 1944 was characterized by an ongoing struggle between the old traditional rightist authoritarian elite and a new radical right and fascist elite.

Prime Minister Bethlen was succeeded by Gyula Gömbös (1932-36) who sought to create a totalitarian fascist dictatorship in Hungary.[27] Gömbös' political philosophy was aggressively anti-Bolshevist and anti-Semitic. He was himself a declared fascist and a great admirer of Mussolini. Gömbös formed a government of 'national reconstruction', and the radical right took over the 'government party', renaming it 'the Party of National Unity.' It was reorganized as a mass party to mobilize support for the new leaders and promote the goal of national (fascist) unity and close cooperation with Germany.[28] Gömbös died in 1936 without having completed his totalitarian fascist experiment.

Some of the Prime Ministers who succeeded Gömbös belonged to the traditional rightist elite and initially tried to oppose National Socialism. They opposed the extermination of the Jews and sought to slow down the collaboration with Hitler's Germany. However, revisionism made many turn about and embrace fascism and Germany,[29] like the example of Béla Imrédy. Finally, Hungary was drawn into World War II as a German ally.

The Hungarian fascist movement under the leadership of Ferencz Szalasi, known as the Arrow Cross Movement, gained considerable strength during the interwar period, receiving 25% of all votes cast in the 1939 national elections. (Cf. table 1 as follows).

Lene Bøgh Sørensen

Table 1. Parliamentary Elections in Hungary 1935 and 1939. The whole country, Budapest and Suburbs

Party	number of seats		votes %					Change in Party support 1,000
			nat-ion-wide	Budapest		suburbs		
	1935	1939	1939	1935	1939	1935	1939	1939 minus 1935
Social Democratic Party	11	5	4	22.3	12.7	33.3	17.1	-20
Liberals	7	5	2	19.0	16.4			0
Smallholders	24	14	15					
Christian Social Party	14	8	3	25.8	5.5	13.5	6.9	-51
'Government Party'	170	179	50	26.0	33.1	35.7	27.5	+31
National Socialists	2	49	25	0.6	29.9	-	41.7	+72
Including (Arrow Cross)	(-)	(31)						
Others	17							
Total	245	260	99	93.7	97.6	82.5	93.2	+32

Sources: Ingemar Glans, *Östeuropas fascistiska förflutna. Fallet Ungern 1920-44* (forthcoming). Data are gathered from primarily two sources. 1. Miklós Lackó, 'The Social Roots of Hungarian Fascism: The Arrow Cross'; and 2. György Ránki, 'The Fascist Vote in Budapest in 1939', now in Stein Ugelvik Larsen, Bernt Hagtvet & Jan Petter Myklebust (eds.), *Who Were the Fascists. Social Roots of European Fascism*, Oslo, 1980, 395-400 and 401-16.

The Arrow Cross Movement had a membership between 200,000 and 250,000 by 1939, drawn from various social backgrounds.[30] The leading echelons of the movement were recruited from among army officers, civil servants and intellectuals.[31] 'Activists' were largely recruited from the *Lumpenproletariat* and criminals.[32] The mass base consisted of middle class and petty bourgeois elements in the towns and villages, semi-proletarians and proletarians with a rural background and, especially from 1938-39, more genuine working class elements.[33] In the 1939 elections the Arrow Cross Movement won the support of a considerable part of the working class.[34]

The comparatively strong working class contingent in the social base of Hungarian fascism is rather unique in an European context.[35] Carsten suggests that the combination of accumulated and unsolved social problems and the absence of a strong left wing in Hungarian politics contributed to working class fascism in Hungary. The Left in Hungary was still weak after the defeat of the Council Republic and the savage repression which followed during the counter-revolutionary period from 1919 to 1921. In 1939, the Communist Party was still banned and the Social Democratic Party was surprisingly weak, receiving only 4% of the national vote. This created a social and political vacuum filled by fascism.[36] Carsten's thesis explains the strength of the Arrow Cross vote in a number of working class districts in Budapest.

Finally in 1944, the German army occupied Hungary and installed the short-lived Férenc Szálasi 'Arrow Cross' government, a regime which perpetrated an unrestricted reign of terror, under which the 'Jewish question' found its 'final solution' in Hungary as well.[37] More than 450,000 Jews were deported to German extermination camps in Poland with the willing assistance of Hungarian gendarmerie and 'Arrow Cross' supporters.[38]

Following the short interregnum from 1945 to 1947, in which free elections were held in 1945,[39] the Stalinist type of political regime and its social and economic system were forced down on Hungary from outside and above. The period of repressive totalitarian political dictatorship during the Hungarian Stalinist period resulted in the destruction of the magnates and bourgeois classes and the complete subordination and control of 'transmission belt organizations' under the authority of the Hungarian Workers' Party.[40]

Following the 1956 revolution, strict control of social and political life was gradually liberalized during the sixties and seventies when Kadar introduced his alliance policy and economic reform policy. Thus, the Kadar period represented a departure from the Stalinist model relying instead on cooptation, market type economic reforms and bureaucratic bargaining. However, no genuine autonomous sphere of organized social life developed. The 'second society' — the sphere of autonomous social and cultural existence in Hungary in the 1970s, analyzed by Hankiss and other Hungarian scholars, had not developed into a strong civil society.[41] Rather, the Kadar regime rested on a negative social contract with the people leading to depoliticization and widespread apathy.

It can be argued that the regimes of the past 45 years, including Stalinism and the softer paternalistic dictatorship of Janos Kadar, reinforced the interwar legacy of a distorted and controlled 'from above' pattern of interest organization and articulation, this time in the service of a different ideology. Elitism has remained a prevailing phenomenon in Hungarian political development along with the tendency to form corporatist structures within the authoritarian framework. Weak democratic mass mobilization and participation has resulted in the failure to develop popular democratic culture. Thus, lacking any significant historical experience in democratic political organizing and practices, the regime change in Hungary in 1989-90 was — as one Hungarian scholar expressed it: '... an adventure into the unknown as well as a 'déjá vu' type appearance of older social patterns already experienced.'[42]

A strong case could be advanced that Hungarian politics and society by the late 1980s most closely resembled the kind of society and politics pictured in the mass society theories.[43] In these theories mass societies are characterized by a strong and dominant elite, a missing intermediate level of a plurality of interest organizations and a weak and apathetic people. History does not dictate that Hungarian political development will forever be condemned to elitism and authoritarianism. Rather, political tradition helps explain why Hungary is struggling to consolidate democracy and why an intermediate sphere of independent social-political organization and a genuine popular democratic culture are slow in coming.

Referring to the present consolidation problems, Ladó points out that the new regime in Hungary in 1990 faced considerable difficulties in creating a new system of industrial relations:

Collective bargaining, as it is known and practiced in industrialized market economies, did not exist in Hungary until very recently. ... Genuine collective bargaining did not take place in the past (because of) the lack of distinct partners having divergent interests and being independent. The concept of 'common interest' and the absence of autonomous trade unions and 'real' employers, rendered any bargaining process impossible.[44]

By the late 1980s, the autonomous articulation and organization of divergent interests was virtually non-existent. Legally based and regularized mechanisms and institutions to arbitrate conflicting interests among autonomous social actors were also absent. However, new parties, new autonomous trade unions and employers' organizations did appear during the transition period and started to compete for influence. Yet, no legal or institutional basis for defining the legitimate roles and rights of representation had been defined. Has time brought some clarity to the problem area of interest organization and representation?

Towards a social dialogue?

In late November 1992, officials from the Hungarian Government, the main trade union federations and employers organizations reached an agreement on a number of social and economic issues. Issues included in the negotiations were the government's proposal to introduce a new value-added-tax system, minimum wage and women's retirement age. The compromise, although it involved only a minimum of issues, was the result of more than a month's intense negotiations among representatives of the Council for the Reconciliation of Interests (CRI). The efforts to negotiate a compromise on employment issues, wages and a tax system were generally regarded as a success. Mihaly Kupa, the former Finance Minister, played a central role in opening up a space for social dialogue. His ongoing efforts in the negotiation process facilitated consensus building.[45] This step was important because it moved Hungary towards a tripartite macro-level forum for economic consultation and interest bargaining.

The event itself signaled the acute need for a social dialogue between labour, capital, and the state in the face of growing social welfare tensions in Hungarian society. Let me here briefly review some general indicators of the economic situation in Hungary since the change of regime. Since 1989-90, industrial production and GDP have declined sharply and *registered* unemployment reached approximately 630,000 by the end of 1992, some 12.2% of the work force. Agricultural production has dropped, and in 1992 exports declined 25% compared to the previous year. Hungary's gross foreign debt is still huge, amounting to 23.4 billion USD by mid-1993.[46] Income inequality has increased and real wages have fallen. Over 3 million people are estimated to be living at or below the social minimum of 9-10,000 Forint a month. According to Andorka, between 1989 and 1991, 'real income declined for half of the population, that is half of the society became poorer, but at the same time there was a strong increase in real income for one fifth.'[47]

In the second half of 1992, there were signs that segments of the Hungarian population were unwilling to tolerate too much suffering in the name of economic reconstruction. In November, a group calling themselves the 'Society for Those Living Beneath the Subsistence Level' initiated a hunger strike protesting against the government's plan to introduce a new two-level VAT tax system. In the same month, railway unions launched a two-hour warning strike against the government's proposed cuts in the 1993 state budget that would lead to major redundancies in the work force in this sector. Both events were covered extensively in the media.

The political articulation of tensions within society that started to emerge in Autumn 1992 pushed the normally anti-union government to become more responsive to social demands. Thus the government's increased willingness to enter into a dialogue with social actors can be interpreted as a response to the uncertainty of how to deal with the social consequences of a deteriorating economic situation.

The background

The idea of a national level 'Great Agreement' between the government, employees' and employers' federations emerged in the spring of 1991. The new Antall government had just experienced its first serious political crisis. In October, 1990, the government's sudden announcement of a major fuel price increase provoked taxi drivers to demonstrate. The government first refused to bargain with 'criminal' demonstrators and threatened police and military intervention. But this attitude on the part of the government only escalated the conflict and for three days the taxi drivers maintained an effective traffic blockade in Budapest and elsewhere in the country. In the capital, the atmosphere was tense. According to some observers, the taxi drivers' blockade gained broad popular support and developed into a general protest against declining living conditions. A public opinion survey conducted in the aftermath of the strike, based on telephone interviews with 1000 people, showed that a majority supported the taxi drivers.[48]

Whether the taxi drivers were in fact concerned with interests other than their own may be less important than the fact that they established a network capable of staging a protest against the government's economic austerity programmes. Thus, they became a voice for many poor and resource-weak people in Hungary.

The government's hostile stand towards the protesters was rejected by the opposition party, The Alliance of Free Democrats and by President, Arpád Göncz, who strongly objected to any intervention by the military. Finally the government had to give in and start talks with the demonstrators.

> **Question:**
> Do you think that the majority supported the government or rather the protesting taxi drivers during the crisis ?
> *Government*: 7% • *Taxi drivers*: 78% • *Neither-nor*: 15%
>
> **Question:**
> Do you agree that taxi drivers were concerned only with their own interests?
> *Yes*: 12% • *No*: 84% • *Do not know*: 4%
>
> **Question:**
> Do you agree that taxi drivers represented public opinion?
> *Yes*: 72% • *No*: 22% • *Do not know*: 6%

However no legally based institution to settle the conflict existed and the character of the conflict itself became difficult to define. Was it a labour conflict or was it a general popular protest against the government's economic policies and deteriorating living standards? What interest organizations supported the protest and were they ready to incorporate and articulate the demands that had been raised? As one Hungarian scholar asked, who should bargain with whom, and in what forum?[49] One structure that could provide a frame for negotiations was a tripartite national council initially established by the Nemeth government in 1988, the National Council for Reconciliation of Interests (NCRI), with representation from the government, the National Council of Trade Unions (SZOT) and several employers' organizations.

In the summer of 1990, the council had been renamed the Council for the Reconciliation of Interests (CRI) and reconstructed to reflect the emerging pluralism in trade unions as well as employers' organizations. The Antall government granted seven national trade union federations and nine employers organizations representation in the council.[50]

On 28 October, 1990, the Antall government convened this ad hoc council to negotiate the major social and political crisis that had erupted with the taxi driver strike and blockade. During the negotiations in the CRI the representatives of the trade unions and employers' organizations united against the government. After intense negotiations that were transmitted by television, the government finally gave in to the taxi drivers' demand and suspended the announced 65% petrol price increase.[51]

The escalation and resolution of the conflict constituted a major learning process for the new government. The new political leaders discovered that not all opposition to their policies could be labelled anti-democratic and thus outlawed. They had to realize that democratic politics do not permit them to impose their own vision of a new economic and political project on the population. Channels for articulating popular demands and an institutional framework for collective decision-making are part of the democratic process.[52] As pointed out by one Hungarian scholar, the newness of the democratic regime was also in itself a disadvantage; the new government lacked industrial relations specialists and had not initially given special priority to this area.[53] Furthermore, the conservative government was hostile to social partners, especially to the National Federation of Hungarian Trade Union (MSZOSZ), the successor of SZOT, which was regarded as illegitimate. As the Hungarian political scientist Mihaly Bihary observes:

The parties and leading politicians of the coalition government at first believed that the entire trade union structure, regarded as a remnant of the party-state, would shortly disappear together with its politicians and organizations and, at most, a few alternative, so called opposition trade unions would survive. Political decision-making would be fully transferred to Parliament and the Government. They had no idea of or affinity to the 'world of labour', to modern corporatism and tripartite system determining the world of labour.[54]

These observations are supported by another Hungarian political scientist who asserts that the Antall government lacked a well-conceived strategy of how to deal with labour and business: 'To illustrate difficulties of analysis it is to be noted that the government's strategy ranged from emphasizing social partnership to exclusion due to the dangers of corporatism.'[55]

For the trade unions, the conflict was an opportunity to reassert their identity and role as 'real' unions representing workers' and common peoples' interests. In particular the MSZOSZ and its chairman Sandor Nagy, gained some prestige through participation in the conflict mediation process as the representative and defender of workers' interests. In Hungary trade unions exerted no influence on the process of political change during the period from 1988 to 1990. Actually, the former official trade union SZOT was admitted as a third party in the round-table negotiations in 1989 leading to the change of regime. However, it was clear from the outset that SZOT would not have any influence on agenda setting or in the negotiations leading to free elections.[56] Trust in trade unions was at a low ebb and it seemed that social organizations as such were delegitimized in the new democratic system because of their incorporation in the past regime. Also important in this context is the notion that because corporatist arrangements existed in the 'communist' regime, such arrangements are detrimental to the new democratic regime. According to Mate Szabo this led to a general weakening of the 'corporative' sphere in politics.[57]

The taxi drivers' blockade provoked the government to reconsider the politics of economic restructuring, now laying emphasis on trilateral conciliation. However, despite much talk of a six-party agreement and a greater agreement on income policy involving social actors, two years would pass before some results were actually achieved in November 1992. That these efforts came to a stalemate so quickly cannot only be blamed on the government. A period of rivalry among new and reformed trade unions concerning unsettled issues of property rights, representation (membership) and legitimacy limited the prospects for real bargaining.

Employees' and employers' interest organizations and the Council for Reconciliation of Interests

In the field of industrial relations, a first step in assessing the new situation in Hungary is to ask who represents whom? Who should be included? In order to answer this question, we must get a clearer picture of the trade unions and employers organizations; but this is not a simple task. One place to start is to look at the organizations that are represented in the CRI and to examine their representativity and legitimacy. Where do these organizations come from? Are they 'real' in the sense that they can be said to represent labour and capital interests? What linkage and support do they have in society?. What follows deals with the labour side.

Trade union federations

In 1990, seven trade union confederations were invited to be represented in the Council for Reconciliation of Interests. They are:

1) MSZOSZ (The National Federation of Hungarian Trade Unions). The successor organization to the old National Council of Trade Unions (SZOT), that officially declared its independence from the Hungarian Socialist Workers Party in September 1989 and dissolved itself in March 1990. The estimated membership of MSZOSZ as of April 1991 was 2.6 million; October 1992, 1.6 million; Spring 1993, 1.2 million.[58] Its president is Sandor Nagy and it represents mainly industrial workers.

2) SZEF (Trade Unions Coordination Forum). A formerly sectoral federation of the old National Council of Hungarian Trade Unions (SZOT), declared independent in May 1990, it represents the interests of teachers, health workers, artists and other civil servants. Its estimated membership as of October 1990, 557,000; Spring 1993, 550,000.[59]

3) ÉSzT (The Association of Intellectual Workers), organizes university and college lecturers. It is a former affiliate of SZOT with estimated membership as of October 1990, 63,218; Spring 1993, 110,000.[60]

4) ASzOK (National Coordination of Autonomous Trade Unions). Also a former sectoral federation of SZOT. Affiliates of ASzOK include, among others, the Federation of Chemical Workers' Unions, the Trade Union of Locomotive Drivers, and The Road Transport Workers' Union. Membership as of July 1993, was 359,620.[61]

5) LIGA (The Democratic League of Independent Trade Unions). The LIGA was formed in 1989 as the first national trade union confederation of new independent unions to appear in the post-Kadar era. Some of the first union affiliates were The Democratic Union of Scientific Workers (TDDSZ), the Motion Picture Democratic Trade Union and the Democratic Trade Union of Teachers. When it was established it was heavily influenced by intellectuals in opposition to the past regime. Its self-reported membership was, as of Spring, 1993, 250,000.[62]

6) MOSZ (National Federation of Workers' Councils). Newly formed trade union federation established in July 1990, with an estimated membership in 1990 of 106,000; Spring 1993, 160.000.[63] As the name suggests, it is a trade union federation incorporating workers' councils of various orientations.

7. Szolidaritás (Solidarity Trade Union Workers' Federation). New Trade Union Federation with an estimated membership of 75,000, was scandalized and lost its seat in the CRI in spring 1994. Whether this organization ever was a trade union or really existed is questionable.[64]

In two years, the trade union movement in Hungary changed from a monolithic to a pluralistic and fragmented structure. This happened as a result of the emergence of new trade union federations and the break up of the former official trade union SZOT. Of the seven national trade union federations in 1990, four had emerged from the old trade union structure SZOT, and three were newly formed. The MSZOSZ, however, maintained by far the largest membership and is today the largest workers' organization in Hungary.

The trade unions: representation and legitimacy

Many questions have been raised as to the representativity of the labour as well as employers' organizations represented in the CRI. Indeed, the CRI itself has taken on the functions of a national level tripartite institution without a clear legal or popular recognized basis. National, regional and local structures of interest mediation are a necessary part of the present process of economic transformation. But the uncertainty surrounding interest articulation and representation in general, and the CRI and the organizations represented in this council in particular, lead to the conclusion that their role is more an accidental arrangement than an expression of an intelligent and well-considered policy concerning industrial relations.

As already mentioned, the CRI was reorganized in the summer of 1990 to reflect the organizational changes that had taken place in the period 1988-1990. The old trade union federation SZOT split, and new trade union federations independent of SZOT appeared. When the CRI was reorganized, no criteria of representation were adopted for admission to the council. The new structure was created on the spur of the moment,[65] apparently without much discussion. As a result, the organizational interests in the council have been suspicious of each other, especially on the labour side. The trade unions engaged in an intense rivalry both in workplaces and at the national level. On the employers' side, there is also some confusion as to whom the representatives of the organizations actually represent.[66]

Of the seven trade unions, only the MSZOSZ had an officially registered membership (1993). Therefore, the above membership estimates cannot be taken at face value. As one Hungarian researcher pointed out in 1992, for many of the trade union federations, the size of membership of the trade unions remained 'top secret'.[67] During the period 1990-93 the seven trade union federations repeatedly questioned each others' legitimacy, and the issue of the distribution of MSZOSZ's inherited assets intensified their rivalry. The trade unions were also put under considerable political pressure from the government to prove their legitimacy and support.

Thus, general distrust of labour organizations as well as power struggles between newly established trade unions weakened the position and role of labour in the CRI during the first four years. Under these conditions, attempts by the trade unions to formulate a common strategy to protect the interests of the people most threatened by the changes in the economic system did not succeed. However, tripartite negotiations proceeded within the CRI, but the arrangement can hardly be characterized as a fully developed corporatist interest mediation system. The conservative coalition government still did not recognize the labour partner in the CRI as legitimate, and the social partners were diversified and weak — not strong and unified — bargaining partners. Furthermore, during this period trade union federations were hardly in a position to effectively enforce compliance among their members. Considering these imperfections, it is remarkable that over the first four years the CRI gained substantial legitimacy and is today a well-established institution of national level interest bargaining between the government and the social partners. As Héthy points out, 'The essential contradiction of the situation is that the neo-corporatist institutions continue to exist and function while the very spirit of neocorporatism seems to be missing.'[68] The CRI has furthermore shown its capacity to deal with crisis situations: solving the conflict brought about by the taxi drivers' blockade in 1990, and the November 1992 tripartite agreements, are evidence of this. This points to the conclusion that the effort to form corporatist structures in the new democratic regime in Hungary was not motivated by the strenght of organized interests. Rather, it should be interpreted as an outcome of the stress that the new political elites faced in responding to economic decline and crisis in the wake of economic restructuring.

When the new socialist-liberal coalition government came into office in June 1994, the question about the legitimacy of trade unions had been settled. In 1993, two elections were held which helped clear the situation: the elections to two tripartite councils, the social security boards and the works/public service councils.[69] In the election to the social security boards, the MSZOSZ came out as the clear winner, getting as many votes as all the other union federations together. The Works Councils elections favoured the MSZOSZ even more, MSZOSZ received 71.67% of the votes. In the election to the Public Service Councils, SZEF emerged as the major public sector trade union.[70] With a 39% turnout, the elections revealed both public support for the trade unions and the relative strength of trade unions. The clear election victory of the MSZOSZ naturally established this trade union federation as the heavyweight labour partner in the CRI, followed by SZEF and ASzOk. In the election to Works Councils, ASzOK received a considerable number of votes from among chemical and transport workers, amounting to 18.57% of the total vote.

Additionally, in the 1994 parliamentary election a number of trade union leaders were elected from the party list of the Socialists and formed a trade union faction within the parliamentary group of the Socialist Party.[71] This premature link between the major trade unions and the Socialist Party was a sign that trade union interests could become more visible in political decision-making.

The new socialist-liberal government also emphasized corporatist interest mediation within the institutional framework of the CRI as important in relation to managing the economic transformation and crisis. A main ambition of the coalition government is to achieve a Social and Economic Agreement. To borrow Lajos Héthys summary: 'The obvious objective (of the Social and Economic Agreement) is to ensure the support of the main interest groups for the measures taken by the government, and thus to avoid the escalation of social tension and [72] The question is whether changed power relations between the government and the social partners will lead to an increase in the efficiency of corporatist arrangements at the national level? In particular, will neo-corporatist arrangements ensue if the trade unions start drawing up alternative economic policies to those of the government? Much is at stake both for the socialist-liberal government that has staked its reputation on concluding a social and economic pact, and for trade unions whose members will expect their organizations to exercise their renewed strength.

Concluding Remarks

The development of the system of economic and social interest representation in Hungary has had a difficult start. The formation of an industrial relations system, including collective bargaining and national interest reconciliation, has only just begun. The historically weak mobilization of social groups and the structures of authoritarianism left little practical experience on which to draw. Employees' and employers' organizations remained weak during the first four years of democratic change, due to the legacy of the past and the uncertainty about the establishment of new social organizations and transformation of old organizations. The 'entry into politics crisis' cannot therefore be explained solely as a result of a conscious attempt by the new political elites to exclude the participation of social interests. Attempts have been made to establish trilateral national fora of interest conciliation in Hungary. These arrangements, especially the institutional framework of the CRI, have shown the capacity to foster conditions conducive to bargaining and interest mediation between the government and the social partners. However corporatist arrangements in Hungary are still embryonic and therefore fragile in the face of the economic structural adjustment including wage restraints and severe cuts in social welfare. On the labour side, one striking feature is the survival of the old but reformed trade union, once considered a totally delegitimized instrument of the previous regime. Key problems of identity, roles and representation have now been resolved. Thus we may expect a clearer position and regularized involvement of the labour partners in the future. The trade unions have been plagued by internal strife so that their energies have not yet been directed at their primary responsibility, defending the workers` interests. In Hungary, a first small but important step has been taken in a long and complicated evolution towards the mobilization and inclusion of social actors in the democratic process.

Notes

1. László Bruszt, 1994. 'The Antall Government and The Economic Interest Groups', in *Balance. The Hungarian Government 1990-94.* Budapest: Korridor, 213; and Zsofia Szilagyi, 22 March 1996, 'Hungary. Communication Breakdown Between the Government and the Public', in *Transition*, Vol. 2 (6).
2. The expression, 'entry into politics crisis' is taken from S.M. Lipset, 1963, 'Social Conflict, Legitimacy, and Democracy': 77ff., in *Political Man*, London.
3. L. Hèthy, 'Hungary's new (emerging) industrial relations system, Trends and dilemmas', unpublished; Andràs Toth, December 1993, 'Great Expectations — Fading Hopes: Trade Unions and System Change in Hungary', *The Journal of Communist Studies*, Vol. 9 (4): 85-87; and Mária Ladó, March 1994, 'Workers and Employers Interests — as They are Represented in the Changing Industrial Relations in Hungary', Institute for Labour Research, Budapest: 12.
4. See the analysis of employers' associations by Géza Kovács, 1994, 'Employers' organizations in Hungary and their cooperation', *Budapest Papers on Democratic Transition*, (80).
5. For the concept neo-corporatism, see Philippe C. Schmitter, 'Still the Century of Corporatism?,' in G. Lembruch and P.C. Schmitter (eds), *Trends Towards corporatist Intermedeation*; and Williamson 1989, *Corporatism in Perspective. An Introductory guide to Corporatist Theory.* Sage.
6. Williamson, *ibid.*
7. Williamson, op.cit.; and Wilson, October 1983, 'Interest Groups and Politics in Western Europe, The Neo-Corporatist Approach', in *Comparative politics*: 105-23.
8. Mihály Bihary, 1994, 'Political System and Party System', in *Magyarország politikai évkönyve*: 41.
9. Bill Lomax, 1992. 'Internal (and External) Impediments to Democratization', paper presented at the ESRC East West Initiative Workshop at Charles University, Prague, 14-17 September: 5-8.
10. See the chapter by Bill Lomax in this book.
11. Philippe C. Schmitter, October 1991. 'The consolidation of Political Democracies: Processes, Rhythms and Types', Stanford University.
12. Ágh Attila, *The Hungarian Party System.* Budapest Papers on Democratic

Transition, (51), 1993; and *The Parliamentary Way to Democracy, The Case of Hungary.* Budapest Papers on Democratic Transition, (2), 1991; and *The revolution of the intelligentsia — Citizenship and Civil Society in Central Europe.* Paper prepared for the conference 'Quality of Citizenship', 20-22 March 1991, Utrecht, Netherlands; Bozóki, Körösényi and Schöpflin, 1991, *Post Communist Transition, Emerging Pluralism in Hungary.* London and New York; Bruszt, László 1991, '1989: The Negotiated Revolution of Hungary', in György Szoboszlai (ed.), *Democracy and Political Transformation. Theories and East-Central European Realities.* Budapest; Bruszt, László and David Stark 1992, 'Remaking the political field in Hungary: From the Politics of Confrontation to the Politics of Competition', in Ivo Banac (ed.), *Eastern Europe in Revolution.* Ithaca and London; and many many more ...

13.   Lene Bøgh Sørensen, 1995. *Political Development and Regime Transformations The Hungarian Case.* PhD dissertation, University of Aarhus.

14.   The Friedrich suffrage was more or less dictated by the entente powers.

15.   According to Bethlen, democracy was not suitable for Hungary, which needed a golden means 'between unbridled freedom and unrestrained dictatorship', here quoted from Andrew Janos, 1982, *The Politics of Backwardness in Hungary from 1825-1945.* Princeton U.P., 211.

16.   Janos, *ibid*: 234-35; and C.A. Macartney, 1956. *October Fifteenth. A History of Modern Hungary 1929-1945.* Edinburgh, 43-44.

17.   Janos, *ibid*: 209-37.

18.   Janos, *ibid*: 217.

19.   See for example William M. Batkai, 1982, *Authoritarian Politics in a Transitional State. Istvan Bethlen and the Unified Party in Hungary 1919-1926.* New York.

20.   For the concept of totalitarianism, see for example Juan Linz, 1975, 'Totalitarian and Authoritarian Regimes', in Fred Greenstein & Nelson W. Polsby (eds.), *Macropolitical Theory, Handbook of Political Science*, Vol. 3: 175-411, especially 187-252.

21.   Juan Linz, *ibid*: 306-13.

22.   *Ibid*: 264.

23.   Juan Linz, *op.cit*: 187-287.

24.   *Ibid*: 289.

25.   *Ibid*: 303-13.

26.   Bethlen was active in forming the 'Anti-Bolshevik Committee' in Vienna, where political representatives of the traditional conservative aristocracy found refuge after power had been handed over to the Hungarian Communist-Social Democratic alliance.

27.   Jörg K. Hoensch, 1988. *A History of Modern Hungary 1867-1986.* London & New York: 127.

28.   Janos, *op.cit*: 287ff.

29.   *Ibid*: 292.

30.   Cf. Miklos Lacko, 'The Social Roots of Hungarian Fascism: The Arrow Cross'; and György Ránki, 1980, 'The Fascist Vote in Budapest 1939', in Stein Ugelvik

Larsen, Bernt Hagtvet & Jan Petter Myklebust, *Who Were the Fascists*. Oslo: 395-400 and 401-16.

31. Miklos Lacko, *ibid*: 395.

32. *Ibid*: 396-97.

33. *Ibid*.

34. Cf. György Ránki, *op.cit*.

35. F.L. Carsten, *The Rise of Fascism*, University of California Press, 1982.

36. Carsten, *ibid*: 170, 174, and 175-78.

37. Janos, *op.cit*: 309-10.

38. Hoensch, *op.cit*: 156.

39. In late 1945 elections were held, which was the first free elections ever held in Hungary. The 'Smallholders Party' got 57% of the votes cast, the 'National Peasant Party' 7%, 17% voted for the Social Democrats and 17% for the Communist party. A small bourgeois-democratic party got 1.6% of the votes Hoensch, *op.cit*.

40. See for example Elemér Hankiss, 1990, *East European Alternatives*, Oxford, Ch. 1.

41. Elemér Hankiss did not suggest either that it would. For the use of the term and analysis, see Elemér Hankiss, *op.cit.*, Oxford, 1990, Ch. 3.

42. György Szoboszlai (ed.), 1991. *Democracy and Political Transformation. Theories and East-Central European Realities*, (preface). Hungarian Political Science Association, Budapest.

43. William Kornhauser, 1968. *The Politics of Mass Society*, London: Routledge and Kegan Paul.

44. Mária Ladó, March 1994. 'Workers' and employers' interests — as they are represented in the changing industrial relations in Hungary', Institute for Labour Research, Budapest: 34-35.

45. Press review on 24 November (The Phare delegation in Budapest). See for background, László Lengyel, 1992, 'Nineteen ninety-one', in *Magyarország politikai évkönyve*: 39-41.

46. See, 'Economic performance of Hungary in the first eight months of 1993', *Commission of the European Communities, Budapest Delegation*. Budapest, November 1993, MV/SP/93; Margit Nielsen, 1994, 'Al begyndelse er svær, samfunds-økonomiens udvikling efter den politiske omvæltning', in *Det nye Ungarn Tilbageblik og Perspektiver*. København: Svantevit; and Lene Bøgh Sørensen, 1993, 'Det går godt i Ungarn, men ikke for Ungarerne', in *Vindue mod Øst*, (22): 22.

47. Rudolf Andorka, 1992. *Social Policy Problems of the Change of Regime*, Budapest Papers on Democratic Transition, (25).

48. Szabo Mate, 'The Taxi Driver Demonstration in Hungary — Social Protest and Political Change': 15, paper presented at ECPR 1992. The article is later published in a revised form in György Szoboszlai (ed.), 1992, *Flying Blind. Emerging Democracies in East-Central Europe*. Hungarian Political Science Association Yearbook: 357-81.

49. The Hungarian labour-market researcher, Mária Ladó raised this question in an interview in Autumn 1992.

50. Preparatory Project on Social Dialogue, *Final report Z92030300.005*, 17 May 1992. The Phare delegation in Budapest. The CRI institution is supported financially by the Phare programme.

51. L. Héthy, 1992. *Hungary's new emerging Industrial relations System, Trends and Dilemmas.* Budapest.

52. Juan Linz has made this observation that what 'often characterizes newly established democratic regimes is the tendency of its supporters (founders) to identify democracy with their own particular social and cultural policies'. In Juan Linz, 1978, *The Breakdown of Democratic Regimes, Crisis, Breakdown, and Reequilibration.* Baltimore.

53. Interview with Mária Ladó, October 1992.

54. Mihaly Bihary, 1994. 'Political System and Party System': 47-48, in Magyarország politikai évkönyve.

55. László Bruszt, 1994. 'The Antall Government and the Economic Interest Groups', in *Balance, The Hungarian Government 1990-1994.* Korridor, Centre for Political Research, Budapest: 213.

56. László Bruszt, '1989: The Negotiated Revolution of Hungary', in György Szoboszlai (ed.), *Democracy and Political Transformation. Theories and East-Central European Realities, op.cit*: 221.

57. Mate Szabo, *op.cit*: 12.

58. MSZOSZ is the only Trade Union Federation that in 1992 had openly registered membership. The estimation from April 1991 is from L. Héthy, *Hungary's New Emerging Industrial Relations System, Trends and Dilemmas.* The estimation from October 1992 is as declared by Laszlo Sandor, Vice President of the MSZOSZ in an interview conducted in October 1992. The April 1993 estimation is from Mária Ladó, *op.cit*: 47.

59. Mária Ladó, *op.cit.*

60. Ibid.

61. According to own accords, estimated from membership fees. ASZOK information sheet. The estimate by Ladó, using self-reported data collected by the CRI, is for April 1993, 410,000.

62. See appendix 1.

63. Ladó, *ibid*: 47.

64. Mária Ladó, *ibid*: 13.

65. This view was expressed by the Hungarian researcher Mária Ladó in an interview in the Autumn of 1992.

66. The first secretary of the CRI, Garsco Lilla, who participates in all bargaining sessions for the trade union side expressed during an interview in December 1992, that there was much confusion as to the representativeness of the some of the employers' organizations.

67. *Ibid.*

68. Héthy, *op.cit*: 24.

69. Mária Ladó, *op.cit*: 25. See also MSZOSZ (National Confederation of Hungarian Trade Unions) information sheets, May 1993 and September 1993.

70. Mária Ladó, *ibid.*
71. László Thoma, 1995. 'The Situation of the Hungarian Trade Unions', in Kurtán Sándor, Sándor Péter, Vass László (eds.), *Magyarország Politikai Èvkönyve, 1995.* Budapest.
72. Here cited from Mária Ladó, 1994. 'Social and Economic Agreement: Experience of Hungary (snapshot of the ongoing negotiations)', paper prepared for the conference 'Negotiations — The Way To Social Pact', Warsaw, 17-18 October: 2.

Bibliography

Ágh, Attila 1991. *The Parliamentary Way to Democracy, The Case of Hungary.* Budapest Papers on Democratic Transition, No.2, Department of Political Science, BUES.

Ágh, Attila 1991. *The revolution of the intelligentsia — Citizenship and Civil Society in Central Europe.* Paper prepared for the conference 'Quality of Citizenship', 20-22 March, Utrecht, The Netherlands.

Ágh, Attila 1993. *The Hungarian Party System.* Budapest Papers on Democratic Transition, No. 51, Department of Political Science, BUES.

Andorka, Rudolf 1992. *Social Policy Problems of the Change of Regime.* Budapest Papers on Democratic Transition, No. 25, Department of Political Science, BUES.

Bihary, Mihaly 1994. 'Political System and Party System', in Kurtán Sándor, Peter Sándor, László Vass (eds.), *Magyarország politikai évkönyve.* Budapest: Nagynovácsy Kiado: 4l7-48.

Bruszt, László 1991. 'The Negotiated Revolution of Hungary', in György Szoboszlai (ed.), *Democracy and Political Transformation. Theories and East-Central European Realities,* Budapest: HPSA.

Bruszt, László 1994. 'The Antall Government and The Economic Interest Groups', in *Balance. The Hungarian Government 1990-94.* Budapest: Korridor, 212-33.

Bruszt, László and David Stark 1992. 'Remaking the political field in Hungary: From the Politics of Confrontation to the Politics of Competition', in Ivo Banac (ed.), *Eastern Europe in Revolution.* Ithaca and London: Cornell U.P.

Carsten, F.L. 1982. *The Rise of Fascism.* Berkeley: University of California Press.

Commission of the European Communities, Budapest Delegation, Budapest, November 1993, MV/SP/93, 'Economic performance of Hungary in the first eight months of 1993'.

Hankiss, Elemér 1990. *East European Alternatives.* Oxford: Clarendon Press.

Héthy, L. 1992. 'Hungary's new emerging Industrial relations System, Trends and Dilemmas', Budapest. Unpublished paper.

Hoensch, Jörg K. 1988. *A History of Modern Hungary 1867-1986*: 127. London & New York: Longman.

Janos, Andrew 1982. *The Politics of Backwardness in Hungary from 1825-1945.* Princeton, N.J.: Princeton U.P.

Kornhauser, William 1968. *The Politics of mass Society*. London: Routledge and Kegan Paul.

Körösényi, Bozóki and Schöpflin (eds.), 1991. *Post Communist Transition, Emerging Pluralism in Hungary*. London: Pinter Publishers.

Kovács, Géza 1994. 'Employers' organizations in Hungary and their cooperation', *Budapest Papers on Democratic Transition*, No. 80. Budapest: Department of Political Science, BUES.

Lacko, Miklos 1980. 'The Social Roots of Hungarian Fascism: The Arrow Cross', and György Ránki, 'The Fascist Vote in Budapest 1939', in Stein Ugelvik Larsen, Bernt Hagtvet & Jan Petter Myklebust, *Who Were the Fascists*. Bergen-Oslo-Tromsø: Universitetsforlaget: 395-400 and 401-16.

Ladó, Mária 1994. 'Social and Economic Agreement: Experience of Hungary'. (Snapshot of the ongoing negotiations). Paper prepared for the conference on Negotiations — The Way To Social Pact, Warsaw, 17-18 October: 2.

Ladó, Mária 1994. 'Workers and Employer's Interests — As they are Represented in the Changing Industrial Relations in Hungary'. Paper, Institute for Labour Research, Budapest, March: 12.

Lengyel, László 1992. 'Nineteen ninety-one', in Kurtán Sándor, Peter Sándor, László Vass (eds.), *Magyarország politikai évkönyve*. Budapest: Nagynovácsy Kiado: 39-41.

Linz, Juan 1975. 'Totalitarian and Authoritarian Regimes', in Fred Greenstein & Nelson W. Polsby (eds.), *Macropolitical Theory, Handbook of Political Science*, Vol. 3: 175-411.

Linz, Juan 1978. *The Breakdown of Democratic Regimes, Crisis, Breakdown, and Reequilibration*. Baltimore: The John Hopkins U.P.

Lipset, S.M. 1963. 'Social Conflict, Legitimacy, and Democracy', 77ff., in *Political Man*. London: Mercury Doors.

Lomax, Bill 1992. 'Internal (and External) Impediments to Democratization', paper presented at the ESRC East West Initiative Workshop at Charles University, Prague, 14-17 September: 5-8.

Macartney, C.A. 1956/57. *October Fifteenth. A History of Modern Hungary 1929-1945*, 7. Edinburgh: Edinburgh U.P.

Mate, Szabo 1992. 'The Taxi Driver Demonstration in Hungary — Social Protest and Political Change': 15, in György Szoboszlai (ed.), *Flying Blind. Emerging Democracies in East-Central Europe*. Budapest: Hungarian Political Science Association: 357-81.

MSZOSZ, 1993. (National Confederation of Hungarian Trade Unions) information sheets, May 1993 and September 1993.

Nielsen, Margit 1994. 'Al begyndelse er svær, samfundsøkonomiens udvikling efter den politiske omvæltning', in *Det nye Ungarn. Tilbageblik og perspektiver*, København: Svantevit.

Preparatory Project on Social Dialogue, *Final report Z92030300.005*, 17 May 1992. The Phare delegation in Budapest.

Schmitter, Philippe C. 1979. 'Still the Century of Corporatism?,' in G. Lembruch and P.C. Schmitter, *Trends Towards Corporatist Intermediation*. Beverly Hills: Sage.

Schmitter, Philippe C. 1991. 'The consolidation of Political Democracies: Processes, Rhythms and Types'. Unpublished paper, Stanford University, October.

Sørensen, Lene Bøgh 1993. 'Det går godt i Ungarn, men ikke for Ungarerne', in *Vindue mod Øst*, (22): 22.

Sørensen, Lene Bøgh 1995. *Political Development and Regime Transformations The Hungarian Case*, PhD dissertation, University of Aarhus.

Szilagyi, Zsofia 1996. 'Hungary. Communication Breakdown Between the Government and the Public', in *Transition*, Vol. 2, (6), 22 March 1996.

Szoboszlai, György (ed.), 1991. *Democracy and Political Transformation. Theories and East-Central European Realities*. Budapest: Hungarian Political Science Association.

Thoma, László, 1995. 'The Situation of the Hungarian Trade Unions', in Kurtán Sándor, Peter Sándor, and László Vass (eds.), *Magyarország Politikai Èvkönyve, 1995*. Budapest: Nagynovácsy Kiado.

Toth, Andràs 1993. 'Great Expectations-Fading Hopes: Trade Unions and System Change in Hungary', in *The Journal of Communist Studies*, Vol. 9, (4), December 1993: 85-87.

William, Batkai M. 1982. *Authoritarian Politics in a Transitional State. Istvan Bethlen and the Unified Party in Hungary 1919-1926*. Boulder: East European Monographs.

Williamson, Peter 1989. *Corporatism in Perspective. An Introductory guide to Corporatist Theory*. London: Sage.

Wilson, Frank L. 1983. 'Interest Groups and Politics in Western Europe, The Neo-Corporatist Approach', in *Comparative Politics*, October: 105-23.

About the Authors

Attila Ágh is a Professor of Political Science and Head of the Department of Political Science at the Budapest University of Economics. He has recently edited three books in English about the Central European Parliaments.

Gerhard Botz was born in 1941 in Schärding, Upper Austria. In 1967 he gained a *Dr. phil.* from the University of Vienna; in 1968 he was Assistant Professor at the University of Linz; in 1979 Associate Professor at the University of Linz; in 1980 Professor of Austrian history at the University of Salzburg; in 1986/87 visiting professor at Stanford University; and in 1997 he became Professor of Contemporary History at the University of Vienna. Since 1982 he has been Director of the Ludwig Boltzmann Institute for Social Scientific History (Salzburg-Vienna). Professor Botz has published extensively on Austrian history with special emphazis on Austrian fascists.

Christiane Brenner was born in 1963 and is a historian. She teaches history at the Osteuropa-Instituit, Freie Universität Berlin. During recent years she has been working primarily on 19th and 20th century Czech history, and on the history of the German Democratic Republic. She is especially interested in the question of historiography and theory of history. She has published many articles on Eastern Europe, with emphazis on the Czech and Slovak history.

Peter Bugge was born in 1960. In 1989 he gained an MA in Political Science from the University of Aarhus, and this was followed in 1994 by a PhD with the dissertation *Czech Nation-Building, National Self-Perception and Politics 1780-1914*. Since 1994 he has been lecturer in Czech and European Studies at the Department of Slavonic Studies, University of Aarhus. Main research interests: Czech history, politics, literature and culture in the nineteenth and twentieth centuries, the history of the idea of Europe and the question of 'European identity'.

Leslie Eliason was born in 1959, and is an associate professor in the Graduate School of International Policy Studies at the Monterey Institute of International Studies in California. A Fulbright Visiting Lecturer at the Department of Political Science, University of Aarhus in 1990, she has published several articles on Scandinavian public policy and comparative welfare state studies while on the faculty at the University of Washington. Her current research focuses on the politics of social welfare reform in eastern and western Europe and public administration education to support democratic transitions.

Heinz Gärtner was born in 1951. He studied political science and communication theory at the University of Salzburg, gaining a PhD in political science in 1977. Habilitation at the University of Innsbruck in 1990. Since 1979 he has been a research fellow at the Austrian Institute for International Affairs, Laxenburg, and is a lecturer at the Universities of Vienna and Innsbruck. From 1987-89 he was a Resident Fellow at the Institute for East-West Security Studies in New York. He was a Visiting Fellow at St. Hugh's College, Oxford, in 1992. In 1993 he was a Visiting Fellow at the Institute for International Relations, Vancouver, Canada, and in 1994/95 Visiting Professor at the University of Erlangen. Heinz Gärtner has published extensively on theories of international relations, developments in world politics, European security, etc.

Eva Hahn was born in 1946 and grew up in Prague. She emigrated in 1968, and has studied in both Stuttgart and London. Since 1981 she has been employed as an academic researcher at the Collegium Carolinum in Munich. She is editor of the journal *Bohemia* and of the *Biographisches Lexikon zur Geschichte der böhemischen Länder* and the author or editor of several books on Czech and central European history and political thought in the nineteenth and twentieth centuries.

László Kürti is an anthropologist (PhD University of Massachussetts, Amherst, 1989) and is currently teaching at the Department of Political Sciences, Eötvös Loránd University, Budapest. He is a specialist in interethnic relations, gender, popular culture and contemporary politics of Hungary. He has co-edited *Beyond Borders: Remaking Cultural Identities in the New East and Central Europe*, (1997, Westview). His articles have appeared in *Anthropology Today, Traditions, East European Quarterly, East European Politics and Societies*, and *Anthropological Quarterly*.

Bill Lomax is a Senior Lecturer in Sociology in the School of Social Studies at Nottingham University. He has published widely on the Hungarian Revolution of 1956, including *Hungary 1956* (1976), on opposition and dissent under the Kádár regime, and on the transition from communist rule in Hungary since 1989. He is currently working on a study of political change in Hungary from the mid-1980s to the present day.

Tibor Pichler was born in 1949 in Bratislava. From 1967-72 he studied history and philosophy at the Comenius University in Bratislava. He is a senior research fellow at the Institute of Philosophy of the Slovak Academy of Sciences, and writes on the history of political thought and nationalism in Central Europe.

Lene Bøgh Sørensen was born in 1959. She gained an MSc in Political Science in 1989, and PhD in 1995 from the Department of Political Science, University of Aarhus. Since 1995 she has been a research associate on a project covering regime changes and democratic development in Central Europe. Her main areas of research include: theories of political development, regime types, East European social and political developments and the transition process in Hungary.

Curt Sørensen was born in 1938. He gained his MSc in Political Science in 1965 and became *Dr scient. pol.* in 1993. From 1965-94 he was Assistant and Associate Professor at the Department of Political Science, University of Aarhus, Denmark, and from 1994 has been Professor in political theory. From 1971-73 he was an Academic Visitor at the London School of Political Science and the Freie Universität, Berlin. He was an Academic Visitor at Stanford University, California from 1991-92. Curt Sørensen has published extensively on Marxist theory, socialism, comparative labour movements and European social and political development. His main works are: *Marxismen og den Sociale Orden*, (Marxism and the Social Order), vols. 1-2, Grenaa, 1976, and *Mellem Demokrati og Diktatur* (Between Democracy and Dictatorship), vols. 1-2, Department of Political Science, University of Aarhus. Curt Sørensen is presently chief coordinator of the research project 'Nationbuilding and Democracy Development in Central Europe', financed by the Danish Social Science Research Council.

Index